Cell Mates/S

STORIES OF PRISON RELATIONSHIPS

Angela Devlin is a writer, broadcaster and exponent of prisoners' rights whose work has attracted wide interest and acclaim: *Criminal Classes* (Waterside Press, 1995), *Prison Patter: A Dictionary of Prison Slang* (Waterside Press, 1996); *Invisible Women: What's Wrong With Women's Prisons* (Waterside Press, 1998), *Anybody's Nightmare: The Sheila Bowler Story* (Taverner Publications, 1998) and *Going Straight After Crime and Punishment* with Bob Turney (Waterside Press, 1999). *Anybody's Nightmare*, the true story of a wrongful conviction for murder, was later dramatised for ITV and featured the character 'Angela Devlin' campaigning for the case to be re-opened (The conviction was eventually quashed and the defendant acquitted after a new trial).

Cell Mates/Soul Mates is based on research by the author over a period of three years into a largely neglected aspect of imprisonment: the development of intimate relationships by 'inside' and 'outside' partners despite the physical and formal barriers. The book contains introductory material and extended extracts from interviews with people who have experienced the phenomenon, which suggest that - against the odds - the partners concerned often remain committed to each other. Notwithstanding the precarious nature of the enterprise - and sometimes hostile reactions from people around them - they stay together and build a new life in which crime becomes a thing of the past, a finding which should be an encouragement to a range of people involved in sentence planning and release decisions.

Cell Mates/Soul Mates
Stories of Prison Relationships
Angela Devlin

Published 2002 by
WATERSIDE PRESS
Domum Road
Winchester SO23 9NN
United Kingdom

Telephone or Fax: 01962 855567
Editorial e-mail: watersidepress@compuserve.com
Orderline e-mail: watersidepress@cs.com
Online catalogue and bookstore: www.watersidepress.co.uk

ISBN 1 872 870 23 6

Catalogue-In-Publication Data: A catalogue record for this book can be obtained from the British Library

Printing and binding: Antony Rowe Ltd, Chippenham

Cover design: Sebastian Devlin

Royalties: All author's royalties from *Cell Mates/Soul Mates* will be made over to the Federation of Prisoners' Familes Support Groups.

Cell Mates/Soul Mates

STORIES OF PRISON RELATIONSHIPS

Angela Devlin

With a Foreword by Claire Rayner

WATERSIDE PRESS
WINCHESTER

Acknowledgements

I would like to thank John Bowers, editor of *Inside Time*, Peter Zimmermann, director of The Prison Fellowship, and Lucy Gampell, director of The Federation of Prisoners' Families Support Groups, for kindly allowing me to place notices in their newsletters; Claire Rayner for taking time off from her very busy schedule to write the *Foreword;* Jane Green for her painstaking and patient editing; Jim Collins of Northants Photographic for his generous permission for use of the wedding photograph; and Roz Hugo and Dave Bullock for their kind help with the cover.

I am especially grateful to all those people who responded to my requests for interviews, whether or not their stories were included in this book. I would like to thank them all for sparing the time to meet me and talk to me, for taking the trouble to check the interview transcripts, and most of all for trusting me with their personal life histories. I hope they will be an inspiration and support to other people in similar situations.

All author's royalties from this book go to The Federation of Prisoners' Families Support Groups.

Angela Devlin
April 2002

Cell Mates/Soul Mates

A note on the naming of interviewees and partners

Where first names only have been used in the interview headings, this indicates that the interviewees wish to remain anonymous. Their names, and any names of people and places that might identify them, have been changed.

Where surnames are included in chapter headings, this indicates that the interviewees are happy to be identified.

The name listed first in the chapter headings is the name of the 'outside partner' and the second name is that of the 'inside partner' – meaning the prisoner or ex-prisoner.

Cell Mates/Soul Mates

CONTENTS

CHAPTER

THE INTERVIEWS

Continued overleaf

Foreword

There are very few writers and campaigners who know as much as Angela Devlin about the wellbeing and problems of people who, for whatever reason, find themselves in prison cells. Few of those who are employed in the Prison Service have her gift for getting behind the facades put up by those (usually) desperately unhappy people who are forced to live in these institutions, and sadly, far too few share her compassion for them. As one who has made some efforts over the past few years to improve the healthcare of women prisoners, I have found her earlier writings on prison issues of enormous value, particularly *Invisible Women: What's Wrong With Women's Prisons*.

Her books are fascinating; *Criminal Classes* was for me the classic 'unputdownable' text; so was *Prison Patter* which is a dictionary of prison slang. Anyone who takes delight in the way the English language can be used and adapted by a closed community to serve its acute need for a private language will share my passion for it.

And now here is *Cell Mates/Soul Mates*. It is a remarkable piece of work: a sociological text which sizzles with love and pain and hope and bitter disappointment and aching loneliness and joy and gratitude and all the other emotions every reader hopes to find in the best sort of novel. And it offers much more than that. It is a work of scholarship, well researched and annotated. The book should be required reading for anyone who works in the Prison Service.

Ms Devlin is clearly aware of the way some people take an almost lascivious interest in the lives of prisoners. She knows how, when a prisoner forms a close attachment with someone from outside the prison and the news gets out, the tabloid papers slaver with excitement and wallow in the story.

But no one need expect to slaver over this text. It is much too well written and too well structured a piece of writing to attract the dribbling classes. I wish it would, in a way. The tabloids only ever speak in the most obvious of stereotypes and in so doing drive an even thicker wedge between those of us who are in prison and those of us who somehow manage to stay out.

And that is a great pity, because nourishing the all too common assumption that people in prison are all wicked and evil and dangerous makes it very difficult indeed for them to get the decent humane treatment their humanity entitles them to. (And I have to say there are some prison workers who share the common assumption and treat their charges unpleasantly, to say the least, as a consequence.)

This book does much to show the absurdity of that common assumption. People in prison are like the rest of us: fallible human beings who can all too easily slip over the line that is drawn between acceptable and unacceptable social behaviour.

Angela Devlin reports from the front line of the modified misery in which most prisoners spend their lives in clear, highly readable prose to provide us all—specialists such as social workers and prison officers (and Governors) as well as the general reader—with these stories of real people and their sometimes chaotic, always complicated lives.

I cannot commend this important book, the result of three years of painstaking and clearly thoughtful effort, too highly.

Claire Rayner

January 2002

CHAPTER 1

Introduction

People who fall in love with criminals are a source of endless fascination. In the months before this book was published, cinema audiences were enjoying two popular films which celebrated prison romances.[1] The BBC screened a deathbed interview with Reggie Kray—his wife Roberta,[2] who married him in HMP Maidstone, at his side. Channel 5 ran a series called *Hard Bastards*, presented by Kate Kray, ex-wife of the late Ron, whom she married in Broadmoor, and based on her eponymous best-selling book.[3] BBC television showed a documentary about women who had formed relationships with the Yorkshire Ripper.[4] The tabloids printed in-depth interviews with Saira Rehman, who agreed to marry the self-styled Charles Bronson, alleged to be Britain's most violent prisoner, without ever having met him and a television documentary about the couple was shown.[5] Venezuelan terrorist Carlos the Jackal, serving a life sentence in a Paris jail, announced that he would marry his French attorney, Isabelle Coutant-Peyre.

These relationships regularly fill a lot of column inches, as I found when I monitored newspaper reports and interviews throughout the three-year period I spent researching this book.[6] Most reinforced a few common stereotypes, generally female: the gangster's moll who unashamedly revels in her lover's notoriety; the obsessed woman who begins by writing to a Death Row prisoner and ends up marrying him; the 'posh totty'—an arty, educated woman who likes her 'bit of rough' and falls for a prisoner; and the 'warder loves lag' variety where prison professionals—male and female—lose their jobs because of their passion for one of their charges.

The media run these stories because they sell newspapers and increase television ratings: many of us are fascinated by people who choose individuals whom the rest of society has condemned, and whom most of us would regard as extremely high-risk partners. For these are not couples who were already together when one of them committed a crime and was imprisoned. On the contrary, these are people who appear deliberately to have sought out convicted criminals and established relationships with them—a decision that seems at best perverse and at worse foolish and dangerous. Whenever I mentioned the subject of this book, people's reaction was dismissive, often angry and always simplistic: 'Those women …'—for people always assumed that only women take such action—'… they must be raving mad!'

But during my eight years of research on prison issues for a number of earlier books, I became aware that the stories that hit the media present only a very partial view of the real nature of such relationships.

REVIEW OF THE LITERATURE

Perhaps for fear of accusations of prurience or sensationalism, academics seem largely to have ignored the subject of prisoner/non-prisoner relationships. There seem to be few research studies, and the work that exists tends to follow popular assumptions by treating falling in love with a prisoner as an exclusively female phenomenon—though there are plenty of men who find the idea of incarcerated women fascinating and who write to them, form relationships with them and sometimes marry them.

Jacquelynne Willcox-Bailey, an Australian journalist who made a television documentary[7] and wrote a book[8] about such couples, confirms the lack of research, though Sheila Isenberg has written exclusively about women who form relationships with incarcerated killers in America, [9] and there are several personal accounts written by prisoners' partners, one of the more recent being a highly-acclaimed memoir, *The Prisoner's Wife*, by American poet asha bandele.[10] Prisoners and ex-prisoners have themselves written more extensively about the influence of non-criminal partners—one of the most famous being Jimmy Boyle, who married Sarah Trevelyan, a psychiatrist, and is now himself an acclaimed sculptor.[11] Murderer Hugh Collins, now a successful novelist, acknowledges his debt of gratitude to his wife, the painter Caroline McNairn, whom he met while on day release from prison. The couple have been together ten years.[12]

METHODOLOGY

My own catalyst for writing *Cell Mates/Soul Mates* was getting to know one particular couple, whose relationship inspired me to look in more depth at the motivation and experience of others who had made this choice. I will call them Jane and Frank.

Jane, a prison librarian, fell in love with Frank, a former violent gangster who had spent more than half his life in prison. Frank was coming up for parole when he began talking to Jane about his poetry and his desire to change his way of life. They married when Frank was finally released, and Jane had to resign from her job and retrain as a teacher. They lived in a rural village far from Frank's former criminal associates in the city, but they went through years of emotional turmoil (the birth of one child, the death of another), financial hardship and social isolation as he fought the hard battle to readjust to life outside, to stay away from crime and to establish himself in a new career. Their marriage has now sadly ended in divorce, but it lasted 12 years—a better record than many 'outside' relationships. Jane suggested it would be worth speaking to other women and men who choose prisoners as partners, to see if there was any commonality in their background and experiences. The choice can often be a lonely one and she also felt that people in this situation—or any parallel one where a relationship is condemned by society—might welcome a chance to read about others like themselves.

I wanted the book to be serious and thoughtful, rather than sensational and headline-grabbing. Of course there are a few 'celeb' marriages like the Krays' and the Bronsons', but most couples want to live quietly, like Jane and Frank, as far away as possible from media attention—the prisoner will often have had enough of that at the time of the conviction. I was more interested in speaking to these couples, rather than those in high-profile relationships, and I was just as keen to speak to male outside partners as females. I also wanted to interview couples whose relationships, like Jane's and Frank's, had continued after release.

But it was not easy to locate them, to gain their trust, or to persuade them to talk openly about their experiences. This study is therefore by necessity qualitative rather than quantitative. Through prison contacts and advertisements in newsletters that are distributed round the jails, I was approached by 50 people who were interested in the project. By a process of elimination (some of their partners turned out to be horrified at the whole idea, some misunderstood my criteria, others withdrew when they saw their stories in print in draft form), I identified 30 people who were prepared to give in-depth interviews, and whose stories were varied enough to interest the general reader. Two of those later decided not to take part for fear of repercussions to their partners who are still in jail, so the final sample amounts to 28. A selection of 23 interviews appears in this book.

Because interviewees were self-referring, they were of course more likely to be people who were happy to talk about their successful relationships rather than those whose relationships had failed: 23 of the 28 couples are still together. Another obvious limitation of self-referral is that the sample cannot be said to be representative in terms of gender (24 of the 28 are female); or sexuality (all the couples are heterosexual); or ethnicity (27 of the 28 outside partners are white Caucasian and one is Asian; 27 of the 28 prisoners/ex-prisoners are white Caucasian and one is mixed-race). This is not in any way indicative of sexual or racial bias: it is just that fewer men, Black or ethnic background couples, and no gay people, came forward to join the project.

With Jane's help I devised a questionnaire,[13] which I sent in advance to people who agreed to an interview. The purpose of the questionnaire was twofold: to give people time to think about their life histories; and to give the interviews a loose structure. In practice people sometimes simply told their stories. I guaranteed anonymity if interviewees wished: exactly half asked for their names to be changed if I published their stories, either because they feared repercussions for partners still in prison, or because their partners were now free and they did not want neighbours and workmates to know their background. Those who are happy to be identified have their real surnames included in the chapter headings. All the other names are invented. All interviewees were sent full transcripts of the interviews and any changes they made were incorporated before the transcripts were edited down to chapter length.

PROFILE OF THE 'OUTSIDE' PARTNERS

The focus of my interviews, and of this book, is really on the 'outside partner': the man or woman who enters a relationship with a prisoner or ex-prisoner. So except in three cases, where it proved to be necessary, I did not go into the prisons and speak to the 17 partners who were still incarcerated at the time of interview (two of these have since been released). But 13 of the prisoner partners had been released at the time of interview, and of those, five wanted to join in the interviews. The other eight released prisoners did not wish to take part, or their partners preferred them not to, or they were simply unavailable on the day of the interview.

What kind of person forms a 'prison partnership'?

Age of outside partners
There are 24 women and four men in the sample. Their average age at the time was 42 years, older than the average age of their partners which was 39. Two-thirds of the outside partners are older than the prisoners. The average age difference is eight years and nine months, but at the greatest extreme one male outside partner is 26 years older than his ex-prisoner wife; another male outside partner is 26 years older than his prisoner wife; one female outside partner is 24 years older than her ex-prisoner husband. There are other large age gaps: two female outside partners are 17 years older than the prisoner/ex-prisoner; and one male prisoner 17 years older than his outside partner. The smallest age gap is a year.

Social background and education
In nearly two-thirds of these relationships there is a considerable difference between the partners in terms of social class/family background/education, and in 80 per cent of relationships where there is this disparity, the outside partner comes from a more privileged socio-economic background. Twenty-one per cent of the outside partners were privately educated (over three times the national average of seven per cent) and a quarter went on to further or higher education. Only one of the prisoners had attended a private school and could be said to come from a materially privileged background.

In some of the interviews it was interesting to hear middle-class partners adopting elements of prison language: at first it seemed incongruous to hear them using words like *cell spin, piss test, bang-up* and *knockback* [14] as if they were a natural part of their everyday conversation.

Employment
The outside partners work in many different fields of employment. For example, I interviewed a primary school teacher, a solicitor, a legal secretary, a bank clerk, a nurse, a refuse collector, a martial arts instructor, a painter and decorator, a paralegal and a security guard. More than one-third work in offices, administration or retailing, 21 per cent are professional people, 14 per cent have manual jobs and eleven per cent do some sort of creative work such as writing. Four per cent work in the leisure industry and eleven per cent were unemployed at the time.

Abuse and trauma
Unsurprisingly perhaps, 68 per cent of the *prisoner/ex-prisoner partners* had a difficult or abusive childhood. But although only one-fifth of the *outside partners* came from a broken home and/or a very large family, a high proportion—half of them—had suffered some kind of trauma in childhood (physical or sexual abuse, illness, early pregnancy or some other form of disruption). Some had been brought up in homes they considered repressive, like this woman:

> My father was very Victorian, very strict and he could be menacing. He always used to say to me and my brother, 'You'll both be hopeless, you'll both be useless, you'll end up on the streets!' I remembered my father one time I was visiting Ben in prison. I thought, What on earth would my father say if he could see me now? I could just hear him saying, 'I didn't expect any better of you!'

Over a third of the outside partners had suffered serious illness or acute personal distress, including the miscarriage or death of a child, at some time in their lives.[15] These high rates of distress may have made them more empathetic to the misfortunes of people in prison, or those who had just been released. During research for this book I interviewed Glen Fielding, an ex-prisoner who during his five-year sentence worked as a trained counsellor to other inmates, often discussing their relationships:

> Quite a high proportion of outside partners have, like the prisoners, also had life problems. Quite a few had been in care as children as a lot of prisoners have, and they had the personal problems that that can cause. Many had been sexually abused too. This meant there was empathy on either side, and this increased the attachment.

Youthful rebellion
More than half the outside partners (15) admitted they had been more rebellious than the average teenager, and several had run away from home, though often this was because of abuse. But this youthful rebellion might have predisposed them to find attractive and to empathise with the ultimate rebel—someone incarcerated for flouting authority. Only one of the outside partners could empathise directly with the prisoner's situation,

having been briefly imprisoned in his youth for a minor drugs offence. A quarter of the outside partners had channelled their youthful insubordination into campaigning of some kind in adulthood (peace and anti-nuclear protests or miscarriages of justice campaigns), which would also indicate a natural empathy with the underdog.

Earlier relationships
Nearly two-thirds of the outside partners had been married previously, 21 per cent of them more than once, and 68 per cent of them had been in relationships that were physically, emotionally or psychologically abusive. Sheila Isenberg found an even higher incidence of previous abusive relationships in women in love with killers.[16] Indeed, the only common thread she found among them was a history of abuse:

> I discovered that most women who were compelled to become involved had abusive pasts—either sexual, physical or psychological abuse—at the hands of their parents (fathers usually) or abusive first marriages or boyfriends. [17]

Where they live
In terms of geographical spread, just over half of the outside partners live in London or the home counties, with a fifth living in the Midlands, one tenth in the North of England, another ten per cent in East Anglia, and one person lives in Scotland.

PROFILE OF THE 'INSIDE' PARTNERS

Who were the prisoners/ex-prisoners these people had fallen in love with?

Serious offenders
There were no serial killers in my sample (though one was a convicted double-murderer), but most of the prisoner-partners had been convicted of serious offences. Over half had been convicted of murder, attempted murder or manslaughter, including one imprisoned on terrorist charges— though three of the convicted murderers claim they are innocent victims of miscarriages of justice. Eighteen per cent were convicted of armed robbery or conspiracy to rob; eleven per cent were in prison for drugs-related offences including importation; seven per cent were convicted of sex offences; one was in prison for kidnap and torture, one for a vicious mugging.

Long sentences
The average length of their sentences was 18 years, though this figure is inflated by the exemplary sentence given to the prisoner convicted of terrorist offences (152 years, reduced to six years through a plea bargain). The shortest sentence was one year.

Previous convictions

Nearly two-thirds had previous convictions. Of the eleven with no previous record, all but one had been convicted of murder or manslaughter.

Time served

The 17 partners still in prison at the time of interview had (up to that point) served an average of ten years. The 13 prisoners who had been released had served on average eight years. The longest time served was by a woman, released after 18 years. The shortest period served, by a man, was just one year, but that was the most recent of a series of other short sentences.

Time since release

On average the number of years since the released partners left prison was three years, but the longest period since release was 13 years and the shortest time was six months.

Previous relationships

Nearly half had been married before, and half had children from previous relationships.

ENDNOTES for *Chapter 1*

[1] *Greenfingers*, about prisoners winning an award at the Chelsea Flower Show, and *Lucky Break*, about prisoners who escaped during the staging of a musical.

[2] Roberta Jones, a Lancashire businesswoman aged 42, married Reggie Kray three years before his death at the age of 66. He is said to have left her the bulk of his estate, including book, song and film royalties.

[3] John Blake Publishing, July 2000.

[4] *Dear Peter: Letters to the Yorkshire Ripper*, BBC1, 9 May 2001.

[5] See interview p. 153. *Charlie's Angel*, a First Sight programme, was screened on BBC2 in December 2001.

[6] For list of media references see *Ancillary Information*, p. 279.

[7] *Barred Wives*, SBS, 1993.

[8] *Dream Lovers: Women Who Marry Men Behind Bars*, Wakefield Press, 1997.

[9] *Women Who Love Men Who Kill*, Simon and Schuster, 1991.

[10] Washington Square Press, 1999 (the author prefers her name to be printed in lower case letters).

[11] See *A Sense of Freedom*, Pan Books, 1977. The marriage ended after 20 years.

[12] See *Autobiography of a Murderer*, Pan Books, 1997. See also an interview in *Going Straight: After Crime and Punishment*, pp. 87-100, compiled by Angela Devlin and Bob Turney, Waterside Press 1999. Collins's latest critically acclaimed novel, *No Smoke*, was published in August 2001 by Canongate Crime.

[13] See *Ancillary Information*, p. 279.

[14] Cell search by officers; urine test for drugs; lock-up in cell; rejection of parole application.

[15] Sheila Isenberg found even higher rates among women in love with killers: almost all of her interviewees had suffered distress of this kind. See p. 169, *op. cit*

[16] See p. 177, *op. cit.*

[17] In 'What Makes Women Fall in Love with these Monsters?', *Daily Express*, 8 May 2001.

CHAPTER 2

Developing Relationships

I asked all the interviewees how they first met and began a relationship with their partner; how much they knew about the offence and what particularly attracted them to such an unlikely choice.

HOW WAS CONTACT FIRST MADE?

Previous links with prisons
Just over half of the outside partners had had some previous connection with prisons before they met the prisoner—they had perhaps visited a friend or relative in jail or they had a professional connection—and those people were obviously more likely to take prison visiting in their stride.

No previous association with prisons
The other half, who had never been inside a prison before, were filled with trepidation at the prospect, not only through revulsion based on their preconceptions, but because they feared seeing someone they cared for in such an environment. These people's reactions to their first visit seemed quite extreme, and they fell into two quite distinct categories. Some, like these three people, felt shocked and appalled by the experience:

> I had never been in a prison before. It was awful! We've all seen prison on the television, but to actually go in there and see those big walls, the officers and the guard dogs, and to get searched! I felt like I was in a dream. This wasn't happening to me.

> The whole thing [visiting Durham women's prison] was quite shocking to me, going through eight or nine locked doors to get to someone you're seeing. It was the whole violence and intimidation, the wretched impression of a big prison like that.

> I was only 18 the first time I went into Strangeways, and oh, it was horrible! Tony was on closed visits behind a screen. There was mesh all round the screen and you could see where people had tried stuffing cigarettes through. There was an officer with a dog behind him, and an officer with a dog behind us. Tony was just 17 years old.

More surprising were those who had quite the opposite sensation. The two women quoted below both have strong religious beliefs:

> I felt a sort of extra peace. It was like walking in and feeling I'd come home. As soon as I walked through the prison door I knew—I just felt at home.

Everybody kept saying to me, 'When they shut those doors behind you it'll feel dreadful!' But I just felt so comfortable that I sat and thought, I'm home.

Meeting through friends and relatives
Eighteen per cent had first made contact through mutual friends or relatives who knew other prisoners in the same jail.

Membership of church groups
Eleven per cent had established contact through their membership of church groups that support prisoners.

Prison professionals
Seven per cent were prison or legal professionals whose work brought them in contact with their future partners.

Meeting outside prison
Eighteen per cent of the couples had met outside the confines of the jail through normal social contact while the prisoner was on remand or on bail, and another eleven per cent while the prisoner was outside on day release. A few couples (seven per cent) knew each other in their early youth but only renewed their acquaintance years later after one had been incarcerated. One man met his future wife just after she was released.

Meeting through advertisements
One inmate met his wife (whom I interviewed but who later withdrew from the project) through advertising in a needlework magazine. The advert began: *Lonely lifer, just started cross-stitch*—though the wife he met through it doubts whether he had ever so much as threaded a needle! Another prisoner answered an advert for soldier penfriends that a mother and her teenage daughter had placed in an army magazine just for fun. When, to the mother's surprise, a letter arrived not from a soldier but from a prisoner, she refused to let her daughter answer. She replied herself and she and the prisoner are now married.

Meeting as penfriends
One in five had met through penfriend organizations—and one man met his partner when he saw the letter she wrote from prison to a national newspaper and responded himself.

It is very common for long-term prisoners to correspond with a large number of people outside the jail. Media reports often focus on people who get a thrill from association with high-profile serious offenders, and of course such men and women do exist. Siôn Jenkins, who has always maintained his innocence since being jailed in 1998 for the murder of his foster-daughter Billie-Jo, was amazed to receive so many letters from women wishing to be his 'friend'. Tony Martin, a farmer who was sentenced to life for killing a burglar who entered his home,[1] was sent 250 letters by a middle-aged widow. Sara Thornton, imprisoned for killing her husband, was bombarded by letters from male admirers.[2]

Prisoners are allowed to advertise for penpals, although they must first seek the Governor's permission. About nine years ago the long-established and highly-respected Prison Reform Trust set up a penfriend scheme for prisoners, to which several of my interviewees had subscribed. Both the prisoner and the outside correspondent had to apply for membership using an official form, stating their interests and—in the case of the prisoner—the offence. The outside correspondent was asked whether there were any kinds of offenders s/he would not wish to write to. The scheme's administrators did their best to match up those with common interests. As a safety measure, all correspondents sent their letters to the Trust which forwarded them on.

Via the Internet it is now possible for people to contact prisoners using a growing number of websites. One of the largest online dating agencies is Matchmakers, and several British prisoners told me they had been contacted by people using it. Though it is a general agency, it publishes links to other sites such as Meet-an-inmate.com, which comes with the tag: 'Lonely female and male inmates desire penpals'. In the USA, websites such as this one, Prisonpenpals.com, Friendsonbothsides.com and Veryspecialwomen.com claim that they are *bona fide* and most publish advice about respecting prisoners, and warn that few inmates have access to the Internet and that their mail is likely to be inspected. But others, such as Babes Behind Bars, sound much more dubious, with salacious invitations to male punters:

> Have you ever dreamed of dating a woman with a rap sheet? I know I have. Not only do I like a girl who takes charge, but one who gets charged— manslaughter, drug distribution—you name it.

Multiple penfriends
Seven of the interviewees said they had corresponded with and visited a large number of other prisoners before they met their partner, devoting much time and money to an activity that became a major part of their lives. One woman had 21 penfriends:

> I got far more from those 21 prisoners who wrote to me than they got from me, though they'd deny it. I felt loved and supported by them.

FIRST MEETING

Delay before meeting
In over one-third of the relationships there was a delay between the couple's first contact by letter and their first meeting. In the most extreme case Aisha, a Muslim woman, married her husband Muhammad, a lifer, by proxy without ever having met him. They fell in love through

correspondence over three years, but they did not meet until six weeks after the wedding. Charles Bronson's[3] wife Saira also agreed to marry him before they met, and the couple had only shared three visits before their wedding. Another couple corresponded for two years before they actually met, and a further six couples corresponded and spoke on the telephone for between six months and a year before meeting. Two couples waited just one month.

Reaction at first meeting

Most outside partners who met through correspondence said they felt very nervous before the first meeting. Aisha was terrified of meeting her new husband, Muhammad:

> I was already married to him but I was terrified—absolutely terrified in case he didn't like me, what I looked like... I didn't know what he looked like at all, to the point that when I spoke to him on the phone I had to ask him what colour he was—I really didn't know. I have a feeling that I asked him that before I married him, not after, but it didn't make any difference anyway because I fell in love with the person, not what he looked like... I went into the visits room and they told me the table number. I was looking for it and I was concentrating so much on finding it, that though Muhammad was standing there calling me, I just ignored him! He kept calling me and all of a sudden it just clicked that it was him and I went and sat down. He sat opposite me and he couldn't even look at me.. he was talking to me but looking over his shoulder to the side. Then he picked up my hand and looked at my wedding ring and said, 'That's nice', but then he dropped my hand really quickly because he felt awkward and I did too.

This trepidation was by no means one-sided. Glen Fielding describes counselling prisoners who faced the prospect with alarm:

> In all probability the prisoner is going to be more nervous than the visitor. I've helped inmates on the run-up to a visit and some were absolutely terrified. I've come across a few who didn't even go on the visit. They were called by the officers but just couldn't cope. Then they went through hell trying to come to terms with the fact that they couldn't cope with seeing the person they really wanted to see.

Three of the interviewees who began as penfriends admitted feeling disappointment because the prisoner failed to live up to the romantic image they had formed and indeed, one in five of all interviewees acknowledged, like the two women quoted below, that the prisoner's appearance was not quite what they had expected:

> In his letters he had written, 'Look—I'm no Chippendale. People have told me I look like a thug. I'm so worried that when you meet me you won't like what you see.' I admit that I just didn't expect the face that turned round and

looked at me and smiled. But once I sat down with him and we started talking it made no difference at all.

From his letters he had come across as this confident person, and I'd imagined this big sort of hunky guy. He looked like his photo but there was none of the confidence—he was like a shy little boy.

The prisoners may well have felt the same sense of dismay: even if a couple had exchanged photographs, they had sometimes chosen very flattering likenesses, and in the prisoner's case, a picture taken many years earlier. Long-term inmates are unlikely to have an up-to-date photo in their possession. Nevertheless, two-thirds of interviewees said they felt immediate physical attraction, while a surprisingly large 36 per cent said they felt love at first sight.[4]

This little guy came through the visits room door, built like an Oxo cube, square as he was tall—and I fell in love with him, just like that, the moment I saw him. Before that, if somebody had told me that that happens I would have said, 'There's certainly no such thing as love at first sight!'

As soon as I met him I knew I was going to marry him. I know it sounds corny but the moment I met him I really knew he was the right person. If you'd said to me, 'Love at first sight' I'd have said, 'Rubbish!' But it felt so right.

The first time I saw him I literally fell in love with him.

I knew instantly he was the right person for me.

The first time I saw him I said, 'I'm going to marry him!' I was only 16.

The first time I saw him I thought: That man's going to influence my life in a big way. I hadn't even spoken to him.

Perhaps the most dramatic example was a woman who fell in love with a prisoner the very first time she saw him working in her neighbour's garden on a prison community scheme:

What I felt was unlike anything I'd ever felt before. It was an overwhelming feeling that I should be with this man. I knew I should be living my life with him. The feelings were so intense, and what reinforced my feelings was the look on his face when he looked at me. It was like everything I was feeling was exactly what he was feeling too.

Instant rapport and ease of conversation were mentioned by a quarter of partners. Seven per cent said they just found the prisoner interesting and quite different from their preconceptions about criminals:

The first time I met him I was terrified. He was a rapist—one of those nasty things you read about in newspapers. But when I saw him I couldn't get over how normal he was. This was the thing that amazed me more than anything else. You expect a rapist to look really creepy, not normal.

VULNERABILITY OF OUTSIDE PARTNERS

The benefits for prisoners of an outside relationship

Prisoners serving long sentences, as most of these were, have a lot to gain and little to lose from having a loving partner outside the jail. It means there is someone to take an interest in them, a particularly welcome prospect for prisoners long since abandoned by their own family and friends; someone to write letters and chat to on the telephone, to bring them clothes and other permitted goods and cash. Some also believe that having a stable relationship and a home outside will improve their chances of parole, and it is certainly true that prisoners need a home address if they are to be released early on electronic tagging.

With all these benefits to be had, it is not surprising to find plenty of anecdotal evidence about prisoners setting up liaisons through their cell-mates.[5] One male prisoner-partner told me about a fellow-prisoner—a lifer—who had established relationships with four women in his desperate (and, according to my informant, ruthless) attempts to find a wife who he thought would raise his chances of parole. Prisoners who become romantically involved with officials in their own jails may hope for special privileges as well as sexual gratification.

Potential for abuse of a penfriend relationship

The Prison Reform Trust (PRT) has now handed the running of its penfriend scheme to a charity solely dedicated to the purpose. One of the reasons behind the move is the need for constant supervision of correspondence because of the danger of abuse. The PRT, while proud to have pioneered the scheme, was pleased to hand it on. Juliet Lyon, the Director, said, 'So many people have benefited from this scheme over the years but, given the risks, we knew we had to find very safe hands in which to place it.' A spokesperson for the new charity told me: 'Having taken advice from the Prison Service and our own lawyers, we are acutely aware that careful selection of participants, strict guidelines and on-going monitoring will always be needed to ensure that a scheme like this is not used unwisely and without caution.'

Lack of social checks

People whose only knowledge of their partner comes from letters and prison visits are bound to be vulnerable in ways far less applicable to a couple meeting outside prison, however long the courtship period. In normal social circumstances there are all sorts of checks and balances that can be applied. People can watch reactions to friends and family members; they can assess how their partners cope with stress at home and at work; they can observe their body language in all sorts of different social situations, and of course they may well live together before making a formal commitment. But in a prison visiting room, social intercourse is confined to a highly artificial environment where there is no interaction with anyone else apart from prison officers. Telephone conversations and letters may be constrained for fear of surveillance.

These observations can apply equally to the prisoner: I remember interviewing for another project a male lifer who protested his innocence. He had married a woman who visited him regularly, claiming to be a qualified lawyer who wanted to help him, though he discovered after their wedding that she was no such thing. She made many other claims that proved to be false, including driving to the jail in her own large car—in fact she could not drive, owned no vehicle and came by train. After the marriage, according to the prisoner, she became abusive and when the disillusioned prisoner applied for a divorce, she made allegations to prison staff which, had they not known the prisoner to be of good behaviour, might have seriously jeopardised his prison status and even his appeal process.

Physical risks

Media reports quite naturally emphasize the vulnerability of the non-prisoner partner, with stories highlighting the danger of jail romances. An extreme example was the tragic case of Margaret Thompson, murdered by her prisoner fiancé in April 2000 when he was on day release, in a crime chillingly similar to the killing of another of his girlfriends ten years earlier.[6] Less dramatically, but still with potentially severe consequences, there will of course be prisoners who exploit their partners outside for money, luxuries like expensive trainers and designer clothes, personal stereos and watches, tobacco and even drugs smuggled into prison. While researching an earlier book on women's prisons[7] I remember interviewing a grandmother in her fifties who was distraught when she was jailed for smuggling cannabis into a prison for her boyfriend. She had never broken the law before but wanted to surprise her lover with a birthday present: 'He said he couldn't understand why I'd done it—he could get any drug he wanted inside prison.'

One of my interviewees for *Cell Mates/Soul Mates*, a woman who suffers from mental health problems, was swindled out of a large sum of money by a prisoner in an earlier relationship. He pretended the cash was to buy him a computer but in reality his family gambled it away. This woman, who has always suffered from low self-esteem and loneliness, found friendship among the many prisoners she wrote to before she married one of them. Although few of the outside partners were as needy as that woman, there were two others whose very first boyfriend was the prisoner marrying. One was raised in a very strict religious family, the other was very shy and lived in a small village with few opportunities for meeting the opposite sex. Their previous knowledge of men was extremely limited.

Three of the 13 people whose partners had been released said they had felt a threat to their personal safety. The other ten felt they had never been in any danger from their released partners.

> I have never, ever, felt threatened by him at all, and believe me, if he was going to kill again, he would have done it to me, because I have pushed him to the limits.

> I've never had the feeling that she would suddenly flare up and attack me.

Was the outside partner fully aware of the prisoner's offence?

A quarter of the outside partners were already aware of the crime before the couple met, and over half of the interviewees said that their partners volunteered information about their crimes, though of course it was up to the outside partner to try to check its veracity:

> He was very open with me about his offence. He said, 'Let's talk about it. Anything you want to know, ask me. Don't listen to anyone else—just ask me'. So we talked about the rape.

> He told me things that could potentially have made me think about ending the relationship. He didn't know how I was going to react but he wanted everything out in the open, so that I was fully aware of all the facts. Nothing he told me made the slightest difference; I was more certain about my feelings for him than I had been about anything before in my life.

There is an unwritten rule whereby, according to jail etiquette, it is considered inappropriate to ask a prisoner directly about his or her offence. This may have encouraged some partners to adopt an ostrich-like attitude:

> I knew from the start that he had been in prison, but I didn't ask what he'd done. I suppose it was a few months before I knew. He did say he'd tell me but I said I didn't want to know, because I knew that when my parents asked, I would have to tell them. I've always been the kind of person that can't tell a lie and I thought, If I don't know, then I can't tell anyone.

Often when they found out about their partners' crimes, people were terribly shocked by the revelation:

> I put the phone down—I was gutted. The worst of all crimes to me is child murder.

> I remember feeling quite dazed and shocked and thinking, What the heck have you got yourself into here?

The male outside partners seemed more likely than the females to take the revelation of the offence in their stride:

> People can make mistakes. On the streets I've come within an inch of killing somebody in a fight. It can just happen when you lose your temper. If she'd been a cold, compulsive serial killer—that's a bit heavy! But a one-off, in an argument when you end up killing somebody—I can quite understand that.

> She has always been honest with me, right from the beginning. I have never felt any danger from her, because I understand completely why she ended up killing.

Concealing the offence
Eleven per cent of the prisoners concealed the nature of the offence and seven per cent only revealed it when the outside partner demanded.

Rationalising the offence
A quarter of the outside partners said they understood why the offence was committed and many attempted to rationalise it (claiming it was caused by drugs or alcohol, by provocation or by being easily led). None condoned the offence, but several, particularly those involved with sex offenders, portrayed the offence as less serious than the jail term suggested. The language they used undermined the severity of the crime. A serial flasher was 'an utter pillock' according to his girlfriend, and there was a kind of forced bravado underlying her robust riposte:

> I said to him, 'If you'd exposed yourself to me, you'd have been wearing your balls for earrings!'

Several interviewees did not feel their partners were criminals at all: they believed they were victims of a miscarriage of justice or political prisoners. Sheila Isenberg said of her interviews with the partners of killers:

> Each woman excused her lover's murder; some concocted fabulous rationalisations to explain how the murder took place.. Others excused the murder by blaming it on social forces or drugs or alcohol. These denials are part of each woman's individual defence mechanism for coping... With women who love men who kill, there is always *although*. There are always circumstances. There are always excuses. There are, mostly, denials'.[8]

Apparent lack of concern by criminal justice authorities
Only one-third of outside partners had ever been asked by police, prison or probation authorities whether they were fully aware of the relationship they were getting into. The two people quoted below were very much the exception. The first woman was just 18 when she went to visit a convicted murderer, and was summoned into an office in the prison:

The probation officer said to me, 'Don't look so worried, this is just a friendly chat. But we're concerned about your relationship with R. It seems to be getting too serious and we don't think it's a good idea for you to carry on.'

Another older woman, whose husband had become eligible to apply for his first home leave, was grateful to be taken aside by the prison Governor:

The Governor said that J's victim had been contacted and she didn't want him allowed out. Then the Governor really thrashed it out with me. He asked me if I was aware of J's offence and he didn't pull any punches with me, and I respected him enormously for that. I did know what J had done, but I felt that in a way the Governor wanted to protect me.

One woman prisoner said the prison staff, particularly the lifer governor, had asked her to wait before marrying in prison a man who proposed to her five weeks after they met. Officers observed the couple on visits and two months later said they were satisfied that the relationship was a safe one.

But nearly two-thirds of the outside partners said they were not contacted in any way, and they were given no information about the nature of the prisoner's offence by any official. Of course, all the outside partners were adults with the right to form any relationship they chose but it seems strange that official concern for protecting the public does not seem to extend to them.

It may seem even more surprising to those outside the criminal justice system that when a convicted prisoner marries, there is no statutory obligation on any agency to reveal the nature of the crime to the prisoner's partner, even when the prisoner is still incarcerated for a very serious crime, when the marriage ceremony takes place inside the jail and when it could be argued that by allowing it, the prison authorities are condoning the relationship.

The Prison Service is very clear on this point. In a written reply to my query about their responsibility, a spokesperson confirmed that:

Under the Marriage Act 1983, now reinforced by Article 12 of the Human Rights Act 1998, people have a right to marry, and consequently the prison's role in considering applications does not extend to the suitability of the marriage of the prisoner and his/her partner, although the marriage will be reported, where it is appropriate, to those responsible for lifers and for prisoners subject to extradition orders.[9]

There are only two circumstances in which the Prison Service may refuse an application to marry, neither of them related to concern for the outside partner's safety. The first is purely pragmatic—for the prison's convenience. An application to marry may be rejected 'if prisoners are due to be released or temporarily released within the month, and therefore do not have long to wait before they organize their own ceremony'. The second has to do with the proper conduct of the criminal justice system: an application to marry may also be turned down 'if the Crown Prosecution Service expresses concerns that the marriage may interfere with the processes of justice e.g. if a remand prisoner wishes to marry a prosecution witness.' But, the spokesperson confirmed:

> In answer to your specific question about whether the Prison Service is in a position to refuse an application to marry where there is a concern that the prisoner may pose a risk to the partner, the ultimate answer is no. However, where a risk is identified, the prison obviously has a responsibility to explore this and the implications for rehabilitation with the *prisoner* [author's italics], and where it is able to make contact with the partner (e.g. if there is an established link between him/her and social services) will do so, although *the prison is not able to disclose the nature of the prisoner's offence* [author's italics].'

Not all staff are happy with this rule. A prison Governor described her concern when a sex offender in her jail formed a relationship with a 15-year-old girl with learning difficulties, considered by social services to be very vulnerable. Her parents seemed happy to bring her to see the prisoner, but the Governor was unsure whether they or the girl knew of the inmate's offences (the rape of his nine-year-old sister and other sex crimes), and she felt very frustrated that she was not at liberty to tell them.[10]

The same rules of confidentiality apply when a prisoner is released and is still under the supervision of the Probation Service. The only circumstances in which the nature of the crime can be revealed at the point of release is if there are child protection issues. Two of my interviewees come into this category, and face having their children taken away if they are still with the prisoner when he is released, and if they permit him to live in the family home—though in both these cases the prisoners have allowed their partners to read their deposition papers, and they seem to be aware of the full extent of their offences. Another woman who fell in love with an imprisoned rapist was—in a most irregular but perfectly understandable departure from the rules—summoned by the man's probation officer to his office and ordered to read everything in her partner's files before he came up for parole. She felt this was a shocking breach of confidentiality as she claimed her partner had told her all about his past—though he denied rape and said his victim had consented.

Like that woman, a male outside partner resented being taken aside by his fiancée's probation officer:

> He said to me in a roundabout way, 'You do know what you're letting yourself in for?' But he didn't know her, and most of the prison officers didn't know her either.

There have been cases where the nature of a prisoner's offence has been revealed only after the couple have married. The fiancé of one woman sanitised his horrific crime and she only found out about it two weeks after their marriage when an anonymous letter arrived with a backdated copy of the local paper reporting it. Another woman avoided asking too many details about her boyfriend's offence because, in her words, 'it made him angry'. Only when her forthcoming marriage made headlines in the press did she discover that he had brutally murdered another woman. She still went ahead with the wedding. Neither man has yet been released.

Another woman, married to a convicted murderer, felt it was up to the outside partner to find out about the offence:

> At the end of the day you're responsible for yourself, and if you don't protect yourself, then you've got nobody to cry to. The prison authorities can't tell you about the offence—they're not allowed to because of confidentiality. I don't believe they should be allowed to either, because confidentiality is an issue that you can't divide. You either operate under the confidentiality rules or you don't. You can't have special circumstances, and if a woman chooses to marry someone and she is not aware of the situation, then more fool her.

WHAT ATTRACTS PEOPLE TO RELATIONSHIPS WITH PRISONERS?

In *Chapter 1* I described the way these relationships are stereotyped by the media in different categories—the gangster's moll, the obsessed woman and so on. Other people who have written on this subject have made their own attempts at categorisation. Jacquelynne Willcox-Bailey describes her own 'crude categories': the 'saviours', the 'martyrs', the 'sufferers for love' and the 'power freaks'.[11] Sheila Isenberg sees women who love killers essentially as victims, repeating a pattern of abusive relationships. Certainly some of these elements exist in the relationships described in this book, but by their very complexity, they defy simplistic definition.

A few of my interviewees are vulnerable people, and half of them have suffered past abuse: the risks to them are discussed above and later in the book. But the remaining half have not suffered abuse, they are not lovelorn obsessives, and many are competent and confident individuals with good jobs and full social lives. So why do they find such relationships attractive?

Friendship
Nearly half mentioned friendship as the basis of their relationship—an interesting finding at a time when friendship in society in general is said to be in decline.[12] One of the male outside partners suggested why a non-

threatening friendship is so important to people who have often been damaged in the past:

> We were building a friendship more than a relationship. In relationships you bring all the garbage from your past and all the defence mechanisms against things that have hurt you over the years. But we were just friends for about 18 months before we married.

Physical attraction
Half mentioned physical attraction which continued after the immediate impact of the couple's first meeting.

Sense of humour
Nearly one-third spoke of a shared sense of humour, which most saw as vital to survive the tribulations of prison life:

> We've got the same sense of humour. He'll make a remark and I'll understand why it's so funny, but somebody else'll say, 'What're you laughing at?'

Shared interests
A quarter of interviewees said they shared similar interests, such as music, art, reading and writing.

Relationship based on honesty
One seventh said they particularly valued their prisoner-partner's openness about his or her past, and one-third expressed their deeply-held belief that the relationship was based on honesty on both sides:

> If I were asked to give advice to other people in the same situation, I'd say the main thing is always to be honest and open with each other, however much you think it might hurt.

Helping the prisoner
A quarter of interviewees said they had a wish to help the prisoner and in most cases their help seems to have been gratefully received, though professional 'do-gooders', however well-meaning, are traditionally regarded by prisoners with scepticism:

> All these people kept coming round and it got on my nerves a lot.

> I called the do-gooders 'twirlies'. My idea of a twirly is a blue-rinse older woman.

Outside partners often claimed a form of exclusivity: they had managed to help the prisoner by establishing an intimate relationship and 'sorting out' their man where nobody else had succeeded:

He never used to let anyone in to himself. Eventually I got through this wall and we're so close now.

In his own words, he's never found a woman strong enough to keep him out of prison. They encourage him to drink—he's always been drunk when he committed an offence.

Many spoke of being needed by the prisoner, vowing, like the brutal Bill Sykes's long-suffering Nancy, to stay 'As long as he needs me'.[13] Women partners seem to be particularly conscientious, writing regularly to the prisoner and always trying their best to be supportive. Many said they found the prisoners' gratitude surprising and touching—very different from the attitude of current partners who took them for granted. In turn their own self-esteem increased:

I sometimes think, Why am I doing this? But I don't mean it. I don't think I could ever leave him. At the end of the day I'm the only person he's really got. He always says how lucky he is to have me.

Why have I stuck with him through all these problems? Because he needs me.

He has said he'd never survive without me.

Frequent telephone contact

Most rejoiced in regular telephone calls which, they felt, also showed how much the person in prison needed them. 'He phones me daily', said one woman, 'and he's so regular I can set my watch by his phone calls'. Sometimes the calls were much more frequent—many times throughout the day if the prisoner could get access to a phone—and such demands on the outside partner's time could be interpreted as worryingly obsessive and controlling—though less so now that so many couples call and text-message each other frequently on mobile phones. The late Reggie Kray is reported to have phoned his wife Roberta five times a day. A controlling personality can exercise that control even from behind prison walls, and I have been shown letters from a male lifer warning his girlfriend (not one of my interviewees for this book) that she will be bound to him forever because he is now 'inside her head'. Helena Kennedy QC writes in her book *Eve was Framed*:[14] 'Some women feel strangely flattered at being chosen by such men, as though they had been singled out from the ordinary run of womankind.' Such abuse of power can be even more dangerous if one partner convinces the other that s/he is emotionally dependent, even threatening suicide to maintain the relationship.

Empathising with the prisoner

These feelings were often described as mutual. A quarter of interviewees said they and their partners empathised with each other and one in six found the prisoner kind and supportive:

> I've had more emotional support from Jeff than I've had from any other man—ever. When my daughter had whooping cough he rang me every day to make sure we were OK.

People trapped in loveless marriages often ironically compared their own situation—imprisoned, as they saw it, in an emotionally sterile home life—with the physical incarceration of the jail:

> I'm sure I could relate to those prisoners because I felt I was in a prison as well.

> At home I felt cut off and alienated. In fact, ironically, I felt like I was living in a wretched prison.

Mothering

Some women showed a strong maternal instinct:

> I do always want to protect. Once a counsellor told me I had the highest rating she'd ever seen for a mothering, parenting attitude. And I said, 'Yes, I can often hear myself. I often say to B [her ex-prisoner husband] before he goes out, "Have you got your tissues?"'

Women partners spoke of buying the prisoner trainers and designer clothes as they would a son. If they complained, it was the kind of affectionate grumble that a mother might make, showing her pride in fulfilling the stereotypical maternal self-sacrificial role:

> In prison men are children: they see the latest thing and they want it.

> I try to go up to the prison once a week, but it depends on time, my shifts, and money. It's a two-hour trip to get there, so there's the petrol. I took £100 with me last Saturday and I didn't have a lot left when I came back. I started helping out when I went up on a visit and he looked like a tramp. He looked absolutely awful! I said to him, 'Can't you get any decent clothes in here?' and he said, 'No, not unless somebody sends them to me.' I don't feel I *have* to supply him with stuff—I *want* to do it.

> I feel sorry for some women whose men seem very selfish. I can remember talking to one woman who used to take a load of kids to visit their dad. One day she showed me a list and on it were written the names of about 20 cassettes that this guy wanted his wife to go out and buy for him—and these were proper shop tapes he wanted, not copies. And she was going to get them too, though the kids had holes in their shoes, holes in their clothes.

Several of the male prisoners had lost their own mothers while they were in prison, often feeling great guilt, particularly when they had to attend the funeral in handcuffs. So maybe there was a kind of surrogacy in their relationship with their outside partners, and the mothering often continued after release:

> In the early days [after his release] it was like having a child in the house—and it still is sometimes. I had to teach him how to use the cashpoint machine, how to write a cheque. I remember the first time I took him to buy a pair of jeans and it was so embarrassing—he wasn't prepared to pay more than £8 and I had to guide him out of the shop. I said to him, 'The last time you purchased an article of clothing was in 1981! Get real!'

Male chivalry

In male outside partners the parental instinct manifested itself in a form of macho chivalry. Three women said their prisoner partners actually addressed them as 'Princess', making them feel precious and special. Earlier I mentioned Sara Thornton, a high-profile lifer before her murder conviction was quashed in 1996. Sara told me:

> I had loads of men writing to me when I was in prison. A man wrote and said he had a big house with five bedrooms and he would look after me. Men want their masculinity affirmed. George[15] wanted to come along like a knight in shining armour and rescue me. He liked that role. He said he would take me away to his castle. But that would have been going from one prison to another.

Enjoying the prisoner's attention

A quarter of interviewees spoke of enjoying the undivided attention they got from the prisoner compared with previous relationships. As Kate Kray told a journalist:

> When women marry a person in prison it's because the prisoner has got nothing else to do but concentrate all their time and energy on the woman outside. [When I met Ron] it was at a time of my life when I'd had a divorce and a hysterectomy and I didn't fit in with Pampers [nappies] and coffee mornings. I suppose subconsciously I was looking for someone who didn't want that from me.[16] .

Many described being enchanted and flattered by the amount of time the prisoner was prepared to devote to writing long letters and talking exclusively to them for two hours during prison visits—where there were no interruptions and nobody else was allowed an audience unless specifically invited. Nearly one-third of the interviewees said the prisoner was 'easy to talk to'. They enjoyed exploring in their letters and in conversation personal and philosophical matters never discussed with their husbands or wives and indeed, in few relationships outside prison do couples find the time to sit down and talk in this way for hours at a time. Long-term prisoners have had plenty of time to think about their own lives and about life in general, sometimes encouraged to do so by offending behaviour programmes. So their conversation is often on a level far more considered than the usual pub banter.

But Sheila Isenberg is more sceptical:

> Men in prison are the best psychologists in the world, because they spend most of their time watching people and reading them... Out of necessity, out of their need to survive, they learn this skill... When a man ... focuses this way on a woman, it's often the first time, for her, that anyone has paid her that much attention.[17]

Building romantic relationships through letters

One-third said the prisoner wrote such good letters that they had fallen in love through their correspondence. It is easy to understand the pleasure a long and romantic daily letter must give to a lonely person, especially now that letter-writing is so often replaced by the mobile phone and the e-mail—though many partners also send prisoners audio-cassettes on which they record their thoughts and feelings. They say they find it comforting to think of the prisoner sitting in the cell listening to them.

But any impression that all the outside partners are sad characters sitting at home waiting for the postman's knock would be mistaken. This lifer's wife has a responsible full-time job in a building society, is a DIY expert and cares for the couple's nine-year-old son:

> Tony and I write thousands of letters to each other—I've got a big box full of his letters. We write five letters a week—two sides of A4 at least every day— and the weekend letter is a big long one. Everybody says, 'What do you find to write about?' But if you write every day you can write trivia, whereas if you only write to somebody every six months you have to tell them something important. He also rings me every night as long as he can get to the phone.

Several people showed me boxes stacked with letters and cards the prisoner had sent them. One man had papered his kitchen walls with cards from his imprisoned wife. Many couples wrote poetry to each other and some of it is included in this book. The prisoners could be just as romantic as their partners: one man designed and printed his own wedding invitations, using the jail's computer equipment to embellish the words with hearts and wedding bells.

The courtship letters, though regarded as romantic and kept lovingly stored, were not all hearts and flowers. Prisoners loved hearing about the minutiae of domestic life, such as the purchase of a washing machine, and one man, who had been jailed years earlier as a teenager, begged his future wife to send him her electricity bills as he had never seen one. For long-termers the letters provided a welcome contact with everyday life outside, and they formed a valuable part of the rehabilitation process for inmates soon to be released. Two women said they took detailed photographs of their own homes and gardens so that the prisoner could piece them together in his cell and get to know the home which would one day be his.

The prisoner as 'protector'

Eleven per cent said they felt the prisoner could somehow protect them, despite being behind bars. This seems to account for some women being attracted to 'hard men'. The most striking example of this is the story of Jan Lamb, friend of the Krays and Charles Bronson, who on the face of it fulfils every media stereotype of a gangster's moll. But her association with hard men dates from her childhood when—fitting the pattern identified by Sheila Isenberg—she was beaten and sexually abused by her mother's violent lover, a man she calls Shaw:

> I think I purposely looked for the bad lads with knuckle-dusters and knives because they could protect me from people like Shaw. Once I met up with Charlie Kray and started going round with his crowd, I can remember always feeling safe and I can remember thinking, No-one can harm me now. If Shaw was ever to come near me now, he'd soon get sorted out. I always feel safe with Charlie Bronson because I know he detests paedophiles like my stepfather. Even now, if anyone tells Charlie someone's upset me, he'll get a letter in the post to them straight away.

A 'safe' relationship

Several women interviewed for this book had suffered years of abuse and they said they regarded their prisoner partner as a safe choice. Using the word *safe* to describe relationships with rapists, murderers and armed robbers may seem strange, unless the word in interpreted literally to mean that the prisoner is safely locked away. But its meaning here may be more subtle. One male outside partner, whose first wife was an alcoholic, was particularly perceptive:

> I think her being in jail and me being outside was like a release for her. The barrier of the jail actually helped. It meant we could say things that we wouldn't have got into as deeply if we were both outside. Basically that's because there was no threat to either of us. We could talk about our problems, what we felt about things, our past—without the problem of actually having a relationship.

Some people, like this man, said they wanted partners who were unable to hurt them or cheat on them. One woman had been badly treated by a series of men:

> I'd been determined to stay on my own, but I needed to know somebody cared for me. And the easiest way was to communicate with somebody in

prison, so I wouldn't have the bad bits that can go with a relationship. The only thing I was interested in was that D was good with women. From his letters he appeared to be kind. He was different from my last one—he didn't appear to be openly violent.

Another woman, who married her husband after he was released, admitted:

While he was in prison it was lovely and romantic because he would phone, then I'd have the letters—it was lovely. Prison was a safe environment and it was all very romantic. I did feel several times later on that we had a better relationship when he was in prison than when he came out. He was inside and I knew where he was. I was outside and I could do what I wanted to do without having to consult anybody.

Although these relationships may feel safe when the prisoner is in jail, all 70,000 people currently in prison—apart from about 25 'natural lifers'—will one day be released. This particular woman's choice of partner turned to be one that was far from safe when the man was first released. Under great pressure and suffering from the trauma of withdrawal from long-term drug misuse he became paranoid and insanely jealous and beat her so badly she had to be hospitalised.[18] He later recovered, they married and are still together, though she confesses:

There are times, even lately, when he's got up suddenly and stood over me and I can feel myself recoiling. Then I'll say how I feel and he'll say, 'No, it's not going to happen again'.

Religion
Religious faith was important to nearly a third of the interviewees, and a quarter said they felt that they and their prisoner partners had been brought together by God. Of the ten who mentioned their faith, two are Roman Catholic, four Evangelical, two Muslim and two Church of England. Sheila Isenberg found that many of her American interviewees were raised in the Catholic faith: 'They need to suffer in order to be saved.'[19] Several of my interviewees said they frequently prayed for guidance:

I said to God, 'If You don't want us to be together, however much it hurts, then take him away and I'll never hear from him again. But if You do want us to be together, please, please let me hear from him'. And within a week of me praying that prayer, he had rung me.

The woman who was violently attacked by her partner when he was first released said she felt this was God's punishment:

Even when B was beating me up I never thought God had deserted me. But I do believe that when you're not living according to God's laws, He does withhold His protection from you. When B and I lived together before we were married we were not living a Christian life, that's for sure. I think the things that happened, happened because God was saying, 'OK, you've gone your own way. You carry on!'

The denial of self for the sake of others was second nature to many of the female outside partners I interviewed because suffering and self-sacrifice were at the root of their Christian beliefs. One Catholic woman's whole life has been shaped by her devotion to a man she fell in love with when they were both 17, just after he had committed a murder and was jailed At Her Majesty's Pleasure. She spoke poignantly of the impact on her life of the strict order of nuns who educated her:

They had a quite an influence on me and I've found they still do today. They have to dig a piece of their own grave every day.

A Muslim wife said:

We believe that everything in your life is predestined. In the Qur'an it tells you, 'We made a mate for each of you.' My husband believes we are the same unit, but we were divided by time. It's funny, because we talk sometimes and I say, 'Really, I don't need to phone you any more, because you answer before I even ask you the questions!' That happens a lot to us— an awful lot.

Fate/Destiny
Over two-thirds (68 per cent) had a very strong sense that Fate had brought them together—their union, they felt, was in some way predestined. Several outside partners spoke of events that were probably coincidences— such as being in the same town on the same day without realising it—as if they were acts of Fate. Nearly one-third said they and their partners were soul mates, and described various telepathic experiences:

He would ring and before I even picked the phone up he would know something was wrong. Before I said a word he'd say, 'What's the matter?'

Such thoughts are common in many courtships, but here perhaps, the intervention of Fate was a way of rationalising a choice that seems so irrational to others. Belief in God or Fate also absolves the believer from responsibility (and blame) for the choice of partner. This woman's comment was typical of many:

I am very much into Fate and karma, and this was obviously meant to be.

ENDNOTES for *Chapter 2*

1 Tony Martin's conviction for murder was later reduced to one of manslaughter by the Court of Appeal on the ground of diminished responsibility.

2 But it is only fair to note that many correspondents write to prisoners for years, just as friends and supporters, and do not get emotionally involved in any way.

3 Bronson changed his name to Ali Charles Ahmed—taking the name of his wife's father—a few months after his marriage when he decided to become a Muslim. See interview, p. 153.

4 A recent survey by the publisher Mills & Boon found that three-quarters of men and women believe in love at first sight and that it will last. One-third claim to have experienced it themselves. *Daily Express*, 24 January 2002.

5 For evidence from a probation officer, see Julian Broadhead, 'Prison as a Dating Agency', *New Law Journal*, November 1999.

6 See *Ancillary Information*, p. 279.

7 *Invisible Women: What's Wrong with Women's Prisons?*, Waterside Press, 1998.

8 See p. 143 and p. 146, *op. cit.*

9 Source: Prison Service Press Office, Autumn 2000. In the USA, for example, inmates have no such statutory right to marry, unless, in some states, the couple already have a child or the woman is pregnant. But Sheila Isenberg describes a test case in May 1989 when a judge overturned a New York state law which previously forbade lifers to marry. The judge said, 'The right to marry in a prison setting is a fundamental one.' (see p. 63 *op. cit*).

10 The governor solved the problem by insisting that the inmate's probation officer accompanied the girl on visits. The law has now been changed. Under Prison Service Order 4400, no Schedule One offender (i.e. which includes a range of sex offenders) is allowed visits from any children other than their own and even these have to be risk-assessed.

11 See *Dream Lovers: Women Who Marry Men behind Bars*, Australia: Wakefield Press, 1999 p. 3.

12 In *Losing Friends* (Social Affairs Unit, 1991) Digby Anderson argues that friendship is failing for a number of reasons: our increasingly busy and transient lives; family breakdown; and loss of trust.

13 From the musical *Oliver*.

14 Vintage Books, 1993, p. 249.

15 George Delf: their six-month relationship is described in G. Delf and S. Thornton, *Love on the wing: Letters of Hope from Prison*, Penguin, 1996. See interview, p. 224.

16 Interview with Cal McCrystal, *Independent on Sunday*, 1 April 2001.

17 See p. 62 *op. cit.*

18 Women's Minister Barbara Roche told a TUC women's conference (14 March 2002) that a woman dies every three days in Britain as a victim of domestic violence, and one in four women has been hit at home at some point. Victims span the whole spectrum from the partners of judges and doctors to the partners of dustmen. The domestic violence charity Refuge receives 1,000 calls a week on its helpline.

19 See p. 89 *op. cit.*

CHAPTER 3

Staying Together

Having made their choice of partner, how easy was it for people to sustain the relationship, often in the face of opposition from family and friends?

Length of courtship
Because media reports inevitably focus on seemingly irrational and sudden marriages like that of Saira Rehman and Charles Bronson, there is a perception that prison relationships must all be impetuous acts of folly. But my research shows that very few outside partners had rushed to commit themselves to the relationship, even if they claimed it was 'love at first sight'. On average they were together with their partners for nearly three years before they made any such decision, with 75 per cent visiting regularly, the same number writing frequent letters and 39 per cent relying on phone calls and sometimes audio tapes.

Conduct of courtship
One of the most interesting features of these case-histories is the almost Victorian formal nature of the courtship period imposed by the constraints of the prison system. Unlike most modern relationships on the outside, where there is no longer much moral stigma attached to cohabitation, these partnerships were forced to develop steadily and gradually, with partners getting to know each other through their letters and—with prison officers acting as chaperones more strict than any nineteenth-century matron—little opportunity for sexual contact. Visiting rooms are now much more stringently policed than they once were, in an attempt to prevent drugs being passed, and if guards think couples' embraces are becoming too intimate, they will put a stop to physical contact. But sometimes there were other chaperones too, in the shape of the prisoner's parents. Two divorced women in their forties describe parental interference:

> Our first meeting was OK—we talked all right. But R was nervous and he talked to his dad more than me, and actually his dad said, 'You've hardly said two words to her!' R said, 'Well, that's all right—I can hold her hand, can't I?' So we held hands and his dad left us alone for a couple of minutes and went off to the tea machine.

> It was probably as much as a year before I managed to get to see him on my own. His mum was hanging on for dear life, so in the end I didn't tell her I was going.

A balance of power

Fifty-seven per cent of the outside partners said they felt they were the stronger half of the relationship:

> He had supported me a lot in his letters, but it was as if once we were together, I was the stronger one. And this was a shock, because I'd expected to meet someone I could lean on. I'd expected this big strong person to lift me off my feet. Now I realise that it was he who was doing the leaning.

However 14 per cent said they felt they were equals. The solicitor said of her prisoner husband:

> Mark is one of the few men I've actually looked up to. He's not educated like I am but he's cleverer than me. I respect him and he is very much my equal. He was never in the least bit frightened of me which lots of men are.

Challenging the prisoner's moral attitudes

Nearly half of the interviewees said they had made such challenges, and the same number said that for the prisoner to give up crime was definitely a condition for the relationship to continue. In my interviews for an earlier book about people who have left crime behind,[1] several ex-offenders cited personal relationships as the catalyst which inspired them to stop offending. Although 'prison groupies' who revel in their partner's notoriety have already been discussed, most outside partners are law-abiding and see themselves as agents for positive change. Many interviewees seemed unafraid to speak to their partners in very robust terms and force them to confront their crimes—and not only while they were still in prison. But, as noted above, women often placed the blame not on the prisoner himself, but on his previous partners for 'failing' him:

> I have found you have to meet R halfway but you have to show him you're strong as well. A weak woman is no good for him because he's not meeting his match. If I'm not happy about something I tell him. I never lie to him. If he's slipping or lax I'll be straight with him and he knows when I'm annoyed with him. I think other women he's been with have let him down.

> I give him ever such a hard time. He's always been with very weak women before, ones he could control. I'm not like that.

> I wrote him a letter telling him I was really angry because he was whingeing about how hard done by he was. I told him it was his own stupid fault. I said, 'I don't have any sympathy for you—think of how your victims felt! You know you can't go through life hurting people and not expecting to be hurt back in return.' I told him that if he goes inside again I don't think they'll let him out next time.

> He said, 'Nobody's ever talked like that to me before!' I think people have all pussy-footed around him in the past.

I told him, 'I'll help you to the ends of the earth. But if I find you do commit another crime, it won't be the police you'll have to worry about—it'll be me!

I said, 'I don't want you to commit another crime, or you would lose me. I'm not going to stand for that.' There would be hell to pay if he went back to crime. I believe if you make a bargain, you mean what you say.

Those ex-prisoners who agreed to be interviewed readily acknowledged their partner's influence:

For the first time in 25 years I know how to work properly, and she made me value money. I started to quite enjoy it. I found I got a buzz from jobs where I was in charge and people were asking me what to do.

Several partners had insisted on the prisoners joining special offending behaviour programmes, particularly at HMP Grendon, Britain's only therapeutic prison.[2]

The nature of Jack's offence had been so violent that I felt that if it didn't get totally resolved then I could be killed. I said, 'I love you dearly but I don't want to end up being killed off by you.' I was very, very hot on him going to Grendon as that would lessen the potential harm to me.

Determination to change their partners

The female outside partners were more likely than the males to mention wanting to effect change. The men seem willing to accept their women just as they are. Maybe that is because all the female prisoner-partners had been convicted of murder/manslaughter in circumstances that could be considered as unique at that time. None were career criminals—indeed, none had any previous convictions.

Of course, women married to prisoners are by no means unique in wanting to change their partners: our whole Western culture encourages such an approach, from the old wedding joke, 'Aisle Altar Hymn' to ubiquitous media articles on how to improve your man by reducing his weight, smartening up his clothes and making him more attentive—usually by stealth.

Interestingly, three of the women partners said they had read the best-selling self-help book *Men are from Mars, Women are from Venus*[3] and had found it very valuable in their relationships. The American author John Gray warns:

The most frequently expressed complaint men have about women is that women are always trying to change them. When a woman loves a man ... she forms a home-improvement committee and he becomes her primary focus. No matter how much he resists her help she persists—waiting for any opportunity to help him or tell him what to do. She thinks she's nurturing him, while he feels he's being controlled. Instead he wants her acceptance.[4]

According to Pastor Barry Goode, an Australian ex-prisoner turned minister ,[5] women who form attachments with prisoners have a particular motive to change their men:

> It's the Florence Nightingale thing that makes these women do this. The worse the criminals are, the more the women think that they can bring a change in them. It's almost like an ego trip. The worse the crimes are, the more prestige the prisoners are given.

Partners valued being in control

Nearly a third of interviewees (all of them women) said they valued being in control while the prisoner was incarcerated. The word *control* was quite frequently used by the outside partners in describing their relationships. The following remarks are typical:

> In some ways I was quite happy with the relationship as it was. I was very much in control and I could go and see him in prison when I wanted to, and if I didn't want to see him I didn't have to. He made no demands.

> There was an attraction because I could call the shots—I was very much in control.

> Somehow nearly all my boyfriends have been younger than me. I think—I know—that I always like to be in control.

People who expressed this view were usually those who felt unable to be in control in their own personal lives. They were currently, or had been in the past, survivors of domestic violence, or their partners were excessively jealous, or kept them short of money, or had lost all interest in them intellectually, emotionally and physically. Now, for a change, they were in charge of everything involving their prisoner-partner—from holding the purse-strings and providing cash and goods, to deciding whether or not to answer phone calls, reply to letters or make a prison visit. But according to Sheila Isenberg, this is only an illusion:

> Being involved with a murderer behind bars gives these women a measure of control. She decides when to make prison visits, whether to accept his phone calls, how much money to give him. This illusion of control makes her feel better about herself, stronger and more powerful.[6]

However Isenberg identifies a deeper motivation:

> They are trying to do over their troubled childhoods. They say to themselves, 'I will make it perfect. I will fall in love with a man who can't drink and can't beat me. He'll always be there for me because he really needs me'. *He's under her control.*[7]

Isenberg only studied women outside partners, but her comments apply also to the men I interviewed, many of whom had been damaged by past relationships.

One of my interviewees analysed her own motives. Like so many of the women in Isenberg's sample, she had been dominated by her father:

> I was always the dominant partner in my first marriage as well, I think because my father was so dominant. I thought, I'm never going to be dominated any more. I've got to be the dominant one in a relationship.

These are women of the kind identified in another self-help best-seller, *Women Who Love Too Much*[8] by the Californian therapist Robin Norwood, also read by several interviewees, showing that they had made some attempt at self-analysis. Like many of my interviewees and Sheila Isenberg's they too had suffered childhood trauma, and Norwood includes herself among their number when she writes about control:

> We have a desperate need to *control* our men, having experienced little security in childhood. A child in such a family will inevitably feel panic at the family's loss of *control*. We need to be with people whom we can help, in order to feel safe and in *control*. [author's italics]

For instance, Norwood describes women brought up by alcoholic parents trying to put right the disasters of their childhood by choosing alcoholic partners, determined to control and change them in a way they could never control and change their families.[9] It may also be true that people who have had to endure periods of chaos in their lives may (consciously or subconsciously) welcome the controlling nature of the jail setting which imposes its own structure on the relationship with the prisoner.

Challenging/having problems with jail authorities

Over half of the people whose partners were still in jail reported challenging prison staff—perhaps another aspect of the tendency to want to control. Several—particularly the highly-educated ones, had made it their business to confront the jail authorities on their partner's behalf, sometimes as part of the role they had defined for themselves as defender, saviour or reformer. By letting prison staff know that there is someone outside fighting the inmate's corner, this approach can put prison staff on their mettle and do the prisoner some good. But far more often it can have the reverse effect, resulting in reprisals against the prisoner.

A woman solicitor acknowledged this downside:

> I think marrying me has in some ways made Mark's life in prison more difficult, because now he's got a very lippy wife. My attitude to prison officers has changed drastically since I've been with Mark. If you go in as a

solicitor they will call you 'Ma'am' because obviously they don't want complaints from a solicitor. But complaints from wives—well, we're just a load of foul-mouthed fishwives, aren't we? They don't think much of him and their attitude extends to you.

This woman frequently incurs the wrath of officers who resent her feisty attitude—and perhaps the fact that she knows the prison rules as well as they do. Another woman was desperate to help keep her partner off drugs:

I used to badger the people in the drug treatment unit, for instance if I was worried about him and I thought he was back on the drugs.

Although such strategies are understandable, they can be risky for the prisoner. The prison authorities may regard a prisoner's partner as a subversive influence and in extreme circumstances this could affect parole decisions. If there were an official forum for families to voice their concerns, there would be less need for confrontational protests, which are often made as a last resort when the outside partner is desperate with worry.[10]

He got himself put down the block to get away from the wing with the drugs problems, and the prison put us on glass visits.[11] So I wrote to the area manager. I caused a real storm in the prison. I was absolutely hated by all the staff. The lifer governor spoke to me on the phone and said, 'You've caused a big stink here!' The staff treated me very badly, making me wait and so on, and I was treated very coldly. They did really stupid things like visiting orders not being sent out to me. I didn't start by rebelling. I was quite polite at first. But as time went on and I saw the way they were treating R, I began to wonder how they could get away with things like that.

When another woman, a writer and campaigner, protested at her boyfriend's treatment, his jail also reacted by placing the couple on closed visits with no physical contact for several months. Increasingly harsh reprimands only stiffened these women's resolve to challenge the system in their partner's defence. But inmates can also be targeted even if their outside partners make no protest at all. I came across two instances where prisoners were put in a higher security category simply because of their relationships with women outside—one because of his affair with a female prison officer, the other because his girlfriend's wronged husband persistently pestered the prison authorities with threats to tell the media about the affair unless they separated the couple.

They gave in to his demands and his rival in love was demoted to a tougher prison many miles away—though of course this only heightened the romance. Some people had also confronted their partner's probation officer in his/her defence.

Others, however, adopt a more pragmatic approach—like this wife:

> I think it's unproductive when partners of prisoners challenge the system by confronting the prison officers. I could make a lot of trouble, but at the end of the day they've got my husband and I'm not going to put him in a vulnerable position because of what they can do.

Prisoners' family support groups have repeatedly called for more opportunities for cooperation between the families and the prison authorities. Family members could, they believe, prove a valuable resource in reducing future reoffending, if they were involved rather than alienated, and—as mentioned earlier—many of my interviewees were dedicated to challenging offending behaviour. This man married a life-sentenced woman five years ago, and it is a now over a year since her release:

> She's out of jail, but it'll take a few years to get the jail out of her. People coming out of jail, specially long-termers, need psychological help to get readjusted into society. After a long jail sentence you need to be debriefed, but all she gets is to see her probation officer once a week. That's not really aftercare—it's just to keep tabs on her so she doesn't reoffend. Any long-termer needs counselling, and if somebody gets involved with a prisoner, as I did, they should be brought into the counselling situation as well. If they are going to be committing themselves to a long-term relationship with the prisoner, then they should be involved in the rehabilitation programme.

Self-sacrifice

Personal sacrifice for religious reasons has already been noted. Nearly a third of the interviewees said they were quite prepared to make sacrifices, particularly curtailing their own social life, to keep the prisoner happy and avoid jealousy. There was also, especially among the women outside partners, an acceptance of deferred gratification—it seemed worth putting up with present hardship with the prospect of future happiness. Enforced celibacy did not seem to trouble many of them—perhaps because few were in the first flush of youth, and many of the women had suffered past sexual abuse. Conjugal visits are prohibited in British prisons, although they are allowed in many other countries.[12] But one interviewee claimed to have had intercourse with her partner many times under the authorities' noses. She says there is plenty of anecdotal evidence that this is not as rare as might be expected, despite stricter security to prevent the smuggling of contraband:

We managed to make love in six prisons. Maybe we should be in the *Guinness Book of Records* but we'd be there along with a lot of other people, I'm sure!

The supreme sacrifice for female partners of childbearing age must be the prospect of childlessness. The courts rejected a recent challenge under Human Rights legislation when a serving prisoner claimed the right to impregnate his wife by artificial insemination.[13] Some interviewees had thought very seriously about this issue:[14]

One of the things we have to think about is having children, because I'm 38 now. I've been told about a DIY method that worked. I met someone on a visit to one of the prisons and she told me that her husband had smuggled semen out on a visit, she'd used it and they'd had a child. Could you argue that semen is not a prohibited substance? I don't know anything in the Prison Rules that says it is—though if the authorities read this it soon will be!

Another couple used a more conventional—though equally illicit—method to conceive their son, now eight, while his father, a lifer, was on a home leave:

It was an accident but it was lucky, otherwise we'd probably never have had any children. Considering that we weren't meant to be left alone at all, it was a bit embarrassing for the escorting officer. When I found out [I was pregnant], Tony had to break it to him and he said, 'Right—the story is, I went to get the car and it happened then—a quickie!'

Self-sacrifice is also a characteristic of Norwood's 'women who love too much', and she gives examples of the way suffering for love is romanticised in popular Western culture. It is endemic in songs like *Stand By Your Man*, opera and soap opera plots, romantic novels and traditional folklore.

GETTING MARRIED

How many couples married?
Over two-thirds of the couples (19 of the 28) had married. According to Prison Service figures[15] 200 serving prisoners get married every year, though the service has no further statistics, for example about gender, age, ethnicity or religion.

Reasons for marrying
Often the impetus came from the prisoner rather than the outside partner: prisoners, as we have seen, have much to gain and little to lose by marrying. Partners often said they agreed because the prisoner or ex-prisoner wanted security:

I thought it would make him feel more secure.

The reason I agreed to marry him was because I wanted to give him all the love and support I could give him. I felt he hadn't been given any real love of any depth in his life. So this was my way of giving him all that I had. I didn't have any money but I had my love and support, and I knew he would need someone to believe in him.

We decided to get married for a number of reasons. We were getting on great together, she was spending quite a bit of time at my place, but she was still very insecure—very, very insecure.

Lucy Gampell is the Director of the Federation of Prisoners' Families Support Groups, the umbrella charity for groups all over the country. She believes the desire to marry is based on the insecurity which both partners may feel:

People outside prison can be together for all to see. But in these relationships the partner outside prison has nothing to show that s/he is in a relationship. So having a piece of paper—the marriage licence—and wedding photos to frame and display are likely to be more important. There may also be other reasons to get married, for instance for outside partners to prove to their families that they are serious about the relationship and they intend to stick with it. For the male prisoner especially there is a cachet about having a wife at home to stick by you. A lot of male prisoners come from traditional working-class backgrounds where there is still a culture of the submissive little wife at home. Then if the outsider partner already has children, the prisoner also becomes an instant father. He can go round saying, 'I'm a dad!' and this can confer further status.

Marriage proposals

In keeping with the 'Victorian' nature of the courtship, nearly three-quarters of the marriage proposals were made in romantic circumstances. Two women were embarrassed when their men went down on bended knee in the middle of the visits room. Others described prisoners who produced the engagement ring as a surprise, after making the secret purchase with the help of an outside associate. The most romantic 'ring story' is that of the ex-prisoner who gave his wife a medieval bronze ring he found with his metal detector. It is engraved with the Latin legend *For my sweet wife*. Yet few of the interviewees were young enough for the first flush of romantic infatuation: the average age of the outside partner when s/he married was 37, the average age of the prisoner partner was 33.[16] Two of the female outside partners took matters in their own hands by making Leap Year proposals.

The formality of the courtship extended, in a few cases, to the prisoner groom asking the bride's father for her hand in marriage:

I actually asked for her dad's approval and he said, 'Yes, but not yet'. I said I wasn't going to rush into it and he was OK with that.

We decided that we wanted to do it properly, although we'd decided to get engaged. We took the rings off and I made an appointment to go and see her dad to tell him this is what we wanted to do. It was awkward, but I think it was appreciated.

Rules for marrying in prison and how they are interpreted

Of the 19 marriages, 13 took place while the prisoner partner was still in jail. Half of these were conducted by registrars inside the prison, usually in a boardroom, conference room or governor's office, while two were held in the prison chapel. Some had applied for a prison chapel wedding but had been warned this could be difficult. A Catholic partner was told she was unlikely to get permission from her church, while a former chaplain of HMP Maidstone always refused to conduct weddings in the beautiful prison chapel. He regarded prisoners who applied to marry as selfish, as no such marriage could be regarded as a complete relationship.

The Prison Service sets out clearly, in Circular Instruction 35/1988, the criteria governing the venue for a prisoner's wedding, the prisoner's own responsibilities in making arrangements, and the security issues involved.

The date and day of the marriage are at the Governor's discretion. Prison weddings have traditionally taken place on Mondays, though it seems they can now be arranged any day. There has never been anything in the rules to specify Monday, but Governors in the past must have found it more convenient, as Mondays are sometimes visit-free days, or are reserved for legal visits.

As for the venue: if the wedding is to take place inside the prison, it is up to the inmate or his/her fiancé(e) to make the necessary arrangements with an outside registrar or with the prison chaplain. Usually two registrars come in to conduct the ceremony, and the prisoner is allowed to request that they use only the private postal address of the prison so that in future nobody could tell from the marriage certificate that the wedding took place in a jail.

Perhaps the most unusual of all weddings was the proxy Muslim ceremony mentioned earlier where the bride was not even present. A strict Muslim, she refused to meet her partner until they were actually married:

> The Imam phoned me and told me, 'Congratulations—you're married!' I was shocked because I was doing housework at the time. Then I was so excited I was ringing everybody up, then my husband phoned and he told me we'd got married at three minutes past four.

A 'reasonable number of guests' (usually interpreted as 12) can be invited, at the Governor's discretion. All their personal details have to be supplied to prison security beforehand, and the Governor retains the right to exclude any guest, though the reasons have to be 'clear and compelling'. In the case of a Category A prisoner, guests are usually checked by police visiting them at home. One outside partner described the process:

> Everybody attending the wedding had to be visited by the police, even my mum, who was in her 60s and wouldn't even cross the road unless the green man told her to! The chapel orderly was a Libyan terrorist and my mum said, 'Oh, he seemed quite nice—what's he in for?'

Children are not to be prevented from attending whatever their age. The prisoner is charged a flat rate fee of £20 to cover the cost of officers escorting guests from the main prison gate. Nearly two-thirds of interviewees' weddings were attended by some of the outside partner's family, while just under half were attended by members of the prisoner's family.

Prisoners given permission for an outside ceremony
About one-third of the prisoner partners were allowed to leave the prison for a few hours to be married in a registry office outside. The Prison Service, perhaps surprisingly, emphasises that ceremonies should be facilitated outside prison if at all possible. For instance, if a prisoner is going on home leave or temporary release within a month, s/he should get married then and needs no formal approval to do so. At the other end of the security spectrum, Category A prisoners and those on the 'E' list—people thought likely to attempt escape—are never allowed an outside ceremony. For those in lower security categories, permission for outside weddings is given at the Governor's discretion.

Governors are instructed to allow low-risk prisoners to attend an outside ceremony unescorted, but if an escort has to be provided, this will cost the prisoner a flat rate fee of £30. The prisoner must be taken to the venue in civilian clothes, the escort must also wear civilian clothes and must perform their duties 'as unobtrusively as is consistent with the needs of security'. As soon as the ceremony is over the prisoner must be returned to the jail.

Of the seven released prisoners in my sample who married, four did so in a registry office and three in a church. They were of course free to make any arrangements that suited them.

The wedding reception
Sixteen of the 19 couples celebrated their marriage with some sort of wedding reception. For those who married inside prisons, the reception arrangements were up to individual Governors' discretion. One bride who wanted to bring in a wedding cake she had made herself gave up the idea when she discovered that this was prohibited and she would have to pay a considerable sum to get one made by the prison. She also rejected the alternative she was offered, to pay an even larger sum to have a cake made

by an outside baker and sent off by the prison to be X-rayed. At another prison wedding the bride had no problems bringing in her cake, but when her groom embarked on the rest of the catering, using skills he had learned in the prison kitchens, he got in a rage when his *vol-au-vents* sank and threw them at the wall. Charles Bronson ordered his three-tier wedding cake from a catalogue but was annoyed when he was not allowed a knife to cut it with.

Prisoners allowed a few hours' leave for a wedding outside the prison usually missed their own reception altogether. A female lifer, married in the local registry office while attached to an officer by a 15-foot shackling chain, left the guests enjoying the party and had to make do with a cake made for her by the prison's kitchen girls. But an officer guarding a male prisoner was more humane: the prisoner's wife told how she and her new husband were allowed to spend an hour consummating their union in the back of a parked wedding car while the officer joined the guests at the reception in a nearby pub! In another wedding inside a prison the officer on guard locked the willing newlyweds in a cloakroom for an hour after the ceremony. With supreme irony he set the burglar alarm so they should not be disturbed!

Indeed, in the dull and colourless routine of prison life, it seems a wedding cheers everyone up and brings a smile to the most stony-faced officers. There are stories of them sharing out the wedding cake to inmates on the wings and sewing up the hems of the groom's hired wedding trousers a few minutes before the ceremony. At a wedding I attended in HMP Littlehey, the groom regaled the wedding guests with stories of his 'stag night' when officers turned a blind eye as other inmates fastened a fake ball and chain around his neck with a label about marriage being a life sentence. This wedding was a pleasant enough occasion, with the two female registrars doing their best to help everyone relax, and prison officers staying outside the room and remaining as inconspicuous as possible.

Security

At the weddings inside the prisons described by my interviewees, security was generally kept to a minimum, with the attending officers keeping a low profile, showing respect to guests, even standing outside the room, and making sure to keep all prison uniforms and window bars out of the wedding photographs. (Photographs are allowed as long as cameras are security-cleared.)

> There were two uniformed prison officers in the chapel and my sister told me afterwards that when I arrived they were just sitting at a table reading the papers. She remembers thinking, I hope they're not going to do that when my sister's getting married—it doesn't seem quite right. But then when we were actually being married they stood up smartly at the back door.

Apart from the woman who remained shackled to an officer, all the other prisoners allowed to marry outside the prison had their handcuffs removed before the ceremony:

> As soon as they came into the registry office building they took off the handcuffs and he walked up the stairs with no cuffs on. The two officers were really excellent. They kept their macs on over their uniforms. We had a video taken of the wedding and they hardly appeared on it at all.

All in all the Prison Service appears to be quite marriage-friendly, though anecdotally more so in male prisons than in female jails—perhaps in the belief that 'the love of a good woman' will reform the prisoner bridegroom.[17]

Changing from maiden name
Contrary to a widely-held prison myth, a female prisoner who marries does have the right to change her name to her husband's.[18]

How long have the marriages lasted?
All but two of the 19 couples who married are still together. On average the married couples have stayed together for six years so far, though some marriages have lasted much longer. In two of the longest marriages—both ten years—the prisoner partners are still in prison; three more couples, who all married when the prisoner was released, have been together nine, 12 and 13 years respectively. According to the counselling service Relate, the average marriage lasts ten years, so these couples compare surprisingly well considering the pressures they have to face. This small sample suggests that their divorce rate is one in nine—a rate three times more successful than the national rate.

SOCIAL EFFECTS ON OUTSIDE PARTNERS

Families' reactions
Half of the outside partners' families were initially shocked, horrified and totally opposed to the union. Their reaction could be very hurtful:

> They believed that I was stark, staring bonkers and very, very foolish.

> I have a feeling of hurt and rejection. It's as if it's an insult to my intelligence, to my judgement. I feel insulted that they regard me as this woman who's lost her mind, lost her marbles.

But eleven per cent said their families were always supportive, and some family members had agreed to see the partner on a prison visit (though most parents found this a traumatic experience):

I can remember taking my parents into a prison to meet J for the first time. It was horrendous. My dad didn't want to comply with the rubdown search and I had to say, 'Well I'm sorry, Pa, but you'll have to, I'm afraid.' He went through it but he didn't like it. He is a private sort of man and he didn't want another man touching him in that way. My mum didn't find it at all easy either, and they both looked as though it was a hell of an ordeal. I think it was very overwhelming for them and it had a lasting effect on my mum. It was so different from anything they had ever experienced.

Nearly a third of outside partners' families finally became reconciled to the prisoner partner, especially if children were born of the union. But one fifth remain implacably opposed.

The problem may not be entirely on the family's side. As one wife said:

I do think people who have been in prison tend to have a chip on their shoulder. Richard thinks some of my family look down on him, whereas I think they have all leaned over backwards to make him feel welcome.

One-fifth of the outside partners concealed the prisoner's background from their families, and twice as many concealed it from friends, neighbours and employers as well as their families. Two-thirds of the prisoners had had problems with their partners' families at some point in their relationships. Several interviewees mentioned pressure from their families for released partners to 'prove themselves' before they could be accepted into the family fold:

I feel very let down by my mother's side of the family because they are not prepared to accept that J has done his time and should be given a chance. They expect J to prove himself—it's as if he's on trial or in a probationary period, and I don't think that's very acceptable.

I feel my family are waiting to see whether he can prove himself and support me properly.

My dad said, 'Look, if you're going to continue with this, I don't want to meet this man until he's out [of prison]. As long as he comes out and proves himself and he can look after you, then maybe this will be all right'.

According to interviewees, their families' objections seemed to be based as much on preconceived views and snobbery as on real safety concerns:

I keep trying to explain to them that he's not some violent thug, but they automatically assume he is, because he's got short hair and tattoos.

Conversely, only a quarter of the *prisoners'* families had difficulties accepting these relationships. Usually the non-criminal partners were welcomed, perhaps in the hope that they would help in the prisoner's reform process:

> We went to see his mum. She loved me! I think she was grateful and so pleased to see him finally settling down, and she saw I was part of that.

Effects on children[19]

Nearly two-thirds of the outside partners had children from previous relationships, compared with 50 per cent of the prisoners. Only a quarter of the couples have so far had children together.

One or two of the outside partners said they had problems revealing to their own children from previous relationships that their partner was, or had been, in prison. One lifer's partner found this particularly traumatic:

> My daughter was about ten when she found out. On her very first visit with me to the prison she was holding on tight to her seat and she said, 'Could I be sitting next to a murderer?' R said it cut him up inside to hear that. When she went up to the counter, he said, 'Let it be me that tells her. I'll tell her when you bring her again.' But by the middle of that week she'd started on me, 'What's he done? What's he done?' So I had to tell her myself. I found it so difficult. I thought, I'm telling my own daughter that I'm involved with somebody that's murdered. I remember her looking at me and she said, 'I asked you if I could be sitting next to a murderer.'

The same woman's son was taunted and bullied at school and indeed, eleven per cent felt their children had suffered at school as a result of their own involvement with a prisoner. The same number complained of the difficulty of bringing up children on their own and having to be the sole breadwinner while their partner was in prison.

Social services became involved with children in two families because of the mother's relationship with a sex offender. In two other cases the outside partners' husbands fought custody battles to prevent the prisoner having contact with the children. Both based their cases on the allegation that their wives were 'unfit mothers' because they had exposed the children to criminals. One mother has won custody, but the other case is still *sub judice*, and the woman, a prison officer who lost her job when she fell in love with a prisoner, has had to withdraw her contribution to this book for fear of prejudicing her case when it comes to court.

Women in the throes of a grand passion were often prepared to travel vast distances to visit their men in prison, and those with children sometimes took them along. One woman had to start out at 6 a.m. and take her two small daughters on three trains, the Underground and a taxi to reach the prison:

> The girls were tired and bored and playing up, and it was complete hell, but I visited every Thursday and every Sunday, getting the train if I couldn't get a lift. I'd have done anything to get to him because I missed him so much.

Another woman went to extraordinary lengths because of her determination not only to see her lifer husband but to keep him in touch with his child, conceived on a home leave:

> I was determined that he should see the baby as much as possible. The furthest away I've ever had to drive was the six-hour drive each way from Manchester to Devon when the baby was two. I used to get him up at 2 a.m., leave Manchester and drive to Devon for the Saturday morning visit. I'd take the baby back to a hotel for the night, have another visit on the Sunday, then drive back to Manchester. I was working nine to five all week and doing that every weekend. It made me ill—I ended up really worn out.

Friends' reactions
A fifth of outside partners said their friends were initially shocked by their relationship and opposed to it, and the same proportion said they had lost friends permanently as a result. Though many friends began by being concerned for the partner's own wellbeing in embarking on such a relationship, it appears that some also feared 'contamination', as if the outside partner was somehow guilty by association and her/his friends might be equally stigmatised by any contact. More simply perhaps, they might have felt genuinely afraid of meeting the prisoner on release:

> I think people can feel threatened. I had a friend I'd known about ten years and after a year of seeing R I plucked up the courage to tell her. I sat down one evening and told her the whole story. She was very nice to my face and I thought, Oh, that was easy! Why did I worry about it so much? Then after a week she phoned me and said, 'I've decided we'll cut ties with each other. We'll have nothing to do with each other any more.'

Work colleagues' reactions
Of the 25 outside partners who were employed, one-third said they had kept their partner's prison background secret from their work colleagues. But the same number said their workmates knew and were supportive.

> I find it helps to be up-front with people. It stops all the gossip, and believe me, the people you least expect can turn out great. Everyone at work knows I'm married to a lifer—I'd rather tell people than have them find out and I've never had any problems, though you never know what people say behind your back.

However three said people at their work were shocked and upset when they were told, and three women had been dismissed from their jobs. When Saira Rehman married Charles Bronson (see interview, p. 153), she was sacked from the women's refuge where she had worked for years. Another woman, a prison education administrator, understood that once she had admitted being attracted to a prisoner she posed a potential security risk. But another, a hospital theatre sister, was shocked to be dismissed when she married a serving prisoner. Although he was not a drug user, the hospital authorities felt he might use her privileged access to drugs to pressure her into smuggling illicit substances into the jail for use as currency. Perhaps in retrospect she might have been wiser to keep her marriage secret. A female prison Governor resigned immediately when prison authorities discovered her relationship with a male prisoner.[20]

Isolation and loneliness

These and other women (eleven per cent of the sample) mentioned the isolation and loneliness resulting from their relationship. Many had married for companionship and ended up having to rely almost entirely on the prisoner. All prisoners' partners are isolated to some extent by being a tiny minority of the population, far away from the person they love, often also feeling anger and resentment at being abandoned and having to cope alone. One wife described 'the silence of my own world, somehow more hostile than any prison wing'. The sense of isolation immediately after a prison wedding was graphically described by others:

> The next day I remember feeling very alone. I really ached because we couldn't be a true married couple. We couldn't go to bed together or be together.

> After we married we had to wait another three years before J was released. The hardest part was being alone, being lonely. But because we'd married, we'd made that commitment to each other, and our love was bonded. We both felt it was right to have done what we did.

> It is so difficult to explain to anyone out here what loving someone who is away from you can be like. It's not all roses and smiles. The loneliness gets to us all, and whatever you want to say cannot be said there and then. Everything goes on hold—most of all your life.

Another woman described the domestic moments that underline her sense of loneliness:

> Silly things do upset me. Last Tuesday I cooked a chicken ... I took it out of the oven and I got quite tearful because I was thinking, He should be here to eat this chicken with me. It's little things like that... It's things like if something goes through my mind I can't ring him up and ask him. I might write it down for later or I might talk on a tape.

Those who have made the particular choice to enter a relationship with a prisoner may experience double isolation, cut off not only from their partner but also—as described above—from family, friends and work colleagues.

There's nobody else in my position that I can talk to, so I tend to have a rosy view of everybody else's life, thinking their life's great.

There is anecdotal evidence to suggest that a 'Them and Us' attitude can exist between prisoners' wives who bitterly resent their unlooked-for predicament, and those who, by choosing prisoners as their partners, appear deliberately to be embracing it. This may mean a hostile reception in the visitors' waiting room and accusations of being a 'prison groupie' - the sort of camp-follower mentioned above, who writes to notorious prisoners for a cheap thrill. One wife, who met her husband while he was (unknown to her) on the run after committing a murder, takes that line:

I'd say 70 per cent of women treat this thing in prison as a drama. They think it's great to go and visit somebody in prison, regardless of what they've done. Some women are only 'married' while they're in the visits room. On the outside they've got their own life, then they transform themselves again the following week.

Another wife described how she had suffered from being labelled:

Because at first there were difficulties with him emotionally, I felt I needed to speak to people who'd been in the same situation, and I went to family support groups. But I think there's a lot of prejudice against people who choose to be with a criminal partner. I know there are people who get their kicks out of visiting prisons, so perhaps that is why I met the attitude that, 'You chose to be with him so you're stuck with your lot.'

Sometimes the social effects of these partnerships were much more extreme. One woman, whose ex-terrorist husband was threatened with his life, was forced to flee to Switzerland with her family at a few hours' notice. They have only recently felt safe enough to return to Britain after seven years' exile. Another woman was warned to leave the area by her partner's criminal associates after he was jailed for drug importation, because she gave information to Customs and Excise officials. She and her three young daughters had to move nearly 200 miles from family and friends. Her prison relationship became too strained to continue and she has recently ended it and moved back to her home area.

THE ECONOMIC EFFECTS OF A RELATIONSHIP ON THE OUTSIDE PARTNER

Extra expense
Most of these problems are no different from those affecting anyone married to someone in prison: the extra costs of visits (mentioned by nearly half of outside partners); other financial hardship (32 per cent); having to

provide the prisoner with goods and money (21 per cent); having to be the family's main breadwinner (21 per cent) and having to work much longer hours (18 per cent). The main difference is that those whose families had severed all contact because of their choice of partner were without the safety net of family financial support, and lacked other benefits of the extended family, such as childcare.

Effect on career

There may be additional implications: as well as the women mentioned above who lost their jobs, one woman, a solicitor, was sure she had been turned down for a post because of her marriage, and another found she had to give up working when her husband was released to support him as he adjusted to the outside world.

PROBLEMS WHEN THE PRISONER IS RELEASED

In any relationship where one partner has been incarcerated there is bound to be a great deal of stress when the couple begin living together. When two already cohabiting people are suddenly separated by a period of imprisonment, there will inevitably be problems when the released prisoner has to reintegrate into the family home. So it has to be remembered that the problems mentioned by the 13 people whose partners were freed are common to many other 'prison couples'. It is just that the stakes are higher. Half of those whose partners had been released said that they found their relationships very seriously threatened by problems in the first few months after release.

Intellectual and emotional relationship without physical intimacy

In some ways the pressures are worse for people who only met when one of them was in prison. Several married couples described the extraordinary experience of getting to know each other very well on an intellectual and emotional level over many years, without the accompanying physical intimacy. One of the released prisoner-partners described the experience:

> When I did get home the adjusting was terrible. I'd had home leaves but they are so artificial. You're not worried about money, you don't know about the domestic problems—you're quite protected. We were strangers really. We'd been sitting at the same table in the visits room for years but we'd never lived with each other—that's what was really hard. When I first came home I even said, "Can we sort out single beds?" because I was so used to kipping on my own. We'd already got married years before but it was like starting again.

Employment difficulties

Top of the list of problems for newly-released prisoners was employment, with half having difficulty finding and keeping a job, and more than a third experiencing serious financial problems—though 85 per cent were in employment at the time of interview, and some couples would claim this was due to the outside partner's influence in supporting the ex-prisoner and helping him/her go straight.

Temptation to reoffend

All the same, 38 per cent said the ex-prisoners had been tempted to return to crime and found it difficult to resist their former criminal associates. In this regard the outside partner's role could be paramount in offering the chance of a fresh start, particularly if the couple's shared home was in a new area:

> He was warned never to go back where he came from. He's known as a hard man there and people would challenge him. I must admit I'm still very protective of him. If he goes out I like him to be back at the exact time he says he'll be back—it's not that I don't trust him, it's just the way I am.

> J has said he could pick up the phone and make contact with people from his former life, and that was something that alarmed me. But he never has done that and I've just had to trust him. I believe he sincerely wants to be straight, and we've made a completely fresh start with our friends.

Drug misuse

Nearly a quarter of the released partners had returned to using illegal drugs:

> He was still smoking pot [in jail], and I had to say to him, 'Look, when you come home there's no way I'm having you smoke that stuff in the house. You can forget it.' He's said, 'There's nothing really wrong with pot', but I say, 'There is actually—it's illegal!' And that shuts him up.

Prisoners' anxiety and communication problems

More than a third talked about their partners' serious problems readjusting to the outside world: their depression, anxiety and insecurity; their difficulties of communication and their tendency, after years of solitude in their cells, to cut themselves off and demand to be left alone. A quarter of ex-prisoners seemed to resent the outside partner's independence and felt they were now redundant. One man, released from prison a year ago, said he felt emasculated:

> I expected to be useful but she made me feel like a eunuch—that's the only way I can explain it. She made me feel not needed, and I'm thinking, What's the point of me being here?

Jealousy

Jealousy of children and other family also caused problems for 15 per cent:

I was jealous because she was sharing herself with the kids and grandkids and I kept saying, 'I married you, not them. Let's just be me and you, let's just you and me enjoy ourselves'.

Anti-authority attitudes
Nearly a quarter of the outside partners said they were annoyed by the ex-prisoner's anti-authority attitudes and felt compelled to challenge them.

Concern about gossip
Fifteen per cent had problems trying to keep the ex-prisoner's background secret from the neighbours and from their own children.

Starting a family
Fifteen per cent also said they disagreed about whether to start a family.

Child custody or access problems
These were mentioned by about 15 per cent.

Violence
Two women had experienced violence from their released partners and several complained of a lack of any support from any professionals.

Lack of gratitude
Eleven per cent felt the prisoner might have shown them more gratitude for the sacrifices they had made. Alongside self-sacrifice there are often very high, sometimes unrealistic, expectations, and people said they had at least expected some sort of acknowledgement for everything they had given up and were disappointed not to get it. This kind of reciprocation may be particularly difficult for released prisoners, many of whom have suffered past emotional damage which has been exacerbated by years of incarceration. For them to adjust to outside life can be overwhelming enough, and to be the subject of the kind of demanding scrutiny made by some outside partners can be disastrous. One wife said of her released husband:

I think maybe I expected more from this relationship than other people might. I think I expected it to be extraordinary, which is silly I know, because maybe it means I get more disillusioned than I should. I think I expected him to be perfect, or close to perfect. I'm not saying I expected him to be really grateful all the time. But I did expect him to be glad, to be more aware that he'd have ended up on his own somewhere.

Three other women gave similar warnings:

> In the heat of the moment I'll admit I've regretted getting married again, though that feeling's short-lived. But all people in prison can see is the light at the end of the tunnel. They think that after getting out of prison, life will be wonderful. But I'd say to them, 'You need to remember that life's harder outside prison than it is inside.'

> I think because I have a readymade home, men see me as an easy target. I have now learnt that not all men are to be trusted on face value. I suppose when Stuart came into our lives and showed us kindness, in a way I jumped at the chance. But now I know better.

> If I was asked if I've got any advice to give to others, it would be this: before you get married to a prisoner, think about it very carefully.

POSITIVE OUTCOMES

Strength in adversity
Nearly two-thirds of the interviewees said they felt that their relationships had been strengthened by the adversities they had had to face. This may be because, as Sheila Isenberg found with women in love with killers, the men represent challenges on which the women thrive: 'Meeting him, earning his love, making the relationship work despite the tremendous odds against it'.[21]

Greater tolerance and understanding
Eighteen per cent of the outside partners said that meeting the prisoner had changed their attitude to prisons and prisoners and left them much more tolerant and liberal. Before they began their relationships many had been as hard-line on crime and punishment as these three women:

> Before I went into a prison I had the attitude, Lock them all up and throw away the key. You think people in there are all totally bad people.

> I had no interest in prisons whatsoever, and prisoners could all go and be hung as far as I was concerned.

> I have had to change the way I think. Where I was brought up, nobody had ever been in trouble with the police. Prisoners? I wouldn't touch them, wouldn't give them the time of day. Knowing Stuart has totally changed me, completely opened my eyes. For me it's a complete turnaround of attitude.

Growing confidence

This expanding of horizons is one of the more obvious benefits of the relationships described in this book, and many felt that through their relationship with the prisoner they had themselves grown in strength and confidence. Interestingly, three of the women said that they had regained their ability to drive a car confidently—lost because of their previous partner's scathing attitude. They had had to overcome their fears in order to drive to prison visits.[22] Many others saw a more general growth in confidence:

I feel I've changed in myself. I've become much more independent. I have a very close relationship with a man I adore and who adores me. We can discuss anything and everything and we're both moving towards the same goals. He's made me believe in myself—he tells me he knows I can do things, rather than putting me down like my husband did. I've found a new confidence and happiness and I finally feel like I've started to live my life.

Through all this I have grown. And I've never had a moment of regret, because I know that that man in prison is the one I want to spend the rest of my life with.

I am more at peace with myself now, and he's helped me try and analyse what I want out of life.

All the *prisoner* partners who were interviewed acknowledged the positive outcomes of their relationships.

Thanks to her my values have changed, and I don't think I will ever go back to crime. She made me enjoy things like getting on a bike and riding round the village. In all the neighbours' eyes it was a waste of time her marrying me, because they were sure I was going to go off. So it was great them seeing us holding hands and walking down the road because I'd proved them all wrong. Honest to God, she has had a profound effect on me. She has made me want to be a better person.

•   •   •

Writers who have studied prisoners' relationships with outside partners have generally been critical, dismissive and sceptical. One of Robin Norwood's case histories is a prison relationship like those in this book—though she writes only about female outside partners. She introduces it as follows:

Prison wives present perhaps the ultimate example of women who love too much. Because they are incapable of any degree of intimacy with a man, they choose instead to live with a fantasy, a dream of how much they will love and be loved some day when their partner changes and becomes available to them ... In the imagination of prisoners' wives, their dream is of magically romantic love. Like their convict husbands they usually find it easier to live with the dream than to struggle to try to make it come true in the real world.[23]

Sheila Isenberg agrees, though it should be noted that she was looking at an even more specific group:

Women who love killers are only *acting* the role of women in love. The men they love are not real: they are fantasies created by the women's psychological and emotional needs.'[24]

Though most of my interviewees would strongly dispute such claims, these are elements of fantasy to be found throughout these case histories. A woman released after serving 18 years for murder admitted of her relationship:

During that time [while I was still in prison] we lived parallel fantasies, though we thought we had common goals.

Living with a fantasy is not confined to women. Two male outside partners actually used the word 'fantasy':

Because of the fact that she was in prison and we couldn't do anything, talking about things outside prison was, in a way, a fantasy.

In one of her letters Sara said that for the other women prisoners and even for the staff, our relationship was like a fairy tale. We did have wonderful dreams about being in a castle with a log fire, playing Sibelius—even going to Finland together. She said in another letter that we were one another's destiny, that we'd get married, and in a kind of way I shared that certainty. But it was odd because of the fact that she was in prison and we couldn't do anything—so talking about things outside the prison was, in a way, a fantasy. Once she wrote to me that some men are only able to love what's unattainable.

But the stories that follow cannot simply be dismissed as fantastic fairy tales which are bound to turn into horror stories. After all, nearly half the prisoner-partners have been released, and some of their relationships have survived all the problems of life outside, lasting longer than many more conventional unions.

Although these relationships are indisputably high-risk,[25] it is important to acknowledge that there is an element of risk in any sexual relationship, and marriages that appear to be made in heaven are often known to fail. If commitment is an important predictor of marital success, then maybe prison relationships have a greater than average chance of succeeding, because both partners often express the strongest possible determination to make them work.

People—especially women—who form prison relationships are commonly described as crazy. But if they are mad, they are by no means alone, for after all, love is itself a form of temporary insanity, as poets have always known. Tennyson writes of 'the cruel madness of love', and Dryden of love as a 'noble madness'. Anyone who has been in love must recall that feeling of light-headed irrational joy that transcends the wisdom of age, common sense and professional judgement. Defying all logic, monarchs in love have relinquished their thrones and politicians their careers.

It is unfair also to assume that prisoners' attachment to people outside the jail is always self-regarding. The interviews in this book suggest that some relationships are genuine love matches, and some have proved to be as successful and lasting as any outside, surviving for many years after the prisoner's release.

So these accounts deserve careful analysis, and acknowledgement of the positive elements in each relationship, as well as an awareness of the risks involved. They are complex personal stories which I hope readers will find fascinating as well as challenging.

Above all, I hope that these tales will help confound some overworked stereotypes and promote greater understanding of the motivation of people who have made such difficult choices.

ENDNOTES for *Chapter 3*

1 *Going Straight: After Crime and Punishment*, Waterside Press, 1999.
2 There are some valuable accounts of relationships between Grendon inmates and their partners to be found in *Grendon Tales* by Ursula Smartt (Waterside Press 2001). See particularly pp. 74ff.
3 Harper-Collins, 1992.
4 See p. 15, *op. cit.*
5 See *Dream Lovers op. cit.* p. 35.
6 'What Makes Women Fall in Love with these Monsters?', *Daily Express*, 8 May 2001.
7 See p. 172 *Women Who Love Men Who Kill, op. cit.*
8 Random House, 1986.
9 See p. 11 *op. cit.*
10 Stephen Shaw, the Prisons and Probation Ombudsman, has complained that visitors to prisons have no right of access to his office (Unlock Conference, 23 November 2001).
11 Closed visits in a glazed kiosk.
12 In the US, for example, conjugal visits are allowed in some states, but only if the couple are married. Maximum security prisoners are banned from conjugal visits. Sheila Isenberg says that in 1989 conjugal visits were allowed in nine states, though sex-related murderers were banned, and in some prisons there are no facilities: see pp. 66-68 *op. cit.* French prison rules will allow the jailed terrorist Carlos the Jackal one conjugal visit a month after his marriage to his French attorney.
13 In April 2001 Gavin Mellor, 30, serving life for murder, had his request to father a child by artificially inseminating his wife Tracey turned down by the Court of Appeal. He had claimed that denial of fatherhood contravened Article 8 of the European Convention On Human Rights, which requires respect for a person's private and family life, and Article 12, which protects the right to marry and start a family. Mexican pop singer Gloria Trevi, jailed in Brazil for sexual offences, is said to have artificially inseminated herself to avoid extradition. In November 2001 she was found to be six months pregnant, despite being held

in a high security prison for two years with no right to conjugal visits (*Guardian*, 20 November 2001). In the USA the FBI found that jailed NewYork mafia members were bribing guards to smuggle their semen out to wives and mistresses (' "Studfellas" father families from prison', *Sunday Telegraph*, 10 March 2002).

[14] In September 2001, a Californian court ruled that male prisoners had 'a fundamental right to procreate' and should be allowed to send their semen to women who wanted to be impregnated. The case leading to the ruling was brought by William Gerber, a 41-year-old prisoner jailed for 11 years in 1997. He claimed his civil rights had been violated in 1999 when the prison authorities refused to let him send a sperm sample to a Chicago laboratory with a view to impregnating his wife. In 2001 the US Court of Appeal agreed with him by a 2-1 majority (*Guardian*, 7 September 2001).

[15] Source: Prison Service Press Office, 5 April 2002.

[16] On the outside, the average age for a bridegroom is 35 and for a bride, 32. (*Population Trends*, 107; Spring 2000.)

[17] In June 2000 a mass wedding was held in a Brazilian jail in an attempt to cool tensions after recent jail riots. More than 100 prisoners were allowed to marry their fiancées in the Carandiru Detention Centre in Sao Paulo, which holds more than 6,000 inmates though it was built to hold half that number. Elgar's *Pomp and Circumstance* was played while a Justice of the Peace read the marriage vows. After the wedding the jail served soft drinks and sausage rolls.

[18] Grace Hall (see interview p. 250) challenged the Home Office when prison officers refused to use her married name, claiming that she must keep the name under which she was convicted. The Home Office confirmed her right to change her name, though the officers persisted in using her maiden name. The myth that women must keep their 'conviction name' still persists. In fact, only the prison number must remain constant throughout the sentence.

[19] For detailed information on the effect on children of having a prisoner in the family, see *No-One's Ever Asked Me* by Kelli Brown, and *I Didn't Think Anyone Could Understand, Miss: Supporting Prisoners' Children in School*, edited by Liz Dibb, both published by the Federation of Prisoners' Families Support Groups, London, 2001.

[20] Following the discovery in January 2002 of a relationship between a female officer and a male prisoner at HMP Doncaster the Prison Officers' Association said its members needed to be warned about their own and the prisoners' vulnerability (*Mirror*, 16 January 2002).

[21] See p. 140 *op. cit.*

[22] When interviewing women prisoners for *Invisible Women, op. cit*, I found that their abusive partners had often tried to undermine their driving confidence as a way of limiting their mobility and making them dependent.

[23] See p. 108 *Women Who Love Too Much op. cit.*

[24] See p. 168 *Women Who Love Men Who Kill op. cit.*

[25] Other high-risk relationships are those formed through Internet chat rooms. However a Bath University study reported at the British Psychological Conference in March 2002 found that romances which began through online chatting were more likely to be successful than those which started through normal social meetings, because couples got to know each other before meeting (*Daily Telegraph*, 16 March 2002).

The Interviews

Sandra and Stuart Watford

On 3 November 1999 I was asked to be one of the witnesses at a wedding inside HM Prison Littlehey, a modern Category C establishment in Cambridgeshire. The bridegroom, Stuart, 33, was nearing the end of an eight year sentence for kidnap and torture. I had interviewed the bride, Sandra, 47, two weeks earlier as she prepared for the ceremony. An office cleaner with three adult children, she was embarking on her third marriage.

At 10 a.m. on a grey Wednesday in November 1999, two weeks after Sandra gave me an interview in a Midlands hotel, she arrived by car at Littlehey prison. She came with her son, daughter-in-law and two-year-old granddaughter. Her blonde hair was elegantly arranged high on her head and she was wearing a beautiful cream brocade wedding dress and a long green velvet cloak lined with cream satin—a splash of colour and opulence in front of the stark brick prison walls. The other guests were Sandra's younger daughter, a psychology graduate, and Stuart's mother and aunt and their partners. After a delay while the photographer's camera and a flower arrangement were cleared by security we were all ushered into the jail and Sandra was taken ahead to meet the registrar in the prison council room. This turned out to be an attractively panelled carpeted boardroom with chintz curtains masking the window bars.

Soon the bridegroom appeared, accompanied by an officer who left as soon as the ceremony began. Stuart was resplendent in a suit with Nehru-style jacket, gold brocade waistcoat and matching tie and handkerchief, a pink carnation in his buttonhole. The outfit had been brought into the jail by Sandra 15 minutes before the wedding. The registrar and her assistant, smiling bespectacled ladies, did their best to make the short ceremony as pleasant and relaxed as possible. We were all asked to stand while the couple exchanged their vows and their rings, and as they kissed, the registrar led us all in a round of applause. Sandra's son and I signed the register as witnesses. The photographer made sure that no bars appeared in the pictures and carefully avoided including a wall plaque bearing the names of the prison and all the governors in its short history. No refreshments were provided and no music was allowed.

Stuart was the first to break the rather awkward silence that followed by regaling us with a lively account of his stag night. In the prison workshop he had been grabbed by an 18 stone prisoner and, fearing the worst, he fought back. Other inmates pitched in and pinned him down while the huge prisoner clipped round his neck a collar with a polystyrene ball and chain attached, bearing a message about the chains of matrimony.

After the wedding Stuart was led back to his cell by a prison officer who apologised for breaking up the party. The rest of us repaired to the local pub where more photographs were taken of Sandra and family near the picturesque village duck pond. By now the clouds had rolled away and the sun was shining brightly. After a pub lunch and the cutting by Sandra of a cake she had made herself she returned to the jail to visit Stuart, still in her wedding dress, and joined regular visitors in the prison visiting room.

•   •   •

I desperately wanted to be married in August, a year to the day since Stuart and I started writing to each other, and we wanted to be married outside prison in a normal wedding where we could have family and friends. Stuart was due for resettlement leave but the prison authorities told me, 'We wouldn't trust him out on release. Give it another 12 weeks and we'll let him have home leave so you can get married outside and spend some time together.' So we settled on November the fifth and I joked about saving money on the reception—I said we could all go to the local firework display and have hot dogs! But it was a Friday and the Governor told us Stuart could only get home leave during the week. If we chose a Friday we wouldn't be able to spend our wedding night together. So we made all the arrangements for November third, a Wednesday.

Then suddenly the Governor refused home leave altogether and said Stuart had to be married in prison. We were devastated—absolutely devastated! The form we'd filled in had said he could be escorted to the registry office, but in the event we were even denied that. We were given no choice—it was a prison wedding or nothing. I'd bought this expensive wedding dress—I wouldn't have spent so much if I'd known the wedding would be in a prison.

The people who run the prison visits centre told us to put in an application straight away for permission to bring in our wedding rings on the day, and to have flowers, and the Governor did write back almost immediately and okayed all that. I was allowed to take in Stuart's ring in advance to see if it fitted him.

I wanted us to have a wedding cake straight after the ceremony but the authorities said I'd have to have it made in the prison and that would have cost between £100 and £200. I actually make wedding cakes semi-professionally for staff in the offices where I'm a cleaner. But if I wanted to bring my own cake into the prison it would apparently have had to be sent to Birmingham where they've got a special X-ray machine—and that would cost nearly as much. So we're just not going to be able to have the cake inside the prison. I've made one and we'll bring it to the pub afterwards.

I only earn just over £100 a week. I thought I would have had my divorce settlement by now so I could pay for everything, but it hasn't happened. Stuart's trying to have 'our' song played at the wedding—it's *Wait for Me* by Kenny Thomas—but I doubt we'll be allowed that either. But as I said to the nice woman who runs the visits centre, 'This is not going to be a sad affair. We're going to make the most of it and we're going to enjoy it.'

Like a lot of prisoners Stuart had a terrible childhood. His father was a boxer and he grew up thinking you solved things by violence. When Stuart was a lad a man pushed him out of the way in the swimming baths and his father went up and broke the man's jaw! Stuart was in prison a few times as a young offender, and when he came out he went to his mother for help. But she gave him the bus fare to get out of her life. His last sentence was for the armed robbery of a post office. And the offence for which he is now doing eight years was kidnap and torture. Somebody owed him thousands and he wanted it back. He saw him in the street after he'd had some drink and that was that.

In contrast my background was very stable. I was the only child of two workers in the local shoe industry who are now celebrating 50 years of married life. They had high expectations of me and I was doing quite well at school. But in 1969 when I was 16 I got pregnant. My parents had been brought up to show no emotion and they didn't show me much love—no affection or cuddles—so I suppose that's why when I was 16 I went to a man five years older than me to get affection.

My mother hid herself away for a fortnight, and I was an object of fascination at school—how could this goody-goody girl get herself into such a mess? I'd always been good at art and one of the art teachers had taken me under her wing and taught me to do oil paintings. My mother burned them all when I got pregnant. My father delivered the ultimatum that either I got married or the baby would have to be adopted.

So I left school and married the baby's father. I went to work in a factory and almost lost the baby—I spent our honeymoon in hospital. In a couple of years I was pregnant again. My husband suffered from ill-health and I nursed him through a major operation. But maybe because of all the pain he turned to drink and I used to get beaten. I used to work nights and the final straw came when I got home one morning and my son's ear was all bruised and he said his daddy had done it. I thought, I've got to get out of this. By the age of 21 I was going through a divorce—I had to give my husband all my savings to get him to leave me.

•　　　•　　　•

My second marriage was even worse because I found out a few weeks after the wedding that my husband was into sado-masochism. By this time I'd started blaming myself—I wondered if I was giving some sort of signal off to men. Still, I stayed in that marriage for 20 years. I'd got a nice house and I was the best off I'd ever been financially. I used to just think, What's half an hour every night? Just get it over and done with. About five years into the marriage the only way I could cope was by practising hypnotherapy. You learn to talk yourself into a nice place—you can transport yourself to anywhere you like. So that's what I would do every day while I was being whipped. It calms you down and gives you an inner strength. People might wonder why I stayed married for another 15 years after that. It was because I had children and I wasn't financially viable on my own. It's easier said than done to leave, and for me it would also have meant admitting to my parents that I'd failed yet again.

But as time went on I knew I would have to leave, because I was beginning to feel like a prostitute. And as the children grew up and were away from home more the whippings became more painful because my husband knew he could get away with it—they wouldn't be there to hear.

I'd always kept up my interest in sketching and I used to like to sketch soldiers at war—I suppose I did it because it brings out so much emotion. Because of this interest my elder daughter, who was 25 at the time and at the end of a relationship of her own, suggested writing off to *Soldier* magazine for penfriends, just for a bit of fun. She said, 'Come on, Mum, this'll cheer you up! I'll write off in my name and I'll reply to the younger ones and you can answer the older ones!' So we put an advert in her name in the magazine asking for penfriends and saying, 'All letters answered.'

I used to open the letters and tell my daughter who'd replied. One of the letters shocked me. I opened it and I remember saying, 'Oh dear—we've got one from a prisoner! No daughter of mine is writing to a prisoner!'

That prisoner was Stuart. At that time he was in a prison called Lowdham Grange, a Category B jail near Nottingham. One of the warders had passed on the *Soldier* magazine to him and he was just browsing through it when he saw our advert. Though I was shocked and didn't want my daughter to reply, it was such a lovely letter that I said, 'Look, we can't ignore this. I'll answer it myself.' What struck me was how Stuart had retained his sense of humour after all he'd been through, and how he was so honest about what he'd done. He wrote, 'I'm still a human being. Please write to me as a person'. So I thought, 'Yes, I will. I will give you a chance'.

●   ●   ●

It didn't cross my mind that this was a relationship that would go anywhere particular, but Stuart was so open, whereas I was with a husband who hardly said six words to me. Right from the start I realised that in Stuart I'd found somebody who understood me. We soon knew so much about each other. I'd write and ask him questions and before he'd even received my letter he'd be writing me the answers. It was so uncanny.

But I must admit that I did something I'm still quite ashamed of. Although Stuart was so honest with me I began by being quite devious with him. Because I didn't think anything would come of the correspondence, I started by writing as if I was my daughter Annette. So he thought he was writing to a 25-year-old woman—and I was 47! He was 33—only three years older than my son!

The crunch came when he told me he was going to get a tattoo with my name on it. I said to my daughter, 'That's it! He's going to go round for the rest of his life with "Annette" tattooed on him, and my name's Sandra! I'll have to tell him.'

He knew already that something was wrong and he kept writing to me and saying, 'Whatever it is, I'll take you and whatever comes with you.' He said it so often and I thought, 'Shall I tell him? Shall I tell him?'

So I did. I sent him a photo and explained everything, all about my real age, my husband and grown-up children and everything. He was marvellous. He said, 'Age is just a number. It doesn't matter.'

By this time we were writing every couple of days and Stuart was sort of dropping hints about asking to be moved to a prison closer to me. He was due to move to a less secure prison anyway but my daughter began to be frightened that I was getting too involved. I was getting hints from Stuart that he did love me, though he didn't tell me at the time. He was too frightened. He thought things were moving too fast, that he would frighten me off.

Finally I wrote and told him I loved him. After I wrote the letter I was in a panic—did he feel the same? He wrote back and said yes, he loved me too, and he begged me to come and visit him. I'd never been in a prison but of course you have these ideas what it must be like—and at first I felt I didn't want to see someone I loved in those surroundings. But he kept writing and saying, 'You've got to come and see me.' Nobody had visited him for quite a while—he hardly had any visitors at all. So I thought, Right—I'll go ahead.

I told my husband I was going Christmas shopping in Leicester and I set out for Nottingham by public transport—I don't drive. Then I took a bus to the village of Epperstone but I hadn't got a clue where the prison was. I assumed I'd be able to get a taxi, but there wasn't even a phone box! Luckily a taxi came along and dropped somebody off and I asked it to take me to the prison, which is right out in the wilds. I'm the sort of person who always likes to be early—but this time I was two hours early and I stood outside the prison in the freezing cold. The warders saw me standing there but nobody told me there was a visitors' centre where you could wait. I felt an utter fool.

After two hours they called all the visitors through to a waiting room next to the visits room. Other people said to me, 'You can look through the window and see your bloke come in.' But of course I hadn't got a clue what Stuart looked like—he'd never sent me a photo. So I said, 'Oh—right!' and felt like a right idiot. Then they called us in and there was this mass of faces. I stood in the doorway and gazed round. He knew what I looked like from my photo, and he called, 'Hello, Sandra!'

In his letters he'd written, 'Look—I'm no Chippendale. People have told me I look like a thug! I'm so worried that when you meet me you won't like what you see.' Annette said, 'He might look awful'.

I admit I just didn't expect the face that turned round and looked at me and smiled. He was medium height, medium build with dark brown hair. But once I sat down with him and we started talking it made no difference at all.

After that first visit I went to see Stuart regularly. I confided in Annette but I didn't tell anyone else. She was a bit hesitant but she realised I wasn't happy with her step-father and all she wanted was happiness for me. My younger daughter was away at university and my son had got married and had his own place. They didn't know a thing about Stuart. Then my son started driving me to the train station. He knew I was going to visit a man but he couldn't understand why this man never came to visit me. Annette said I shouldn't tell him. But in the end I did and he took it marvellously, marvellously. He said, 'So what? As long as you're happy!'

•   •   •

Meanwhile things were getting worse with my husband. If I was ten minutes late getting home I would be whipped—he used any excuse to do it and his attitude became even more dominating. My eldest daughter and my son guessed what was happening and they got so frightened for my safety. Annette and her partner never hesitated—they offered me a home with them. My youngest daughter had no idea what her father was doing. Finally Stuart coaxed me to leave. He said, 'Look, you've got to get out of this.'

So I planned my escape. About a month before I left I confided in my parents about what was going on in my marriage—though I still didn't tell them about Stuart. I organized theatre tickets in London for my husband and youngest daughter—that was something I often used to do—and on the day they went, my father came and moved all my furniture and clothes to Annette's house. I left a note for my husband telling him I'd left, and saying my solicitor would contact him. I didn't say where I'd gone.

But my husband didn't find the note—my youngest daughter did, and she was in a terrible state. I didn't want to tell her why I'd left, but in the end I had to—she needed to know. Unfortunately she soon found out about Stuart as well—that was by accident too. I had arranged to visit the prison and to stay with some prison visitors in Nottingham who did bed and breakfast accommodation. They rang my old home to confirm the arrangement and got my husband. Though he dismissed the call and said, 'Nobody in this house knows anyone in prison', my daughter overheard and guessed that I was going out with a prisoner. She still sobs her heart out though I think she now accepts that Stuart is part of the family. He's written to her and explained that he understands how she feels because he went through his own parents' break-up.

•   •   •

My parents know I'm getting married again, but they've never met Stuart and they assume he's in the Forces. I go and see my parents and I must admit I'm in a dilemma over them. They're both old—in their seventies—and I think it would break their hearts to know I was marrying a prisoner. And I don't want Stuart pre-judged. I want them to meet him and for him to be treated as an equal. If they find out afterwards, at least they'll have got to know him already. I do believe basically in telling the truth, but it would cause my parents so much hurt. I've spoken to people at the visits centre at Littlehey and they advise you to tell the truth. Someone who's weaker-willed than I am might take their advice and find they're totally shunned by their families. So many women I've spoke to have become outcasts. Do you hide the truth and remain part of the family ? Or do you tell the truth and find your partner is immediately condemned and you are as well?

Stuart has spoken to my mother on the phone and he's sent birthday cards. I think once they meet him they'll realise that he'll be a valuable asset to our family. I've got three grandchildren and Stuart loves kids—he can give them so much time, help them with their homework, play with them.

I think my parents do suspect something. My father drove me up to Littlehey the other week and dropped me at the bus shelter, but conveniently there's an RAF station in that village. After that my father sat me down and there was a lot of emotion in his voice when he said, 'Is he really in the Forces?' I was taken aback—I didn't know what to do, and I said, yes, he was. I just didn't know what to do for the best.

•   •   •

I wouldn't say I have any doubts about me and Stuart. I've never regretted saying I'll marry him, though my track record isn't very good, I must admit! I've tried marriage two different ways. First time I married in a hurry, the second one I did it all 'right', courted for a few years, got married—and yet that marriage was a disaster. So why shouldn't this one work? This is the happiest I've ever been. I'm positive we'll get on all right because we're both prepared to give and take.

I think the more knocks we get, the stronger we are, the more determined to prove people wrong. When the wedding was cancelled, that was an all-time low, but it has made our love stronger. We are bonded in that way. We both have an unusual sense of humour and we can talk about anything and everything. We both have time for each other. I think in a relationship like ours you've got to give everything, else it fails, it's liable to go astray. I could go off with somebody else and because Stuart's in prison he wouldn't know anything about it. But I wouldn't betray him, not that way. That's probably because I'm a strong character. If you were a bit weak you could give way.

•   •   •

I have had to change the way I think. Where I was brought up, nobody had ever been in trouble with the police. The police were the best—they never did anything wrong. Prisoners? I wouldn't touch them, wouldn't give them the time of day! I would even have been in favour of capital punishment. Certainly I used to think, Lock 'em up and throw away the key!

Knowing Stuart has totally changed me, completely opened my eyes. Stuart talks about his friends in prison and I've spoken to them myself. They are ordinary people though of course they have done some terrible things. But now if ever I could help them in any way I would, because I don't think they get the help they need. So for me it's a complete turnaround of attitude.

Mind you, once I knew Stuart and I were getting serious I did give him an ultimatum. I said, 'I don't want you committing any other crimes, or you would lose me.' I told him, 'I've had enough trouble in my life. I'm not going to stand for that. You've got to make the choice.' There would be hell to pay if he went back to crime. I believe that if you make a bargain, you mean what you say.

I admit I'm having problems coming to terms with his past girlfriends, specially because one of them had his child. Stuart is more capable of coping with my past than I am with his. I think once he's released and we're together we'll be all right. I don't have any fears that he will be violent to me. His mother has emphasised that he wouldn't do that sort of thing.

But Stuart has never had one home leave in the eight years of this sentence and understandably he's scared of coming out. I know he's going to find it so difficult and I'm not getting any help from anywhere. His probation officer hasn't even been to see him about his release. It's little things that shock me— like when I visit and put money for refreshments on the table and he looks at a £2 coin and says, 'I've never seen one of these!' Quite honestly I dread to think what kind of job he will get. I think it's going to be very hard for him to accept that people may not want to employ him because of his record. I think I will try to be at home for him during the day, so if there's any problem we can spend more time together and I can help him. If I worked all hours he'd be left on his own and probably he'd feel completely lost. He's told me he may suffer from post-traumatic stress.

I don't think you can ever completely change anybody. But if Stuart really wants to change, he will. I know I've got to guide him and I know it's going to take a hell of a lot out of me. But the effort has to come from him as well—it's not got to be one-way traffic. He's having a chance and I think I can say it's the only chance he'll get. But I'm optimistic this will work. I suppose it's because I'm a very determined person.

•   •   •

Postscript: Stuart was released in March 2000 and immediately got a job as the manager of a snooker club, where he worked for five months before being made redundant. He began training as a forklift truck driver and was confident that he would have no problems getting employment. When Stuart was first released Sandra, full of trepidation, finally told her parents about his prison record. Her father said he had known all along. Stuart has now been accepted by Sandra's family, though her younger daughter still finds the situation difficult. In August 2000 Stuart and Sandra had their wedding blessed at a ceremony in their local church. All the family were there, the reception was held at Sandra's mother's home and it was a very happy occasion.

In November 2001 Sandra contacted me again. Stuart was finding it very difficult to get a permanent job: 'Life is terribly stressful. To be honest, I don't think the Government want ex-prisoners to succeed.'

Diana and Mark

Diana, a qualified lawyer, fell in love with one of her clients, Mark, a life-sentenced prisoner. They have been married six years and Diana has noticed a remarkable change in the way prison officers treat her.

Diana is a practising solicitor working on criminal cases in the London courts. An attractive woman with shoulder-length brown hair, blue eyes and an animated expression, she looks much younger than her 39 years. The day we met she was casually dressed in loose trousers and a striped top. She lived alone in a large flat on the top floor of an apartment block in London with stunning views of the distant St Paul's Cathedral. Diana had just sold her flat and was moving to a terraced house south of London.

Diana is the eldest of the three daughters of a Norfolk painter and decorator and his wife, who worked in Littlewoods. Diana did very well at school and went on to do a law degree at London University and to qualify as a solicitor. In 1990 she had been practising for three years when she met her future husband Mark, now 35. She took over from the regular duty solicitor at a London police station and was asked to represent Mark, who had just been brought in, charged with trying to rob a post office. However it soon emerged that he had absconded from a police car in Somerset while being taken into custody on a murder charge. Diana then lost touch with Mark until he rang her out of the blue two years later. He had been convicted of the murder and was a Category A prisoner serving a life sentence in a top security jail. He was facing a further charge of prison mutiny and wanted Diana to represent him. She agreed, they fell in love, and married inside prison in 1996.

Their wedding photographs show a strikingly good-looking couple, with Mark wearing a kilt and Diana in a beautiful white dress with full-length veil. Since their marriage Diana has had access to all the papers in Mark's case and she now believes him to be innocent of the murder. She has investigated the case and has sent the papers to the Criminal Cases Review Commission.[1] Diana and Mark are waiting to see whether the Commission will refer the case back to the Court of Appeal.

•   •   •

I've always had a slightly rebellious streak. I remember being very, very annoyed when I was about nine and I was watching the Queen on the telly. I asked my mum when it was going to be her turn to be Queen, and when she said no, it didn't work like that, I remember feeling absolutely furious—because my mum couldn't be Queen.

I would never quite do what my mum and dad thought I should. I wanted to leave school at 16. It was quite a strict grammar school—I'd passed the 11-plus to get in there—and I was always in trouble. When my A level results came out they were better than I thought they'd be. I thought, What shall I do? *Crown Court* was on the telly and I was watching it and I thought, I know what I'll do! I'll go and be a barrister! I applied to read law in London and I got in.

I don't think I had a proper idea of what I was letting myself in for. Perhaps it's not so true these days, but with the Bar it's a question of who you know—and my dad was a decorator and he didn't have connections in chambers. I let myself get scared off by that and decided I would go and be a solicitor instead. After I finished my articles I always had jobs doing criminal law. I'm a solicitor-advocate now, because solicitors have rights of audience in the higher courts. So now I've ended up where I always wanted to be.

I had two long relationships throughout these years. I met my first boyfriend when I was 17 and I was with him for five years, all through university. Then I had a seven year relationship with someone but it was a disaster.

•　　•　　•

I met my future husband on 31 July 1990 in a police station cell. I wasn't the duty solicitor but in those days firms could send what they'd call reps, so I got sent off to this nick and met Mark—except he didn't give that name—he said he was called John Jones. I turned up to Marylebone Magistrates' Court next day and I put in a bail application. Mark thought I was quite amusing because although I didn't know his whole story, what he was supposed to have done was bad enough. He'd tried to rob a post office and he was of no fixed abode.

I went down into the cells after the hearing. One of the officers came up to me and said, 'His name's not John Jones—it's Mark Roberts and he's on the run for murder!' So I went into his cell and I said to Mark, 'Oh, hello, Mr Jones—or should I say, Mr Roberts?' And he said, 'Oh—they know, do they?' And I said, 'Yes, I'm afraid they do.' He looked at me and said, 'I didn't do it, you know'. That was the first comment he ever made to me about the situation. It meant nothing much to me at that moment and I thought, Oh well, perhaps you didn't.

But there was something about him that intrigued me. I thought he was an interesting character. And there was definitely something physically attractive about him, though he didn't look like he does now. He's got long black hair but because he was on the run he'd cut it short and dyed it a sort of brown colour. I asked him who his solicitors were and he told me, and I said I'd get in touch with them and tell them what had happened. Then they took him off to Brixton prison.

Looking back now, I think the very first sign that there was something between us was that second time I met him, locked in that tiny cell with him at Marylebone Magistrates' Court. The building used to be a swimming pool, and I've had a theory that the cells must have been the old changing rooms, because they were so narrow. There was only one seat so you'd have to decide who actually sat on it. Mark was sitting on the seat and I said, 'Oh, don't get up!' and I parked myself on the floor. I'm not very tall but I couldn't straighten my legs—that's how narrow it was. I remember sitting there and just talking to him about legal stuff generally. But I do remember a point when we looked at each other and neither of us said anything, and everything went quiet for slightly too long. Then it passed and we carried on as normal. I think I'd describe it as if something in the air seemed to shift.

We went back to the court the next week. By this time the circus had started. The Flying Squad escorted Mark to court and he came into the courtroom handcuffed to two of them. I had to explain to the magistrate what all this was about, and I remember there were two or three people in the public gallery who gasped. They all thought it was magnificent that a man had escaped from prison, though really he had just slipped the lock on a police car.

After that Mark's solicitors sent the papers up to me and asked me if I would take instructions for them on the murder. I read the papers and thought, he's not going to be convicted for this, is he? This is nonsense! He was supposed to have murdered an itinerant French hippie who had turned up in the West Country and stayed with a group of New Age travellers—of whom Mark was one. This guy disappeared one night and about ten days later his body was found in a ditch.

By one of those curious little quirks of fate, I was in that area of the West Country on New Year's Eve 1990. I was with my boyfriend who worked for a film company. On New Year's Eve we went from pub to pub. I had to go and see Mark a couple of times while he was still on remand in Brixton, and one of those times I discovered that he'd been in the same town that same night, going from pub to pub. We've always had this idea that we might have seen each other in the crowd. I do believe in Fate, though I'm not a complete fatalist. I think some things in life are going to happen, whatever you do. Some things are set in stone.

Then Mark got taken back to a prison in the West Country and that was the last I saw of him for about two years.

I left the firm I was with because I got a better job at another firm, but I remember asking a solicitor at my old firm to let me know if he ever found out how the Mark Roberts case turned out.

•   •   •

About two years later I was sitting in my office one day when the phone went and the girl downstairs said, 'I've got someone called Mark Roberts for you'.

'Never heard of him!' I said. So she said, 'I'll put him through.' Then Mark came on the line; he explained about the murder trial and said that he'd got 14 years—and the penny dropped.

He was ringing from a prison up north to say he was up before the local magistrates in two weeks' time—one of 14 men charged with prison mutiny. So I said, 'All right, I should be able to sort out an agent for you by that time.'

'Oh no,' he said, 'you don't understand. You've got to come yourself.'

So a couple of weeks later, off I went to visit Mark. I was quite shocked at how he seemed to have aged. I thought, God, he looks different! For a start his hair had changed. I'd seen this guy with shortish, blondish-brown hair, and suddenly he'd got all this long dark hair. He looked very pale—he's got this Celtic colouring, pale skin and dark hair. He gave me a load of papers and I started to go through them.

•　　•　　•

The next time I saw Mark was at the Crown Court. I went walking up to the court with all the other solicitors and there were two or three men on the roof with sub-machine guns and loads of police with Alsatian dogs. I said to another solicitor, 'They must have some big case going on here—I wonder what it is?'

'It's ours, you idiot!' he said. Of the 14 men on the mutiny charge, five were Category A prisoners.

I was literally sick with nerves. I went and threw up in the loo. When I got into the court, there were all these very eminent barristers who'd all done prison cases, and all these other solicitors who had been qualified for about ten years. I remember being very, very frightened. It's one of the few times I've had really bad stage fright.

When I finally got to see Mark in the cells I sat down and he said, 'You look pale, are you all right?'

'No!' I said. 'I'm not up to it! I'll get hold of chambers and get a good person up here in a couple of hours.'

Mark looked at me and he said, 'Now listen to me very carefully. All you have to do is just go upstairs and ask some questions!' He talked me into it very gently.

And it was OK. I didn't make a complete fool of myself at all. In fact I enjoyed doing it. They were committed for trial, which didn't happen for over a year later. Mark got moved to a prison in the Midlands and I used to go there every couple of months, supposedly to take instructions for him. In fact they were more like social visits than legal visits. Mark's a very engaging person with a certain amount of charm.

•　　•　　•

Mark was born in Glasgow and he lived in Scotland till he was eight. His father was a park keeper. His mum died of cancer when Mark was 14 and just before she died he was sent to a detention centre. He'd started appearing in court when he was ten or eleven, and when I went to visit him at that prison in the Midlands, one of the officers said to me, 'I've known him since he was a lad, you know!' He was rather precocious and was always hanging around with older boys. His previous convictions were things like TDA—kids' stuff.

I've seen quite a lot of his old social inquiry reports, and I've even seen a psychiatric report on my husband. I would advise any wife to get one of those! His reports all said things like, 'Mark is intelligent, he has got a good average IQ, but he has underachieved substantially at school.'

He didn't bother going to school after a certain point. So he's not educated like I am, but he's cleverer than me. Mark is one of the few men whom I've actually looked up to. I respect him and he is very much my equal. He was never in the least bit frightened of me, which lots of men were. He's very articulate and there isn't much he can't talk about. I see us as equals.

Mark was 24 when he was convicted of murder. Before that he'd had quite a lot of jobs. He'd been a hod-carrier for a while. He used to work in a kitchen and as a cashier in a petrol station, and when he was arrested he was busking.

During these visits we talked about all sorts of things. He told me his relationship with his girlfriend was starting to go wrong. She wasn't visiting him as often as she should. When he mentioned that to me he said, 'What about you, then? Have you got a boyfriend?' And I said, 'I can't discuss that with you! I'm your solicitor!'

'Well, I've told you all about me!' he said.

'Well—that's different!' I said. And I wouldn't tell him.

•   •   •

This went on for about a year and then as it was coming up to the mutiny trial I went up on a visit and I took a woman barrister with me. We'd got the coffee on the table and she'd forgotten to get sugar, so Mark went back to the serving hatch for it. While he was gone she leaned over to me and she said, 'Diana! You and Mark!'

'What about me and Mark?' I said.

'It's electric, what's going on between you!' she said. 'You can almost touch it.'

I remember getting a lecture all the way home on how there was going to be trouble. I spent the whole two hour journey denying that anything was going on. There was that thing in the air that time in the Marylebone cell, but we'd never discussed it. And I really didn't think I was ever going to do anything about it. I mean I was vaguely aware that I quite fancied Mark physically, but so what?

Nearer the court date I went to the prison again with the same barrister. When we arrived, Mark gave me an astrological birth chart he'd made for me. He'd taken a lot of care with it and drawn it and coloured it for me. It was quite touching, and without thinking I lurched forward and kissed him on the cheek—and then went bright red.

All the way back to London in the car I got told off again by the barrister. 'The prison officers were all there,' she said, 'and they'll be after you for that.'

When it got to the trial, it was stopped after the second day because of some problem with the jury. But for those two days Mark was very withdrawn and quiet—and he's not usually quiet at all. I kept asking him what was wrong and he kept saying it was nothing. I told Mark I was going back to London and he said, 'Will you come and see me in prison before you go?'

I knew something was wrong so I did go back and visit him and I said, 'What's the matter? Have you fallen out with the barrister or something?'

And he said, 'No. I'm going to tell you something. I've got to say it, and once I've said it you can forget it. But I'm going to say it. I've fallen for you, you know! I've been thinking about this a lot, and I remember you telling me that sometimes female solicitors get letters from loony clients who fall in love with them. I would never want you to think I'm one of them. I know you're my solicitor and I shouldn't be saying this to you. The only reason I'm saying it is that I don't think it's one-sided. Am I right?'

'Yes,' I said. 'Yes, you are.'

It was about seven o'clock in the evening when the visit finished and I left the prison. It's a good four hour drive back to London and I drew up outside my flat and I couldn't remember anything at all about the journey. I'd driven down to London in a complete trance! It was one of those moments when you know something has happened to you that is going to change your life. It's happened, it's done. You can't run away from it.

I never questioned it, but I felt rattled by it, disturbed by it. I won't call it fear—that would be wrong. It was just the sense that something very important had happened, and nothing was ever going to be the same again. It was something big, it was something completely new.

•   •   •

Mark was acquitted on the mutiny charge and he was moved back to the prison in the Midlands. Then he asked me to help him with the murder charge. So I turned up at the prison.

It's my theory that the officers had it in for me because of the mutiny. They may have thought they'd seen the last of me, and now here I was again. After that visit my female boss got a phone call from one of the prison governors, saying, 'Who is this woman? Is she a solicitor? Because we don't believe that was a legal visit—we're sure things were going on.'

My boss called me into her office and she said, 'Now what's happening?' I said, 'As I left I kissed him on the cheek, but I've done that before and they've never remarked on it.' Solicitors are not like doctors anyway—we are allowed to have sexual relationships with clients. There are plenty of divorce lawyers, usually male, who have affairs with their female clients.

So I wrote a letter to the Governor telling him what was what. He wrote back saying he found the whole thing very unusual, but he would allow me to come back on a legal visit as long as I behaved in a professional manner. I was really annoyed by this. I didn't think it was for him to tell me how I should behave with my clients.

But I did say to Mark, 'Look, I'm trying to sort out this murder conviction for you. I can't be a girlfriend and a solicitor. I've got to be one or the other—and to be honest, in some ways I think I'm more use to you as your solicitor.'

On my first visit after the incident with that governor, when I came to leave we both stood as far apart as we possibly could and shook hands very vigorously.

•   •   •

Then in 1995, after a year of this silly business, Mark got moved to another prison and I said, 'This is a good time for me to visit you as your girlfriend.'

I had to apply for security clearance because he was still a Category A prisoner—he still is to this day. It was quite funny being cleared, because I had a detective from my local nick coming round, and I didn't recognize him. He said, 'You do know what he's in for, don't you?' I said, 'Yes, I used to be his solicitor. I've seen his previous convictions and his psychiatric reports.' He seemed quite happy with everything and I got cleared to see Mark, he sent me a VO [visiting order] and off I went.

That was in September 1995 and I hadn't mentioned anything to my family, but I did tell my closest friend. I said, 'There's something going on between me and Mark,' and she said, 'Tell me something I don't know!' My mum had seen it coming for some time as well but I think my family thought it would fizzle out.

Just before I started visiting Mark as his girlfriend he sent me this ring that I'm wearing. He'd got his dad to go and buy it for him and send it to me. It probably didn't cost him more than five pounds but it was all the money he had in the world at the time.

When I had been visiting him a few months, one of us—and I don't know which of us it was—said, 'When are we going to get married?' It wasn't a big thing—it was something we both knew, we'd always known.

•   •   •

The prison he was in then was a pretty horrible nick and I said, 'I don't want to get married in here.' In fact for a while I said, 'Let's wait till you come out. I don't want to get married in a prison.' But gradually I relented because I thought, I am going to marry him, and it doesn't matter where we get married.

So we'd decided in general terms to get married, and Mark was saying, 'When?' and I said, 'Well, I don't remember being asked properly!'

At that, in the visiting room full of people, he went down on bended knee and proposed!

I said, 'Get up! Get up before anyone sees what you're doing!'

Then I moved his ring to my ring finger, and when he got moved to a more laid-back nick, we set the date for 2 December 1996, 15 months after I had started visiting him as his girlfriend.

I went out one night with another of my close women friends and I told her that I wanted to marry Mark. She gave me a right bollocking! She said it would have an effect on my career—they would never make me a judge! So I said that was fine, I didn't want to be a judge. Then she said, 'You don't really know him! How do you know he won't come home and drink himself stupid or take drugs and steal from your family? There are going to be people who won't have him in the house. How do you feel about that?'

I think I was quite shaken by what she said, but she's mellowed as time's gone on, though I don't think she'll ever think it's a terrific idea. Other people have reacted in different ways. The gossip round the magistrates' courts of

London was rife. In some circumstances you almost become a minor celebrity because people want to know everything and they ask you the most personal questions.

I went to see my boss one day and I said, 'I'm going to marry him—do you want me to resign?' He was lovely. He came over and kissed me on the cheek and he said, 'No, that's absolutely fine. Can I buy him a colour telly as a wedding present?' And I said, 'He's not allowed a colour telly, but can we have helicopter, please?'

●　　●　　●

We got married on a Monday morning in December. Mark had asked the Governor about the cake I'd ordered and he said that was fine. The extraordinary thing was, it wasn't even delivered from the shop. I collected it from there, along with a stand I'd hired—it was a three-tier cake. When we got to the wedding reception I half expected to see a slice cut out and carefully replaced! The really mad thing was that the bottom layer ended up on D wing for all the prisoners to eat—I could have laced it with absolutely anything. I took my bouquet in with me as well.

Our wedding invitation was printed in Celtic script and very carefully worded. It just said, 'The chapel' and the name of the road that the prison was in. It didn't say anything about prisons. And that's what it says on our wedding certificate too.

We were only allowed 12 guests so I asked my sister to take the wedding photographs. I was starting to get very paranoid about the story getting into the papers. I thought if someone else had the negatives the temptation to sell them would be very big.

Everybody attending the wedding had to be visited by the police and security-cleared. There was my mum, who was in her 60s and wouldn't even cross the road unless the green man told her to! There was my one sister, who's a chartered accountant, my other sister, who's a personnel manager, a friend who's a solicitor, another who's an account manager and another who's married to an RAF officer. Mark's dad is now a local government officer, and none of his family has any previous convictions. Mark's best man was his mate who was doing seven years for the possession of a shotgun. My godson was my ring boy—I sent him down the aisle carrying the rings on a little cushion.

We were married in the prison chapel by the prison chaplain in a Church of England ceremony. It was a normal church service but we didn't have hymns. I promised 'to love, honour and protect' Mark—not to obey!

I wore a long white dress with diamond lattice embroidery on the front and a pearl tiara. I wasn't going to have a veil, but Mark had this fantasy of lifting the veil up after we were married and kissing me. So once I'd agreed to have a veil I didn't mess about—I had the whole full-length thing—and he did lift it up and kiss me when we were pronounced man and wife. It was cold so I also had a long green velvet cloak.

We had the reception in a little side room off the chapel. We weren't allowed to bring in any food apart from the wedding cake, but Mark can cook, so he'd prepared quiches, biscuits, cakes and sandwiches, which he had to pay for out of his prison wages. He phoned me up one day and said he thought we'd have *vol-au-vents*. 'But we can't take food in, Mark, so we can't have those!'

'Oh yes we can, I'm going to make them!'

'But you can't do puff pastry!'

'Yes I can, I used to work in a kitchen!'

But the *vol-au-vents* went horribly wrong and got thrown at a wall in the prison, so we never did have them. We had no alcohol of course, just Coca Cola, tea and coffee.

The chapel orderly was a Libyan terrorist and my mum said, 'Oh, he seemed quite nice, what's he in for?'

•   •   •

I think marrying me has in some ways made Mark's life in prison more difficult—because now he's got a very lippy wife. The officers don't get into discussions with me if they can possibly help it. One of my friends said, 'Well, of course they don't like it. You come along, you're a solicitor, you've obviously got a decent income—and you're with *him!* They don't understand it and they resent it.'

My attitude to prison officers has changed drastically since I've been with Mark. Going into prisons before as a solicitor, I would be cordial with the prison officers and obviously their attitude was different. If you go through that door as a solicitor they are more careful. They will call you 'Ma'am' because they don't want complaints from solicitors. But complaints from wives—well, we're just a load of loud-mouthed fishwives, aren't we? Why listen to us?

But of course I'm still the same person. I don't change when I go through a different door. Perhaps my friend is right—the officers think I don't fit the picture of what a prisoner's wife should be.

We have been subjected to deliberate hassle and I've complained about it. On visits we've been told, 'Stop this, stop that, stop the other,' while other couples doing exactly the same thing were left alone. One day Mark put his hand on my knee and a very young officer told me not to let him do that. I said, 'Please don't speak to me like that! I'm probably old enough to be your mother!'

Then they stuck us on closed visits because I had an argument with the Governor. They said we were too intimate. I was absolutely *incandescent* with rage! I was considering suing them for misfeasance in a public office.

•   •   •

From the point of view of my career, there are people who take a certain sneering attitude and there was one job I didn't get because I told them I was married to Mark. I felt I had to disclose it because I didn't want to have a 'terrible secret'.

Being married to a prisoner does mean that I feel more sorry for clients, no matter what they've done, though I still recognise someone who's telling me a load of horseshit. You don't always like your clients—some of them are pretty horrible. But no matter what they're like, when you wave them off to the nick for three years or so you still feel bad. And I feel sorry for their families, though I've only ever disclosed to one client's wife that I'm married to a prisoner.

I'm also an outsider to most of the other prisoners' wives. It's partly a class thing I think. I suppose because I'm a professional and I speak with what they think is a posh voice—which I need to do to be effective in the courts—I probably come over as snotty, though I come from a working class background. I get the feeling they think I'm one of these prison groupies. Chatting with them in the women's toilets they've asked how long I've been married, and how long Mark's been inside, and they soon worked it out and they have the attitude: 'We have to be here, you don't. Why did you marry him?' But what they don't realise is that I knew him eight years before we got married.

•　　•　　•

After we married I set about trying to get Mark's murder conviction overturned. I spoke to his former solicitors and they were very happy that I was helping him and I went down to see them and got all the papers.

I think I would have probably fallen in love with Mark even if he really had committed the murder. I remember just before I got married, one of the solicitors I worked with said to me, 'If you find out that he did this, don't let it spoil it. You have fallen in love with him.' And I said to this guy, 'Well, if that happened, I suppose I'd want to know why he lied to me for so long.' One day, a good few years ago now, Mark and I had a conversation. I was still his solicitor then and I said, 'I shall say this only once. Did you do this murder? I'm willing to do a lot of work for you, but don't waste my time. Did you do this?' And he said, 'No, I didn't. If I'd done it I would have offered a plea of manslaughter and I've have been out by now.'

There are times when I wish he had done it. That's a really weird thing to say—that you wish your husband had killed somebody. If he had done it there would be some sense in all of this. But because he hasn't, it's like madness. There are times when I've had a bad day and maybe the officers have hassled us, and I feel like saying, 'Right, I've had enough of this! The joke's gone far enough—he's coming home with me!'

•　　•　　•

Mark's been in prison eleven years now, and the worse case scenario is that he just stays there, on and on and on, keeping on applying for parole and never getting anywhere near it. He's got four years left on his tariff and if only I knew that he was coming home then!

One of the things we have to think about is having children, because I'm 38 now. I've been told about a DIY method that has worked. I met someone on a visit to one of the prisons and she told me that her husband had smuggled semen out on a visit, she'd used it and they'd had a child. Mark and I talked about this and I said if they caught you, you'd probably be put on closed visits for three months—but then again, could you argue that semen is not a prohibited substance? I don't know anything in the Prison Rules that says it is—though if the authorities read this it soon will be![2]

•   •   •

I'd be lying if I said I thought there would be no problems when Mark is released. I wouldn't want to underestimate how difficult it might be for a while though I'm often quite surprised at how much he does know about the real world. He reads newspapers and he's got TV in his cell. Though when I was selling my flat he was amazed at the house prices when I showed him the estate agents' details. He'd be amazed at all the trendy wine bars and pubs too.

I can see changes in him—after all, I met him when he was 24 and now he's 35. I think he may find it difficult to adjust to having a wife who earns more than him. He keeps saying that he's no gigolo! I do think about all of these problems but I don't worry too much. What I do know is that we will just muddle through it as best we can. Because we really fancy each other—and after all, we're mates!

Postscript: Six months after this interview Diana phoned to say she had settled in well in her new house and had taken photos of rooms she had redecorated to show Mark. 'His project is the garden. I'm no good at gardening and he knows about plants, so he's got to design it.' Mark has moved prisons since the interview—much to Diana's relief as that prison had twice banned her on suspicion of bringing in drugs. She complained to the Prison Service and the allegations were withdrawn.

ENDNOTES

[1] The Criminal Cases Review Commission reviews alleged miscarriages of justice, usually after a first appeal has been dismissed by the Court of Appeal.

[2] See pp. 61-2, Endnotes 13-14.

Shirley and Ben Cheng

Shirley is 67 and is the widow of a former police officer to whom she was married for 25 years until he died of cancer at the age of 47. Widowed for ten years, in 1998 she married a Chinese former drug dealer 24 years her junior.

Shirley lives in quiet Norfolk village with her husband Ben Cheng, who used to be a heroin addict and drug dealer. Their 130-year-old beamed cottage, shared with a Tibetan *lasa apso* dog called Penny and a cage of finches chirping away, is idyllic. The interview was conducted over a delicious lunch with Shirley and B, as she likes to call Ben, in their cosy kitchen, opening out on to a small but well-designed garden. Shirley, her greying hair subtly highlighted, was wearing a loose shirt and trousers and looked the picture of a middle-class country lady. She has a very soft, calm voice, and was educated from the age of five at a private convent girls' school in Surrey. She did most of the talking as B's understanding and command of English are still rather limited, though she always made sure to bring him into the conversation. His comments are included here.

The walls of the beautifully furnished sitting room are lined with photographs. They show Shirley and B at their wedding in a local registry office, B in a smart dark suit, bought for the occasion by Shirley—'the first suit he ever owned!'—and Shirley in a red dress and white jacket. They are standing under a rose-covered arbour in the registry office garden. B is a handsome, slim man with olive skin and high cheekbones, who looks much younger than his 43 years. When I tease Shirley about getting herself a 'toy-boy' she laughs and agrees. Other pictures show B's son by his first wife, with a younger boy, his wife's son from another relationship.

B got involved with drugs at the age of 18. He was sent to England by his desperate Hong Kong family at the age of 28 to stay with his sister who had married an Englishman and lived in Norfolk. B remained drug-free for a few years, until he met his addict wife. During their six-year marriage he became more deeply involved in drugs. He ended up serving a long prison sentence for drug dealing.

Shirley met B in the chapel of HM Prison Wayland, the Norfolk jail near her home which held the late Reggie Kray until his release on compassionate grounds in August 2000. (Coincidentally Kray's wife Roberta moved to the same village as Shirley and the two women have met—Shirley found Roberta 'very quiet, very nice'.) Some friends of Shirley's belonged to the Prison Fellowship, a Christian ministry to prisoners, and they invited her to join them for a service being held in the prison. Eventually B asked her to bring his young son and step-son to visit him and after a few months he declared his love for her.

• • •

The first time I saw B he shone! His face was beaming and he literally shone. We were only just introduced by another inmate—we said hello and how are you and that was about all, because his English was limited. We didn't even sit together. Then he stopped coming to the chapel for quite a long time. But I never forgot his face.

My husband Peter had died of cancer at the age of 47. We married when I was 31 and he was 21 and an officer in the Metropolitan Police. We had been married 25 years and I was devastated by his death. We had both become Christians after we moved to Norfolk and I held on to God to get me through. My late husband used to go into Wayland prison with a local worship group, and I did ask him once if I could go with him. But he didn't want me to, and I felt quite hurt by that. Then a few years after his death I felt God calling me to go to the prison. I tried to get in with the Prison Fellowship, but all the doors seemed to remain shut to me at that time.

About three years later I found out that a neighbour of mine used to go into Wayland chapel every Sunday and when I asked her for a lift, she agreed.

The very first morning that I was in the chapel I thought, Yes, I know I'm in the right place! The chapel at Wayland is beautiful, large and airy with open windows and a great sense of peace and light. As soon as I walked through the doors, I knew—I just felt at home. Everybody kept saying to me, 'When they shut those doors behind you it'll be dreadful!' But I just felt so comfortable that I sat and I thought, 'I'm home!'

After a while I started going in to the chapel on Tuesday evenings as well as Sundays. I made friends with one particular inmate and it was he who introduced me to this Chinese man called Ben. I also started working as a volunteer in the visitors' centre, and I loved this work.

●   ●   ●

Ben's children, who were aged about seven and ten, had been in foster homes since their mother died and were then living with a family friend. I thought it was very sad, so I asked one of the chaplains if it was permissible for me to bring the boys in and he rang me the next day and said it was fine, as long as I knew I was responsible for them.

I used to go once a month. My friend came with us as I hadn't got a car and we gave B time with the boys. We got on really well and became like a family. After a few months I knew I was feeling more than friendship for B, and one day I asked the co-ordinator in the visits centre if I could go into the prison and visit him, which I did. I just had this feeling about him—it was quite extraordinary. It's strange—I can't explain it. I was really wanting to hear him say something.

On the Tuesday nights we all used to give each other a hug after the service as the men were going back to the wings. One Tuesday night we were doing that as usual and B said to me, 'I love you!' Just like that!

B: This come from my heart, that I love Shirley, so I say, 'I love you'. I think it's because she come into chapel, and then I met her when she bring the children in and then we build up a relationship slowly. And then when I saw her in the chapel I say, 'I love you'.

Shirley: It was a wonderful surprise—I was so happy! I actually came out of the prison walking on air! Then I asked the co-ordinator if I could go and see B again on the wing. That second time I went to see him he held my hand, and of course that was picked up by the officers, and I was asked by the prison authorities to stop going into the chapel, because I was a Prison Fellowship member and a volunteer at the visitors' centre, and I was getting friendly with an inmate.

I was upset but I knew at that stage that my feelings for B were much greater. I had two choices, and I went to see B and I told him the options. I said, 'Either I don't see you at all until next May when you come out, and you can just write to me and phone me. Or I give up working in the visitors' centre.' And B said, 'Whatever you want to do is OK. You decide what you have to do.'

I decided to take the first option—to go the prison's way. I went home and for the next ten days I had no peace, none at all. I used to get down on my knees and pray to God, and every time He would say to me, 'Don't listen to men, don't go the way they want you to go'. So in the end I phoned up the co-ordinator and I said, 'Can I change my mind?' and he said, 'Yes, but I think you're doing the wrong thing.' And I said, 'No—I'm not', and I wrote a letter of resignation and put it on his desk.

•   •   •

So in 1996 I gave up working in the visitors' centre and going to the chapel, but for the next year I used to visit B once a fortnight for a couple of hours. He would phone me two or three times a week and he used to write me letters. I've got boxes of beautiful letters which took him hours and hours to write. He would say that he loved me and he missed me. Because his English was limited they were quite repetitive but they meant such a lot to me and I've still got them all. It was lovely and romantic because he would phone, then I'd have the letters—it was lovely. Prison was a safe environment and it was all very romantic.

I did feel several times later on that we had a better relationship when B was in prison than when he came out. Because he was inside, I knew where he was. I was outside and I could do what I wanted to do—I didn't have to consult anybody.

Both my parents were dead by the time I met B, but when I told my brother about him he thought I was crazy. I've got a cousin I'm very close to—we're like sisters. She was quite happy when I told her about B. Her husband was OK to start with as well. But after B was released, things happened that neither he nor my brother were happy about, and after that they didn't want anything to do with him.

•   •   •

When my brother and I both lived at home we were quite close, but I can't say I had a happy childhood. Though my parents both loved us in their own way, they could never express it. I don't ever remember being cuddled or told that I was loved.

My father was very Victorian, very strict, and he could be very menacing. My brother and I were frightened of him and we had to be careful what we said and how we behaved. He often kept a cane on the table in case we misbehaved and he would use it to smack us if we were naughty. He always used to say to us, 'You'll both be hopeless, you're both useless, you'll end up on the streets!' and to my brother he'd say, 'You'll end up a dustman.' He would never praise us. I remembered my father one time when I'd been visiting B. As I stood outside the prison visits room with various assorted people I thought, What on earth would my father say if he could see me now? He'd probably say, 'I didn't expect anything better of you!' I can just hear him saying it!

My father was a works manager and we had a comfortable life, always the best food and clothes. I was born in Weybridge, Surrey, and we had a lovely house with a separate tradesmen's entrance and a beautiful garden. Then the war came and my brother was born in 1940 when I was about seven years old—and somehow life changed. Soon after the war my father became very stressed at work and eventually had a nervous breakdown.

I went to a private convent school in Weybridge where I was taught by the nuns. I was very timid as a child and I was glad I was at a girls-only school. I was a very average pupil but I always felt that my father wasn't very happy with my progress. He always made me feel I was a bit thick and I could never come up to his expectations. I think my brother felt the same, though he did pass for the grammar school in Woking.

My brother was very placid and he would do anything to keep the peace. In fact I used to think he was really cowardly. But I used to stand up to my dad sometimes and that's why there were such violent rows. I used to be quite aggressive until I became a Christian—as a small child I can remember throwing a rice pudding at the wall in a temper! I think I was in my twenties when my father and I actually had a stand-up fight!

•   •   •

I was only 14 when I left school. I couldn't wait to leave because I didn't like school, and I went to train as a librarian in Boots, though I was still living at home. I stayed working there for over 12 years and eventually I did well and reached senior librarian status, with my own branch.

I had a lot of friends and boyfriends but if any got too serious I called it off. I was engaged three times but I always decided I didn't want to be tied down. Then when I was 20 I became pregnant. The baby's father was 18, which was under-age at that time. This meant he was still under parental control and he was not allowed to have any more to do with me. I didn't dare let my father know or he would have completely disowned me. My mother knew and she supported me. I went away to north Devon, supposedly to work at another branch of Boots. But in reality I stayed at a friend's home until I had the baby in a mother and baby home. The baby was adopted.

Just before I left for Devon I'd become friendly with another man. He supported me through the pregnancy and later we became engaged, and it lasted six years. But then quite suddenly he went off and married someone else. I was very upset, but work was good—I was always confident in my work.

Then I started working for the National Health Service in various hospital departments and I worked for three different GPs. I loved every minute and progressed up the ladder. I was determined to show Dad that I could make good. My brother also had a good job in insurance and did very well too.

During this time I had various affairs with one man and another, sometimes one-night stands. I always seemed to pick the wrong people until one year I went on holiday and met Peter, who was in the Metropolitan Police. He was 21, ten years younger than me, and when we got engaged my father accused me of baby-snatching. Somehow nearly all my boyfriends have been younger than me. I think—I know—that I always like to be in control.

Peter and I were married nine months later and the marriage lasted 25 years until his death. After my marriage my relationship with my father greatly improved. Marriage was comfortable though we had our ups and downs. I couldn't give love easily, because of my background. Peter would say, 'Give me a cuddle', but I hated touching people. We chose not to have any children. I'd had that one child before I was married, but by then I wasn't very maternal.

When we'd been married about 15 years we both got baptized as Christians. I was 53 and I'd always believed in God, sometimes read the Bible and always prayed when I was in trouble. But I'd never gone to church, and my life before had been far from Christian—sleeping around and drinking. We both enjoyed our Christian life and I know we both felt changed—I'm still changing. After my husband's death I continued going to church and it was a support after his death while I was grieving, and of course it was through the church that I came to go into the prison chapel and meet B.

•   •   •

When it was time for B's release in 1997 I was getting very excited. I bought a car and took driving lessons so that I could go and pick him up. I'd had a licence years earlier, but I hated driving so I'd never renewed my licence. Then I started to feel that God was saying to me—and several people had said— 'Why don't you start driving again?' So I sat my test and passed.

B had been moved to an open prison, so the day he was released he came back to Norfolk by train and I drove and picked him up at the station.

Then a lot of things happened that might not have if the social worker looking after B's boys had not insisted that they come back to us straightaway. B came out of prison and after only a week she said, 'You really ought to have the boys back.' I think it was putting too much pressure on him altogether.

The boys went to school in a nearby village and they came to church with us. They had been in the same room when their mother's boyfriend died, then their mother died in hospital from septicaemia soon after. Their social worker said it was surprising that they'd grown up so well considering the trauma they'd had. But then things started to go wrong. B suddenly said he wanted to go and live up north near his sister. So we went and found a house there and I put my bungalow here on the market and it sold very quickly. B took the boys up there and he was given a place in a hostel.

Then one day he rang me and said, 'I'm coming down!' I thought he meant he was coming to help me move, but he said, 'I'm bringing the boys with me.'

'Why bring the boys?' I asked.

'I'm coming back! I don't want to live up here!'

'But you can't come back!' I said, 'I've sold my house. The buyers are pushing me to move out and I'm going into private rented accommodation and there's no room for you and the boys!' So when he came back, he had to take the boys with him and present himself at the housing department and say he was homeless with his two sons. They immediately gave him bed and breakfast accommodation and a week later they found him a beautiful council house.

•   •   •

But very shortly after that the pressure got too much for B and he started beating me up. He became very paranoid. He accused me of having affairs with every man I knew—literally. When I wouldn't say who it was—because of course I *couldn't*, as there was no-one—he would just get worse. He would also beat his own son up as well as me, though not his step-son. After that my brother and my cousin's husband didn't want any more to do with him.

The last time B beat me up, he did it really badly in his sister's home, and his brother-in-law went mad. He told B, 'You've caused all this trouble!' and B's sister said, 'I'm not having this any more. I'm calling the police and you've got to have him charged. The best place for him is back in prison!' So she rang the police and I had to make a statement and then I had to go to hospital.

B was charged with actual bodily harm and they sent him back down to Norfolk and I stayed with his sister till she came back down with B's son. B was told he mustn't see me on any account, but he disobeyed.

By this time I was totally frightened of him. I was *petrified* of him, so I can well understand battered women. I was very, very frightened. Where I was living by then was way out in the country, very isolated, and I felt terribly vulnerable. B would come over in the middle of the night, having left the boys on their own, and he'd run upstairs to see if I'd got a man in my room. He would even go round picking imaginary hairs out of the bed. I became terrified of him.

B: I don't know why I did that. I felt suddenly totally different.

Shirley: Even B's sister said, 'This is not my brother.' He did take two lots of heroin after he came out of prison. A so-called friend gave him some for driving him somewhere. He did tell me he'd taken it.

B didn't beat me up again but he was still behaving badly. He'd come over and then he'd just walk out. He'd say, 'You'll never see me again. I don't love you any longer!' And off he'd go. By this time I'd got the cottage we're in now and the boys had gone to B's sister to live. They've been there for two years now and they're doing very well.

I never stopped loving B and if I went out I'd come home and the first thing I did was to pick up the phone to see if there was a message from him. Yet when he'd say he was coming over, I'd think, I don't want you here because I'm too frightened of you.

One day I went into town to meet him for a meal. We were coming out of the restaurant afterwards and he started accusing me of all sorts of things. And I said, 'That's it! Just get out. I'm going home on my own.'

When I got home he rang me and he said, 'I've just rung to say goodbye. I'm leaving—I'm going back to Hong Kong.'

I was absolutely distraught—that's the only word I can use. The only thing I could think of was to ring him back and tell him he'd still got some of my garden tools and I needed them back. He brought them over that night and he was really quite sweet, but I was absolutely beside myself. Next day I tried ringing B's flat but the phone had been cut off—he'd already gone, leaving his flat and everything in it. I was devastated because although I had become frightened of him, I still loved him and I was afraid I might never see him again.

• • •

Fortunately some people from my church stood by me and prayed for us. One of the ladies said, 'You know, Shirley, you've got to let B go. God's got to take him away from you because you've done all you can. God's got to work on B on His own without you around.'

So I said to God, 'If You don't want us to be together, however much it hurts, then take him away and I'll never hear from him again. If that's what You want then I'm willing to go down that road. But if You do want us to be together, please, please let me hear from him.'

And within a week of praying that prayer, B had rung me. The phone went about a quarter past seven one morning and it was B ringing from Hong Kong to say he was sorry and it was all sorted out—he was OK. He said, 'I've missed you. I'm fine now.' He had gone to stay with some Chinese Christians he'd met during the second part of his sentence.

While B was still beating me up, before he went off to Hong Kong, a lady who used to counsel me said to me, 'You know, Shirley, perhaps you and B should make a date for getting married, even if it's six months or a year ahead. It would be something for you to work at—and go to counselling.' I thought it was a strange thing for her to say at the time. B did say he'd be willing to go to counselling, and he had actually asked me to marry him, but I'd said, 'Not while you're like this!'

But during the time that B was away I asked the Lord one day, 'Should I have said I'd marry him when he asked me? Perhaps I did the wrong thing?' I sat there and the answer came back to me from God: 'Well, I didn't wait till *you* were perfect, did I?' And I thought, 'No, You didn't'.

So when B rang from Hong Kong that morning I said, 'I'll come out to Hong Kong to see you! Do you still want to marry me? Because I'd like to marry you!' He was so surprised.

I made arrangements to go over at the beginning of May 1998. In the meantime I used to phone him every Sunday at his mother's, after I came back from church.

●   ●   ●

I went out to Hong Kong for two weeks and I met B's mother. His father is dead and he's got two brothers but I didn't meet them. His mother can't speak any English but I got the impression she didn't like me very much.

B: She was all right—she just can't speak English so she can't talk.

Shirley: Hong Kong is a very vibrant place and everybody seems to live life and enjoy it to the full. But B is very passive and he's a very serious person. Even when he's with his own people he doesn't talk a lot. They're much more voluble than him. His sister's told me he's always been a loner.

In Hong Kong we got engaged—we bought our rings out there. We thought it would be nice if we could get married there as well, but I found out I'd have to be resident for 17 days.

So I flew back and B flew back two days later. I asked him, 'Would you have come back anyway if I hadn't come out?' and he said, 'Oh yes, because I was missing you.'

We got married on 11 July 1998 at our local registry office, and in the afternoon we had a service of blessing in the church. We could have got married in church but we felt that because we had already lived together, it wasn't right. In the registry office we just had my friend who's always supported me, and her partner, and B's step-son and his girlfriend. My two main memories are the bacon butties we had in a café together before the wedding because we were early—and the fact that I spilt coffee over my jacket and as soon as I got to the registry office I had to go into the ladies' and sponge it. Then B had forgotten the rings—he'd left them in his shirt pocket in the car! So I had to borrow my friend's rings!

But it was a lovely day. In the afternoon the church was full for the service of blessing and they did a lovely reception for us afterwards with a cake. Later we had a party here in our house for about 20 of our friends. The following Saturday I said, 'Oh, I could go through all that again!'

●   ●   ●

My brother's still not happy that I married B because of B's treatment of me earlier. He now runs a pub about half an hour from here, but he won't ever have B in his pub, because he says B used to be a drugs dealer and my brother has a lot of prison officers coming in who might know him. So I seldom see my brother.

B's sister wouldn't speak to me for a long time because she thought everything that happened was my fault. Nor would her husband, because he thought we'd caused such an upset in the family. But that's fine now. The boys still live with them, they've got their own friends in the area and last summer they came to stay with us for two weeks. I said to B, 'The boys know who you are, you're still their dad, but they've moved on now.'

B has a full-time job cutting and packing vegetables. He's been in that job nearly two years now. We live comfortably—I have a state pension and we don't have any problems financially. I did go back to work at the prison for a short time last year, in the visitors' centre. But once more I was stopped by the prison authorities.

We both go to the same church, and it's lovely that B is with friends there—some of the people have known him longer than I have. They say, 'Goodness me, B is growing so much, he is changing so much!' Because I'm so close to him I can't see it myself, though I know he has changed.

I do still sometimes say to B, 'You haven't taken anything, have you?' I suppose it's still there, that fear that some time he might go back to drugs. But he says, 'How can I? I'm at work all day, I'm with you all evening and I haven't got much money!' But there's always that feeling that he might go back to what he was before. There are times, even lately, when he's got up suddenly and stood over me and I can feel myself recoiling. I'll often say how I feel and he'll say, 'No, it's not going to happen again.'

B: Once I find Jesus, Jesus keep me straight, help me to stop taking drugs. I will never go back to taking drugs.

Shirley: It's very difficult for us to have a discussion proper, because of his English and his understanding. Sometimes I feel frustrated about that, and it can make me quite irritable, saying something several times. He'll look at me and grin and say, 'What did you say?' I say it again and he's switched off before I've finished. So we don't do a lot of talking. It's about patience and tolerance and being there for somebody and trying not to be judgemental.

•   •   •

Even when B was beating me up I never thought God had deserted me. But I do believe that when you're not living according to God's laws, He does withdraw His protection. When we lived together before we were married, we were not living a Christian life, that's for sure. I did try and back out of it several times, and B would agree, but then we'd both fail again. I think this happened because God was saying, 'OK, you've gone your own way. You carry on!' I feel God really took charge of it and took B away, because I was just getting in the way. What had to be done, had to be done where B had his roots.

What happened was also a teaching. I feel you can always turn things to the good. At least I can understand how it feels if in future I ever have to deal with battered women. Now we do everything together, shopping and gardening, preparing food and washing up—B is a very good cook and we have people over to eat with us. We sit together in the evening and watch television a lot. Because of the language barrier he prefers something where he can just sit and watch the pictures, like nature programmes. I'm very interested in politics and current affairs and I love programmes like *Casualty*.

But we like being together, we like doing things together. I say to B, 'Don't you find life with me boring sometimes, after such an exciting life?' But he says, 'No'. We sit together and hold hands, something I never did with my first husband. From quite early on Peter and I had separate bedrooms. I didn't like being in the same bed with him, even when I was first married to him. But with B it's so different. Yes, you could say I've got myself a toy boy—and people do tease me about it!

I do always want to protect. When I had some counselling I filled in a questionnaire and the counsellor told me I had the highest rating she'd ever seen for a mothering, parenting attitude. I said, 'Yes, I can often hear myself.' I say to B before he goes out, 'Have you got your tissues?' as I would to a child. I was always the dominant partner in my first marriage. I think because my father was so dominant I thought, Right, I'm not going to be dominated any more. I've got to be the dominant one in a relationship.

B has completely changed. He is a gentle, quiet, non-aggressive man, loving and kind. Everyone who knows him likes him. He works hard and enjoys his work. We have a wonderful marriage in spite of the difference in our ages—24 years. Age does *not* matter when you really love each other. I pray that we will have many more years together.

My relationship with B is something I've wanted all my life and never had— a real love affair.

Postscript: A few days after the interview Shirley sent me a poem she had written in 1997 when B was still in prison. Here is an extract:

> I met him in the prison
> This quiet Chinese man,
> Little did I realise
> What God had in His plan.
> I stepped across the boundary line
> That by the law was laid
> And that was when my life began
> That's when the price was paid.
> We are growing strong together
> Learning to trust and give
> Learning to love together
> As long as we both shall live.
> I thank God for new life and a future
> For B and I and our sons.
> Forever and forever be faithful
> Forever and forever be one.

Jonathan and Caroline

Jonathan, 52, does not want his real name or that of his wife revealed for the sake of his family, some of whom are unaware of his wife's background. He married Caroline, 26, at the beginning of December 1999, just over a year after her release from a six-year prison sentence for manslaughter. She had stabbed to death an elderly woman (her boyfriend's mother) while under enormous stress as the single parent of a young child.

Jonathan is a stocky man with a ready smile, bright blue eyes and shoulder-length, curly, greying hair. He comes from a comfortable background—his father was the managing director of a large car sales company—but went through a rebellious stage in his teenage years, getting involved with drugs in the seaside town where he grew up. He went to art college and at the age of 20 during his 'hippy' phase he was sent to prison for a short time for being in possession of cannabis and supplying it to a friend. He and Caroline live in a cosy maisonette in a quiet residential area with their baby daughter, born in February 2000, two months after Jonathan gave this interview. The living room is full of books and in the corner is the computer on which Jonathan does his writing. After years as a factory worker and lorry driver he has built up a new career through his interest in computers and martial arts. He has written a number of books on Taoist philosophy as well as a novel, and he runs a monthly Internet magazine. Jonathan met Caroline through his work as a martial arts instructor when she attended one of his classes a few months after leaving prison, where she had qualified as a fitness instructor. Jonathan has two adult daughters from his first marriage which ended in divorce when he was 35, and Caroline's son, who lives with his father, is now aged nine. He visits Caroline and Jonathan occasionally.

•   •   •

The first thing I noticed about Caroline was her eyes—lovely bright, shiny eyes, full of energy and wanting to learn and excitement. That was in November 1998. I'd turned up to the club as usual to teach my karate class and I saw this girl sitting outside. I just remember seeing her eyes and thinking what a nice girl she looked—a cracking girl! I had about 18 regulars in my class, varying from teenagers to people in their sixties. Caroline had seen a poster in the city information centre and she'd already been the previous week when I was away and another tutor took the class. Now she was just sitting outside waiting for somebody to turn up.

At first she was just a pupil. I thought she was a nice lass. I've always been shy. I've never had 'the chat'—I've always left that sort of thing to women. I think I gradually realised that Caroline was interested in me. It was just the way she sort of sparkled when she was talking to me. She was very attentive and her eyes were like tea saucers. She came to the class regularly twice a week and she was the only woman there. I admired her because although any woman is welcome to join in, not many women do. Caroline was very keen but she'd only done weights and aerobics before—and she was quite difficult to teach! She thought she knew the lot! What I didn't know then was that she'd been a gym instructor in the prison. When I found out I appreciated how difficult it must have been to make the transition to pupil.

But it was some time before I knew anything about her background. After a few weeks I told her she could come to the pub with me and another student—I used to go to the pub with him regularly after classes. She declined, and I found out later that she had to be back at her hostel before 'lock-up' time. She lived in temporary accommodation run by nuns for women in need.

After a while she accepted my invitation and we went out to the pub with this other guy. I tried to bring her into the conversation as much as possible but she just sat there quietly and didn't say a lot. I didn't know why at the time, but she was reticent, especially about her past—where she had been, what she had done— for reasons that became obvious later. But I could see she was interested in me. I felt comfortable with her and I could see she felt comfortable with me as well.

•   •   •

One night we were talking about food and places to eat and I mentioned a particular restaurant where I used to go to get myself a decent meal once a week. She said it sounded nice and asked me where it was. I said, 'If you like I'll meet you down there and buy you a meal and a cup of tea and we can have a chat'.

So a few days later we went out to this restaurant for lunch. It was just a matter of weeks that I'd known her, but we got on like a house on fire—just like old friends. After the meal I offered her another cup of tea but she said, 'I live just down the road. Let me make you a cup of tea there.' By this time she'd been given her own key so she let us in, not the nuns. She was still being wary—she explained it was a sort of hostel and her father, having religious connections, had managed to get her in.

I was supposed to go off and meet a couple of friends later that day but we got on so well that I never went. She was talking about living in one room, and—whether it was extra-sensory perception I don't know—I told her about me having been in prison years ago.

That did it! She told me she'd been in prison herself and I asked her why and she told me she had killed her boyfriend's mother. I just accepted it. I didn't push her for details as I didn't want to make her feel uncomfortable. It didn't seem to fit with Caroline as I knew her, but I accepted it because these things happen. Not all of us have supreme self-control. She explained that she did it because she was under such pressure. I didn't want to upset her by pushing so I just gave her a cuddle. I didn't get home till one o'clock in the morning. We just really hit it off in every way. I think we needed each other.

I suppose it was a bit of a whirlwind romance. It was a very short period of time between her starting training in November and us going out for that lunch and ending up spending the rest of the day together. That was on 5 December 1998.

I just liked everything about her. She has this meek little look about her, but she's honest, she's bright and intelligent, and motivated—that's the word. To tell the truth I wasn't concerned about her past—not at all concerned. I felt totally comfortable and at ease with her. I was more concerned about her future.

After that, everything came out over a short period of time and I tried to be supportive. I totally understood everything that had happened to her and why she'd felt the way she felt. I understood why she was trying so hard at everything—as well as my classes she was doing an Open University degree which she'd started in prison. I understood why she was obviously trying to find her identity and a new life.

•   •   •

I'd had quite a few relationships since I broke up with my ex-wife. She obviously put me on edge and on guard. Some were easy, some tough. It's quite strange but not at any time did I feel threatened by Caroline. Obviously I was unsure about how the relationship would go—if we got into a deeper relationship. I was a bit wary and 'on my toes'. I enjoyed Caroline's company and her friendship but in my own thoughts privately I was very wary and very cautious because I didn't want to get involved and then let her down. I remember thinking, I've got to be very, very careful about this one. I've got to make it clear that we're friends—even if we become sexual friends.

My concerns for myself were whether I would get hurt again. So I expressed any fears I had and we had some good open talks. I was open about feeling insecure and uncertain about rushing into relationships. But Caroline put me at my ease, and we've just got closer and closer. We are perfectly suited to each other. We just get on so well. We've got similar tastes in everything. Our age difference never worried me. For some strange reason most of my girlfriends have been younger than me. My ex-wife was about eleven years younger. I like to feel that I'm younger than my years in my attitude in life.

We decided to get married for a mixture of reasons. Caroline and I were getting on great together. She was spending quite a bit of time at my place, but she was still very insecure—very, very insecure. The thing about marriage came up because we were getting on so well. I'd had no intentions of ever getting married again, not unless I met somebody who was really right for me. To be honest, I couldn't fault Caroline. We think the same, we've got the same sense of humour, we like the same things, we do the same things. In every respect we are compatible. When the possibility of marriage and children came up, it wasn't too difficult a decision to make.

We got married on 1 December 1999, which was near enough the anniversary of the day we first went out. The wedding was in a registry office and I was grinning from ear to ear the whole time because the registrar was so pompously insincere, starting off, 'We are gathered here on a *very* solemn occasion.' I think Caroline was petrified! She was wearing a long purple dress—a maternity dress because by then she was already pregnant. After the wedding we went to the nearest pub and the reception was a few sarnies! We didn't go on a honeymoon—we both came down with flu that night. The Monday after the wedding Caroline lost her wedding ring—she's still looking for it!

A while later I told my friend—the one I used to go drinking with—about Caroline's background, just in case it slipped out, and so he could be more diplomatic about asking her about her past in company. He just shrugged his shoulders. He's fairly cool with things.

I didn't tell my mother. My father died years ago when I was in my twenties, but my mother is still alive. She came to the wedding and she gets on famously with Caroline. She's happy with her, thinks that she's a lovely girl with a lovely face. There's no way I'd tell her that Caroline was in prison. If I did, it would finish her off. She's 89 and she's had breast cancer and she's also got heart trouble. Hopefully she's not going to find out, which is one reason why I wanted my name changed for this interview.

I told my older daughter about Caroline's past. She can be a bit of a gossip, but I told her not to tell anybody. When I told her Caroline had stabbed her (sort of) mother-in-law, at first she gasped, then she kind of laughed nervously and made a bit of a joke. She said, 'Nice one!' because she's got a very awkward mother-in-law who's always sticking her nose into everything.

Now she and Caroline get on famously. And my younger daughter now knows and they get on famously as well. I think my younger daughter was quietly shocked. It came out when she was sitting here with me and Caroline. I also mentioned a bit about my own past—she didn't know I'd been busted for dope, because I tried to keep that quiet from my girls whilst they were younger in case they thought it was a licence to go out and do drugs themselves.

They've both been instructed not to tell either my sister or my mother what happened to Caroline. My sister can be a trouble-maker. She came to the wedding as well but I tell people on a 'need to know basis'.

•   •   •

I think it's been very helpful to Caroline that I had some experience of prison myself, though it was years ago and I feel I went there because my beliefs were different from those often pompous and arrogant people who represent the law. But my experience meant I knew how Caroline felt. I told her that when I was released from prison I was picked up by a friend in a van and taken to a pub for a few drinks. Afterwards when I stepped out into the town centre I just flattened myself up against the pub window, because people seemed to be running around like headless chickens. I felt totally insecure at that moment in the midst of the general public. The place struck me as like a madhouse, total mayhem and madness. People walking around the town looked so mental—

they really did. I suddenly realised that inside prison I'd been cosseted and protected from everyday life. Over a period of time I think that has helped Caroline because I could relate to how she felt—though obviously I couldn't relate to the amount of time she'd spent away from society.

When Caroline was first out of prison she needed to be assertive and get on her own feet. There's been times when she was assertive with me—not many, but two or three—to the point when she would shout at me and say, 'Listen to me! Listen to me! Hear what I've got to say!' and I'd say, 'Go on then, carry on.' And then she'd say her piece and if it was valid I'd say 'Yes, OK.' Or if it wasn't valid I'd say, 'Right, now shut up and listen to me!'

Eventually I think a little bit of my calmness rubbed off on her. We got to talk about things and we've had no serious upsets. Essentially I could see when she was going through a tricky phase and I'd either give her some space, or give her a cuddle, or sit down and have a heart-to-heart, whatever was needed. In the context of prison I think personal space is something you get far too much of, though in there you are not in a position to utilise it. Whereas when you come out you have that personal space but it's hindered by fear and doubt—you always have a doubt that you're not going to make it in society. Or you fear that you're going to have to do something wrong to go back into prison. You can't handle society, because you've been kept away from it. It's a pretty useless system really which keeps people away from society rather than teaching them how to become part of it.

I think I discovered that Caroline needed somebody whose shoulder she could lean on and trust. I think I just allowed her to bounce ideas off me — whatever her feelings. When she said she was going to give up her studies at the Open University I said, 'Are you really sure that you want to do this? Why do you want to do it?' We discussed it and I said, 'Well, you'd better take your time and think about it.' But she'd already got her mind set on it. She'd made her mind up and once she's made her mind up to do something, that's it. I felt she was actually moving away from study and work and perhaps clinging on to relationships for security. There were a couple of times when she told me fibs for the sake of her own steadiness or security. She admitted it later. And I said, 'Well, you know, I thought as much'.

And then there came a time when she stopped taking the Pill without telling me at first. Obviously I was a bit shocked and I didn't know whether I was ready or even thinking about having kids and all that sort of stuff again at my time of life. But I thought, 'What the hell—I'm happy with Caroline and whatever makes her happy makes me happy'.

•   •   •

There may not have been serious problems, but there were lots of 'down' moments, when Caroline started to show her depressions in front of me. There was one day when she suddenly changed from apparently being happy. She started joking about there being a little teddy bear on the floor with all the stuffing ripped out. At first I thought she was joking and I lifted up this bit of tissue—and there was a teddy bear with its stomach ripped open and its stuffing ripped out. She was giggling maniacally, nervously, about it. I really couldn't get to the bottom of why she did it. But it was another form of her depression and fear coming out. I think that was a breaking or turning point because after that we gradually spent more and more time together, and then she started to become a bit more settled. She began to give up the idea of university and thought of going in for fitness training more seriously. I've always expected bounces and rebounds and you do get that. You bounce from one side to the other and eventually the bounces get smaller.

I'll admit I've had to make big sacrifices in allowing Caroline into my space, into my life, sharing my belongings and time and everything else. I mean, I gave up my personal space for her to share. I was living on my own in this house we now share. This is a lovely area of the city and after moving here I felt happy and comfortable for the first time in my life. It's taken me years after my divorce to get these meagre sticks of furniture together. So I had to think hard about the prospect of sharing it with somebody. The thought is always in the back of your mind that you can lose it, or half of it.

But overall I haven't been worried about this. I really don't feel threatened by Caroline, and I think she deserves my love, because she is a kind and loving and very special person.

• • •

I've mentioned the low points—but oh, there are lots and lots of lovely moments! For a start, Caroline and I can talk about virtually any subject. It's like having a friend and an adviser, somebody that you can talk to. I've probably conversed about more subjects with Caroline than I have with anybody else in my life.

Essentially I've always been a thinker. I've always studied social endeavours, attitudes and moral philosophy. I've made it my life study. So I think I understand most situations, whatever they are. I've rubbed shoulders with everybody—the good, the bad and the indifferent—and got on with all equally, because I accept people as they are.

I used to be quite removed from people. I used to be quite self-contained and I didn't think most conversations were necessary, apart from those hippy days when we used to sit around stoned and chatting on forever about philosophy and had principles about everything. But with Caroline I can just sit and have a chat about everything and everyone. It's good—we empathise. Our relationship is perfect, absolutely perfect.

Postscript: When I called Jonathan and Caroline for an update their daughter was three months old. Caroline says she is a good baby and she finds her easy to cope with. Caroline has set up a very successful personal fitness business using the Internet. She and Jonathan now see her son more regularly and he is becoming close to his new half-sister.

Jenny Peacock and Nick Tucker

Jenny, 49, is a customer services adviser for a large electrical company. She is divorced with a married daughter and small granddaughter. She met Nick, 50, in September 1996. Next day he invited her out, and at this second meeting he told her he was on bail for murdering his wife.

The case of Squadron Leader Nicholas Tucker had hit the headlines six months before he and Jenny met, though Jenny was not aware of it. In July 1995, Nick and his wife Carol were involved in a car accident in which Carol died. Police became suspicious because of irregularities at the post mortem, and Nick was charged with her murder.

Jenny believed Nick's claim that he was innocent. During the 14-month wait for the trial they became close, he asked her to marry him and she accepted. Nick's lawyers were convinced he would be acquitted but the jury convicted and in 1997 he was given a life sentence with a 12-year tariff. Jenny continues to believe in him and to campaign for his release. His first appeal was dismissed and his case is now with the Criminal Cases Review Commission.[1] The couple became engaged on Valentine's Day 1998 and plan to marry on Nick's release.

Jenny lives in a neat house in a quiet close. A pleasant, warm person, she has fair curly hair and blue eyes. It was her day off work, and she told me she was more casually dressed than usual, in an olive green top and black trousers. On her left hand was the diamond ring that Nick put on her finger in the prison visiting room. Jenny showed me a silver-plated photograph album charting the couple's 14-month relationship before Nick was sent to prison. On the front is a picture of them at her brother's wedding, both looking so smart and happy that at first it appears that the wedding was their own. Inside is an equally poignant mix of pictures. Several show the couple at Nick's parents' home in Wales, with its beautiful garden overlooking the sea. The most recent shows them with Jenny's daughter and granddaughter, taken in the visiting room at HMP Gartree.[2]

Jenny's home is immaculate and she takes a delight in decorating it in the latest colours There are lovely flower arrangements everywhere and on the walls are paintings done by Nick in prison. I interviewed her in her cosy kitchen. She is clearly a hospitable, friendly and popular woman. The youngest of seven children, she still lives in the area where she was brought up, and is used to family and neighbours constantly dropping by and phoning. Yet Jenny has a low, quiet voice and the rather self-deprecating manner of someone who has never rated her own qualities very highly. Her marriage at the age of 20 to her first steady boyfriend, who had affairs and could be violent, further lowered her self-esteem. She smoked throughout the interview and admitted being nervous. Shy by nature, she says that until she became involved in Nick's case she could never have imagined having the courage to give media interviews.

The first time I saw Nick I noticed that he'd got this nice smile and blue eyes. I was out with a friend at a local pub and I don't know why I noticed him, but then I thought no more about it.

My friend and I went on to another place where there was dancing. I went up to the bar to get a drink—and there he was again! I said, 'Didn't I see you at the other pub?' and he said, 'Yes, I was there,' and he said he'd noticed me too. He was with some RAF chaps and they were all going on to a party, but just then he was on his own. And I don't know what it was, but I was attracted to him and we started chatting. I said, 'What's your name?' and he said, 'Nick' and I said, 'Are you married?' and he said he was a widower. I asked him where he worked and he said the RAF, and then I backed off a bit.

•   •   •

I'd had enough of the RAF because my ex-husband was in the RAF. We'd met in our late teens, I married him at 20, had a daughter and moved to Germany when he was posted there. He drank and then he would become violent and I was scared of him. He'd come back home and be moody and if I said the wrong thing he'd have a go at me, and one time he put scissors to my throat. One Sunday he was out and I went round to friends, and when I came in and went to my wardrobe it was completely bare. He said he'd got rid of all my clothes. He hadn't—he'd put them all in suitcases and hidden them! Then when we moved back to England he started having affairs and I just couldn't hack it any more.

So when I was 27 we divorced and I brought my daughter up on my own. We had no money so I went to work at the local bacon factory. I was in my mid-thirties before I had another long-term relationship. I was with that man for ten years, but I think he just wanted a housekeeper. He used to go off and do his fishing and golf every weekend and in the end the relationship just died and in 1995 I left him—we parted quite amicably. By the time I met Nick I'd been on my own for about 15 months.

•   •   •

To start with Nick and I had a conversation about the RAF, then my friend came over and I introduced him to her. We went on chatting and before he left I gave him my phone number.

He rang up next day and invited me out for the evening. We went to a village pub and almost immediately he said, 'I've got something to tell you, and when I've told you, you probably won't want to see me again, and I'll understand'. He told me that he and his wife were in a car accident and she had died, and I felt really sorry for him.

But then he said, 'The police think that I killed her.'

I was like—oh—the shock!

Then he started to go through it all. He told me they'd been out to dinner, he was driving the car, then a deer came out on the road and the car went in the river. He said all he could remember was water coming up at the windscreen and then being in the water and shouting to Carol. He went over with me what had happened that night, how he got taken to the hospital and they wanted to keep him in, but he said, 'No, I've got to get back to my children and tell them!' His daughter was 17 and his son was 15. He had the padré with him at the time.

Then he went on to tell me what the police had said—that he had killed Carol because of his affair with a Serbian girl when he was out in Bosnia. But he said, 'It was nothing! It was stupid and I regret it, but I loved my wife, I'd never do that to her. I can't believe they think I killed her! My only guilt was coming out of that restaurant and saying I would drive as she'd had two glasses of wine and I'd only had one non-alcoholic beer. If I'd let her drive, maybe this wouldn't have happened. She could have been driving at a different speed, the deer might not have come out on the road. That is the only guilt I feel.'

• • •

The accident happened on 21 July 1995 and I met Nick on 21 September 1996, 14 months later. In March 1996 he had been arrested, charged with murder and bailed. At the hearing the judge had said, 'Show me the evidence—I can't see the evidence here!' He couldn't understand that this was a case that was going to go through, and he gave him bail. But the police just kept going on and on. At first they had treated Carol's death as a normal road traffic accident. It was only after the post mortem that they found some little haemorrhages in her eyes, which were unusual in a case of drowning. That's what sparked them off. Then they were suspicious because in the September after the accident Nick fell to pieces and had a mental breakdown and had to be admitted to hospital. He'd only been out of hospital eight days when they took him in for questioning and they questioned him for eight hours solid, which they shouldn't have done, because he was still in a bad way.

He told the police about this girl he'd got involved with in Bosnia, this Serbian interpreter. That has been half his trouble—he's so open, totally open. He just tells it like it is. People don't understand the situation in Bosnia and places like that. You could be dead the next day and this fling with the girl was something that just happened. He brought her to England for a week's stay. He had booked a place to stay with Carol in London, then she said she wouldn't come, and I think he was a bit peeved, thinking, I'm only over for a week—why can't she come? So in passing he said to this girl that he'd got this week booked, and she said, 'Oh, I'd like a week in London!' and it went on from there. Apparently she had flings with lots of men and was living with a guy in Bosnia.

I believed what Nick was saying. After all, there was no need for him to tell me anything at all, but he sat there for two hours telling me everything. At the end of the night he said, 'Look, now you know all this, obviously you may not want to see me any more. I leave it in your hands if you want to give me a ring.'

• • •

After that first date with Nick I told my family everything. I spoke to two of my sisters and they had varying views. One said, 'Everybody's innocent till proved guilty.' The other said, 'Don't have anything to do with it.' I spoke to my daughter and she said, 'Mum, I know you're a good judge of character. If you believe him then I'll believe him.' I said, 'I want you to meet him and then you'll know how I feel.'

I left it a few days and thought about it. Then I decided I wanted to carry on seeing Nick. I thought, We get on well and I think we could get through this. And all the while Nick's lawyers were convinced that the case would never get to court. They kept telling him it would get stopped half way.

Nick was still in his RAF house a couple of miles from where I lived. He couldn't go far because he had to report to the police every day as part of his bail conditions. He used to come over to my place a few times a week and we'd go out for drinks. Or I would go over to his place for weekends. I'd cook him a meal or he'd cook for me—he's a very good cook, very domesticated.

A few weekends we went to stay with his mum and dad in Wales and I got on very well with them. They were devastated by all this. His brother is very supportive and we'd go and visit him and his family as well.

I'd say Nick comes from a middle-class home. He did very well at school and he was very young when he started in the RAF. He had risen to the rank of Squadron Leader and he was actually going to be made Wing Commander when all this happened. People have said he was a 'desk man' but he wasn't totally. He was out in Bosnia and he was in the Gulf. But he's quiet and he always says to me that he's boring. In fact he knows how to enjoy himself, but he's just a very nice guy. He collects medals and he's a member of the Orders and Medals Research Society. He likes looking back over history, and he writes books on the subject. He'd just had a book published when I met him.

I just felt so easy with Nick, and he said he felt easy with me. We could talk to each other about anything—there was nothing we couldn't say. I've never been treated so well by anybody. He'd been married 20 years and he had a very good relationship with his wife—he always used to say she was the rock of the family. Because she'd served in the RAF herself, she understood about RAF life. Apparently she was more bubbly than me, more outgoing.

•　　•　　•

In December 1996, a couple of months after Nick and I met, we went to Cambridge for the day and we were walking around the city, holding hands and talking. And he said he loved me.

I thought, I love you too. But I think I held back a little bit, partly because of my previous experiences, and partly because of the situation we were in. There was always this cloud hanging over our heads all the time and we were wondering what was going to happen. I kept thinking, Why do I meet the man of my dreams when there's all this happening?'

Quite quickly our relationship had turned from being just friendship to being physical. I felt we had this chemistry—you don't realise it can happen until it happens to you. We liked hugging, holding hands. We would sit and watch television holding hands and we became very close.

Nick met all my family—I'm the youngest of seven children so there's a lot of us, though my mother died of multiple sclerosis when I was 18, and my father only lived a few years after her. Nick and I went to my brother's wedding, then Nick met more of my family at Christmas time, and my sister had a big birthday party in a hotel on the coast. All my family soon knew so much about the case, and they all think Nick is innocent. Right up until the trial Carol's brother was fine with Nick as well, but then he changed.

On my birthday in June 1997 Nick asked me to marry him. I think that was my best moment, though I was quite surprised he did it. He said, 'Obviously with all this going on I'll understand if you don't want to give me an answer—if you'd rather leave it till after the trial.'

But I immediately said yes. On many occasions he'd say to me, 'You can walk away—I'll understand.' But I felt he was so genuine and such a nice person that I couldn't face the thought of that. We didn't get engaged then, because Nick said we ought to wait. But in our minds we'd started making plans, we'd even started looking for houses. So it was half exciting, because the lawyers kept saying there'd be no problem, and half having this cloud hanging over us.

The worst thing that happened was that a month before the trial Nick's barrister was taken off his case, because he was on another case at the Old Bailey and it carried on. Nick had had a whole year with this barrister working through everything. We even went to the judge to see if Nick's case could be deferred but this wasn't allowed.

•　　•　　•

The trial began in November 1997 in Norwich. The lawyers told me not to attend, so every day I was trying to go to work, but I was constantly worried and my brain was just not focusing. In court the police used Nick's mental breakdown to say he was like that because he was guilty of murder. His daughter was a prosecution witness—I think the police got to her and I suppose she wanted to do something to get back at him because of his affair. Nick's son wanted to go to court because he was 100 per cent behind his dad. He says he knows his dad wouldn't have done anything like that. He says, 'People forget this is my mother we're talking about.' But Nick's barrister wouldn't let him go and give evidence. He said it would look as if we were playing Nick's son off against his daughter. Now we really wish James had gone to court.

Nick's original barrister didn't want me known about, but the new barrister decided it might look good. So when Nick was in the dock the second week of the trial, his own barrister said to him, 'We believe you've started a new relationship?' and Nick said he had. In my opinion, that made it look worse—people might say, 'Oh, he goes from one to another'.

They didn't name me in court, but by dinner time that day the *Daily Mail* had come round to my place of work and knocked on the door. Obviously the people there didn't know who this reporter was, but he asked for me and I went out of the door and he said, 'I understand you're Nick Tucker's fiancée.' I said, 'Where have you got that from?' and he said, 'I'm from the *Daily Mail*—would you give me a quote?' I said, 'No, I don't want to talk,' and he said, 'I've got a photographer in the car—if you could just give me a picture?' I said no and started to go inside.

But they must have snapped me because next day there I was in the papers. I went into work and I told my boss what had happened and he said, 'Look, they're obviously going to hang about and wait for you, so stay here for a little while, then when it gets dark I'll drive you to your daughter's house.'

That evening I spoke to Nick on the phone. Every day after court he used to go to his house and his parents, his brother and sister-in-law were there with him. Nick said, 'They've found you so you might as well be over here with all of us.' My boss was brilliant—he told me to take off whatever time I needed. So I stayed at Nick's every day while he went to court, and in the evening he would come back and they'd go through everything that had been said. I'd have the dinner ready for them, then we'd watch it on the television. It was horrible.

That weekend my friend phoned me up. She only lived round the corner and she told me to look outside and see if there was anyone around. I looked and there was nobody so she came round to get me and we went to her mother's in Clacton for the weekend just to get away from it all. But next day in the papers there was a picture of me coming out of the flat. All this was horrendous—it was a nightmare.

Then we got to D-Day—Friday the fifth of December. The day before, the jury had gone out and hadn't made their decision. Nick came home that night and we had that worry. Nick said, 'No, they just can't convict me on this—there's no way!'

Next day I was with my daughter when the guilty verdict came over on the radio at midday. It was a majority jury verdict—ten to two. I just couldn't believe it! I went hysterical. My sister came flying round because she had heard it, and she went to my doctor to get me some tablets to calm me down. I said, 'I've got to get back to be with Nick's dad!' His mum had gone to court every day but his dad couldn't face it. He said, 'I can't go there and watch.' That day I had left him to go to my daughter's and I had to get taken back to Nick's place. I couldn't drive because I was in such a state. People were phoning and the media were knocking on the door. The media had set up camp, they had television cameras everywhere. We were just inundated with phones ringing.

That day there was obviously no way for me to talk to Nick until late afternoon. His mother, his brother and sister-in-law had been in court and they went down to see him in the cells. Then he was allowed to phone me. He just said, 'Forget about me, just forget about me, get on with your life.' I said, 'No way, I'm not leaving you.'

Then his mum and his brother and sister-in-law came back and we were all stunned. We just couldn't believe it. Nobody wanted to speak to the media at that time because they had slagged Nick off so much in the papers. So we just thought, What's the point of speaking to them? They're only going to make it worse. That Friday was horrendous—to me that was the worse day of my life.

•   •   •

Next day I went with Nick's father and brother to see him in Norwich jail, and that was horrific. I had never been in a prison before and it was awful. We've all seen prisons on the television, but to actually go in there and see those big walls, the officers and the guard dogs, and to get searched! I felt like I was in a dream—this wasn't happening to me. When we finally got in to see Nick he was just crying constantly. He couldn't speak, he just couldn't stop crying and saying sorry to everybody. I kept saying, 'You don't have to be sorry, it's not your fault. This is the justice system that's done this.' His brother and father left us alone for about ten minutes and we just cried together.

I booked to see him the following week, and then I got into the routine of visiting him once a week. He was in Norwich from the December till the following August, and the first month he was in the prison hospital because they thought he was a suicide risk—but he wasn't. Another reason they kept him in the hospital so long was because they were worried about the other prisoners, because they used to shout out things to him. I think it was the way he'd been treated in the newspapers—that's what did it.

Because of the way Nick is, and what he's been through, it didn't actually take him long to get over that first devastation. He used to come out with things like, 'All right, they've put me in prison, what else can they do to me? They can't shoot me! In the RAF I could have been shot no end of times.' He got onto an Enhanced regime[3] very quickly because he kept his nose clean and did whatever he was told.

•   •   •

On Valentine's Day 1998, we got engaged. I went into Norwich one day and chose my ring, a diamond cluster, and I got Nick a three-coloured gold ring. That day I came into the prison wearing his ring on my finger, and in the visits room I gave him my ring to put on my finger. Then I put his on for him—and it was too big! I had to keep going back to the jeweller's to get it changed and they kept saying things like, 'Why can't he come in himself?' I said he was working away. He's been wearing the ring ever since.

In August 1998 he was moved to HMP Gartree, which is better than Norwich prison. The majority of the officers are very good and I have quite a good rapport with them now. At first when I went to Norwich I never spoke to any of the other visitors. I've tended to keep myself to myself. But this last year I've started to speak to people more. It takes me about an hour and a half to drive to Gartree and I go on weekdays or weekends, whichever fits in with my work.

Nick works in the prison Braille unit. He picked it up easily and he's translated things into Braille in Spanish and Russian. He's taken up art and he's done a lot of watercolours.

We used to write a lot but now he phones every night. I have said I would marry him in prison, but he doesn't want us to do that because he doesn't think it's fair on me. He thinks it's a bit tacky, and he thinks he will be out in the next year or two. It was his birthday in January and I managed to get him a cake made, but that was all. I do take clothes in for him but they've really cut back and you can't take much in now.

• • •

In November 1998 Nick had an appeal, but he lost it. He's been with the Criminal Cases Review Commission since January 1999 but they haven't yet assigned a case worker to him. In late 2000 the Channel 4 *Trial and Error* programme about Nick's case was shown, and after that Nick cheered up a lot, though he's had his ups and downs over the years. The officers obviously know his case and they've seen things on the television and they've got a different approach to him now. They even ask him how it's going, and I think they actually respect him. I've had neighbours coming and knocking on the door and saying, 'Saw the programme, it was good.' I haven't had any adverse reaction from anybody, though there are probably some people out there who think I'm stupid.

Over the years we've realised we've got to use the media, though I'm the kind of person who's shied away from things like that. I've always felt I was quite shy—I don't even like having my photo taken. But I've got to do all this for Nick. I've done radio, though I still get nervous at interviews, and I've done a lot with the local newspaper. Before Nick lost his appeal I was asked to go on *The Richard and Judy Show* and the thought of that was scary. In the event they cancelled the invitation, but I would have done it if it was going to help Nick. A few years ago I could never have imagined that I would be doing all this, talking to the media. I just couldn't have thought about it.

But through all this I think I have grown. And I've never had a moment of regret, because I know that that man in prison is the one I want to spend the rest of my life with.

Postcript: In Autumn 2001 Jenny rang to say that a CCRC case worker had finally been assigned to Nick's case, three years after his first appeal—but, she added, the waiting seemed endless.

ENDNOTES

[1] See Endnote 1, p. 82.

[2] Some prisons arrange for officers to photograph prisoners with their families.

[3] The highest of the three regimes under which prisoners are held. It allows privileges such as extra visits and spending money as rewards for good behaviour. The other two levels are Basic and Standard.

Alison and Richard

Alison, 47, was a divorcée with two adult children, who has for many years been a valued employee of one of the major UK banks. Six years ago she married Richard, 41, who was serving eight years in a Scottish prison for attempted murder. He was one of Alison's 21 prisoner penfriends. They have a small daughter.

Alison and Richard live in a council house on an estate in the Hampshire town where Alison was brought up, the eldest of the three daughters of a storeman and a cleaning lady. The house has been decorated to a high standard by Richard, who has been working on it since his release from prison three years ago. Alison and Richard married while he was on his final home leave in February 1996. He was released later that year, just in time to be present at Sarah's birth. Alison is a small, chatty woman whose bubbly manner and neat appearance seem at odds with a life filled with emotional traumas. In her early twenties she was abandoned by the father of her first child and had an abortion. She set out to get pregnant again immediately, her relationship broke down and she brought up her daughter Marie alone. Now 24, Marie has just graduated from university with a law degree, and a framed graduation photograph proudly displayed on the mantelpiece shows her in her academic gown.

When Marie was six Alison married a serviceman penfriend she had met through *Soldier* magazine, though she had grave doubts after discovering just before the wedding that he was a compulsive liar who had not told her he was married before and had two children. Alison immediately became pregnant but her husband abandoned her for another woman straight after the wedding. Alison and their son Jon, now 18, have had very little contact with him. Alison has always been very involved in the church, and became interested in writing to prisoners when she visited the local prison with her church drama group.

• • •

I first went into the local prison with James and David, two young men from our church drama group. We used to put on plays with a religious message and we were going to discuss doing one for the inmates. I'll admit I only wanted to go into a prison out of sheer interest—nosiness I suppose. We went on a Sunday and the minute I walked in, I felt a sort of extra peace. It was like walking in and feeling I'd come home. We were taken across to the chapel and I was immediately overwhelmed by the love in that place. I remember thinking how different it was from an outside church. In prison there are no trappings, no 'busy-ness' going on—nothing else but what people are there for. I was amazed by it. We went to the service and then sat and chatted with the prisoners. They wanted to talk about what was affecting them in everyday prison life, but what really surprised me was how much they cared about what was happening to us outside as well. I came away feeling stunned. I knew I'd have to go back there. I knew it couldn't just be this once.

I couldn't wait to see James and David to plan our next visit, and when I saw them I said, 'Wow, wasn't that great!' But they said, 'No! We never want to go there again!' They were these two huge six-foot guys and it turned out they were intimidated by speaking to the prisoners! But that confirmed that my wanting to go back to the prison wasn't something that everybody has, and now I look back I believe it was God's way of getting me inside to do the work I did afterwards with prisoners. So I started going to the prison Sunday service a couple of times a month.

Before I went into a prison I had the attitude, 'Lock them all up and throw away the key'. I was just ignorant. You think people are all in there because they've done something really awful—that they are totally bad people. And of course they're not. When you meet them you just know them for what they are on that day. You get to know the good side of them. Sometimes I would know what crime they had committed, but when you're with them inside prison, you feel that the crimes are separate, because they were done outside.

· · ·

A woman from the church gave me a list of chaplains she had built up a good relationship with, and I wrote asking if they knew of prisoners needing someone to correspond with. Over the next year or so I wrote to prisoners all over the country and I'd go and visit some of them in prisons as far away as Manchester. Usually we gave our church curate's address, but there were three prisoners I trusted enough to give them my home address. And there was one prisoner at the local prison that I used to meet if I was shopping in town. Some of them were allowed out to work in the community and I'd go and meet him and we'd have fish and chips.

It was quite an exciting time. Every time I got a first letter from someone I'd take it to the other women from the church. We'd started writing to American prisoners and I got one letter from there that they felt was very strange and I decided to stop writing to him. But I never had any dodgy letters from prisoners in this country. I always used to give a description of myself to the chaplains, saying I was a Christian and I had children.

· · ·

The day I got that dodgy American letter, I also got my first letter from Richard, who was a prisoner in Glenochil prison in Alloa, near Glasgow—the only Scottish prison I'd approached. By this time I must have been involved with prisons for about two years and I was writing regularly to 21 prisoners. But right from the beginning I knew there was something different about Richard's letter. It was only an introductory letter but he said how nice it was that somebody was interested in prisoners—it gave them a bit of hope.

In fact it was amazing that Richard ever wrote to me at all, though he didn't tell me that until quite a while later. He had had the kind of religious experience that I think quite a lot of prisoners have. One night soon after he was convicted he felt he really repented of his crimes, he got down on his knees and his cell was filled with light. So he became a Christian and he used to talk to the chaplain. One day the chaplain went up to his cell and they sat chatting. As the chaplain got up to go he dropped a letter—my letter—and when Richard picked it up for him the chaplain said, 'Oh, that's what I came up here to talk to you about. Would you be interested in writing to this woman?' But Richard said he wouldn't, so the chaplain took my letter away. Then the following Friday after one of the chapel meetings, the chaplain went up to Richard again and said, 'Wouldn't you reconsider?' I don't know why he did that. There were 400 men in that prison and he could have gone up to anybody. So Richard said, 'If you really think she'd be interested in a prisoner up here in Scotland—then OK', and he wrote to me. That was in September 1994.

After that first letter it was a while before there was a second one, because Richard's mother was very ill and in fact she died in the November. They let him out for the funeral handcuffed to an officer and he was allowed to go and put a rose on the coffin. I got a Christmas card saying he was sorry he hadn't been in touch, he'd had family problems. But he asked me to keep in touch and after Christmas we started writing regularly. Richard's a brilliant letter-writer— it's like reading a book.

•　　•　　•

In the letters Richard told me it was the second time he'd been in prison. Both offences were heat of the moment things—he'd got involved in fights. The first sentence was four years—he was in a fight in a house. The second one, about two years later, was more serious and he got eight years for attempted murder. Again it was a similar thing. Somebody owed him money and he said they started a fight just to get out of paying him. By the time I started writing to him he was nearing the end of his sentence. He was released a year after we started writing.

After we'd been writing for a few months I had a strange letter from Richard, saying, 'I don't think I should write any more because I'm feeling more than friendship for you.' I think that was probably a ploy, and afterwards he admitted that sometimes prisoners would do that, just to test how much the other person cared. He also wrote that he thought I was moving in higher circles now and I was too good for him. This was because by this time I'd got involved with the Prison Fellowship, which is a Christian ministry that supports prisoners and their families, and I'd been invited to represent the organization at a charity function at the House of Lords. You do forget perhaps that prisoners sometimes over-rate a lot of things that happen outside. It was just a tea for people involved in charity work.

So I wrote back and said, 'OK, if you think going to the House of Lords is such a big deal then I won't go.'

That was the last letter I wrote for a while, because after sending it off I had to go into hospital for two weeks for an operation—I'd told Richard I was due to go in.

I had the operation and in the middle of the night I was coming round from the anaesthetic and feeling very sick when a nurse came in and said, 'A Richard James phoned. He said he'd ring you as soon as possible'. My first thought was, How does he know which hospital I'm in? My address is in Hampshire but I was in a hospital in Surrey.

Later he told me that he was so gutted when he got my letter, and was so worried about me going into hospital, that he couldn't go to his usual prison job, and he begged the wing officer to let him use his phone for an urgent call. He then spent ages on the phone trying to find out which hospital I was in. Finally he tracked it down by ringing our local police station.

•   •   •

My relationship with Richard really started from this time. After the operation I stayed with my mum for a couple of days and I rang Richard's dad to let him know I was OK. Then Richard rang me at my mum's and I heard his voice for the first time—I heard his Scottish accent. We talked about everything, non-stop. Because he was ringing from Scotland he kept using up his prison phonecards.

The next day I went to stay with my sister in South Africa for four weeks. Before going into hospital I'd got very run down and lost a lot of weight and I needed a rest. So I asked my mum to have the children stay with her—Jon was 13 and Marie was 19 by this time. While I was out there I was still writing to a lot of prisoners. I'd given them all airmail letters so they could write to me. I've always said that I got far more from the prisoners who wrote to me than they got from me, though they'd deny it. But I felt loved and supported by them. Every day I'd walk half a mile from my sister's house to the postbox and collect their letters. Richard's was the very last to come. I was there four weeks and it didn't arrive till the day I left. He'd pulled a muscle in his shoulder, and there was also a delay in the post.

While I was out in South Africa I felt I had to decide one way or the other about Richard, though I'd never even seen a photo of him at this point. But coming back on the plane I knew—I'd decided about Richard even before I knew what he looked like. Then he sent a photo and it was if I recognized him—he looked familiar, and I felt as if I knew him already. It was a black and white photo and he had short hair and a beard and moustache, and though I've always disliked those, I felt he wouldn't look right without them. Soon after I got back I went to visit Richard in Glenochil. This was July 1995 and I stayed with his dad, who came with me on the visit.

It was very strange to meet Richard for the first time. I'd seen the photo of course, but because like the other prisoners he'd supported me a lot in letters, he'd come across as this confident person, and I'd imagined this big sort of hunky guy. He was tall—about five foot ten—and yes, he looked like his photo, but there was none of the confidence I'd expected after reading the letters. He was like a shy little boy. It was as if once we were together, I felt I was the stronger one. And this was a shock, because I'd expected to meet someone I could lean on. I'd expected this big strong person to lift me off my feet. Now I realise that it was he who was doing the leaning.

That first meeting was OK—we talked all right. But Richard was nervous. He talked to his dad more than me, and actually his dad said, 'You've hardly said two words to her!' Richard said, 'Well, that's all right—I can hold her hand, can't I?' and so we held hands and his dad left us alone for a couple of minutes and went off to the tea machine.

•　　•　　•

After that I started going to Scotland once a month, and people began realising this was something different, though I still went on writing to other prisoners and visiting them as usual. Richard wrote to my mum and introduced himself—my dad had died long before—but she was naturally wary. She told me to be careful. It took her a while to come round to the idea of me getting involved with somebody like Richard. It wasn't so much what she said, it was more a case of what she didn't say.

In the last week of September 1995 I went to visit Richard and stayed with his father as usual. I got home on the Sunday and as soon as I got in I phoned his dad as I always did to say I'd got home all right. But there was no answer. After a while I got the neighbours to go round and see. Whenever I visited I used to go in to see them, and the woman used to say, 'Oh, I did pray that Richard would find a nice Christian woman! I'm so delighted for you both!' In fact later on they came to our wedding. So they went in and found Richard's dad had died of a heart attack. I had to ring Richard in the prison and tell him. It was awful to think of him lying there while I was on my way home.

The death of Richard's dad actually speeded things up a lot. By this time Richard was in an open prison on the Scottish borders and they gave him a week's compassionate leave because he was coming up for parole, and the bank I worked for gave me a week's unpaid leave so I could go straight back up there.

So we had a week together, which was spent arranging his dad's affairs. The first night I got there, Richard said, 'You know this changes things?' It turned out he felt I would stay with him now, but only out of duty. He'd got no other family, nobody. And I said, 'It doesn't change anything—it just speeds things up'. By this time we'd talked generally about getting married, though not in any detail.

But now the prison said they had a problem because with the death of his father, Richard had no home address to go to when he got parole. I'd lived in my house in Hampshire for 13 years, so I told the prison they could assume Richard was coming to live with me.

His father's funeral was in October, so it was November before he could get another home leave, and he came down to stay with me for the first time. It took him all day to reach me.

•   •   •

That first home leave we got engaged. Richard asked me to marry him in front of everybody in a Harvester restaurant! We'd invited my mum and she was still a bit wary till she met Richard, then she was okay. We'd also invited the guy who was going to be best man—he was a friend of mine from church—and one of my sisters and her husband. Richard was very shy but then he produced this ring—which he had paid for but I'd actually had to go and buy myself—and in front of everybody he asked me to marry him!

We decided to get married in February 1996. We knew he wouldn't be out of prison by then but I thought it would make him feel more secure. We wanted to be married here in my church, and the prison agreed to allow Richard an extra day out. I was left to arrange everything and as with most weddings there were problems. One day I was getting really stressed out and I was in tears. At times like that there seemed to be a kind of telepathy between me and Richard. He would ring and before I even picked the phone up he would know something was wrong. Before I said a word he'd say, 'What's the matter?'

In the end the wedding was lovely, everything went perfectly. I wore a long white dress, but no veil. As soon as I saw the dress I knew it was perfect. We had 40 guests at the reception in a very nice hotel, where they gave us a room for the night after the wedding. It was all very different from my first wedding, which was in an army church with the reception in the officers' mess.

There was a lovely incident with our wedding rings, though we didn't know about it till the best man made his speech. He said, 'Some of you may have seen me disappearing into the vestry, pretending to have a coughing fit!' I hadn't noticed, but apparently when it was coming up to the time for him to produce the rings, he felt in his pocket—and there was only one ring there! He panicked! He dived into the vestry and pulled Richard's ring out, turned his pocket inside out and was on the point of ripping the lining to see if the other one—my ring—could have fallen through. Then he looked more closely and saw that my ring was stuck inside Richards's, where it fitted perfectly.

So the wedding was lovely and nobody said anything unpleasant about Richard, though people were curious. I just used to say he was in a fight, it was a spur of the moment thing—and that was that.

•   •   •

I was 44 when we married, and I didn't want any more children. I didn't want to start taking the Pill, so Richard applied to have a vasectomy, but these things take time. We were only together for 48 hours every month, and at my age I was only supposed to have a one-in-eight chance of conceiving.

But then I got pregnant almost immediately! Richard was delighted, but I was very shocked. I felt under a lot of stress because of the fact that he was still in prison. He was due out in September and the baby was due at the end of November. Because I'd recently had an operation I was booked for a Caesarian and I thought, Oh my God, what happens if he's not out when the baby's born? I really did go through a bad time at first. I went on working full time at the bank until the start of the eleven-week maternity leave. I was sick a lot of the time, partly due to stress, but also because I'm prone to sickness anyway. I get ill when I'm pregnant and during this pregnancy I was in hospital twice. I remember one night particularly I tossed and turned, I couldn't rest and I was really depressed. It was so hard to trust and have faith.

Then at the end of September Richard phoned me at work to say he'd got his parole. He was stunned—he didn't really think he'd get it. I was so relieved! I went up to Scotland to stay overnight and I picked him up. It was great because Sarah arrived four weeks early, on October 13, and Richard was present at the birth. He'd gone to the job centre immediately he was released and got a job on the night shift at McDonald's. He told them he'd got a criminal record and they said that was all right. I was worried he'd be at work when the baby came, but as it happened she arrived on his day off.

Richard soon got very fed up at McDonald's. Most of the staff were 17-year-olds and I hated the night shift because he'd be in bed half the day and it was too disruptive. So he went back to the job centre and applied for a job at an engineering firm. As he was being shown round he told them he'd been in prison, and they had no problem with it and he got the job. It's a pump maintenance place and he goes all over the country fixing underground water pumps.

I went back to work in the bank full-time as soon as Sarah was born, but with the cost of childcare it wasn't worth it. Then my mother looked after her but she's been ill twice and that meant I couldn't go to work. Now Sarah's been offered a place in a day nursery and the bank have rearranged my hours so I can fit everything in and keep my job.

•　　•　　•

When Richard first came to live here I was nervous about people on the estate knowing about his background. I'd been here on my own for so many years and was known for going to church and never having men to stay or anything—and this was all so new and so different. I know people can be friends with you one day and look the other way the next, so I didn't want Richard telling the neighbours. But he did and it was fine, though my neighbour's brother is a prison officer. Now Richard's been living here six years I'm not so worried—it doesn't bother me. Sometimes it crosses my mind whether in years to come any of Sarah's friends will know, and I wonder whether that will be a problem. I don't think I'll tell her, but I don't know whether Richard will or not.

My son is an outgoing sort of person who took to Richard straight away. My elder daughter Marie was a bit slower. She was always quite polite to him but she's very withdrawn. She was at university at the time of our wedding and she wasn't sure if she'd come. She did come, though she was very nervous.

• • •

We have had quite a few low points in our marriage, but I'm not sure whether that's because Richard's been in prison, or if it's just him as a person. He can get days when he just won't speak and that gets me down. I would rather have an argument and clear the air, then just get on as normal. One of the things I think prison does to people is to make them learn to switch off. So Richard can cut himself off and I find it really hurtful sometimes. When he goes into one of his silent moods he'll cut himself off from Sarah as well. Yet if I want to go upstairs and read for a bit he thinks I'm giving him the cold shoulder! He's normally a really boisterous, outgoing, friendly, loud, life-and-soul-of-the-party sort of person. We'll go out to a pub and he'll strike up a conversation with anybody. When he's quiet it's the very opposite. He'll act like nobody's here. He'll come in and ignore people and if he's fallen out with me he'll go off upstairs. And this makes me feel very resentful. Sarah's lovely, but she's hard work and I didn't really want any more children, and there are times when I wish I'd been a little more careful. I blame him that she's here with me and he can just walk away. I think, How dare you!

I think being on my own for almost 13 years has made me independent, and I think we women are stronger than the men. But I do resent the fact that I do 99 per cent of the work. I come in from my job and take over Sarah, and he comes in from work and does nothing, except take her to the park on Saturday mornings. It gets to the point every couple of months that I'm in tears from sheer exhaustion. Then I say to Richard, 'If you'd just get her ready for bed one night a week', and he says he'll do it—but it never happens. Only yesterday I got really annoyed. I said, 'My mum's been ill, I've been running up and down looking after her. I've had all this worry about whether I'll carry on working and how we'd miss my money, and who would look after Sarah.' There's nobody else in my position that I can talk to, so I tend to have a rosy view of everybody's else's life, thinking their life's great.

I do think people who've been in prison tend to have a chip on their shoulder as well. Richard thinks some of my family look down on him, whereas I think they've all bent over backwards to make him feel welcome. But I think part of this is also because he's an only child and he hasn't had the normal arguments and making-up that I had in my family. So he often feels he's been slighted, and where anybody else might not even notice, for him it'll be a major thing. Because Marie's not the gushy type, he felt at first that she didn't like him, and he had a period when he felt very down over that. She wasn't even living at home, but whenever she came back at weekends from university he'd find some reason to argue with her. She'd just be voicing her opinion on some point they disagreed on, but he got awful about it.

This got really bad a few Christmases ago and it led to Richard leaving me. He did actually leave. It was when Sarah was about 18 months old. Richard had another argument with Marie and he said he felt I was siding with her. He walked out and found digs somewhere and stayed there for a few weeks and I had to start claiming rent benefit. Looking back I should have said, 'Marie hasn't got to prove herself to you! It's you that's got to prove yourself to her!' He couldn't quite break away and he kept coming round and I kept going and meeting him. Looking back, I don't think I should have run around after him so much.

Also being an only child and a boy, Richard's been used to having a mother who does everything for him, and when he was in prison, if Richard wanted anything his dad would get it for him. In prison men get childish—they see the latest thing and they want it. One time I remember he wanted a watch so his dad got him one but it wasn't the right one—he wanted a different one. So his dad went and changed it. Then somebody in the prison had a personal organizer and Richard just had to have one too, so his dad got him one of those. And two months later he gave it away to somebody—and he's still doing that kind of thing now!

I think looking back I started off on the wrong foot when Richard first came to live here. I used to try and shield him from anything I thought would upset him and I realise now that that was a big mistake. Now I've had enough of walking on eggshells and I think it's about time he grew up. I think most of our problems have been because of misunderstandings and different expectations. I think maybe I expected more from this relationship than other people might. I think I expected it to be extraordinary, which is silly, I know, because maybe it means I get more disillusioned than I should. I think I expected Richard to be perfect—or close to perfect. I suppose that's because I felt we'd been brought together by God. He did say once, 'If it wasn't for you, if we hadn't got married, I'd be homeless', and I said, 'Oh no you wouldn't. I'm sure the Lord would have done something else for you.' I'm not saying I expected him to be really grateful all the time. But because of where he came from I did expect him to be glad, to be more aware that he could have ended up on his own somewhere.

•　　•　　•

I can't see Richard ever committing an offence again. I think his life is so different now. I've never weighed up the pros and cons of being involved with people. If I like someone I'll be with them no matter what others think—I have a couple of friends that other people think are odd. In the heat of the moment I'll admit I've regretted getting married again, but that feeling's so short-lived. When I married Richard I felt I was walking a chosen path—and I just have to remind myself of that from time to time.

All that people in prison can see is the light at the end of the tunnel. They think that after getting out of prison, life will be wonderful. But I'd say to them, 'You need to remember that life's harder outside prison than it is inside.'

Joy and Paul

Joy's wedding to Paul in a Scottish prison had to be postponed for a month after tabloid newspapers discovered the date and printed graphic details of the crime—strangling a prostitute—for which Paul had already served 18 years of a life sentence. Although this was the first time Joy knew the full story, she went ahead with the marriage, despite strong family opposition.

Joy, 33, lives in a council flat in Edinburgh with her two green budgies and a large collection of soft toys. A large, diffident woman with short dark hair, she was wearing a loose, white tee shirt and baggy, patterned trousers. She has always lacked confidence and suffered from a poor self-image since she was teased and bullied at school for being overweight—so badly that at the age of 17 she took an overdose of drugs she had been prescribed for depression. Joy is articulate and pleasant but she suffers greatly from anxiety: before the interview she made many worried phone calls about my travel arrangements.

Joy has worked as a tax assistant for the Inland Revenue and as a nursing auxiliary and carer, but is now registered as incapacitated and unable to work. She comes from a middle-class background. Her father is a maths teacher, her mother a nursery assistant, and her younger brother an accounts manager for a big financial services company. Joy says her parents never approved of her friends, and family relationships broke down almost completely when she decided to marry a life-sentenced prisoner ten years older than her. She showed me her small collection of wedding photos. She is shown smiling in her smart wedding dress and jacket and hugging her new husband Paul, who is wearing a suit and tie. He has receding hair and a small toothbrush moustache.

The couple have now been married four years but the relationship has been a troubled one, with both partners instituting divorce proceedings at different times. The depressive illness which has troubled Joy since her teens has been greatly exacerbated recently by difficulties in communicating with her husband. Soon after the interview she was due to go into respite care for a week to alleviate her anxiety.

•   •   •

I'd first contacted Paul through the Prison Reform Trust penfriend scheme[1] and he was one of a lot of folk they sent me. But my first contact with prisons came a while before that. When I was in my early twenties I worked in a hospital and one of my work colleagues committed a crime and got sent to prison. I felt sorry for him and I used to write to him, though I never visited him in prison. Then a childhood friend of mine was imprisoned in America. He used to live near here before he went to America to stay with his dad. He was convicted of setting fire to a flat in which a child died, though there's a lot of evidence to show that this child started the fire herself. He was put on Death Row and he's serving a 65-year sentence. I wrote to him for a couple of years,[2] till it got into the papers that I was writing to him, so I stopped.

Then I became a volunteer for SACRO.[3] The men I'd been writing to had got too emotionally involved with me, and I wanted to do something officially. That's when I first visited a prison, travelling free of charge on the SACRO bus. I went to Edinburgh prison to visit a man I'd been writing to for about five weeks.

I was apprehensive about going into a real prison. You see the prison staff and you smell the place. I got on all right with this prisoner till I found he had lied about his offence. He'd said he was in for murder but I found out from another prisoner that he was in for rape. Another prisoner I wrote to asked me to send £50 a week to an outside address to buy him a computer. I did it for about eight weeks, which added up to £400 I sent him. But it turned out that a member of his family was spending the money on bookies. I confronted the family but they wouldnae give me my money back. He was just using me.

Once my mum and dad found out I was writing to prisoners they put a stop to it. When I was working on a night shift they went through my room and searched for the letters. So then I got in touch with the Prison Reform Trust penfriend scheme. They sent me a form so they could match up my interests with prisoners who had the same interests and who were about the same age. They tell you the person's sentence, but not their offence—they're not allowed to tell you that—and they advise you not to ask outright what the person's in for. You can put down your preferences and I said I would write to women as well as men.

Through that scheme I was writing to about six prisoners. Some of the letters were quite short, but others used to send 20-page letters. The longest I ever had was 30 pages! I went to see four of them, the ones in Scottish prisons. I did get invites from English prisons but it was too far for me to go, and with my nursing work my time was very limited.

So by the time I went to see Paul I'd got to feel quite at home in prisons. In my first letter I just said, 'Hi there! How are you?' I told him my name, my age and my interests—reading, writing letters, music, watching telly and videos.

When my letter to Paul arrived at his high security prison, he'd gone on the run. That was the second time he'd absconded. The first time was when his mother was ill. This second time, he hadnae returned from a home leave because he'd found his girlfriend in bed with her ex-husband and he'd gone on the drink, then gone AWOL. The prison kept my letter and he got it when he was recaptured and returned there. He wrote back and said he'd been recaptured and would I go and see him. By then he must have been in prison 12 or 13 years. What attracted me about his letter was that he seemed to have a sense of humour. So I said I'd go and visit him.

Though Paul was in a high security prison, the visiting room was very relaxed. It was spotless and it was massive, with low tables and chairs, and a table where the officers sit. There were officers standing round, and CCTV cameras. They searched you as they do in all prisons. The only thing that was different was that they gave you a rub-down search.

I went up to the desk and said Paul's name, and I told the officer, 'I don't know what he looks like!'. They waved to him and he came and met me. He just looked normal, about the same height as me, quite thin, with a moustache. I thought he had a nice cheery face.

We managed to get easily into conversation, talking about our interests, our tastes in music. I told him about my job and my family.

After the visit he wrote to me saying he'd enjoyed it and he really liked me. Then he said he wasnae getting any younger, and how about he and I giving it a go? I liked him, so I thought, Why not?

After that our letters got more detailed and more intimate, and I used to go several times a week to see him. After a while we did hold hands and have a kiss and a cuddle—that's as much intimate contact as you're allowed.

Then when I'd been visiting and writing for about six months, he said, 'How about you and I getting married?' I was a bit taken aback because I didnae think it would last. I didnae think it would go as far as it did. I said to him I couldnae believe that somebody wanted to marry me, because I was insecure about myself, lacking in confidence. I just thought, Why does he want me? From Paul I was getting friendship and the fact that I could be myself with him. I didnae have to put on an act. I suppose what he was getting from me was companionship, somebody to talk to. And we had in common that we'd both been hurt in previous relationships. I don't consider myself to be what the average man would want, because I'm big and not very attractive.

•   •   •

The boys used to tease me a lot at school, and there was one time when two boys took advantage of me in the woods on the way home from school. I told my mum and dad and they went to the guidance teacher, but the two boys denied what they did.

My first boyfriend I met when I was 18 and we were actually engaged, going to get married. But when I was 20 I split from him because he beat me up for no reason. I met the next one when I was 21 and that lasted a year, till he broke my nose. He had an alcohol problem. When he was sober he was all right. Even after he broke my nose he asked me for a tenner to go out and get pissed again.

Then I got a summer job in the parks department and ended up going with somebody I worked with just for the one night, and I fell pregnant, but I lost the child at three-and-a-half months. It was a relief at the time because I was wondering how I was going to cope. But now I regret I lost the baby, and I still think about it.

After Paul asked me to marry him I thought about it on the way home and wrote him a letter that night. Yes, I would marry him. I got an engagement ring for myself but I kept the engagement to myself, kept it low key.

We were engaged for about a year before we married. What I knew about Paul's background was very limited. It's still limited, mainly to what I've read in the newspapers about him. I know he comes from Glasgow, I think from a large family, though they don't have any contact with him now. His father died years and years ago, but he was very close to his mother, though he's never really spoken a lot about it. Before his mother died he used to go and stay with her on his home leaves. She was ill anyway, but she became even worse when she heard he'd absconded. The police were called to let her know. After that she wouldnae have anything to do with him, but he did get to go to the funeral. That was about two years before I met him. If I tell him I think he's been funny since his mother passed away, he gets upset.

To be honest Paul's never told me very much about his offence. I did ask him but he wouldnae talk about it. He just said he didnae want to discuss it and he got real angry. So all I knew by the time we got engaged was that he'd murdered someone in the Glasgow area. I think he's got a problem addressing his offence. He's done all the prison offending behaviour courses and the alcohol counselling, but he feels he knows more than the whole prison.

He had a release date for 1984 but because he absconded he lost it. If he gets released I wouldnae feel in danger because he'd be on a licence for life. He's never shown any violence to me and I've always felt perfectly safe with him.

· · ·

I had to write to the prison requesting permission to get married, and Paul had to put in a request to the Governor. The Governor agreed, and then we had to get in touch with the chaplain. Then you have to pay at the registry office for your banns.

We were supposed to get married in May 1996, but then a story about us appeared in the papers so we had to put the wedding off till the June. Not long before the May date for our wedding, I was at a pub down the way with some friends who were also married to long-term prisoners. Some of them were going to be my witnesses at my wedding. We were all out together, and one of them must have phoned up the media to make a bit of money, because the newspapers reported on conversations I'd had with my pals on this hen night.

Then I had the reporters round here at this flat, and they were hounding my neighbours, so I went out to them and told them to clear off. I ended up smacking the reporters to smithereens and the paper printed a picture of me attacking one of them. A reporter phoned me here and taped our conversation, so I had to get my number changed. The prison were going to look into how my number had leaked out. I know some prison officers do work under cover for the papers.

Next day there was a wee bit in the local paper, but a national tabloid paper had a full report. They'd printed all the background to Paul's offence, and it was only through the papers that I found out that when he was about 24 or 25 he'd strangled a prostitute at a hostel where he was staying. They dragged up all the details about Paul's case, and yes, it was a shock for me to read all that. The headline was something like, 'I'll marry killer'.

When this all got splashed in the papers one of my friends rang me up and said, 'I hope you know what you're doing!' But I didnae bother what she said. I'd only told my parents that I was getting married the night before the newspapers printed the story. I had already told them I was going to a wedding that day, but I didnae say it was my own! I told them one of my friends was getting married, and my mum bought me my dress and jacket. Then after the papers had been on at me I rang them up and told them.

My dad got on the phone to the prison to tell them to stop the wedding. Then my dad gave me the ultimatum—it had to be either them or Paul. And I chose Paul. My mum wouldnae have anything to do with me at all, once it appeared in the papers about me marrying a prisoner. It was quite a shock to them to read it. I never asked them to the wedding and they never offered. They just phoned the Governor to try and stop it and the Governor told me that's what they'd done. They had also somehow got hold of the chaplain's number and they tried to bribe him, though I don't know the ins and outs of that story.

My dad ended up phoning me and telling me not to bother going near them again or phoning them, or they were going to get a court order taken out against me. That's the type of people they are—middle class, they like to look good. They don't like to feel embarrassed. But I've always got on better with my dad than my mum, and I got back on speaking terms with him in a couple of days.

After all this publicity I was up at the prison visiting Paul when we got told that the Governor wanted to see us. We were called into a private room and the Governor said, 'The wedding's cancelled!'

'Excuse me?' I said, 'I've had to pay money for my banns.'

'Well, let's say the wedding's postponed,' he said.

When the papers found out the wedding had been put off, the journalists waited for me in the prison car park one day and they caught me and asked me how I felt about my wedding being postponed. The prison staff wanted to chuck out the reporters but because the car park's not prison property they weren't allowed to touch them. But then some visitors from Dundee came to my rescue and they walked across the path with me and I hid behind a statue till the reporters had gone.

Our wedding, on 11 June 1996, was a media circus as well, because the papers found out when it was. What they do is, they go down the registry office and all they have to do is to look at the list of banns they've got put up there. So when I got outside the jail after the wedding the press were waiting for me again. They were all crouched down at the back of the car park. But this time I just waved to them. They just did a wee bit of a report with a photograph of me coming out of the prison. They said I was flashing a gold ring and that I had a camera full of snaps.

Still, I enjoyed our wedding. It was in the prison chapel, which is up in the clock tower. I just wore a normal dress and jacket, not a wedding dress, and Paul was wearing a suit. We had a cake which I bought in a shop. The chaplain had to take it in for us. For our first wedding date I'd had a cake specially made but it wouldnae keep until our actual wedding. The prison officers were the witnesses—because I couldnae have my pals as I was planning. The Governor was there as well. It was all over in less than ten minutes, then because of the hassle we'd had with the press, we were allowed to have our visit up there in a room next to the chapel, while Paul's personal officer and the chaplain sat in the main chapel.

•　　•　　•

Now it's four years since we got married and now and then I've regretted marrying Paul because of the way he carries on sometimes. I think Paul felt that he was wanting somebody to come home to. A lot of prisoners think that getting married will help when it comes to their parole, but that's not the case. Whether they get parole depends on how they do their sentence and how they present themselves. It's not because the prison thinks they're going to have a stable background to go out to, though a social worker will come here and do a special report on the home circumstances. I think Paul was wanting to prove to people that he wasnae all bad. He does try, but he doesnae always go about things the right way.

When he gets depressed I try and get the conversation away from his parole. I talk about what I've been doing, what he's been doing, what he's hoping for. But if *I'm* depressed I don't get much support from him at all. I do look forward to going and seeing him, because I get a laugh out of him, and if I want to talk about something, he's there, he listens—but then he goes off on a different subject.

I don't know whether it's because of the length of time Paul's been in prison, but he just takes things for granted—he takes me for granted. He thinks, She'll always be there for me. He says in his letters how much he misses me, how much he wants me. He says that when he gets out we'll be together, then I'll know how much he really does love me.

But now our problems are about communication, which I think started for Paul when his mother died. There was one letter relating to his mother—how he felt about her death—which was quite upsetting. I told him he needed a bereavement counsellor, but he's had that before and he's ended up telling the counsellor not to come back and see him. I actually thought he had mental health problems, to be honest. But there's only so much I can do. I think I'm supposed to be mother, wife, counsellor—the lot. He wants me to be everything, but with my illness I just can't do that. I did do a counselling course because I felt it would help me deal with the problems I'm facing with my husband in a clearer way. Sometimes I can see other people's problems clearer than they can, and even now I'm ill, I'll sit with people and help them.

On visits, when I ask Paul about things, he changes the subject, and as a result I have to end up phoning the prison to find things out. He'll keep in contact regularly for a couple of months by phone and by letter, then he'll stop, and I'm lucky if I get a letter every couple of weeks. I'll get on to the prison about it, they'll go away and speak to him again till they're blue in the face, but then it'll be periods of stop-and-start contact again.

One day I was on a visit and Paul brought a lawyer's letter down to the visits room with him which said that he had started divorce proceedings against me.

I was gobsmacked! I didnae know what to say or where to look. My first reaction was to burst into tears and I asked for the prison chaplain. The Roman Catholic chaplain came down and sat with us for a while. He knows us both really well and he got on to Paul about it. In the end Paul's solicitors closed the file because he hadnae responded to their letters. In their letters they said he hadnae given any grounds for divorce. He hadnae given any real reason why he wanted to divorce me.

Last year I decided to start divorce proceedings against Paul myself and I really meant it, because I felt I'd had enough of the way he'd been treating me. I asked a social worker to go with me on a visit, and he arranged a private visit. That's when I told Paul I wanted a divorce, and all he said was, 'That's up to you!' So I left the visit in tears.

Then I got a letter from him, wishing me all the best. He said that my visits were still booked, and did I want to go up there? And because I'm a softie I gave in to him. Me being me, the letter pulled my heart strings and I went up to see him. Then he promised things would be a lot better, a lot different, and he started phoning me regularly. Then he was moved to a Category C prison and for the first few weeks he used to phone me up regularly every Thursday night. But once he made friends in the hall, that wasnae happening any longer. This has just happened recently, in the last four weeks. He's not contacting me properly again.

All the Scottish prisons have now got family contact development officers and I've approached them for help with our communication problems, but they weren't really any good. I think they're better at practical problems like how you can arrange transport, and they give advice on things like benefits. I contacted Aftermath[4] as well but they're very short of counsellors and I was lucky if I could speak to my counsellor even once every six months.

A lot of prisoners' wives are frightened to talk to other prisoners' wives about their problems when the husbands are in the same jail. It might end up that things get distorted when the husbands talk to each other. In the last jail Paul was in, there was a lot of bitching going on amongst prisoners' wives. There's a visitors' centre where you can go for a cup of tea before your visit and that's where all the bitchiness and gossip starts. As a result people wouldnae even speak to each other and a lot of us stopped going to the centre. We used to congregate at the bus station café instead.

•   •   •

Since Paul was moved to his C Cat, it's a lot further away for me to travel. If I visit him it's a ten-hour day for me and because of my illness I'm not supposed to go on public transport. He has come here on a home leave and I made dinner for him and the officer who came with him. One of my neighbours came in and had a cup of tea and we sat around talking about prison and life in general. The officer, who was an older man and really nice, said that rather than get prisoners into trouble he'd prefer to help them. That's the first prison officer I've ever heard say that. Paul's next home leave is in August.

Sometimes I feel I'm bashing my head against a brick wall. Last night I was so worried about Paul because I hadnae heard from him, and I phoned up the prison and said, 'Can you tell me if my husband's there?' and I gave his name. And Officer Smartass who answers says to me, 'Is there any reason why he wouldnae be here?' I says to him, 'No, but I'm entitled to know!' I thought, Why should I have to justify myself to any prison officer? But I do get on very well with most of the prison staff. They know me well and they know about the problems. The chaplain has offered to get me put up at a convent near the prison because of my transport difficulties.

We've been thinking that when Paul comes out he's going to have a whole lot of problems adjusting, because of his lack of communications skills. But the earliest he could get out is another two and a half years, and he's got no release date yet. We don't know when he's getting out, because he's absconded twice and in his last prison he was downgraded for experimenting with cannabis, though that's all the drugs he's ever done.

Paul wants to have children but at the moment I don't feel that I'm well enough to be able to cope with a wee baby. But when I say that, he really thinks I'm talking a load of rubbish. He says, 'What's all this shit you're talking about?' He knows I've got depression problems but he doesn't realise the severity of it. He probably thinks, Oh, she'll get better tomorrow. But that's not going to happen and sometimes I feel as if I'm about to go back to square one.

• • •

I've become worse since I married Paul. My community nurses know that. They understand about it and they've tried to help, but they say it's not for them to make decisions. It was my decision to marry Paul. He's my husband and it's up to me to decide things—it's not up to them. But they do say that if the problem wasnae there I'd get better a lot quicker. My self-confidence has shattered and I don't have any defence mechanisms left. Before, when I was working, I was the head carer in a care home. I was on a higher rate of pay than the other carers and I was looked on by my employer as a team leader. People who had problems would come to me for advice. But now I'm about to get a carer myself, to act like a sounding board and help me plan things so I don't get in such a flap. Paul doesn't want a carer to come in for me, but I think she'll be able to make me see things from a clearer point of view and help me work my way through my problems.

In December 2000 Paul got a two-year knockback. I spent Christmas with my mum and dad though my relationship with Paul is still a very sore point with them.

Being a prisoner's wife is really difficult. Nobody understands the difficulties we face. You have to take each day as it comes, because each day brings its problems. At every visit, each prisoner's moods are going to be different. I saw Paul yesterday and he's very down at the moment. Sometimes I just can't see what the future will hold. If I was asked if I've got any advice to give to others, it would be this: before you get married to a prisoner, think about it very carefully.

Postscript: In September 2001 Joy wrote to say she and Paul had divorced:

He said he couldnae cope with my disability any more and he wrote me a letter saying he had started divorce proceedings against me. I thought that was a poor excuse—his heart was never in our marriage and the way he treated me got worse, specially on his last escorted visit home. So I took things into my own hands and in July I put in for a divorce, and it was finalised five weeks ago.

I've got some happy memories and I never felt I was in any danger from Paul, but I got fed up with the emotional blackmail and I felt smothered. I'm glad I'm out of the marriage and my parents are relieved. I wish I'd listened to them and I'm never going to write to prisoners again. I'm never going to get into a situation like that again and like I said before, anyone who's involved with a prisoner should think about it very carefully indeed.

ENDNOTES

[1] See *Chapter 2*, pp.18 and 21.
[2] There are an estimated 3,000 British women who correspond with American death row prisoners. There is an organization, Lifelines, which provides such prisoners with penfriends. A speaker at their conference, in 1998, was Sister Helen Prejean, who inspired the film 'Dead Man Walking' ('Death Row Penpals', *Daily Express,* 14 March 2002).
[3] Scottish Association for the Care and Resettlement of Offenders.
[4] A charity which helps offenders' families.

Sue and Andy Horwood

Sue, 36, is a primary school teacher, the privately-educated daughter of a self-made businessman. She faced bitter opposition from her family when she decided to marry Andy, 46, then recently released from the latest of a number of prison sentences. They have just celebrated their twelfth wedding anniversary.

Sue greeted me at the front door of the house in the Midlands that she shares with her husband Andy and their ginger cat, Garfield. Sue has worked for 12 years in the same local primary school. She is a very warm person with long, fair hair and an all-embracing smile that lights up her whole face. You feel that the disadvantaged children she teaches must be very fond of her.

Andy joined us for part of the interview. He is a large, genial, bespectacled man and was wearing the work-clothes of his trade—he is a painter and decorator. The couple have fitted out their kitchen-diner with attractive pine units and there is a large table at which much convivial entertaining takes place when ex-prisoners and other friends come to stay. In one corner of the kitchen on a purpose-built wooden unit is Sue's computer. Andy was able to buy it for her recently when his hobby, metal-detecting, yielded an amazing find. In the fields near his home, he and two friends discovered an earthenware pot containing a hoard of stunning Roman silver—he showed me photographs of beautiful deep-bowled spoons and coins. It was reported as treasure trove and the friends shared a substantial reward. Andy delights in antiquities and showed me various artefacts he had dug up. When I left he presented me with a touching gift—a delicately engraved medieval bronze ring. He had found one for Sue bearing in Latin the legend *For my sweet wife*.

Andy's background is very different from Sue's privileged upbringing. He came from an impoverished family, rarely attended school and at an early age followed in his father's footsteps and became a petty thief, serving a number of prison sentences. The last offence was more sinister: Andy was jailed for mugging using a knife and sent to Dartmoor.

• • •

Sue: Andy wasn't the first prisoner I'd met. In the holidays from teacher training college I used to drive a minibus taking inmates and prison officers from the local courts to the jails. I must have been about 18 when I started. My dad ran a transport company and he had this contract: in those days they didn't use secure vans like Group 4 and Securicor do these days.

I remember the first time I had to do a prison run. I think there'd been something in the news about security, because when I went into the prison an officer said, 'We'll have to do a search on you!' and I remember thinking, Are they having me on, or is this for real? And yes, they were having me on. On the way back to prison the prisoners in the bus used to say, 'Turn this way!' and of course you'd make a joke of it because you knew they were telling you the wrong way. But apart from that I never talked to them at any length, and that was all I knew about prisons.

Then when I was still in college I heard that a man who used to run a local village post office had been sent to prison. The post office had been robbed and he got the blame, but I believed him when he said he wasn't guilty. He and his wife used to attend the same church as I did when I was home from college, and I started writing to him and visiting him with his wife, then the man got released and the three of us became friends.

It was through this couple that I met Andy. They'd heard on the radio about a group called the Prison Fellowship, a Christian ministry to prisoners, and decided to go to one of their meetings. I said I'd give them a lift though I was thinking twice about going to the meeting. But I thought I'd got to bring them back anyway, so I might as well go.

The meeting was held in a Christian centre being run as a kind of hostel for people coming out of prison. I was quite nervous because I didn't know anybody there. Andy was staying in the hostel—he'd been out of prison about a month—but he didn't come to the meeting because he thought it would be full of do-gooders. He just did the refreshments.

Andy: When I first came out of prison there were all these people that to my way of thinking were do-gooders. I was trying to start a new life. I'd done three lots of prison and I didn't want to do any more. So I moved to a place 100 miles away from where I lived to try and get away from the crime scene. I'd got no choice but to live in this house because of my parole, but all these people kept coming around and it got on my nerves a bit. I called the do-gooders 'twirlies' and my idea of a twirly was a blue-rinse older person. Then this bird comes in and she was an absolute corker, all dressed in red, with blonde hair. She was a stunner! I couldn't take my eyes off her. So I zoomed in and said, 'What would you like to drink after the meeting?' and she said, 'Orange squash, please'. During the meeting I kept going to the door and listening. Then when the meeting finished I came in with the drinks and went straight up to Sue and said, 'There's your drink' and said, 'Help yourself' to the others.

Sue: We started talking but I didn't notice that Andy was zooming in on me and hadn't offered a drink to anyone else! We were just talking general talk. The next time I saw him was when he turned up in my church.

Andy: I found out the address of the couple Sue had come with to the meeting and the next Sunday I walked the ten miles to their home and asked if they knew where she lived. 'Oh, she's just been here today for lunch!' they said. 'Why don't you come to church with us tonight and you'll see her'.

Sue: So he turned up at church and I was surprised to see him—I thought, Oh my goodness! It was only then that I was aware that he was interested in me and I thought, Oh, where's this leading? What am I getting involved in? I was about 24 and I'd never really had a serious relationship before then. I used to be very shy, and also not long before I'd met Andy my younger sister had died and that had quite a significant effect on me. She was 18 and she was mentally handicapped and because of that she was like the hub of our family, the one that everything revolved around. Andy was fun, he'd got a good sense of humour and made me laugh, and he was giving me the attention I needed.

Andy: After that it was a continuation. I used to walk the ten miles to her church every Sunday to make sure I'd see her.

Sue: Then one time he said he was going to come and visit me at my house. I said OK but I was on tenterhooks. It was pouring with rain and while I was waiting I was getting worried. When Mum saw him she said, 'Well, who is he? Hasn't he got any other clothes he can change into?' and I said, 'Well, no—I don't think so.' So by now she's really thinking, 'My goodness, whatever has my daughter got into here?' I'm sure I must have talked to her about him but in our family we never talked on a level of feelings, only on the level of things that were happening. I don't think my parents said too much in the beginning because I suppose they thought it would all blow over—they hoped it would.

My dad had built up his own business from scratch—minibuses and removal lorries—and we lived in a reasonably big semi-detached house. My father is a strong character—a *very* strong character! My elder sister and I went to a private girls' secondary school, and my younger sister to a special school. There was an expectation that we would do well, though they didn't push us. I was more hard-working than my sister.

•   •   •

Andy: I had a very different background. My dad was a lorry driver but he was also a heavy gambler so he gambled most of the money away and we had a relatively poor upbringing. I've got two sisters and a brother, all older than me. Crime came relatively early into my life. My father was a thief as well as a gambler and he went to prison for it several times. He died when I was 15. But the rest of the family were fine—I'm the black sheep. I got involved in shoplifting early on, then breaking and entering. I did time for that in 1977 and then I got a six-month sentence for stealing a doctor's car. Then I got two-and-a-half years for mugging some Asian guys and I began that last sentence in December 1985. I was into booze and drugs as well—amphetamines and barbiturates and a bit of LSD. And I got into witchcraft and black magic as well, and on occasions that turned terrifying. And in relationships with women, all I was interested in was sex.

•   •   •

In prison a lot of lads will go to church just to get out of their cell, and that's what I'd been doing. Then I started taking a bit of interest—it was just sort of gradual. Because of the nature of my last crime and my violent attitude, they sent me to Dartmoor. From there I'd applied to go to a place for ex-cons in Cardiff, but then, three months before I was due out of prison, that place shut down and I'd got nowhere to go.

The night I heard that, I went back to my cell and after lights out I threw down a challenge to God. I was throwing my arms about, shouting and bawling and I said, 'Why are You doing this to me? All You're doing is shutting places down!' I was five floors up and there was nobody outside on the landing. Then I heard this loud booming voice. I got down on my hands and knees and buried my head in the bed. The voice said, 'I want all of you or nothing at all!'

Next morning when I came out of my cell, my aggression seemed to have gone. I felt different. The screws said, 'What's the matter with you then? There's something different about you.' I was forever getting nicked—I was a stubborn bastard—but when they tried to wind me up that day I didn't spark off at them. Then when I came out of prison and went to live in the Christian Centre they helped me immensely. They taught me all the things I'd missed out on—I didn't even know how to read a phone book. Then I got myself a job and I've gone on from there.

•　　•　　•

Sue: My grandmother went to the Anglican church in the village regularly. My parents didn't go to church but they sent us to Sunday school. So we'd had a church grounding. I'd started to explore Christianity for myself and I'd been teaching in the Sunday school, but it was really make or break for me when I went away to college. Was I really going to stand up and say, 'Yes, I am a Christian?' Luckily there was a strong Christian fellowship in the college that I went to, and in the second year I helped to run it.

In my younger days I wanted to please my parents—I always very much wanted what my parents wanted for me. Now I know who I am as a person but then I didn't know who I was at all. I'd always thought I had a good relationship with my parents, though Dad was always working and he was very intense when he was working. I think I did go through times when I resented that. I enjoyed being at college—I enjoyed being away from home, finding out who I was. But when I met Andy I was living back at home again. It was February 1987, part way through the school year, and I'd just got a supply teaching job.

Andy and I used to go for walks round the town. Neither of us had much money so we didn't go to the pictures or anything like that. Andy started visiting our house quite often and my parents were picking up that it was getting serious. It all happened quite quickly, from the February when we'd met towards the summer time—probably six months or less. Then my parents said to Andy, 'We don't want you coming to the house'. I can't remember the conversation but I just remember these things happening and it made it very difficult. I know at one stage he was waiting at the bottom of the road because they didn't want him in the house. And when Andy and I decided that we really wanted to be together they did *everything* possible to try and put us off.

I knew from the start that Andy had been in prison, but I didn't ask about what he'd done. I suppose it was a few months before I knew. He did say he'd tell me but I said I didn't want to know, because I knew that when my parents asked, I'd have to tell them. I've always been the kind of person that can't tell a lie. I thought, If I don't know, then I can't tell anyone.

The only people I really talked to about Andy were my friends from the post office, because I knew they had some understanding of prison and prisoners. The husband was out of prison by then, and the wife just listened to me.

●　　●　　●

About six months after we met, Andy moved into a flat of his own. I was working away from home by this time and travelling back each day, and I used to go to the flat and we used to cook dinner together. I was still living at home: because of my Christian morals I was very determined that I was going to stay a virgin and I was going to do things properly. On one occasion my parents must have said they didn't want me to go and see Andy, because I remember having a fight with them. It sticks in my mind because it was the only time that we've ever fought physically. I was struggling to get away, and I did go to him.

Because by that time I'd been to college and been away from home a lot, I was a much, much stronger person. I think really Andy got the blame for that more forceful element that was coming out. But because I'd been away from home, my parents hadn't seen how much I was changing.

At the end of that summer we went to visit Andy's mum. She loved me! I think she was so grateful and so pleased to see Andy finally settling down, and she saw I was part of that.

Andy: My mam stood by me through thick and thin and she wouldn't have anything bad said about me. She died in her seventies, but I was blessed to have her at our wedding.

●　　●　　●

Sue: We decided that we wanted to get engaged, so we went out and bought two rings. This was that same summer, the summer after we met in the February, so it was all quite quick. Then we decided that we wanted to do it properly, we wanted to tell my parents. So although we'd decided to get engaged we took the rings off and Andy made an appointment to go and see my dad to tell him that this was what we wanted to do. It was very awkward, but I think it was appreciated.

We got married the following year, which was also a bone of contention because my sister had already planned to get married in the June. With me being a school teacher, the summer holidays are really the only time you can get married. But my parents stipulated that because my sister had already planned her wedding, we shouldn't get married before her. So we got married in the August, about six weeks after my sister.

My sister's husband was already working for my dad in his business. He was very much approved of, and after their wedding they were moving into one of my dad's properties. Andy had a job by this time. His first job on leaving prison was general maintenance at a truck builders but the money was poor and we were finding it difficult to find somewhere to live. Andy had got county court judgements and debts as well. So we asked my parents for help and my dad gave me an ultimatum. He said, 'Do you want the money for a house deposit, or do you want the wedding?'

I did feel very hurt because my sister was having both, and it was a very difficult decision for me to make. We have a very big extended family, and although we're not that close, because my parents were paying they would want to invite everybody as they had to my sister's. I think it was only because of my faith that I said, 'We'll have the wedding'. I really believed that was right, and I believed that God would look after us, no matter what.

And then just before we got married, Andy went to meet a friend of his called Kirk who was married to an American woman. They attended the same church as us and they lived in the house that we are living in now. Andy was sitting in a chair over in that corner of the living room and he felt God saying to him, 'One day this house will be yours.' This is at the time when we were struggling to find somewhere to live, and everywhere we looked was much too expensive.

Then a few days later Kirk came up to us in church and told us he and his wife were going back to America and said, 'If you can raise the money you can have our house.' The figure he quoted was far below market value. Another friend in the church introduced us to a friend working in a building society who helped us to pay off Andy's debts so he could get a mortgage, and Andy moved into this house a few weeks before we got married.

We were married in the Pentecostal church which we still attend. The service was shared between the Pentecostal minister, my minister from the Baptist church I used to go to, and the minister from a church Andy had attended. The three ministers had never met before but it was all so beautiful and fitted together so well.

My wedding dress was a long cream-coloured satin dress and I had yellow and cream flowers. By this time my parents had come to terms with my marriage. They realised it was going to happen and if they wanted to maintain their relationship with their daughter they were going to have to accept it. My father gave me away and my parents invited the whole family—there were a couple of hundred guests. My parents' house had a huge lawn and like my sister we had a big marquee in the garden. It was all beautiful. We did it all properly with speeches and everything.

I think the closer members of my family knew about Andy's background. I suppose it was part of the family discussion, maybe at my sister's wedding only six weeks before. But I never discussed it with my sister. As I said, we've never really been a family that discussed our feelings.

I think that's one thing that Andy makes me do. Normally it's the other way round, isn't it? Women talk a lot about their feelings. But I think he made me talk about what I felt, and I think that was definitely good for me. He's made me discuss things that in the past I would probably have kept very much to myself and dealt with in my own very quiet way.

We borrowed somebody's tent and went to Brighton on our honeymoon, but when we got there we found the tent hadn't got a fly sheet! So we just slept in the car for a few nights instead.

•   •   •

Of course there have been problems. In the early days Andy used to go out of the house if he felt he couldn't cope with a situation and thought he might get violent. It upset me a great deal and I used to cry a lot when he got like that, and crying would make it worse because he said I was trying to manipulate him.

Andy: My mam used to do that—she used to cry continually if something wasn't going right. She used to cry and try and make me feel sorry for her. But it made me worse, it made me more angry.

Sue: I always knew that when he got angry it wouldn't last too long and he would calm down. So I would just wait quietly till I knew, or I'd keep testing the water to see what his reaction was, and I'd think, It's not time yet—give it a bit longer. There have been a couple of occasions when he's got angry and broken a window or thrown a cup, but not at me. I don't think I've ever thought that he would hit me, though I do remember him saying once that he felt like it.

Andy: I've never hit a woman—I'd put my fist through the wall first. When I feel I want to lash out at somebody I just walk away. Usually my anger threshold is very high—it takes a long time to get me going. But if I'm tired it's instant and it's a very volatile situation. It could be a simple little thing that could spark it.

Sue: Then there were knockbacks at work for Andy.

Andy: The truck building company closed and I got a job with a company down the road driving a dumper truck. Before I went to prison I got certificates to drive excavators and dumpers. I stayed there for over two years. I've taken numerous jobs since. If I can't get work I go self-employed as a painter and decorator.

Once when we'd been married quite a few years I relapsed back on to drugs. It was only a bit of whizz [amphetamines]. I was working long hours, 19 or 20 hours a day—so I took it to help me do the work. But even though I'd stopped, I just couldn't contain it. I had to tell Sue.

Sue: It was over and dealt with by the time I knew, so I was able to see that he had fallen, gone against his own principles, but it had stopped. My supply teaching turned into a full-time job and now I've been at the same school for about 12 years. Money was a difficult one, because money was often tight. Those were the only times I felt that Andy resented me being the main breadwinner. I think problems have only come about when we haven't had enough money to make ends meet, and Andy hadn't got any money in his pockets. But Andy always knew that he had a problem with money—he's always been very honest about that—so he would let me deal with it. Another big problem was sex—he'd had a vast array of experience and I'd had none. So to start with I was very, very tense. And then we found out we couldn't have children. That was a very difficult one, a big depression time, specially as it was to do with Andy not me. He had a bad accident once and he wondered whether that was the cause.

There have been times when I've found this very hard, specially at my school when lots of my colleagues were leaving to have children, and when my sister had her two children. But I worked through it. As well as teaching full-time I'm very involved in prison work. We have ex-prisoners living here with us, and we have prisoners' relatives staying when they come to visit them. I go into our local prison to take bible study classes on Wednesdays, and Sunday services.

Another very difficult time came for Andy when he was stopped from going to that prison himself. He used to go in and walk round the wings and talk to the men. But one day he was talking to a guy who was in a uniform with stripes, showing he was at risk of trying to escape. Andy was just having a laugh and a joke with this guy and the officer on the wing. The officer pushed the guy in his cell and pulled the bolt across and Andy, carrying on the joke, pulled the bolt back again. Another officer who was right over the other side of the wing saw what happened, though he didn't know the background, and he reported Andy to the Governor for trying to help an E-man[1] to escape. I think the Governor might have been on Andy's side, but he had to back his men up, so Andy was banned.

There have been times when it's been tough but they have brought us closer together. We have certainly never regretted marrying each other and Andy has said he'd never survive without me. I think the best thing about our relationship is that both Andy and I have a heart for people. We both have the same attitude towards life and now we have someone to share it with. You've got somebody to come home to, whatever you're feeling like. I think that's the best feeling. We give each other enough space—we trust each other enough. Of course we've had lots of arguments but we were always determined never to let the sun go down on an argument, even if it meant staying up all night. If I were asked to give advice to other people in the same situation as us, I'd say the main thing is always to be honest and open with each other, however much you think it might hurt the other person.

Andy: We never had a TV set when we first got married, not for years, so we had plenty of opportunities to talk, and this gave us a good base to build on. Every night we used to play a couple of games of scrabble and we built up a really good relationship where we were able to talk and share our hang-ups with each other.

Sue: At the end of the day we know that we love each other, and we know that it's right with God.

ENDNOTE

[1] A prison word for an inmate who has made escape attempts or who is suspected of planning an escape.

Amanda and Jack

Jack, 42, has been in and out of prison since his teens. He was serving a 17-year sentence for attempted murder when he was attracted by Amanda, 36, an administrative assistant in the education department of the prison where he was held. When Amanda, who was in an unhappy marriage, admitted she felt the same about Jack, she was asked to leave her job. Jack has been out of jail for two years and said he would like to take part in the interview.

• • •

Amanda and Jack, who live in a small flat in east London, chose to come to my home in Kent for the interview. Amanda is a pretty, cosy-looking woman with fair wavy hair and an 'English rose' complexion. Her normally placid expression can become very determined when she is expressing strongly-held views. When she speaks of her love for Jack her face lights up. Her manner is particularly polite and she speaks in a soft, careful voice that is best described as ladylike; she sometimes giggles in a quite girlish way. On the day we met, Amanda was neatly dressed in a pale pink skirt and black top. She is the only child of middle-class parents and since leaving her selective school in Bristol she worked in a number of responsible office jobs before specialising as a medical secretary. Back in 1994 she had been working at her local prison for about six months when Jack declared his love for her in a message on her computer screen.

Jack, a slimly-built man about the same height as Amanda, has dark hair and a moustache. He was smartly dressed in a blue shirt and cream-coloured trousers. The couple appeared to be very much in love and often held hands during the interview.

Amanda's parents were horrified when they heard that their only daughter had fallen in love with a serving prisoner. Her ten-year marriage had already broken down, and she says her self-esteem had suffered badly because of her first husband's controlling nature. She can still appear rather diffident, though having listened courteously to Jack's views during the interview, she was quite prepared to contradict and correct him politely when she disagreed with his views.

When Amanda got her divorce in 1996, Jack was allowed out of prison for their wedding. He was finally released in August 1999, having served eleven years of his sentence.

The couple have suffered considerable financial stress, with Amanda retraining as a medical secretary and becoming the breadwinner to allow Jack to complete a course to qualify as a computer engineer.

• • •

Amanda: One day in the spring of 1994 I arrived as usual at the prison education department where I'd been working since the February, and one of the prisoners, Jack, who was a computer wizard, told me the computer was all set up ready for me to use. I looked at the screen and I saw this message from Jack saying that he loved me! It was deliberately set up for me to find.

I was like, 'Oh my God!' I was absolutely horrified but part of me was flattered too. I didn't respond to Jack at all. I didn't even acknowledge to him that I'd seen the message, but I did report it to my boss. She said, 'Don't take any notice. It's just his way of having a bit of fun. These chaps do these sorts of things to test you out!' Jack had a trusted position in the education department and he used to help me with all the admin I had to do. He was very bright and he was a godsend to me.

Jack: It was a professional relationship, then we developed a friendship. I suppose initially it was a sort of impishness when I wrote that message on the computer screen. I suppose I chose 'I love you ' to put Mandy to the test and to cheer her up a bit, because there was some kind of vibe I picked up from her. Mandy had got a sort of aura about her and I felt very protective of her. If any other inmate might give her hassle, I'd be around. When she first came into the prison, her naivety was one of the first things that struck me. I found that nice but concerning too. This was why I wanted to protect her.

•   •   •

Amanda: I'd been married for ten years by then. I got married when I was 20 and Norman was 23. We had teething problems from the word go. He wasn't physically violent but he was a hard, cold man. He worked in the City as an accountant and we had this exquisite, beautiful, four-bedroomed house on a lake, but I felt cut off and alienated. In fact, ironically, I felt like I was living in a wretched prison. Norman was a control merchant: he was very dominant and he put me down a lot. I didn't feel loved by him at all.

Around the time of our tenth wedding anniversary in June we had a big bust-up, and I began to realise that the only person I wanted to be with was Jack. But I never linked in my mind that Jack was the cause of our break-up, and I don't believe he was. I was having a hard time at home, and I do honestly believe that even if I hadn't met Jack I would have somehow got free, because—again ironically—the prison job gave me a sense of freedom.

I went on working in the prison and I loved what I did. The job boosted my confidence because I was treated decently and people were respectful to one another. I felt totally equal to the guys I was with, and to all the staff. In fact I'm sure I could relate to those prisoners because I felt I was in a prison as well.

•   •   •

Since that message on my computer screen, Jack had never said anything to me about his feelings and I had never said anything to him. We worked together and we had some good chats, and I got to know him quite well on a certain level. We'd never expressed how we felt about each other at all, except perhaps by looks. But obviously I was aware that I was drawn to Jack, so I made it my business to find out about his crime, and I went and had a look at his notes.

Jack: That was inspired by what happened one day when I got very angry. I was doing something on the computer in one of the offices one morning and I was due to do the wages. Mandy came in with the wage books and made some comment like, 'I'd like these done pretty damn quick!' And I thought to myself, Hold on—there's somebody here who's taking me for granted! This isn't my job—I volunteered to do it! So I picked up the wage books, walked back to Mandy's office, dumped them on the desk and walked out.

Amanda: He was *exceedingly* angry— I could see the anger in his eyes and it gave me a bit of a shock. So that was why I checked him out and went to read his notes. As I read them I felt pretty sick, almost not believing it could be the same person I was working with. When I first knew what he had done and the seriousness of it I remember feeling quite dazed and shocked going home that night, and part of me thought, What the heck have you got yourself into here? He had spent most of the past 20 or more years of his life in prison, since he was about 17. He was in and out, in and out, and progressively the offences got worse and worse, and then it resulted in this attempted murder. He was involved in a house burglary that went wrong and he panicked. The victim was a woman. So I was very shocked indeed. But then I think I focused on the man I was working with, and I tuned into his vulnerabilities which I could sense. I felt that Jack thought he'd failed dismally, no-one would ever want him, no-one would ever be bothered with him or give him a chance.

Jack: I did feel like that. It's a feeling that is part and parcel of prison life.

•　　•　　•

Amanda: Then one day in September 1994 when I was having a particularly hard time at home, I was in the office at work and I momentarily put my head on Jack's shoulder. I know I shouldn't have done that.

Jack: That particular day we were alone in the office. Mandy was trying to get to grips with some software on the computer and I was showing her what to do, so we were sitting next to each other. We were just chatting as we normally did, then she just gently leaned over and put her head on my shoulder. Since I'd put that message on the computer screen, that was the first real sign. I was confused for a while and I thought, Do I cross this boundary or not? Because there has always been that invisible line that you do not cross with a member of staff. It crossed my mind to put my arm round her shoulder and give her a little hug. It was tempting but I thought, No—just in case. Then Iris, the boss of the education department, walked in.

Amanda: I am rather amazed that I did that, because I am the kind of person who, whatever work I do, I try to be professional, and in no way would I compromise that.

Soon after that my boss Iris confronted me. She asked me if I was aware of Jack's feelings towards me. Did I think he was attracted to me? I said, 'Yes, I think he is'. She said, 'Well, how do you feel about it?' and I said, 'Well actually—it's mutual.' And I burst into tears.

She said, 'You'll have to go home. I want you to think very seriously about everything over the weekend and tell me on Monday what you feel.' She told me I would be asked to leave my job, but she didn't know when. I think Iris was a very intuitive woman with a lot of experience with inmates, and she was bitterly disappointed that I'd allowed myself to become fond of Jack. But she had the integrity to know that if she asked me how I felt, she would get an honest answer from me.

With Jack I became attracted to and fell in love with the man I was working with, not with the man who'd committed all those crimes. Obviously Iris was aware of his past, and she was probably also aware that he could be beguiling and charming. I think she was genuinely concerned for me—what on earth was I doing?

The next morning I went in as usual and I was told within an hour that I had to go. Iris came and thanked me for all my hard work and gave me a really lovely reference. But she was still concerned that I was going for second best. Two of the women prison governors came to see me and they said they totally believed that nothing unprofessional had gone on and I was given a glowing reference by the main Governor. But all the same it was absolutely horrendous and wrenching: obviously they regarded me as a security risk and I think they felt I had been beguiled by Jack.

Jack: As far as the Prison Service is concerned, an emotional attachment means a sexual attachment. There's an automatic assumption that if someone has formed a relationship, there's going to be a sexual aspect.

Amanda: I remember thinking, How can I let Jack know I'm not going to be here any more? I went to see Stuart, a civilian welding tutor who I think had sensed that I was fond of Jack from the way I spoke about him. I said, 'Stuart, I've got to go today. It's been nice knowing you—goodbye'. Then I took down a lovely picture that Jack had done, and I took it home as a sign to him. I somehow wanted to let him know I was going, and that it wasn't just for a day or so.

Jack: That morning I realised something was up, because Mandy came in and to me she seemed very offhand, and she made some comment about me being a joker. Then in the afternoon there was no sign of her. I picked up on her message, that she had taken the picture. So I also went to see Stuart and he told me she'd left because of me. This came as a big surprise to me—it was all so quick.

Amanda: When I left that day I remember sobbing my heart out. I suppose it dawned on me that I wouldn't be able to work with Jack, or be with him. I'd never had that degree of friendship with any man before and I felt broken-hearted because I didn't know if I'd ever see Jack again.

As soon as I left the prison I wrote a carefully-worded letter to Jack. I told him that my boss had spoken to me and I'd had to leave. I wished him well and I hoped everything would work out for him. I think I said, 'If you ever want to let me know how you're getting on, you can contact me.' I didn't say, 'I love you' or anything like that, but he read between the lines.

Jack: That letter arrived around lunchtime on Friday 21 September, 1994—it's one date I've got engraved on my memory! I sat there and read it and reread it and reread it. It was signed 'Mandy' with kisses at the bottom and it had her address and telephone number. In the evening I phoned Mandy, and from that moment onwards, from 6.30 on Friday 21 of September 1994—there was no looking back.

Amanda: I was really surprised and elated to get that phone call the next day, the day he received the letter, because apart from those couple of kisses I'd put, I hadn't conveyed how I felt. He said, 'It's Jack'. I said, 'Jack! *Jack!* Oh my goodness me!' I was just totally amazed and absolutely thrilled. You could tell by the change in my voice.

After that he used to ring me and we'd have chats, and within a very short space of time we were able to compare our feelings and started writing to each other regularly. The very first card I sent him had the words *Simply the Best—* because I remembered when my boss said goodbye to me she said, 'Don't go for second best'.

I got a letter from the prison authorities after I left and was told that before I could visit Jack I would have to wait till the end of my contract. So I first went to see him on 19 October 1994, a month after I left the prison.

•　　•　　•

Jack: As soon as I walked into the visits room I realised that the staff weren't the normal wing staff. Every one of them was a member of the security staff. Mandy walked in and I noticed a few officers looking at her and then over at me. I greeted her with a big hug, and that was our first real physical contact.

Afterwards I was expecting strip-searches, cell spins, random searches, but I didn't get any of them. Next day I had members of staff coming up to me and saying, 'Saw Amanda on the visit. Nice to see her!' This totally gobsmacked me. It was really nice, that staff were actually congratulating me on the visit.

Amanda: I really used to absolutely eyeball the prison staff when I came in on a visit. I thought, I've done nothing wrong, I've got nothing to be ashamed of—it's not as if it's all about sex in the cupboard or anything like that. It was a strange experience, going in and seeing all these people I'd known in a professional capacity, and now going in as Jack's friend. But I held my head high. I didn't feel ashamed or embarrassed. I discovered later that there had been rumours that I was pregnant. Some malicious person had made up stories about me and I felt hurt to think people would be nasty to me.

But I suppose from the prison's point of view, they felt that if I'd become fond of Jack, he'd want to butter me up and get me to get the keys and let him out. I would potentially be a risk.

Jack and I would discuss whether or not he would get parole—but because of the sort of crime he had committed I thought, I have no problem if he's got to do the whole lot of his sentence. I felt that what he'd done was absolutely horrendous. Because of the seriousness of the crime I wanted him to do the extra time and get it over with, then when he came out, to be given that love and support that he needed to make a go of his life.

The only person I told about my relationship with Jack was my friend Sheila, who used to work in the prison as a counsellor. She'd moved to another prison nearby but she still used to come back once a week and visit the guys in our prison. I was truly grateful to Sheila, to be able to talk to her and trust her implicitly.

Jack: I had Sheila's friendship as well. She used to come in once a week to the education department and sit down and talk. She was a great listener. She was one person you could trust completely.

•   •   •

Amanda: When I told my parents about Jack and about losing my job, their reaction initially was one of horror, though my mother was not surprised. A few weeks after I left my job, she'd come to stay with me because I had to have a small operation. Jack phoned through to the hospital with a message which was brought to me by a nurse. It was a quotation from *Jane Eyre* and that made my mother very suspicious.

I've always been very close to my mother and I could always talk to her about anything. But when I told her about my relationship with Jack, though she wasn't really very surprised, she was obviously very concerned.

With my dad it was really more a reaction of shock and horror. He wanted to know if Jack was the cause of my marriage breakdown and I told him he wasn't. I think it was my grandmother who realised the true extent of how I felt about Jack, even more than my parents. She said to them, 'Surely you don't want to lose her?'

I come from a middle-class background and I'm an only child. My father was a senior architectural technician who worked for the same large building company for 30 years. My mother was a state-registered nurse.

I went to a very, very good Church of England school in Bristol with high standards and values. When I was about 15 or 16 I went through a bit of a rebellious stage, but I'm not the sort of person to be deliberately rebellious or to upset my parents. I suppose that phase went on for about 18 months, but after that I was very close to my parents. They have since been through a great deal of pain and hurt, and my love for Jack rocked the boat for me with them. Now they love Jack as a son, and there couldn't be a better mum and dad in the world, and I love them to bits.

I remember taking my parents into a prison to meet Jack for the first time. It was horrendous. My dad didn't want to comply with the rub-down search and I had to say, 'Well, I'm sorry, Pa, but you'll have to, I'm afraid.' He went through with it but he didn't like it. He is a private sort of man and didn't want another man touching him in that way. My mum didn't find it at all easy either and they both looked as though it was a hell of an ordeal. I think it was really very overwhelming for them and it had an effect on both of them—a lasting effect on my mum. It was so different from anything they had ever experienced. It was nerve-wracking for me too.

• • •

My parents had liked my first husband because he went to church and I suppose you could say he had good prospects. I had a big wedding and they thought Norman was a nice chap, and they had the security of knowing I'd have a reasonably good lifestyle.

But now I'd lost my job and I really was in dire straits. After I told my husband I wanted a divorce I didn't get another single penny from him. It was hard going on living in the same house as him when I had no money, no job and I was absolutely crazy about Jack. I went and rented a room and I had to do bits and pieces of work where I could. One of my jobs was packing dog bones. Then someone said to me, 'Why don't you try and get work as a medical secretary in a hospital?' I went and did a test and I got very good marks and they sent me off to a job in a psychiatric hospital. Since then I've done my medical secretarial diploma which was a huge achievement for me.

Jack: By this time I had done one third of my sentence so I was eligible to apply for home leave. I got the okay from the Number One Governor. He called me into his office one day and told me I could go. As I was leaving the office he said with a smile on his face, 'Don't kill her, will you?' But before I could take the leave I was moved to another prison, and there came a letter from the Home Office banning the home leave.

Amanda: I asked the Governor of the new prison why Jack wasn't allowed home leave and he said that Jack's victim didn't want him allowed out. Then this Governor really thrashed it out with me. He asked me if I was aware of Jack's offence and he didn't pull any punches. I had some very frank chats with him. I did know what Jack had done, but felt that this Governor wanted to protect me. He warned me that if Jack didn't get help to address his behaviour, and if he got out and committed another crime, he would go back to prison for life. The Governor felt, as I felt, that it would be very sensible for Jack to go to Grendon,[1] the therapeutic prison. From what Jack had shared with me I felt that maybe there were things he hadn't resolved. The nature of the offence had been so violent that I felt that if he didn't understand why he'd committed it, potentially—if he was to 'blow'—then I could be killed.

So I had a frank talk with him about it. I said, 'I love you dearly, but I don't want to end up being killed off by you'. I said I believed that there was only this one prison, Grendon, that would probably help him understand why he had behaved in that way. That would lessen the risk of potential harm to me.

Jack: I hadn't addressed the reasons for my crime and I did lots of soul-searching and then I said yes, I did want to go to Grendon.

Amanda: I really did have a fear that I could get killed. I don't hold that fear at all now, because I know that he has had such intensive therapy at Grendon that he understands why he did what he did. Then in 1995 Jack and I decided to get married.

Jack: We'd thought of waiting and getting married when I got to Grendon. But the prison staff warned me that we'd have to wait till I'd been there six months. I'd saved enough money to get Mandy an engagement ring. I sent the money out to a prison visitor and she arranged to bring it in on Mandy's next visit. On the visit I got the box out of my pocket and I said, 'Have a look at this!'

Amanda: I was absolutely thrilled to bits! My divorce had come through in March 1995, but we didn't get married till December 1996. I think Jack would probably have wanted me to marry him sooner, but I needed time. Although I loved Jack without a doubt, I had a lot of anger left, and I had to deal with it before I could marry again. Through counselling I managed to do that, and Jack was a tremendous support to me. Ideally my parents would have liked us to wait until Jack came home and proved himself.

Jack: I actually asked for Mandy's dad's approval and he said, 'Yes, but not yet. Let her get over things.'

Amanda: The reason I agreed to marry before Jack went to Grendon was because I wanted to give him all the support I could give him. I felt he hadn't been given any real love of any depth in his life. So this was my way of giving him all I had. I didn't have any money but I had my love and support, and I knew that he would need someone to believe in him.

Jack: We married the day after Boxing Day, 27 December 1996, then less than two weeks later I was transferred to Grendon.

Amanda: I didn't tell my mother's side of the family about the wedding until the night before I got married, because I really wasn't sure what their reaction was going to be. In fact they believed that I was absolutely stark, staring bonkers and very, very foolish.

On our wedding day, Jack was allowed out of the prison for a couple of hours so we could get married in a registry office. He had to be escorted by the van driver and two officers, but as soon as they came into the registry office building they took off the handcuffs. The two officers were really excellent. They kept their macs on over their uniform. We had a video taken of the wedding and they hardly appeared on it at all.

Jack was wearing a suit and tie and he looked immaculate—the prison had given him the suit and a friend sent him in the tie. The wedding service was very tastefully done, and Jack and I were each allowed to choose a piece of music. I chose an Irish song called *When you were sweet 16*, and Jack had an instrumental called *Wedding*. It was a very poignant occasion.

Jack was incredible. You would never have known he'd just come from prison. He hadn't been out for years, and none of us could believe how he adapted to the situation.

Jack: For a couple of hours I felt free. The registry office was on the first floor and I looked through the windows at the lovely view. They were large windows and they weren't barred. It was one hell of an experience to look out at the trees through windows with no bars after so many years.

Amanda: I just glowed! It was very different from my first wedding because I arranged it all myself. I wore a red suit and a pretty cream blouse and a black band in my hair and a lovely bouquet of white roses. I felt I looked nice and pretty.

It was very intimate because it was just the nearest and dearest. After the ceremony I was allowed a private visit to Jack in the jail. It was totally unexpected and that was the perk of the day. We had two officers as our 'minders', hovering round us and making us coffee, and a couple of the governors came over and congratulated us. We were in this huge visiting area but Jack and I were able to sit and cuddle. After that I went and met up with my family and treated everybody to a very nice lunch in this lovely village pub—but without Jack of course.

The next day I can remember feeling very alone—I really ached because we couldn't be a true married couple, we couldn't go to bed together or be together. I remember that hitting me quite strongly.

• • •

After we married we had to wait another three years before Jack was released. The hardest part was being alone, being lonely. But because we were married we'd made that commitment to each other and I think our love was bonded.

Jack: It was so nice to have this relationship where I totally trusted Mandy. I used to listen to other guys who'd had a phone call or a letter from their wives or girlfriends and they'd say, 'She's going out. Who's taking her home?' and I used to think, I don't have this worry with Mandy.

Amanda: I didn't believe I would ever be unfaithful to Jack. I love him deeply and I couldn't bear to hurt him. There's a much closer bond with him than in relationships I've had in the past. The reason I was able to cope with whatever time Jack still had to do was because I knew he'd done wrong and I believed that he was sorry and wanted to change.

Jack: I think it would have been possible for me to change without going to Grendon, though it would have taken a lot longer and I wouldn't have been so stable. But I don't think I would ever have been any risk to Mandy or to any other woman.

My first venture out of prison after our wedding was in November 1998 when I had an escorted day out and I went from Grendon down to London for the day. We went home to Mandy's little flat in Bethnal Green. I cooked a meal and the officer just sat in the lounge and let us do our own thing. So that was my first escorted visit.

On my first home leave the next month, I made the journey from Grendon to London on my own, and I felt ten feet tall that day. That first night I got toothache and as Mandy's flat was a studio flat there was nowhere to go, so I went out for a walk. It felt so great to be walking round the streets at five o'clock in the morning, with total freedom to do what I wanted to do, when I wanted to do it.

I was released in August 1999. That was when I walked through those gates for the last time.

Amanda: The day Jack was finally released was very emotional. I remember driving like mad to go and pick him up from the prison, and I got delayed in traffic behind a tractor and when I got there he was already walking up the road. I felt absolutely dreadful because I'd said I'd be there as soon as he came out of the gate. Still, it was very emotional driving away from the prison and saying, 'Goodbye prison forever!'. We played Simon and Garfunkel music and we were very, very quiet and very, very moved.

I prayed that Jack would feel at home in the flat and he said he did. The flat was rented furnished and I think maybe that helped because in a sense the place was no more mine than it was his. I wanted it to be cosy and welcoming, to be nice and homely and feminine.

Within a week or two of Jack's final release we went away on our honeymoon and that was a real highlight. We had a lovely little cottage in Devon and it was so nice to be just the two of us, with no phone, and being able to go walking together.

One fear I'd had was that when Jack came out I wasn't sure whether he'd still want to be with me. But when he did come out, we were able to feel comfortable with each other and we've been able to talk things through, We're able to be quite blunt with each other, but I know with Jack that he's not putting me down as my husband used to, even if we do flash a bit with each other at times.

Jack has said he could pick up the phone and make contact with people from his former life, and that was something that alarmed me. But he never has done that, and I've just had to trust him. I believe he sincerely wants to be straight.

When I first met Jack he was still smoking pot, and I had to say to him, 'Look, when you come home there's no way I'm having you smoke that stuff in the house. You can forget that!' I wouldn't put up with him coming home and smoking it. He's said, 'There's nothing really wrong with pot,' but I say, 'There is actually—it's illegal'. And that shuts him up!

Some people at my work know about Jack's background. My boss has met Jack and she hopes he will be able to get work. I have a lot of colleagues who know about him too, though not the details.

The hardest bugbear is the money side of things. Jack's sense of the value of money is different from mine—so if I'm honest, the financial side of our marriage can be a strain.

•　　•　　•

Jack: I've been out of prison two years now, and even though Mandy and I have got a damned good relationship, life isn't a bed of roses. In fact it's one hell of a struggle because of society's attitude to people like me. I will always have a criminal record—it is never spent.

Amanda: Of course I've had to make some sacrifices. When I fell in love with Jack I had to give up my job, and when I left my husband I had to leave a very nice house and everything that went with all of that—like being able to buy very nice clothes.

But it's equally important that Jack has time to do his computer engineering course and to adjust in his own way and not feel pressured to get work, when he needs time to study for his exams and get the grades. At times, if I'm honest, I feel a conflict, because I'd love him to get a job—because it's all so wobbly. But I also feel I've got to give him time and space to adjust.

My dad's side of the family have been fine, but I still feel very sad about my mother's side because they are so prejudiced against Jack. I feel very let down by them because they are not prepared to accept that he's done his time and he should be given a chance. They expect him to prove himself—as if he's on trial or in a probationary period. I have a feeling of hurt and rejection, as if it's an insult to my intelligence and my judgement. I feel insulted that they regard me as this woman who's lost her mind, lost her marbles!

With my mum and dad Jack now has a good relationship, and that's something I'm mega-relieved about. They like Jack and in fact only recently my mum told him how much she liked him. I was very touched by that.

I think I have been an influence on Jack's decision to go straight because for the first time in his life he's found somebody who loves him the way he is. I fell in love with a man I was working with—not because he was a criminal. There was no attraction to me in him being a criminal.

When I fell in love with Jack I felt that here was this man who felt he would probably never be wanted by anybody. He was a wizard with the computer, he could have been Mr Flash Guy. He can read something once and take it in, whereas I'm not like that, I really have to slog. But underneath it all, I'm sure he felt that nobody would ever really want to have him, to be with him. He felt he would never be given a chance. And I thought, You're wrong. You have so much.

Jack was very kind to me in the prison, very helpful and hard-working, and I respected him. I felt he was worth believing in, and he needed somebody to be a good friend to him and to love him. Neither of us has ever regretted getting together. I love him dearly and I wouldn't swap him for anybody.

ENDNOTE

[1] See *Chapter 2*, p. 39 and endnote 2, p. 61. Also pp. 186, 193, 195.

Jan Lamb and Charles Bronson

In 1992 Jan Lamb met the man who was later to become known in the media as 'Britain's most violent prisoner'. Charles Bronson, born Michael Peterson, took his new name from the star of the violent Death Wish films. He has spent time in all three secure psychiatric hospitals—Broadmoor, Rampton and Ashworth—and has been moved around the prison system 150 times because of assaults and roof-top protests. He was given a life sentence in February 2000 for taking a prison teacher hostage in the spartan Woodhill close supervision unit (later condemned by prison inspectors and now closed). When he met Jan in a pub nine years ago he was between sentences and they had a nine-month relationship before he was arrested for a post office robbery. The pair have remained close ever since, though Charles Bronson has since married and changed his name again.[1]

When I went to interview Jan she had just moved to a small, quiet village in the south-east of England. Born in north Devon, she lived for many years in Halifax where her only child, a daughter now in her 20s, was born. Later she moved to Kent to be near her close friend, the late Reggie Kray, then in HMP Maidstone. Her exceptionally soft voice is accented with different regional overtones, as is her singular use of certain words and phrases.

Jan loves the peace and quiet of the country but alternates it with parties in London and the North where her social circle is the criminal underworld. In many ways Jan fits the old cliché of the 'gangster's moll' which, she says, she has often been called. With Kate Kray, ex-wife of Ron, she recently started the first UK *Gangsters Moll* web site. She has her own site and she desktop-publishes her own headed writing paper with the legend *Angel of the Underworld*.

Jan, still glamorous at 52 despite having to wear gold-rimmed spectacles, is a statuesque woman with long, blonde hair. The day we met she was wearing skintight denim jeans and many rings on her manicured fingers. Her flat was quite sparsely furnished: in the living room was a silver-grey Dralon suite and a TV she said she rarely watches, preferring the radio and the company of her affectionate tortoiseshell cat, Zia .

Only the dozens of photographs on the walls gave any clue to Jan's character and unusual social life. Her 'rogues' gallery', as she calls the display, showed her in the company of some of Britain's most notorious gangsters including the Krays, 'Mad' Frankie Fraser, Howard Marks and Dave Courtney.[2] Jan attended the funerals of both Kray twins. There were also photos of actors like Mark Bannerman and Mike Greco who play the di Marco brothers in the TV soap opera *EastEnders*. Jan loves to recount anecdotes about her encounters with the infamous, though she is careful not to give away any secrets. She refers to her friends as 'the chaps' and 'our lot'.

But behind the 'moll' stereotype is another even darker story: Jan's childhood sexual abuse by her brutal stepfather. In that abuse lies the clue to her early involvement with violent young gang members, whose company she sought for protection and perhaps as a family substitute. This pattern has continued throughout her life. Repeatedly during the interview she spoke of the respect and protection she has always been given by the criminal fraternity. Now rather an isolated figure, she has suffered serious health problems in the past and a recent illness saw her alone in her top-floor flat, dependent on benefits and on support from social services, sustained only by phone calls from 'the chaps'.

•　　•　　•

I met Ron and Reg Kray by accident. I were 17 or 18 at the time and I'd moved from Devon to the East End of London where I were working in a shop that sold school uniforms and sportswear. I shared a flat in Walthamstow with a girlfriend and we'd heard about this good club, so we decided to go there. As we got to the door, two chaps came out and one of them said, 'Are you two young ladies going in here?' We said we were.

'Oh no you're not! It's not good for ladies.'

'But we're going there for the dancing!'

'Not in that club you're not! There's too many fights and things! We'd rather you go to..' and they told us another place.

My friend and I had no idea who these chaps were but they had this 'Don't mess with me' sort of look about them. And I liked that. Later we discovered we'd met Reg and Ron Kray.

About a year after that I met their brother Charlie and I came to be really good friends with all three brothers. They were always there, they always looked out for me and my friends. It's a sort of protection if you're in a set with people like that. Of course, two or three years after I first met Reggie, he were sent to prison.

•　　•　　•

Even before I met Reg and Ron and Charlie, my friend and I used to go round with guys who were all carrying a piece on them—some sort of weapon. I felt great with them. I felt at ease.

That all started when I were about 14. I started mixing with 'the wrong crowd', and I were told, 'You shouldn't go about with them! You're going to end up a gangster's moll!' There was some lads at school who used to carry chains in their pockets and had knuckle-dusters and I used to hang round with them, because I felt safe. I thought, They've got knives and baseball bats in the boots of their cars so nobody'll touch them. I'm safe.

I needed to feel I were protected from my step-father. My mother's marriage to my father broke up when I were a year old and she married a man known as

Shaw. He were a really evil man and he used to beat my mother. He'd start drinking Special Brew when he got up at six o'clock in the morning.

When I were about five or six my mother tried to get away from Shaw. She went off with me to Dawlish and got a job looking after someone's children. The family put us to live in a small caravan in the garden and I remember waking up with spiders on my face—the place were crawling with them. We stayed with my nan for a bit but then Mum and Shaw got back together again. I suppose she stayed with him just to keep a roof over our heads.

Shaw would punch us and grab us both by the throat and pin us against the wall. At one stage we had a house at the top of a hill about a mile from my aunt and uncle and I've lost count of the amount of times that I used to run down the hill in the pitch dark to my aunt's and I'd bang on the door and shout, 'He's beating my mum up again!' Other times when I were little I'd run out to the police station in my nightie, even in the pouring rain. The police used to put their jackets over me, take me back the house, take Shaw and keep him in a cell overnight, then let him back home in the morning. Whenever they came he'd always say the same thing: 'Sorry, mate, I'm tired. I been driving all day and I had a few pints. It's all right, everything's fine.' And my mother'd be sat there huddled up, terrified.

There were one time when Shaw were laying into my mother, really punching her in the chest and she were losing her breath. In those days we had coal fires and I remember running over and picking up the poker and beating him on the back. And I remember thinking, 'I can't stop!' And I couldn't. My hand kept going with this poker on his back and I remember thinking, I'm going to kill him! I *want* to kill him! Then he turned round, grabbed the poker off me and punched me in the face, knocked me flying. Sometimes I think that if I had killed him it would have been worth it.

My mother's said quite a few times over the years that I did harden as I got older and I think it's because of the things I've gone through and seen my mother go through. People used to say to my mother, 'Jan's very quiet, isn't she?' and my mother would say, 'Oh yes, she's very quiet, but if you get on the wrong side of her you'll wish you'd never met her.' I've often said to my mother and my friends, 'I wish I'd been like that years ago.' Ever since my daughter were able to understand what I was saying, I always brought her up so she would be able to look after herself. I taught her that her fist is for punching, her feet are for kicking, her knee's for kneeing someone, her head's for head-butting. She's had a few problems but she's never been in any trouble with the police. She's 20 now and she's just got married.

•   •   •

My mum worked hard all her life, in old people's homes and mental institutions as well as looking after children. But that meant I were left alone with Shaw, which were frightening. I were only about seven, but he used to pull his trouser zip down and then he'd grab me by my hair at the back of my neck and make me suck him off. I used to tell my mum but she'd always say,

'Don't tell anyone. We don't want the neighbours pointing the finger at us. We'd be in the papers!' I used to get very angry but I understand more now how she must've felt at the time.

The abuse affected me at school as well. Some teachers were men and when you're small and sitting at your desk and a teacher comes and stands beside you and you turn round, your face is level with his zip. And of course because of Shaw that frightened me. I always used to think, What's he going to do?

My mother eventually told Shaw's parents what he were up to and they had a go at him and threatened him with the police and his dad actually punched him. But like my own mother, Shaw's mother said, 'If you get the police involved it's going to be in all the papers and everyone'll be pointing and saying, "That's that family! That's that little girl!" ' Back in those days people didn't like to do that sort of thing. But it meant I grew up thinking, My mother didn't do anything about all that.

As I got to be a teenager I started rebelling. Like if we went on a day out, the camera would come out and my mum would tell me, 'Stand next to Shaw so I can take some photos'. I just wouldn't and that would cause enormous arguments. And then he kept saying, 'You should call me Dad'. I'd say, 'I'll never call you Dad. You're not my father and you never will be! My father's a perfect gentleman!' I never knew my father but I had this image of him being the perfect gentleman who would have sorted Shaw out if he'd known what were going on.

Things changed when I were about 14 because I think my mother must have said, 'Enough's enough!' She left Shaw for a man called John who were a country and western singer. He had a really good family and a lot of friends. When Shaw found out where we were living he turned up. I heard his voice and I was terrified. But John and his family and friends chased him off.

We moved up to Halifax, and that were when I started hanging out with the wrong crowd. I think I purposely looked for the bad lads with knuckle-dusters and knives because they could protect me from people like Shaw. There were gang fights but when our lads were fighting, us girls were always told to go into one of the cafés and stay there. They kept us out of things like that.

But at 16 I left school and I left home and went to work as a nanny in Middlesex, and eventually I got the job in the uniform shop. Again I got in with guys who carried weapons and again I felt safe.

•　　•　　•

Once I'd met up with Charlie Kray I started going round with him and his crowd instead. I didn't actually know they were involved in anything illegal, though at times I used to think to myself, There's something going on here. One minute we'd all be sitting chatting away, then the next minute another chap would walk in. All of a sudden there'd be a nod of the head, others would go over to him and they'd sit whispering. Then it were back to the chatting again. And I'd think, I wonder what they're up to? But I can always remember feeling safe within that crowd, and I can remember thinking, No-one can harm me now. If Shaw was ever to come near me now, he'd soon get sorted out.

The Krays had a lot of respect for women. All the gangsters were like that. They only ever did things to people of their own kind, when it was a case of either the others would get hurt or they'd get hurt themselves. It's like in the case of Ron with George Cornell. George were threatening to kill Ron so it was a case of Ron or George. It were the same with Reg and Jack McVitie.

I never lived off them or any other men—I always worked. After the shop I worked as a nursing auxiliary in a London hospital till I was 28, then I worked in a shop that sold evening gowns, where I worked my way up to be head seamstress. Then when I was 30 I fell pregnant with my daughter Michelle. Her father was half-Italian and I'd been with him about a year and a half. But he were a mummy's boy so I just walked away from him.

I went back to Halifax to have the baby and got a house up there. My mother looked after Michelle and I got a job running a taxi office, which I did till Michelle were about eight. My mum knew all about my friendship with Reg and Ron and she never worried about me because she knew they were the old school type who didn't believe in hurting women or children or elderly people. She met Reg once, when he were at Gartree. She went and visited him in the prison and he were a proper gentleman to her.

•　　•　　•

It were about this time that I visited a prison for the first time. The son of a friend of mine got remanded to prison and because I had a car I used to take his mum to visit him.

I suppose the next time I visited a prison were when I went to see Ron in Broadmoor. One of the chaps said, 'I'm going to see Ron. Want to come along?' Ron were sentenced in 1968—then he got taken from the prison he were in and put in Broadmoor because they said he were insane. But Ron knew exactly what were going on. Ron were always a mile ahead of everyone. He would sit very quiet but his eyes were all over the place, taking everything in. He knew exactly who was who and what was what. He knew what was going on where.

Broadmoor were dismal, a cold unfeeling place, not like a hospital at all. But Ron were Ron—he were just his usual self. I think he liked to show that he were cheerful, to keep his visitors happy. He were that type of person. That first time I went, some very weird people would come up and ask, 'Who's this, Ron?' He would just look at them. His eyes said it all: 'Go away'. He'd only introduce me to those he got on with. Some nurses and doctors really respected Ron.

•　　•　　•

One day when Michelle was about ten her father contacted us and wanted to see her more often, so we moved up to Falkirk to live near him. I stayed there three years but I didn't like it and I spent every weekend travelling back south to visit Reg in prison, and to see my other friends. Michelle only saw her father about five times the whole time we were in Scotland and in the end, when she were about 13, we moved down south again and lived in Maidstone where Reg were in prison. He got someone down here to help me find somewhere to live.

When Reg married Roberta[3] and she got a house in Maidstone, Reg asked me if I would go and see her and welcome her to the area. But Roberta didn't want to know any of us, right from the start. I went to the door and asked if she'd like to come for a coffee or a meal, or a drink down the town, but the answer was no, no. So I just turned and walked away. To be honest, I think the reason they married was that Reg thought he would get a better chance of parole if the prison thought he was going to get married and settle down when he got out.

● ● ●

It were coming up to Christmas 1992 when I first met Charlie Bronson—he'd been released in the November. He'd been out of prison for a period of time in the eighties as well. I were sitting in a pub on the Isle of Sheppey with a male friend of mine. We'd been there for five or ten minutes when in walks Charlie. I'd never met him before but I knew who he was from his reputation. Even then there were a lot in the press about what a dangerous person he were. Charlie didn't have his beard in those days though he did have hair on his head and he had a moustache. I think he were wearing jeans and a tee shirt or jumper.

He knew the man I were with, and when he came in he noticed his friend and he came over and he says, 'Who's the bird?' That's typical of Charlie! My friend introduced us and Charlie went and got some drinks and came and sat with us. I thought he were really nice. I said to my friend, 'He's not at all like they make him out to be in the papers! He's pretty sweet and he's got a brilliant sense of humour.'

Charlie said to me, 'I'm not long out of the nick. Doesn't that bother you, sitting here with me, knowing the reputation I've got?'

I said, 'I never go by what other people say. I like to find out myself what the person's like.' As we were leaving Charlie asked me for my phone number and he said, 'I'll give you a ring some time and we'll have a chat!'

He phoned me up the next night and asked me if I fancied going out for a drink. So that's what we did. We just went to the pub and that were it. We just hit it off and it went on from there. We got into a sexual relationship very quickly and he's written about that himself in his own book.[4] But it weren't just that—I think it were just the way he is. He sits there so relaxed and he's got such a tremendous sense of humour, just like mine. We spoke about when he were inside and the brutality that went on. Things he had seen, people he had met. He'd just finished serving a sentence for armed robbery—I think it were about seven years. He knew I knew Ron and Reg. He and Ron were good mates, because at one time they were in Broadmoor together and they got on really well. Charlie had a lot of respect for Reg as well.

Charlie had a lot of notoriety then and it's got worse since. The press like to make it as bad as they can because they want to sell papers. He had beaten some inmates up and people have said to me since, 'He even beats up other prisoners!' But they don't realise that it's paedophiles that he's beaten up. I never told him what happened to me as a child. Now I feel I can talk about it more but even two or three years ago I couldn't sit and talk about it. I would just burst into tears. But I always feel safe with Charlie and at the back of my mind I think it's probably because I know he detests people like my step-father. Even now, if anyone tells Charlie someone's upset me, he'll get a letter in the post to them straight away.

Charlie and I had a good time in those nine months he were out. We used to walk along the beach on the Isle of Sheppey. He had a caravan there and I stayed with him in it with my daughter. Michelle thinks the world of Charlie. It were a big caravan but it were a bit cramped with the three of us. But Charlie's very good with kids.

We'd go out for a drink or a meal. We like most kinds of food. Charlie likes steak though I'm not so keen on that myself. I like Chinese and Indian food and I love Italian food. My mother knew all about Charlie though she never met him. She just said to me, 'If you're happy that's fine.' After all I was in my forties by then. Charlie loves his own mother—he loves the ground she walks on—and I found her very nice.

By the time Charlie went off to rob a post office and was arrested and sent back to prison I'd moved out of the caravan. Charlie's a real keep-fit fanatic. I don't mind that because I like guys that keep fit but with Charlie it were just too much. It were exercise, exercise, exercise all the time. I said to him, 'I've had enough. You've got all your keep-fit stuff in here and it's getting beyond a joke.' So we left, but we're still very close friends.

I didn't know he was back in prison till a friend told me. I wasn't really surprised. The circle of friends I've got, some of them have been in and out so often that you just accept it. When I heard I sent him a letter saying, 'Sorry to hear you're back inside.' He wrote back and we've kept in touch from then on.

Charlie's had a very bad time in prison. In 1993 he got attacked by ten officers and they broke his fingers and did all sorts of damage to him. Then his father died and the officers went into his cell and beat him again and they shouted at him, 'Your mother's dead!' though she weren't dead at all.

Charlie's got a bad reputation but he's got a heart of gold and he's just a terrific guy. He'll do anything to help anyone. He'll go out of his way to phone guys up to help. But I don't think we'd have stayed together even if he hadn't gone back inside. I think we'd always have been close friends like we are now, but we'd have gone our separate ways. We've got too much in common I think, that's why.

•   •   •

About a year ago I started the Bronson Mania fan club. By that time I'd been writing to Charlie for the six years he'd been back in prison. We've got quite a lot of members now and I've started doing a newsletter. Charlie and I also write a page for a magazine that goes round the pubs and clubs in Sussex. He does a piece one month and I do it the following month. Charlie wrote a book which sold brilliantly. I think it sold about 10,000 copies in the first week or so. I don't think all of this glamorises crime or influences young boys to try and copy guys like Charlie, because most of the members of his fan club are Charlie's age or even older—and you have to be over 19 to join.

I'm writing a book myself, about miscarriages of justice. I had a book of poems published in 1996 as well.[5] A lot of my friends who read it thought the poems were sad, and one of them said to me, 'These poems are about you, aren't they? They're about your life.' At first I said no, but then I admitted it.

I attended Charlie's trial in February 2000 at Luton Crown Court. He got lifed-off [given a life sentence] for taking a hostage, but now he's got a new solicitor who's working on his appeal. Charlie's really confident. He's only got five years of his previous sentence left to do, and in every letter I get from him, on the bottom he writes, 'I'll be out in five!'

• • •

I felt it was very sad that Charlie went back to prison after those nine months outside, but I would *never* ask him why he did what he did. It's just not the done thing to ask. There's definitely a certain code and I've brought up my daughter to respect it: that if you hear anything you don't ask questions. I think it's the way the guys show their respect for us. If they are up to something they want to keep us out of it.

Although Reg and Ron and Charlie and others have been my friends, I'm not part of what they do. The guys have their own thing and we girls are not part of that. We're part of the social scene every day. But if the guys are going off talking in corners, that's up to them. We just don't ask questions and they don't discuss things with us. It's a guy thing. It's nothing to do with us if they're going to do something.

Sometimes when people know who I am they can react in very different ways. When I first moved into this flat my new neighbour called in to see if he could help me, but when he saw my 'rogues gallery' of photos on the wall he just made an excuse and went off.

Then you get people who can't be friendly enough. Some people do want to know all about me because I've mixed with famous people—actors and singers and people like Reggie and Charlie. But to me they were just normal friends.

I last saw Reg about a year ago but he phoned me a week before he died. He were quite breathless but he said not to worry about him. He could only get a few words out at a time but he said to me, 'Keep your chin up, don't let anyone use you.' He asked how his little princess was—that was my daughter—he always used to call her that.

He died at seven o'clock on the Sunday morning and I got a phone call straight away from two of our lads that were with him—one of them were holding his hand when he died. After the funeral I think I felt at ease, I feel that now Reg is free and him and Ron and Charlie are all together again. He's not suffering any pain, he's free from the system.

After Reg went, Charlie Bronson said to me, 'Don't be too upset, Jan. Ron and Reggie and Charlie, they all loved you, you know.' Weren't that a lovely thing to say?

Postscript: My next meeting with Jan was at the wedding party of Charles Bronson and Saira Rehman at the club owned by Jan's friend Dave Courtney (see footnote 2). By this time Jan's health was much improved, she had moved into the centre of Maidstone and was, as she put it, 'in full circulation again'. She is now excited about the number of hits on her own new web site and is busy sending out signed photographs and adding a merchandising page to sell *Angel of the Underworld* calendars.

Drawing sent to Saira Rehman (see next interview) © Charles Bronson 2001

---

[1] See next interview p. 153.
[2] A legend in his own lifetime, Courtney is said to be the model for Big Chris, the character played by Vinnie Jones in the film *Lock, Stock and Two Smoking Barrels,* and to have been advising Lord Archer how to avoid trouble in prison. See also next interview.
[3] See p. 15, endnote 2.
[4] *Silent Scream,* Mirage Publishing, 1999.
[5] *Feelings,* Avon Books, 1996.

Saira Rehman and Ali Charles Ahmed
(previously known as Charles Bronson)

Saira Rehman, 31, a Bangladeshi divorced mother, attracted much media interest when she announced her engagement to Charles Bronson, allegedly the UK's most violent prisoner, before even meeting him. Photographs of their wedding on Saira's birthday in June 2001 were on the front pages of most national newspapers. I interviewed Saira a few days earlier.

Saira lives in a small, neat, terraced council house in a Luton street in the heart of the Asian community. It is furnished very simply in a modern, Western style with plain, painted walls and just a few pictures, including several of her fiancé, cut out of newspapers. The most striking is a large cutting of him in his boxing days—the one Saira saw when she fell in love with him. Another framed cutting shows him with his mother. Saira is a very attractive woman, slim and pretty, with shoulder-length dark hair and a vivacious manner. She was wearing a simple and elegant shalwar kameez in lilac and grey. She was brought up in a well-off family near Dacca but her strict Muslim mother forced her into an arranged marriage at 19. Her husband, a British Bangadeshi man, brought her to England to live with his family eleven years ago but became violent. After the birth of her daughter she divorced him and since then has supported herself and her child by working in a women's refuge, as a translator, and by dancing at parties.

The interview took place in Saira's kitchen, a stylishly simple room with plain blue walls and transparent chairs. She cooked a delicious curry and we were joined by Sami, Saira's ten-year-old daughter. Sami seemed a friendly, happy child with her mother's vivacity—only once dulled for a few moments when she described bullying by pupils at her school because of her mother's relationship with a high profile prisoner. After the interview Saira showed me the traditional Indian wedding dress she would be wearing.

A few days later—at 9.30 a.m. on Friday 1 June 2001—she wore it at her wedding at HM Prison Woodhill. All the newspaper reports the following day commented on the bride's beauty and expressed amazement at her choice of husband.

On the wedding evening I attended their party, held at a club in Woolwich owned by Dave Courtney,[1] former associate of the Krays. Free drinks flowed as the club filled up with dark-suited gangland hard men and a two-piece band blasted out music. Saira, still in her wedding sari, sat quietly at a table in the corner with her new mother-in-law. None of her own family attended. Sami, now wearing jeans instead of her bridesmaid's skirt, mingled with tattooed men in black and helped herself to snacks. There was a flurry of excitement when veteran campaigner Lord Longford arrived, frail but mentally alert despite his 95 years.[2] Later in the evening the party moved to an upper room and Longford sat on a red chair in the middle of the dance floor—a surreal figure bathed in swirling reflections from the mirrored ball spinning above his bald head as he made a speech about how much he and everyone else in the room loved Charlie Bronson, and how wonderful it was that now he had a beautiful bride. Saira stood beside him, smiling demurely. The quiet bride in the sari seemed a million miles away from the feisty woman I had interviewed just a few days earlier.

•　　•　　•

Five years ago I saw Charlie's picture in a local newspaper. I had never heard of Charles Bronson before, because I usually read Asian newspapers. The article was in there because Charlie was born in Luton.

I remember it was the school holidays so my daughter Sami was in the house. I was having my breakfast and reading the newspaper and there it was—Charlie's picture. It was very small, just head and shoulders. That's why I get annoyed when people these days ask me silly questions, like, 'Was it physical attraction?' How could it be, when I couldn't even see him properly?

In most newspaper pictures of Charlie that I've seen since, he's shown wearing dark glasses—but in that picture he wasn't. It was the well-known picture of him in his boxing pose, but I couldn't see the pose—all I could see was him from his chest up. He had very short hair and there was something about his eyes in the picture. I couldn't take my eyes off him. I could physically feel something *here*—where my heart is. I can't explain anything more than that.

Then I read the report, so I knew why he was serving his sentence. It said that Charlie had done an armed robbery. This was about five years ago—long before he took a prison teacher hostage.

Over the next few weeks I dropped that newspaper article in the bin several times and I closed the kitchen door. But I always went back again and picked it out of the bin. That picture really got to me.

What's strange is that I never fall for people like that. I believe in falling in love and having something mentally and spiritually special. I've always had it in my mind that there was somebody out there for me. I met so many people, but I couldn't put that imaginary picture to any of them—not till I saw Charlie's photo.

•　　•　　•

I had a very happy childhood in Bangladesh. I had three brothers—two older and one younger, and I was my parents' pet. Back in Bangladesh, if you've only got one daughter she gets most of the attention. I was very, very close to my dad—he died nine years ago. He used to be a politician, then he was a college professor, then he was the manager of a garden where tea was grown, not far from Dacca. That tea garden was the most beautiful place on earth.

So from an early age I was very privileged. We used to have lands in the countryside where rice is grown. We were quite rich and my dad used to give away a lot to the poor, specially at Eid time—that's a festival a bit like Christmas. A few days before that time my dad would be buying clothes for the poor and paying for their food —not just for his employees, for anyone who came along—and he used to give money to every single charity there was. Poverty was everywhere and we were taught by my dad to be sympathetic to people who were less well off, or to people who had problems.

My mum didn't work—she was a traditional Muslim woman. My dad, my older brother and I used to be very close, but I wasn't very close to my mum. She wanted me to cover myself up from head to toe from a very early age and to learn the Koran and become very Muslim. She didn't want me to mix with boys. She wanted me to finish school and then get married.

I went to a girls' secondary school and I did very well academically. But I always wanted to become a dancer from a very early age. I've always done what I believed and followed my instinct, and up to now I haven't made any mistakes. But when I was a teenager I wasn't allowed to train as a dancer. I only started to do my dancing about six years ago since I came to England.

After the girls' secondary school I went to a mixed college, but I was only there six months, then my uncles and my mum decided—and they influenced my dad in this—that it was time to get me married off. All I wanted to do was to have some freedom to study and become somebody, but they put a stop to that.

After they stopped me going to college, I had to stay at home for a year. That year, from the age of 18 to 19, is a time I'll never forget. I was forced to wear head-to-toe cover by my mother, and she would watch me all the time so that I didn't speak to any boys.

We've got this middle-man system in Bangladesh for arranged marriages, and he brings all the proposals to the girl's home. I had so many proposals at that time, including several from America, a few from England and one from Austria.

I would be dressed up nearly like a bride and they would take me into a room and one of these middle-men would come along with the boy's mum, and she had to have a look at me to see if I was good enough for her son! It was as if they were going to the shops to buy sweets! One day the boy's mum actually pulled my hair to see if it was a wig! She had a look at my nails to see if they were false or not! And she looked at my fingers, to see if I'd got six fingers or something! It was disgusting.

The husband my family chose for me was a Bengali man of 26, living in England. His family presented him as being very well off, with his own house and his own restaurant.

So my first wedding, when I was 19, was in Bangladesh. My husband came over and we got married, and as long as I live on this planet, I'll never forget the trauma, the nightmare of it all. I got a marriage made in hell, and getting out of it was like trying to escape from a nightmare. Every single minute of it I hated.

Seven months after the wedding we came to this country and that was quite devastating for me. I couldn't speak one word of English. We came to live in Birmingham at first and it turned out that his whole big family all lived in one house. There was no privacy at all.

A couple of months later I found out that I was pregnant, and after that my husband used to disappear for weeks at a time. I used to ask his family where he had gone and they'd say, 'Oh, he's working in some restaurant earning money.'

One day when I was seven months pregnant he came home and he pushed me down the stairs for forgetting to put sugar in his tea. Now I know he was ill at that time—I found out later he had manic depression—but he was a right bastard to me.

Luckily the baby wasn't harmed and she was born safely two months later. But I'll never forget the three nights I spent in hospital. Nobody was there with me and I didn't speak a word of English.

The morning after the birth my husband came to see the baby. With him were three police officers—I didn't know why but in fact it was a child protection team. They took me into a room and all these people asked me questions. I had given birth to a baby the day before, so you can imagine my mental and physical state. A translator was sitting holding my hand and she told me that my husband had abused his niece when she was nine years old, two weeks before he went to Bangladesh to get married to me! His family thought he was doing it for the sex—so they took him to Bangladesh to get him married off!

Within 12 hours I had spoken to a solicitor and I said, 'Give me the options for divorce.' I never went back to my husband. I went straight to a women's refuge. My ex-husband has tried to get access to Sami but as long as I live, as long as I breathe, I'll try not to let him do that. I know he's biologically Sami's dad—but no—she is mine.

•   •   •

At first I lived in the refuge after Sami was born, but three or four months later I had a council house and social services supported me. I still couldn't speak any English, but I used to have English friends round to my house and I picked up English quite well. I suppose I must be good at languages. I speak three other languages—Bengali, Hindi and Urdu. I also understand Punjabi and I can speak it a little bit. I understand Gujarati but I can't speak it. I've got temporary work as a translator at the moment. I do the translating in a community group.

About six years ago, when Sami was four, I moved to Luton to get away from my ex-husband. Every time he was out of mental hospital he used to hassle me, and once he turned up at Sami's school. So I changed my name and moved here.

During this time I had two other relationships, normal healthy relationships. Despite my experience with my marriage, I've never ever felt bitter towards men, because I've always believed there is somebody out there for me. That was my strongest belief ever.

• • •

I didn't tell anybody how I felt about Charlie after seeing his picture because I felt stupid. At that point I actually thought to myself, Either I'm being stupid, or there's psychologically something seriously wrong with me, because I've never done anything like this before—I'm a very realistic person. I still didn't really know anything about this guy Charles Bronson. But by then I knew that I was in love with him.

So I decided to try and contact him. I never knew anything at all about prison or prisoners before. In my work I came across a lot of women whose husbands were in prison, but I had never been in a prison and I knew nothing about prison life. I also used to work with a dance group in London and the manager was a prison officer. So I said to him, 'This lady in Luton, she wants to write to Charles Bronson. What's his address?' But the prison officer said the 'lady in Luton' was stupid to want to write to a guy like that.

So I thought I'd better try other options. I must have rung so many places to find out where Charlie was. Then one day another newspaper article said he was in Whitemoor Prison in Cambridgeshire. I rang the prison and asked how I could write to Charles Bronson. They said I could write to the Prisoners' Location Service and they would ask his permission—so that's what I did.

Meanwhile that prison officer I used to work with said, 'Charles Bronson's got his own web site. Why doesn't that woman in Luton look at that?'

I'm not on the Internet, but a week before Christmas 2000 I went to stay with a friend in London who is. One night at half past four in the morning I was sitting in front of the computer with my friend. She was falling asleep and saying, 'Look, why are you so crazy about this guy?' I lied to her, and I feel bad about that, but I didn't want to tell anybody, because I thought they would think that I'd gone crazy. So I said, 'I'm on this project—it's to do with charity'.

Then suddenly there was his picture! I just couldn't believe it. I was sitting there crying—I don't know if they were tears of joy. I thought, It's him! It's the man that I was looking for all those years! I had his blown-up picture in front of me on the computer and I was asking him, 'Why didn't you find me? Why did *I* have to find *you*?'

From the web site I got to know Charlie's whole story. Here I was at half past four in the morning, reading everything, and I just thought how unfairly he had been treated.

I stayed with my friends for a few more days and every single night I went to the web site and I just looked at Charlie's picture. In my mind I would actually talk to that picture. There was a mobile number there to ring so you could get to hear Charlie's voice. Every single night I heard that voice, God knows how many times! The phone bill was enormous!

I was thinking, I know this is right! I'm 30 years old, I have experienced all this crap in my life—and it makes you an experienced person, when you've been through so many things. You know what you're doing—and I kept thinking, This is the one for me. Whether he likes it or not, I'm just going to get it out of my system and tell him, because where I come from—what my culture, my values taught me—is that love is unconditional. If someone came to Bangladesh and they were hungry and I was sitting with a plate of rice, I wouldn't think whether I was hungry or not myself. I would offer that person my last bit of rice. That's my culture. So I didn't expect anything from Charlie.

•　　•　　•

On New Year's Day I came home and I found waiting for me a letter from the Prisoners' Location Service with Charlie's prison number and I wrote to him—four pages.

I put in everything—who I am, where I come from, my marriage, Sami, the two relationships I had, and that because of Charlie being in my mind all the time, these relationships had to stop.

I put my mobile number in the letter and a picture of myself wearing black shirt and trousers, and on the back of the picture I wrote, 'Not that I'm trying to impress you. I just want you to see the person behind this letter.'

Charlie got the letter, and he said later that he read it at least 100 times. He tried to ring me that same day, but my mobile was switched off. Then he tried again the next day but he couldn't get through.

Two days later I got a letter back from him—a four page letter like mine. First he was trying to bring some sense into me, as if to say, 'Why are you trying to get involved with a man in my situation?' Then he asked me, 'Next time you write, can you send me a picture of you, close-up? There's something about you, Saira, I just don't know what.' He gets hundreds of letters. Women send him half-naked pictures but he just puts them away. He told me a long time ago that they are just weird women. He saw immediately that I was different.

•　　•　　•

The first Saturday morning in January I was asleep downstairs. I decided I was going to sleep downstairs because that's where the phone was and I had this gut feeling that Charlie was going to phone. And that Saturday morning at 9 o'clock he phoned for the first time—it was the happiest day of my life.

His voice was a very, very deep and sexy and he said, 'Saira?'

I said, 'Yes? Who is this?' Then I said, 'It's Charlie, isn't it?'

He said, 'Yes, it is! Finally! Three times lucky!'

I just didn't know what to say for a few minutes, and then he said, 'How are you? Are you okay?' And I said, 'Yes, I'm all right now, yes!' And then he said, 'How's your daughter?' and we chatted about Sami. He was very easy to talk to. It was like we'd known each other for years. We were on this phone call for about 15 minutes.

Then he said, 'You took three years, Saira! You took three years to come to me!' Because it was three years since I first saw his picture.

A few letters later he wrote, 'I know what it is. It's you I've been waiting for all my life. All these women I've known, the other relationships I've had—nobody has ever had that power over me like you do!'

At times he does get angry in his letters. He feels really, really angry about what I had to go through in my life. It's almost like he lived with me through it all. We've got this very, very strange connection between us. It's like two bodies with one soul. Sometimes we end up saying the same thing in our letters and we don't even know that we're posting it at the same time. It's amazing. We write every day—sometimes it goes up to ten pages. In fact we could talk hours and hours and never stop! What we both say these days, is, 'We have to come back again and again and again, because one life is not enough to love you'.

I tell him the details of my life and we also argue in the letters—silly little arguments like any couple will do. So our relationship is not all about fantasy as people seem to think. We actually live a bit of life in the letters. Our recent argument is that I want to have a baby boy, he wants a little girl! We even argue over the names!

• • •

We applied for me to visit Charlie in prison from the beginning, when I started to write to him, but first I had to go through a police check. The police intelligence officer came to my house to interview me. He was quite a genuine person and he said, 'I'm not here to judge you', and he never asked me if I knew what Charlie had done. He checked my passport, everything in my background, to see I wasn't some terrorist. Because I married a British citizen I am a British citizen too.

It took a couple of weeks for us to get security clearance and I actually met Charlie for the first time on the 4 March this year [2001]. By then I had met Tracey, who was his secretary. I went to the prison with her and her husband because there were a lot of press people outside waiting. That first visit Charlie wanted me to wear black, so I wore a black dress and trousers—English clothes.

Charlie is still in solitary, but they let him come out to the visiting room. People have asked me millions of times, 'Were you nervous? Were you scared?' I'd say, 'Why? I couldn't wait to see him! It's like I'd known someone for years and I hadn't seen him for a long time.'

It felt like ages, waiting and waiting. Then I walked in first and there he was. He was exactly as I expected. Straightaway he put his arms round me and I put my arms round him at the same time. Normally it's a quick hug the first time you meet someone. But he just didn't let me go and I didn't let him go. I gave him a kiss on the cheek, but then he turned round and kissed me on the mouth, a proper kiss. The officers didn't stop us because they had checked my mouth and hair everything on the security check.

I didn't even notice the prison officers at first. That particular day there were 12 officers in there, and he was the only prisoner. It was a room a bit bigger than my kitchen, with all these officers and cameras, cameras, cameras!

The visit lasted an hour and a half. All the way through the visit, even though Charlie was talking to Tracey about business, he was holding my hands and looking at me. After half an hour Tracey said, 'We'll leave you two guys together and we'll disappear.'

Since then I've been to visit Charlie seven times. He's allowed two visits a month, but last month they allowed us an extra visit.

Sometimes I get looks from the officers. I wasn't born yesterday and I can tell these looks mean, 'Who the hell do you think you are?' I look back at them as if to say, 'Who the hell do *you* think you are?' But mainly they are nice. Quite a few of the prison officers get on well with Charlie and I feel they're on my side.

•   •   •

A month and a half after that first visit we both said at the same time, 'Okay, let's do it—let's get married!' Charlie didn't get down on bended knee to propose or anything—he would have loved to, but in there he's not allowed to move much because of security. But we'd decided to marry even before we met. I think on our fourth conversation, about a month after I started writing to him, he said, 'Do you know what, Saira? One day we will get married.' I said, 'How do you know? It's amazing'. So from then on it was an understanding that we would get married. He asked Tracey to send him a catalogue of Indian gold rings. He wasn't allowed to have the ring in there so he asked me to bring it in and wear it on another finger, so he could put it on my ring finger.

He was actually going to propose to me in public on the day he went to the court in London for his appeal—on 3 May 2001. He was going to propose inside the court room—something that nobody's ever done before! He was going to shout out in the court room, 'Will you marry me?' But they never allowed him to go into the court. He was gutted—he was very angry. I went to the court but I didn't see him because they wouldn't allow it. The newspapers took a picture of him outside. He just wanted to see me in the cell in the court, in the dungeon, just for five minutes. I tried to go in with his barrister but the court officer wouldn't let me. But I knew by then why he wanted to see me.

Charlie chose the day for our wedding—my 31st birthday, 1 June. He asked me, 'Saira, would you wear traditional Asian wedding clothes?' and I said, 'How did you know that's what I would have chosen myself?'

By this time Sami knew about Charlie. Sometimes she reads newspapers, and one day she saw his picture and she said to me, 'Mum, I think I feel sorry for him'—this was before she knew I wrote to him. So I said, 'Sami—that guy—I actually wrote to him and I like him'. Sami and I are quite frank—we talk about almost everything. She said, 'Mum! You never told me!' And then she said, 'Is he going to like you back?' I said, 'I don't know—let's just see. We might just be friends—because you can't force somebody to like you.'

•   •   •

I've lost a lot of my friends and relatives in Bangladesh because of Charlie. They don't want anything to do with me any more. It's because of the media—the story is everywhere, even in Pakistan. Recently some Islamic Fundamentalists said that if this had happened in Pakistan they would have stoned a woman like me to death.

I lost a lot of friends, but that proves who are your real friends. All I've got left are two very close women friends. At the moment they're far away so you can imagine how lonely I get. Most of my other friends don't want anything to do with me any more. They told me they think that Charlie's some kind of monster and I'm making the biggest mistake of my life.

Before I spoke to my mother myself she'd heard crap about me through the news headlines—as if Charlie is some sort of woman killer—and she actually became ill and ended up in hospital. But when I rang the hospital and told her the truth from the beginning, she was happy for me. Two of my brothers are happy too, but the brother I brought over to England wants nothing to do with me now.

Sami does get hassle at school. When all this about me and Charlie first came out in the papers, 14 or 15 kids at once started to pick on her. But she's a very confident kid, she does karate and she can look after herself. The school haven't shown any understanding or help. They have got such a big attitude problem with me. They had actually suggested to me that I should become a parent governor, and now they don't even say hello to me. I went to them and said Sami was getting hassled and they said, 'We are trying our best'.

I also lost my job. I'd been working in a women's organization for about five years, mostly voluntarily. One day I went to work as usual and the whole management committee had got together and they said, 'We think you should leave for 12 weeks.' They said it was because they were supporting the victims of domestic violence, and this was to do with Charlie's history. But Charlie never ever harmed any women and children in his life. He's even got his own children's charity, called Bronson's Children.

•　　•　　•

It's true that I'm not going to be together properly with the man I love, but I come from a country where I've seen women every day whose husbands have been living abroad for years. That's part of my culture and that gives me strength. I wouldn't choose to be apart from Charlie, but I am strong enough to do it. I have said this in every single newspaper interview and they just don't publish it.

The other thing is that sex isn't everything. It's not just about physically being with Charlie. There are all the letters, and I go and see him, I speak to him. I'd rather be like this and be the happiest woman, than give up Charlie and be unhappy.

Since we went to the court Charlie now does have the right to appeal—which means that he might go for re-trial, or he might even automatically get his life sentence reduced. He hasn't killed, he's not a paedophile.

When he does get out he wouldn't break the law again. He's said to me so many times that he wouldn't—and he's a man of his word. I am never, ever going to question Charlie and ask, 'Why did you do those things?' He has paid for all the crimes he has committed. He says to me, 'Saira—I would even work on a building site, just to be with you!' And that means a lot to me. I would do anything to make sure that he doesn't go back inside.

•　•　•

We've been together now about five months. If people asked me whether that was long enough to get to know a person before you marry them, I would say to them, sometimes you live with a person 20 or 30 years and you still don't know them.

What do we have in common? What *don't* we have in common! We've got almost everything in common, except he likes dogs and hates cats and I hate dogs and I love cats. We've had an argument about that already.

Of course we have our silly little arguments as any couples do. But as Charlie said to me the other day, 'Saira, the good thing is that we never let an argument become a problem. We finish it, and we have understanding and respect'. I love Charlie the way he wants to be loved. I understand him the way he wants to be understood. That's what we share.

I have been through so many pains and Charlie has taken half of those pains away. In one of the newspaper articles he read how I spent those three days in the hospital when I was having Sami—the loneliest three nights of my life. He wrote back and said, 'Don't worry, babe—when we have our baby, I'll be there with you every single second, holding your hand, no matter what.' I felt like it didn't hurt any more—after all those years.

When I read his books, and when he tells me some of the things about the past, I can take his pain away too by being sympathetic and by the words I use.

•　•　•

At the wedding they will let Sami come into the prison, and Charlie's mum's going to be there, and his cousin and some close friends and Tracey and her husband. Charlie has got his mum and his one brother—he had another brother who died.

Charlie's chosen to wear all black—a black suit. It's not going to be a religious ceremony because I'm from a Muslim background so I wouldn't want a Christian ceremony. We can't have a Muslim wedding because Charlie would have to become Muslim. He said, 'We'll just do the normal registry wedding now.' But when he comes out he wants to have a proper Bengali traditional wedding.

We don't get any special rights after we're married and no prisoner gets conjugal rights[3]—Charlie said that would be like a dream come true. But it's not going to happen and it really doesn't matter. Our relationship and our beliefs are beyond that.

I don't get any financial help from Charlie because he doesn't have any money. There's such a lot of crap in the newspapers about that. He said, 'Saira, do you know how much I've got?' I said no and he said, '£2.50!' If there is any money between us it'll be me working hard to earn money for our future.

We are going to have a wedding cake that Charlie ordered out of a catalogue. But the prison are not providing a knife to cut it with. The reception party after the wedding has been arranged by Charlie and Dave Courtney somewhere in London. There'll be 150 people there. Of course Charlie can't be there, and that'll probably be the hardest thing I've ever done in my life. But he wants me to do my dancing and later on he will get to see the video. We are only allowed 12 wedding guests at the ceremony inside the prison.

I don't know if I'll be accepted by all Charlie's friends who have known him for years. At the party I'll find out. I met Dave Courtney already and he's such a nice guy and so down to earth. I haven't met Charlie's mum yet but I've spoken to her on the phone. She's a very nice lady. She wrote to Charlie saying she hopes for me and her to become close friends one day.

But at the end of the day, as Charlie says, 'I just simply don't care. If people can't accept us, they can all leave us.'

• • •

A week after this interview, Saira and Charlie were married in a blaze of publicity. The following day Saira, wearing a dazzling traditional Indian wedding dress in red and gold, had her picture in all the national newspapers and television news programmes. I spoke to her a few days later.

• • •

The wedding was lovely. I had to wake Sami at quarter to four in the morning so we could be at the prison by 8.30. A car came to collect us and take us to the home of one of Charlie's friends where I got myself dressed in my traditional Indian wedding dress with all the jewellery as Charlie wanted. Sami helped me do my hair and fasten my blouse hooks and put on my bangles. The wedding was at 9.30 a.m. and we went off in a huge cream stretch limousine covered with pink and white ribbons. A TV camera crew were with us all the time, and they travelled in the car with us—they are making a documentary about us.[4] But obviously they weren't allowed into the prison.

There were a lot of reporters and cameramen waiting outside the prison and they kept asking me how I felt. I just said I was very happy. Then some prison officers came out and one of the governors came and introduced himself and said he would be helping me and the guests, and they took us all through the gate without making us show our passports or other ID. The governor even arranged for a car to take me, Sami and Charlie's mum across from the main prison to the special unit where we were getting married, though it was only a four-minute walk.

I must say the prison staff really put themselves out for us. They had made the room really lovely by decorating it with vases of flowers everywhere. There were about 16 officers in the room but they kept well back and didn't hassle us at all. They gave me a cup of tea as I sat waiting. I wasn't nervous about the wedding at all, though I was nervous about meeting Charlie's friends and family because I thought some of them might not accept me. Five minutes later the other guests came in, then Charlie arrived. That was the best part of the whole day, because Charlie was there with me.

He looked so handsome—he's a very good-looking man though you can't tell that from the newspaper photos. He's 48 but he looks about ten years younger. He was wearing a black, collarless shirt and black trousers. He still had on his dark glasses. Everyone thinks they're sunglasses but really they are prescription glasses which he has to wear because he can't look at the light, as his eyes have been made weak by spending all those years in solitary confinement, and the prison fluorescent lights are really bright and they hurt him. But even through his glasses I could still see his eyes and he looked so happy as we made our vows. There were two lady registrars and they were really nice. The main registrar asked us if we would like to hold hands and we did—we held on to each other tight through the whole wedding. Then he kissed me. Then he sang me a song—*What a Wonderful World*—and the officers took some photos.

At the reception the prison put on a really good spread for us—all sorts of sandwiches, biscuits and small cakes, and fruit juice—obviously we couldn't have anything alcoholic to drink. We had the three-tier wedding cake that Charlie ordered out of a catalogue. It was white with lemon roses all round it. Charlie said he wanted to save one of the tiers for when our baby is christened. Then he showed his strength by picking up the whole table with the cake on top to move it into the middle of the room so the officers could take pictures. One of the tiers was taken out of the prison by Charlie's friends so we could cut it at the evening party later. We had about ten guests and we were all allowed to stay till about 10.30, then the others left, leaving me and Sami and Charlie's mum alone with him for another two hours, which was lovely.

When we came out of the prison there were even more press—it was amazing to face so many flashing cameras. I must say I got annoyed when they kept asking me very embarrassing personal questions, and I got really upset when one of them trod on the back of my dress and tore a big piece out of it. That really was too much! One of Charlie's friends' girlfriends had to sew it up.

We went back to Charlie's cousin's house which was full of people and the TV camera crew filmed all the time. I couldn't eat anything at all. In the afternoon I was allowed a two-hour visit alone with Charlie. He was a bit tense at first but he relaxed later. We both felt relieved the wedding was over and we felt closer than ever.

In the evening there was a big party at the Manhattan Café in Woolwich— the club owned by Dave Courtney—and loads of Charlie's friends were there, including Lord Longford who made a lovely speech about Charlie and me. The whole evening was videoed so Charlie could see it later, and towards the end of the evening I got changed out of my wedding dress into a red and black costume and did one of my traditional dances.

Now I've been married exactly two weeks. Last Sunday I had my first visit to Charlie as his wife. The officers were all very nice and respectful to me. Charlie took off his dark glasses on the visit, though the light hurt him. At the end he said it was the best visit he'd ever had. I felt closer to him and more in love with him than ever.

Postcript: I remained in telephone contact with Saira in the weeks following her wedding. The media interest continued and sometimes she was very upset—for instance when one Sunday newspaper reported that only 18 days after the wedding, the marriage was already on the rocks and Charlie was seeking a divorce, Another ran an interview with Charlie's first wife saying he was terrifyingly possessive. She was quoted as saying she was not surprised at rumours of a divorce and of Saira she said, 'All she wants is to become famous by being linked to him. I knew he'd realise sooner or later.' Saira ignored the reports and continued visiting her husband. In October she announced that he had decided to become a Muslim and had taken her own father's name, because his previous name was being exploited and identified with violence. His new name would be Ali Charles Ahmed and the couple were hoping to arrange a Muslim wedding ceremony soon.

But in February 2002 the *Mirror* newspaper reported that Charlie, now in HM Prison Durham, had banned his wife and other family from visiting him, saying their visits were 'mental torture', both for his relatives and himself, and that he would not see them again until he was freed. Saira confirmed the story. 'He is on closed visits and we can't touch or hug,' she told me. 'But we still write every day, and if that's Charlie's way, I have to go along with it'.

ENDNOTES

[1]   See endnote 2, p. 152.
[2]   Lord Longford died just a few months later.
[3]   See pp. 61-62, endnotes 12, 13 and 14.
[4]   *Charlie's Angel,* shown on BBC2 in November 2001.

Jenny and Kevin O'Neill

Jenny, 52, works as an educational welfare officer for an inner London borough. In 1988, she was working on justice and development issues in the Diocese of Southwark and visited Wormwood Scrubs prison, where she met Kevin O'Neill, 17 years her junior. The couple fell in love and married four years later in HM Prison Hull. Kevin was a Category A prisoner, jailed for life in 1986 for murdering a 19-year-old youth with whom he shared a London squat. On the night of the murder there were nine people in the squat including Kevin and his girlfriend. Kevin had reading and writing difficulties and had been in trouble from a young age. On arrest he made a statement to police but it was not recorded and no solicitor was present. Though he withdrew the statement before the trial he was found guilty of the murder. Now aged 35, he has spent half his life in prison, the last 16 years for a murder he has always maintained he did not commit. Jenny successfully fought for him to be removed from Category A status, and continues to run the campaign for his case to be referred to the Court of Appeal.

Jenny was divorced from her first husband. She brought up her four children—all now adults—in two rooms and then in a small overcrowded flat until the family was rehoused. Her small, bright kitchen has a window looking out on some of London's most popular tourist attractions. The sitting room is simply furnished with a few splashes of colour, but the room is dominated by two stunning oil paintings by Kevin, to whom Jenny has now been married for eleven years. One shows a single white dove, the second two doves flying together. In the first picture the dove represents Jenny coming into Kevin's life. In the second, painted for their first wedding anniversary, the two doves represent the couple together. Kevin's work has been exhibited in London and in his native Scotland.

On the day we met, Jenny had just rushed back from a long day at work—a job where she tries to help parents get the support and education they want for their children. She was wearing a mid-calf-length dark skirt and turtle-neck jumper, and with her fresh complexion and smiling face, framed in her fringed elfin-cut hair, she looked much younger than her years. She was welcoming and hospitable and spoke articulately and with animation about her relationship with her husband. All her adult life she has fought for causes: she is in the Peace Movement (she was particularly active in the eighties) and helped with the Birmingham Six campaign.

●　　●　　●

In June 1987 I got a three-year appointment as the justice development worker for the Anglican Diocese of Southwark. I was asked to attend the first Birmingham Six appeal on behalf of Bishop Peter Hall on the days when he wasn't in attendance. Bishop Hall had been a rector in Birmingham at the time of the bombings, and he'd had concerns about the whole issue from the start.

After the failure of that first appeal I got invited to Mass in Wormwood Scrubs, and that was how I first met Kevin, the first Sunday I was there, in March 1988 in the prison chapel. He was playing his guitar and I was sitting up at the front. There was a rapport—our eyes did meet briefly that first time and the chemistry was there from the start. Then it came to the point in the service where you have to go and greet people and offer each other the sign of peace, so there was a direct contact.

Kevin was 23 and I was coming up to 40, and I was desperately aware that I was so much older and that I had four kids. The youngest was eleven and my marriage annulment had come through four years earlier. So though I was attracted to Kevin I didn't know whether to get involved. I used to go into the Scrubs on Wednesdays as well as Sundays and always on the Wednesdays there were other younger women there, and I was actually jealous when I saw them talking with Kevin. It's the only time in my life I can remember feeling passionately jealous like that.

•   •   •

The knowledge that Kevin was probably an innocent party was there from the start. I already knew Richard McIlkenny, one of the Birmingham Six. Kevin was on the same wing as Richard and later on, after the Scrubs, he was held with IRA prisoners. Because Kevin had an Irish name, it was wrongly assumed by some people that he had been jailed for terrorist offences. Kevin is from the west of Scotland, but his family were from Ireland and he was a born Catholic.

Kevin wouldn't have found it very easy to talk to anybody about his case— he would always have found it much easier to write. But he probably said enough to Richard, and then he came up to me and said, 'Richard told me to tell you about my case.' He does not find oral communication easy, and he gave me a very garbled account, so I had no real sense of the case, and I didn't know anything about legal work. But I said I would work on the case, and I meant that. Kevin had always had people who would say they'd do things, and then nothing would happen. Because of his oral communication problems, he wasn't easily going to be able to establish a relationship based on the kind of limited meetings you have in prison. Instead I found I was getting to know him through his paintings, which is a quite legitimate way because he is a totally visual person. That November there was a preview of an exhibition of all his paintings at St James's, Piccadilly, and he wanted me to go to it, and my children went with me. Some of the paintings expressed something of his spiritual life, but a lot were political and social comments. There was stuff on prison and homelessness, because he'd been on the streets before he was in prison.

•   •   •

Kevin comes from Paisley near Glasgow. He doesn't come from a criminal background, but his family was living in overcrowded circumstances. One brother has now fallen foul of the law but it wasn't a family where you'd assume their children are going to get into trouble with the law.

Kevin's birth had its own dynamics and its own consequences for the family. He was two months premature and he had a distressed birth, so for his first ten weeks he was in a hospital in central Glasgow. His being slow in developing affected family life, by his mother's account. He was the fourth child in quick succession. His father had suffered a motorbike accident at 19 years old, and his mother had specific problems with literacy skills—she is clearly an uneducated but intelligent woman who has passed her strong visual thinking skills to Kevin. Sometimes I say I think he is on an autistic continuum and there's a contrast between what he is able to communicate orally and his written ability.

Before he came into prison on a life sentence, Kevin had been in borstal. Then he was a young offender on probation and should have been in Paisley, but instead he did a runner and was in Ireland with his girlfriend. He came back to Scotland but by then his parents had split up and suddenly he'd got nowhere to live. Then he was rehoused on an estate in Barrhead, which is where you don't want to be if you're from Paisley. So that was the other reason why he ended up in London in the Elephant and Castle area.

At the Old Bailey in May 1987 Kevin was convicted of murder and sentenced to life imprisonment. His co-accused were two young French guys and they were convicted of ABH and jailed for four years. The judge recommended that thought be given as to whether Kevin should ever be released.

Though there was a fight at the squat it wasn't Kevin's fight, and Kevin was with his girlfriend when the victim was killed. As a neighbour who knew Kevin from childhood said, 'Kevin's a lover not a fighter.' Later I knew what she meant! He hadn't dabbled in drugs before he arrived in London, then he tried heroin once and he nearly died. At trial he made the association between the words *heroin* and *addict* and agreed that he was a heroin addict. But in fact it was drink that was the problem. Where he's got anything on his record for assault, it's for assaulting police officers when they're trying to arrest him when he's drunk. But all these labels, including the label *psychopath*, are in files which are still following him.

•   •   •

In the March when I met Kevin in the Scrubs he was still a Category B prisoner. But just after I met him he got his tariff, and I became aware of the fact that he'd got this incredibly long sentence. He was told, 'Come back in 17 years. We'll give you your tariff then, but don't ever expect to get out.' In Scotland then, the average life sentence was ten years, so he wasn't anticipating facing 30 years and he didn't realise the enormity of it. He didn't become Category A [high security] till the July—I presume because of the length of his sentence, and because of the trial judge's letter. I think the judge had gone along with the psychiatric evidence—and who needed a prosecution if you'd got a defence solicitor who stood there and described Kevin as the most malignant personality he'd ever met! The psychological assessment of Kevin at the time of the trial suggested he was suffering from a personality disorder and was under the influence of drugs.

In the July, after he was made a Cat A prisoner, Kevin came up to me and asked me to work on his case—that's probably what prompted it. Being Cat A meant that he was watched and limited and everything was recorded. It obviously built up and up until it erupted over something that had nothing directly to do with his case, and the following January he set fire to somebody's cell. That day was a Wednesday and when I arrived at the Scrubs that evening for a prayer group, it was very late starting because of the fire, and because of Kevin being taken over to the block. Then he was ghosted out[1] to Albany prison on the Isle of Wight and I didn't see him for a year. Ironically, the Sunday before that I was sitting in the church and I saw him come in and I had a sense of knowing potentially where the relationship could go.

•   •   •

Although on the face of it I come from a very different background from Kevin's, there are some similarities. We are both of rural stock where parents or grandparents have moved into urban settings. I was brought up in a small cottage in Dorset. My father worked as a commercial traveller for a builder's merchant and my mother was at home until my teenage years when she did some part-time work in a doctor's surgery.

When I was about 19 I went to work as a volunteer with a group ministry in Glasgow. I was baptised an Anglican and brought up as a Methodist, though later I became a Catholic. I've always had a faith, a spiritual life.

I joined CND and the Labour Party. It feels like I've been rebelling in some kind of way all my life. It feels like I've always known that the air you breathe or the water you drink is political, and that the personal and political are inextricably linked. There was a strong strand of the anti-establishment in me.

At the age of 21, in the summer of 1970, I went to work on a play scheme in the Loyalist Shankhill Road in Belfast and that's where I met my first husband. He was 25 and involved in community work.

We lived in Belfast for four years and then we came to London. He had been in a seminary but he'd opted out of it and was studying for a degree in divinity. I supported his studying, then I got a grant from the local authority to do a one year full-time course in pastoral theology. We had three children by then and we all lived in two rooms in a condemned Church Commissioners' property.

Maybe my first husband was somebody who should never have married. He was educated by the Christian Brothers and anyone who knows about them has spoken about the absolute violence. There was the threat of violence in our relationship, but I felt I was psychologically rather than physically abused, and my self-estimation was plummeting.

In the eighties I became heavily involved and very active in the anti-nuclear/peace movement. At one point I was Co-chair of Christian CND and I had to be very careful about being arrested because I was having a lot of hassle with the father of my children. Had I gone to prison I would never have met Kevin, as they wouldn't have allowed me into the Scrubs.

After we'd been together seven years I left my husband. By then we had four children aged between two and seven. When I left I was desperately wanting somebody who could love me—I wanted to be loved.

I did a variety of jobs, then I worked in Southwark for four years with unemployed teenagers, using my qualifications for the first time in a long while. It was soon after this that I got the job with the Diocese of Southwark as a justice and development worker, and that was how I ended up at the Birmingham Six appeal which led to me being invited into the Scrubs and meeting Kevin.

●　　●　　●

When Kevin was moved to HMP Albany from the Scrubs I started writing to him. I never wrote him long letters because I sensed he would have problems. There was an openness in my letters but Kevin never properly picked it up. I got some lovely letters back, full of good, poetical thoughts from an innocent prisoner, but Kevin's not somebody with whom you can expect to have the kind of written correspondence where it grows. It's very much of the moment, so if you ask a question in a letter you won't necessarily get the answer.

While Kevin was in Albany he was very much around people involved in miscarriages of justice. He spent months in the segregation block. There have periodically been complaints that he takes himself off towards the seg, and I think that's because it's the only place where he can get away. I'm more worried when Kevin's on the wing than when he's locked in his cell, where he becomes more creative.

●　　●　　●

During that year while I was writing to Kevin I had an on-and-off relationship with a journalist, which lasted from February to November 1989. I saw Kevin again that same year when he came through the Scrubs on his way to the special unit in HMP Hull. He looked terrible, very thin and withdrawn.

I knew Kevin was going to Hull, and I said to him, 'Look, if you can get me cleared by security I will come up and visit you.' I knew how difficult it was to get to see people who were Cat A prisoners. He must obviously have put in for my clearance, because in March I got a visit from Special Branch.

They rang up to let me know they were coming, and the Special Branch officer who came was actually very helpful. He was surprised to find that Kevin wasn't an IRA prisoner—he'd just heard the length of the sentence and the Irish name and put two and two together. A lot of people made that assumption. This guy said, 'Now, why do you want to visit?' I thought, What shall I say? I'm not a relative. I'm still going into the Scrubs and as a visiting professional you're not supposed to write to prisoners and maintain contact. So I said, 'Usually I wouldn't, but I felt in this case that it might be a useful thing to do.' So he wrote down, 'For reasons of moral and religious welfare.'

I got the clearance and it was sent to Hull and it sat there for months. I wrote and told Kevin that the Special Branch man visited me, but that didn't mean to say I was cleared. I still didn't realise all Kevin's problems of communication so I just thought, He probably doesn't want to see me.

I was involved in publishing some poems for Richard McIlkenny as part of the campaign and I sent this book of poems up to Kevin. Then he phoned! That morning I had just arrived back home having stayed with the journalist overnight, and I thought, That's it—the relationship's finished. Then Kevin phoned and said, 'Thank you for the book!' It's interesting the way things come together because Kevin had never phoned before! I asked about visiting him and it emerged that the prison had the clearance but they hadn't sent it over from the main gate to the special unit.

I went to visit him there just before Christmas 1990—I hadn't seen him since January 1989—and we talked about his painting and about his case. Kevin had stopped painting in Albany because the prison started analysing his work in a very negative way. Because there's a surreal element in some paintings they made assumptions that he was into drugs. Then somebody in Albany must have thought a place where he might get help is Hull. He spent two years in the special unit there, where he had his own studio space for a while and did a lot of painting. His work appeared in exhibitions in Hull and he did some work for Amnesty International.

I've always been very aware of coming out of the prison afterwards in that special light of late December. It was a cold, crisp day in Hull and I remember thinking—knowing—that I was going to have to work out how I felt. I knew I was committed to getting this guy out of prison, but I was going to have to sort out my own feelings too. The visit was totally platonic, but now I know that from the time at the Scrubs, Kevin was aware of how I felt.

●　　　●　　　●

Over Christmas 1990 and early New Year after I came back from the Hull visit, I worked my way through my reasons to see if I was prepared for this relationship, and if it was right. I didn't want to make a mess and enter into a relationship which was unequal or wrong, and I knew I shouldn't enter it for the wrong reasons—the 'need/care' reasons. At that time I remember reading a book called *Women Who Love Too Much*.[2] It was about women who enter different kinds of need/care relationships and thrive on difficult circumstances—such as someone whose parent is an alcoholic and she marries an alcoholic because she thinks she can sort him out and change his life. Maybe I was just trying to tell myself that I did know what I was doing.

I did send Kevin a very platonic Valentine card, then after Easter 1991 I started visiting him fortnightly. Because Kevin was Cat A and in the special unit, there weren't a lot of visitors. It was unusual for there to be two visits going on at the same time, and I was aware that there were only us and two officers in the visits room. Kevin and I had a hug at the beginning and that was it. I was there for moral and religious welfare, wasn't I! There was a chemistry there but Kevin wasn't articulating it and neither was I. It just sort of hung in the air. I suppose now I can look back and realise there were lots of reasons, including the lack of trust. And the last situation Kevin needs to be in is stuck at a visits room table with somebody. It's the most distressing place for him to have a relationship, because you have to sit and talk for hours.

I can remember feeling, He needs to know that I am actually vulnerable and not strong, and that I am accessible. I'm 17 years older than he is, so I was very aware of wanting us to be equal. He'd experienced so much of being thought 'the stupid one', 'the lesser one'. I had to spell this out in a letter, and I suppose it did sink in.

Then he went off to Long Lartin— Hull sends prisoners off to see how they cope in a mainstream prison. When he was there it meant we were away from the setting where the officers were watching all the time.

When Kevin got back to Hull, it was wonderful because we just clicked—it literally just happened! Once the relationship had changed, it all happened very quickly. Later Kevin said to a friend, 'It just kind of happened. I never actually proposed to her!'

The physical relationship only began when we'd decided to marry. One minute we were just formally together, and then suddenly I was sitting on his lap! You're not supposed to do that and it was a great shock to the officers—they were so taken aback at the speed with which this relationship had gone from one thing to another that they didn't immediately say, 'Stop!' The good thing about Hull was that we had more closeness at that stage than we might have had elsewhere.

In those early days there were times when we able to have a close physical relationship in the midst of everything. The very first time we properly touched, in Hull, we suddenly realised how compatible we were. We had reached a point where we'd decided we were going to get married and then we had this physical thing—wow!

•   •   •

We got married in September 1991. Kevin made all the wedding arrangements. Had I appreciated his sequencing problems and information processing problems I might have said or done one or two things. Some people from the wing missed the ceremony as Kevin had verbally shifted the time of the wedding from the time arranged! In a lot of prisons you had to get married on a Monday morning[3] because they had that as the time for weddings, but we got married one afternoon. We didn't have a religious wedding because the chaplain at the Scrubs advised me against it when I went to him and suggested it. He said, 'It's a long process and the chances are you won't get permission.' With Kevin's background he reckoned it would be quite difficult to get married in the Catholic church, and maybe we should just have a civil ceremony.

Kevin's best man was Ricky, his friend from Paisley who'd been visiting him regularly. Ricky's younger brother and my younger daughter, Hannah, were the other two guests and as they were under 16 they didn't have to be security-cleared. Hannah had already come up to Hull with me. I thought, If this relationship is going where I think it's going, I want to know how Kevin can relate to somebody other than me. They got on fine and it was lovely to see them together.

My eldest daughter Ruth was between school and university at this time and as she was abroad she thought she was the last one to know about my relationship with Kevin. In fact I was writing to her and telling her, so she actually knew more than the others. But it wasn't until a month or so after we married that she realised that I was happy and the marriage was good for me. She was the last of my children to meet Kevin, about a year later.

My son John was about 16. He has a lovely dry sense of humour and when I told him about Kevin he said, 'Does that mean I might wake up one morning like this?' and he made a slit-throat gesture! My other son would have been 18, and he was very much, 'Oh well, if Mum's involved in a relationship she won't be worrying about me and I can get on with my life.' They were protective of me but I suppose they had a sense that their lives would have moved on by the time Kevin would be released.

My father had died just before I met Kevin. I think my mother was worried—a serving prisoner! Why couldn't I do something nice and respectable? She and my brother both wondered, 'Why on earth?' My brother actually voiced it by saying, 'Why do you actually have to *marry* him?' and I said, 'Because that's where the relationship is at. It can't be anything else.'

Our wedding was a really nice ceremony. The registrar was a woman who had worked in the Hull special unit as a teacher, so she was quite relaxed. There were so many people I'd never met. We were only allowed two guests from outside, but there were also the people from the education department, Kevin's wing and another wing. I wasn't sure if we'd have any photographs, but in fact one of the officers was determined to do it properly. He got people into groups the way photographers traditionally do at weddings. At least Kevin wasn't handcuffed, whereas if we'd got married outside there would have been guns, the lot.

I wore a Paisley pattern suit which I'd only ever worn once before, and Kevin wore a suit which I brought in. After the ceremony we had a reception. The cake was made by the education department and they'd laid on the food. It was a small unit and they didn't have many weddings.

We also had the pleasure of walking round the exercise yard. It was a lovely early September afternoon and we were surrounded by people shouting out of all the windows. We were walking round hand in hand and they didn't expect a woman to be there, but they didn't shout anything obscene! Once I would never have been able to stand up and kiss somebody in front of everyone, but I got used to it. Then everybody else went away and Kevin and I had an extra hour together.

•   •   •

In May 1992, eight months after our wedding, Kevin was moved to Long Lartin prison in Worcestershire. In every prison Kevin goes to, his cell is his protest. He generally never cleans it and in some prisons he's never even unpacked. Whereas other people make their cells homely and comfortable, he will not, because it would make him part of the system. This started when he was made Category A, because that was an injustice on top of an injustice. For the same reason he won't do any offending behaviour courses and he's never entered any of his paintings for the Koestler Prize competition for prison art, because he won't recognize himself as a prisoner—he won't say, 'I am a prison artist'. He's been in prison 16 years and all this is as true now as it was then.

I don't seek confrontation with Prison Service officials. I deal with situations that arise. I'll write to governors and deal with the Home Office and Prison Service Headquarters and I'll be very straight and fight my way through. But I've rarely had personal problems with officers. Maybe that is partly because Kevin doesn't enter into confrontational relationships with staff, although he will stand his ground on his innocence, and the way he deals with his cell annoys the system. But generally he has got on okay with wing staff. Of course, some officers absolutely hate him and the Irish issue has always impacted on him. Kevin stayed in Long Lartin till April 1993, then he was moved to Whitemoor prison where he stayed till December.

That year my eldest daughter went through a life-threatening operation to remove a large acoustic neuroma, and Kevin was very, very supportive. That has had its whole dynamic and its effect on my life. It didn't help my campaigning, but it did mean I had to be much more measured.

Kevin was then in Full Sutton prison till October 1994, in the segregation unit. The reason he was in there was partly because we made love in the visits room toilets! We'd already had sex on one of the visits in Hull. One good thing about prison visits as they were then was that you could end up with long foreplay so to speak! Since then of course the whole drugs issue has meant that there has been less and less physical contact, but at the time Kevin was absolutely determined that it was going to be possible and he was delighted that he proved it. I warned him, 'Look—there'll be repercussions!' And the repercussion was what led him into the Full Sutton seg.

This is how it happened: I went out to the toilet first and then there was just a moment when there was a distraction, so Kevin got to the toilet after me. At the time there was a certain laxity and anarchy about Full Sutton and you can see how it happened. In fact there are numerous children who have been conceived in the prison system—it's not that unusual. We managed to make love in six prisons—Hull, Full Sutton, Long Lartin, Whitemoor, Gartree and even in Parkhurst we managed until security got tighter there. Maybe we should be in the *Guinness Book of Records*, along with a lot of other people, I'm sure!

In Full Sutton that was a quickie! We were locked in the toilet and no way could they get us out. They realised Kevin had left and they were all outside the toilet door but we weren't leaving! I even got back into the visits room and completed our visit! I just walked straight back into the visits room and the officers decided they didn't want a confrontation there and then. But they told Kevin when he went back on the wing that he'd be on closed visits from then on. I knew that would be the consequence, but it had never crossed his consciousness that this would happen and he was so angry.

He decided to set fire to his cell, both because he'd been put on closed visits and as a protest at the delay in getting his case to the Appeal Court. He had a very careful cell fire but—again because of this lack of connection—he could have killed himself that night. I know he wasn't intending that because he was on good form at the time. But it never dawned on him that because he was a Cat A prisoner they might not get him out as soon as another prisoner. If it hadn't been for the other guys on the corridor he could well have died. That night he was taken to hospital in York suffering from smoke inhalation and the hospital staff asked if he would be cared for if he was taken back to prison. The prison has a good hospital wing but when Kevin got back they just dumped him in the seg.

All this happened on a Saturday. On the Sunday I went back for a second visit. Nobody told me what happened and there I was, sitting at a table in the visits room when a prisoner came across to me and said, 'I think you're going to be on closed visits. There was a fire last night.'

That was one of the worst moments for me—realising there's somebody they've taken from hospital and dumped in segregation, he's suffering from smoke inhalation, he's nearly died—and it's all about the non-connectiveness of his mind. That's why he's in prison and that's why he shouldn't be there.

Kevin was moved to Parkhurst in October 1994 and he stayed there till 1998, and it was in Parkhurst that he got taken off Category A status.

• • •

Although the judge had said at Kevin's trial that the Home Secretary might never want to release him, when he had written his letter a year later he had actually recommended 18 years, which meant the sentence should be reviewed at 15 years. Suddenly, here was something that was different and more positive and not so dead-ending. Someone at Parkhurst told Kevin to put in a submission, but then he got a letter saying basically, 'Forget it, you're going to be Cat A'.

Kevin gave a very literal response to this letter. He said, 'I'm going to be Cat A. There's no way through it.' It was good for me to see his reaction to the Cat A letter because I didn't too often have experience of his reactions to words on paper. It gave me an inkling of what had gone on when all the papers were piling up in his cell before the trial. Now I said to Kevin, 'Okay, now I can do something. Now they've got this wrong I can write and spell it out. Before that I couldn't do anything.'

I don't think I ever thought it would be easy, but what I didn't realise was how difficult the whole system is in terms of learning difficulties, and the wariness of the legal profession. By this time I'd got a report on Kevin's dyslexia. We had tests carried out by Dr Harry Chasty, who was at the time the Director of the Dyslexia Institute. Dr Chasty concluded that Kevin had 'auditory memory difficulties which would lead him to misunderstanding and responding inappropriately to long questions. The acceptability of his statement is very questionable. I therefore conclude that there are serious dangers in the conviction of Kevin O'Neill on this evidence alone.' I presented all this stuff and the result was he was taken off Category A.

•   •   •

There was a period when Kevin wasn't painting at all. He was writing instead. At Long Lartin he started on a computer and he hasn't looked back since. The computer becomes like an extension of his mind. At Parkhurst he first did desktop publishing, then he started writing novels. You can see how it frees up his mind and takes him forward, and how comfortable he is with it. He now knows he would like to do animation, and he has a sense of an ability, a future.

One day it will be a relief to be able to live and do ordinary things and relate in everyday circumstances. Kevin and I have different strengths and abilities. We can't live by ignoring the way either of us thinks and functions, but it will be a relief to be able to live on our own terms and explore and discover things in different circumstances.

•   •   •

I have a small network of people that I communicate with for Kevin's campaign, but it's very fragmented and it takes a lot of energy. When you're married to someone unjustly convicted you can't take holidays, though sometimes I stay outside London with friends for a few days. Developing and sustaining anything much of a personal or social life is difficult but I try and sustain it as best I can, as it's important for our future to have friends and family.

I think one of the very worst times was in January 2000, by which time Kevin was in HMP Maidstone. The Criminal Cases Review Commission[4] had made the decision not to refer Kevin's case to the Court of Appeal. Usually they only look at cases where an appeal has been lost, whereas nobody had ever launched an appeal for Kevin. But the CCRC looked at it under exceptional circumstances because it had been so long at the Home Office.

A case worker had intended that I should get a copy of their decision before I went to visit Kevin. But it got sent out second post, which meant that I had to go on a visit before reading it. By the time I got to the prison, Kevin had read bits of the decision over the lunchtime before the visit, and he was feeling that all this paper weighed against him. He was saying things I had no way of dealing with, as I didn't have the information. So there has been the hell of having to deal with all this mess. But you know that regardless of everything you're actually okay. We've been through so much together and we've still survived.

It is a very particular experience being married to an innocent prisoner and it has very particular demands and strains. One hits one's lows, but they haven't seriously lasted for any length of time, and I have never for a moment regretted marrying Kevin. In truth he would hate it for me not to be there, but periodically when he's feeling low he says, 'I don't want to hold you here', and I have to say, 'Look—I don't want to be anywhere else. I couldn't be anywhere else other than here.' I think Kevin does recognise that he could so easily have been lost in the system, and that he is now in a better position in terms of self-esteem. And he puts this down to my being in his life.

Postscript: Jenny wrote in autumn 2001:

Kevin and I celebrate our tenth wedding anniversary this September, which we should have been doing outside the confines of the prison system. Kevin has moved prisons again. Changes are difficult for him, and no easier with the years. He desperately needs to have his voice heard. This continuing injustice is going on far too long. It is made all the more difficult for Kevin by my involvement in the campaigns of people long free. He has seen so many released and he wonders when his day will come.

ENDNOTES

[1] Spirited away to another prison, usually overnight or early in the morning, with very little, if any, warning.
[2] Robin Norwood, Random House, 1986, see also pp. 41, 59-60.
[3] See p. 46.
[4] See endnote 1, p. 82.

Maria and Adrian

Maria and Adrian married ten years ago, the day after Adrian was released from prison at the end of his life sentence. He had been jailed at the age of 19 for killing his girlfriend's father in a fight and burying the body on the moors near Manchester. Maria knew nothing about prisons until she went to visit a friend who had been jailed for amphetamine possession. This man befriended Adrian and asked Maria to write to him.

Maria, 33, is a small, jolly, bespectacled woman who laughs a lot and has a strong Midlands accent. The only unconventional feature of her appearance is her gold nose-ring, which at first seems rather at odds with Maria and her surroundings—she, Adrian and their black-and-white-cat, Iggy, live in a well-furnished and tastefully decorated new house on a Midlands estate. The back lawn with its neat flower beds is kept very private by the high wooden fences which Maria has put up all around it. She gets on well with her neighbours but does not want them knowing about her husband's background.

When you meet Adrian, Maria's nose-ring fits into context: Adrian's brow is pierced with gold studs and his earlobes are laden with gold rings. Heavily tattooed, he is a slim, tanned man who on first sight looks younger than his 38 years. But his face is deeply lined and his anxious expression only relaxes after a while.

Maria's background is very different from her husband's. Her family were hard-working and respectable and she attended a strict Catholic school, while Adrian's father was a Glasgow criminal and Adrian was raised in a poverty-stricken tenement where several families had to share an outside toilet. Maria has worked hard all her life, mainly in secretarial jobs. She comes across as much more confident than her husband.

She is now registered disabled and the couple do not have children, but since her marriage to Adrian she has become involved with a number of voluntary agencies. She is still an active campaigner in one miscarriage of justice case. Two years ago she qualified as a counsellor and hopes soon to take a degree in counselling.

Around their comfortable sitting room are photographs cataloguing the couple's life together, including their wedding photographs with Adrian looking anxious in a dark suit and Maria radiant in a beautiful white dress and flowered headband; and their belated honeymoon in Tenerife in 1999, eight years after they married.

•　　　•　　　•

As soon as I met Adrian I knew I was going to marry him. I didn't know how, but I knew I was going to! I know it sounds very corny, but the moment I met him I really, really knew he was the right person. It just felt so right. I was never like that before. If you'd said to me, 'Love at first sight' I'd have said, 'Rubbish!' But it felt so right and Adrian seemed such a lovely man. He'd done this horrific crime but he wasn't at all threatening—he hasn't got a threatening bone in his body.

By the time I actually met Adrian I had been writing to him for about four months. I'd first gone to the prison, about 50 miles from where I lived, to visit a male friend who had a serious drug problem and who was caught in possession of amphetamines. So I went with this friend's wife.

I'd never been inside a prison before but the jail we went to is a very relaxed one with no high walls or barbed wire. The visiting room was comfortable and the officers were all very friendly, especially when you got to know them. I used to write to this friend and one day he wrote back and said he'd met this really nice man in there whose mum had just died and he'd got nobody—and he asked me to write to him. So I wrote Adrian a friendly letter.

At that stage I was 24. I'd broken off a long-term engagement which lasted from when I was 17 till I was 21, and I was in another relationship in which I was very, very unhappy. The man was quite a bit younger than me and he had huge problems. I'd been with him probably about 18 months, but I knew it was a relationship that wasn't going anywhere.

When I started writing to Adrian, it was only friendship—there was never any intention of a relationship. But even as a friendship there was an attraction because I could call the shots—I was very much in control. It was up to me when I wrote to him. He'd write to me, but I could either write back straight away or leave it a couple of weeks.

I started writing in July 1990, and he was at the stage in his sentence when he was allowed days out. In the December he'd got an unescorted town visit and he wrote and said, 'How about meeting me? How about spending the day together?'

Although I'd never visited Adrian in prison I felt as if I knew him. I trusted the judgement of the friend who had introduced us and I was as sure as I could be that I would be safe.

•　　•　　•

He'd been totally honest about his crime through his letters. I didn't ask him, he volunteered that information. He's never hidden anything about why he was in prison. He was 19 when he killed his girlfriend's father, back in 1981. The man was a very violent man and he very much objected to Adrian being with his daughter. One evening Adrian went to their house in Manchester and this man opened the door with a hammer in his hand and went to attack Adrian. Adrian took the hammer off him and hit him back and killed him. In his panic he disposed of the body—he took it to the moors and buried it in total panic—he didn't know what else to do. It turned out it wasn't the actual moors, it was a farmer's field, and the body was discovered six days later. If he'd gone to the police and confessed, maybe he would have got manslaughter. But he accepted that he had killed a man, he was convicted of murder and he took the punishment. He had never been in trouble before at all, not so much as a parking ticket. I believe that if his family had been informed enough to get him a decent legal team, things might have been different.

Adrian's background is very different from mine. I had a very stable family, whereas Adrian was brought up in Glasgow and his father was from a criminal background, part of the gangs. His mother worked very hard but it was a violent relationship where alcohol played a major part. There are differences too in our attitude to authority.

After school Adrian had a brief period in the army, then worked in the cotton mills in the north of England. I think he'd been out of the army about six months when the crime happened. He served time in most of the prisons in the north. His girlfriend, whose father Adrian killed, wrote to him for a little while but things didn't work out. They were both very young and she must have felt so confused. Adrian's mother stuck by him until she died. He'd served over nine years by the time I got to know him.

●　　●　　●

In our letters we had shared thoughts and feelings. Because at that stage there was still no intention of a relationship we could be very open with each other. There were no strings: he wanted nothing from me and I wanted nothing from him, apart from friendship.

He helped me through the last days of the unhappy relationship I was in. I was clinging to it because I didn't really want to be on my own, but he helped me finish it.

Adrian was a good letter writer—he'd write chatty, funny letters. I wrote to him every day. The important thing was to post him something daily, even if some days I was so busy I'd only got chance to write one page during my break.

It was like writing a diary or a journal. I'd write, 'Oh, I'm fed up—I had the gas bill today!' I've still got the letters upstairs and I could read them through now and think, Oh yes, I remember that day! We were building a friendship. Just as you might get home and spend half an hour on the phone, I'd write a letter instead.

Adrian wanted to hear everything—the phone bill, whether I'd been to the petrol station and filled up the car. The things that are mundane to the rest of us are like escapism to a prisoner because they are things they don't do—they *can't* do. I think that Adrian got normality from reading my letters. He was able to 'escape' from prison in that way. Towards the end of his time in prison I used to have to take my mail to show him. I used to say, 'This is the gas bill, this is the electricity bill, this is how it all works'. He was sent to prison when he was 19 and he was nearly 30 when he was released, so he'd never had any of these responsibilities.

●　　●　　●

When his day out came in December we arranged to meet in a café just down the road from the prison. I'd given him my car registration number because I hadn't seen a photograph of him and I hadn't got a clue what he looked like, and he hadn't got a clue what I looked like either—no idea. I just sat there in my car waiting.

And then this man started walking towards the car and I thought, 'Oh, promising!'

He wasn't what I expected at all. He was medium height, very slim, fair-haired, neat and tidy with a moustache—a very timid-looking man.

He didn't have an officer with him—he was allowed out on his own. Our first words were sort of shy I suppose. But after that it wasn't awkward at all, because we really did know each other from our letters. We came back to my house, an hour's drive away, and had lunch, then we looked round the shops a bit, then we went round and saw the friend who'd introduced us—he'd been released by then. There was nothing physical between us at all. At the end of the day I just took Adrian back to the prison and said goodbye, said I'd write again. But I did write to him after that first day out, saying I thought this could go a bit further.

He wrote back not really encouraging me, just saying, 'Wait and see what happens'. I think, looking back, that he did want a relationship but he didn't quite know what to do and maybe he was a bit scared. He'd had a lot of hurt in his life.

And at that stage we didn't know how long he'd got left to serve. By then he'd done about nine and a half years, but the way I'd been brought up, I thought a life sentence really meant life.

•   •   •

None of my friends or family knew about me and Adrian—it was very much my secret and I didn't want to tell anybody else. I was leading almost a double life. I had a close woman friend but I didn't tell her and I didn't tell people at work either. The only hint to anyone was that I stopped going out so much. I just wanted to stay in and write to Adrian. I felt disloyal going out enjoying myself, though Adrian encouraged me to have a life of my own.

When I did tell a few close friends later on, they reacted surprisingly well. Most were absolutely brilliant and supportive. One or two decided they didn't want to know, and stopped coming round to see us. They couldn't have been real friends and they are no loss at all.

In some ways I was quite happy with the relationship as it was. I could go and see Adrian when I wanted to, and if I didn't want to see him I didn't have to. I was very much in control of the relationship—very much. Adrian made no demands. It was also in the days when there were not so many phones in prisons, so he couldn't phone me. But his letters were definitely getting warmer and more loving.

•   •   •

In January 1991, about a month after our first meeting, Adrian was due for a home leave, and he asked if he could spend it with me. I had to fill in a lot of forms and be checked by probation officers and I was approved, because obviously I hadn't got any criminal background at all. We decided to split the weekend up with a couple of days in the Cotswolds and the last night in Manchester. There was still nothing physical about our relationship, not even a kiss, until I dropped him off at the prison gate at the end of that home leave—and that's when we kissed for the first time.

After that I used to visit him in prison as often as I could, sometimes two or three times a week. On the visits we were still very much communicating, talking a lot and holding hands, not so much kissing because I'm not into public displays of affection.

About six weeks after the Cotswolds weekend Adrian told me he'd got a review coming up. I didn't understand the system so I didn't realise this could mean he'd be getting out. Then I had a letter from him one morning saying he'd had the review and he'd been given his parole and he was going to spend nine months in a pre-release hostel—and provided that all went okay he would be released afterwards.

He went into the hostel at the end of March and he used to be allowed out for weekends. I had been house-sharing, but I then moved into a flat which Adrian and I chose together. All the neighbours thought he worked away from home during the week and just came back at weekends.

I took him to meet my parents at their house and my mum took an instant shine to him. My dad liked him too but kept him at arm's length—I was my dad's baby girl after all, and he would have been the same whoever I was with.

At first I didn't tell my parents that Adrian had been in prison, but I did tell my elder step-brother. Unfortunately he told my younger step-brother who told my parents. My parents confronted me with what my younger brother had said, and at first I denied it. But then Adrian and I decided to get engaged so I realised I'd got to come clean. We actually got engaged on 31 May 1991. We were in my flat and he went on bended knee and said, 'Will you marry me?' Then we went out for a drink with a couple of my friends to celebrate.

So then I took my parents out for a meal and I said, 'Last week we spoke about Adrian and you asked if he'd been in prison and I denied it. Well, actually—it's true'. And I told them the whole story. At the time Adrian committed his crime there had been a fair bit of publicity, but it was local to his own area rather than nationwide, so they weren't aware of the case. My mum, as if trying to make it better, said, 'As long as it's not for rape, that's okay!' It was as if it was more socially acceptable to kill somebody!

My dad's attitude was always very much: 'Lock 'em all up and don't ask questions'—and I was like that myself before I met Adrian. I had no interest in prisons whatsoever, and prisoners could all go and be hung as far as I was concerned. But now my father has his own perception of Adrian's crime and he can cope with that. Now he thinks Adrian's absolutely wonderful. He's with a new partner since Mum died and she accepts Adrian as well. I don't really have a lot to do with Adrian's family. I think his sisters see me as a sort of threat. We had an awful row with them a few years ago and one of them told me I was too intelligent for my own good. I think they very much believe I took Adrian away from them.

•   •   •

We planned to get married the following year in August, but then Adrian heard that his final release date was actually Christmas Day 1991—though they brought it forward to Friday 20 December. He decided he wanted to come and live with me, but I refused to let him live with me unless we were married. So the wedding was brought forward.

We were married the day after his official release, on 21 December 1991. He was released and we got married all within the space of 24 hours, and I was on a high which lasted for about a week afterwards—it was absolutely brilliant! I was 25 by then and earning good money doing secretarial work. But we were still on a very tight budget and we weren't going to have a reception. But then a friend said we could have our reception in her house.

We married in a registry office and the wedding was very simple and very quiet, with about 20 guests—my parents, Adrian's dad and sisters and their husbands, and a few close friends. My friend made a heart-shaped cake and I wore a below-the-knee dress and a very pretty headdress with flowers.

Adrian definitely didn't love me and I knew he didn't. He admitted it the day he married me. I think that was because he was incapable of love at that time. He couldn't show love as he'd never been shown love himself.

Before we married, towards the end of his time in the hostel, we did have a major breakthrough when he said to me, 'Do you know, I felt all funny when I saw you walking into the car park today—all sort of butterfly-ish.' That was as near as he got. Now he will tell you he worships me, and I know a hundred per cent that he loves me. But it took him a long, long time and he's only been able to tell me so in the last couple of years.

So when Adrian was first released he was very cold. In those early days there was such a huge wall around him and it took years and years to break it down. It's probably only in the last three or four years that that wall has really, truly started to come down. It wasn't only prison that had built that wall, it was his whole life. All prison did was to strengthen the wall. Cracking it down was—oh, an enormous task!

Adrian is very much damaged by his life and by the prison system. He'd be the first to tell you that he'd been dragged up. His dad was in and out of prison—he was a man's man who would give Adrian the slipper but he was not allowed to cry. Then Adrian went into the army and then into prison himself, so all his life he's had not to show emotion. He is still very angry against anybody he thinks is in authority, and he instantly puts that wall up. He was expected to confront people and if he hadn't, he would have been a soft touch with the officers and with his mates. I don't think that's unique to prison—it happens on the streets as well.

Now Adrian is good at exploring his feelings. To the outside world he's the strong and silent type, but to me indoors he's a great talker. I've very much had to prise things out of him. He is open with his feelings but sometimes he just doesn't know how to express them, and he gets very frustrated. I've since gone on to train as a counsellor. I spent three years in college and now I'm a qualified counsellor, so if there is something going on under the surface with Adrian, I use my training to prise it out of him.

I have taught Adrian to love, by showing what you do for somebody when you care for them. From me he's learnt what he should probably have been learning from when he was a small baby—but he only started learning it at the age of 30. It's hard work but it's rewarding, and if you're committed to someone it's what you do—unconditionally.

I do find that Adrian is too grateful to me and I don't like this attitude. He often says that if it wasn't for me he'd have ended up back in prison, and I'm the one that kept him on the straight and narrow. But all I have done is loved him. He knows he committed the most appalling crime and he had to pay for it. I don't think he'll ever forgive himself

He's been out of prison ten years now and he's given no cause for concern, but at any time his licence[1] could be revoked if he was involved in any offence punishable by custody. For instance, if he went to the pub and somebody started a fight and he got involved and was arrested, he could in theory go straight back to prison—no police station, no court, no trial, nothing. It could be as simple as the neighbours saying 'There's this man next door and we feel threatened by him.' He's not 40 yet and if he lives to the age of 90 he'll still have this hanging over him, and I think that is so cruel. I used to work in the pub trade and I did look into the possibility of Adrian and me sharing the licence to a pub. But it turned out that the brewery wouldn't allow him to live on licensed premises. This was because of the restrictions of his life licence. If there was a fight and he needed to protect the pub he wouldn't have been able to take charge of the situation for fear of what might happen.

•   •   •

A major low point in our marriage was when a close friend of mine was murdered. This brought up strong feelings for Adrian. He had feelings of guilt and to some extent he even felt responsible. It gave him an insight into the other side of someone being killed in a violent way. At the time he felt it wasn't appropriate for him to attend the funeral. He felt he would be a hypocrite.

Another major low point was three years ago when Adrian lost his job. He was sacked because of his attitude to authority. I was not sympathetic at all—I was very angry, very upset, very confused. All my counselling skills didn't help me at all, not in the slightest. But I didn't have to handle the situation for very long, because he found a job about a week later. He is a good worker.

Adrian's very good at arguing at work, but he won't argue with me, he won't raise his voice in the house—he'll just sit there and watch the telly. But if we do fall out it's never for more than an hour. I'll say, 'Come and give us a hug!' or he'll come and give me a hug. I have never, ever felt threatened by Adrian at all, and believe me, if he was going to kill again, he would have done it to me, because I have pushed him to the limits.

In the early days it was like having a child in the house—and it still is sometimes. Adrian had never had a bank account, and I had to teach him to use the cashpoint machine, how to write a cheque. He'd never done a week's grocery shopping in Tesco's. I remember the first time I took him to buy a pair of jeans and it was so embarrassing! The lady wanted £30 for one of the cheaper pairs, and he wasn't prepared to pay more than £8. I had to guide him out of the shop! Outside I said to him, 'Adrian—the last time you purchased any item of clothing was in early 1981. We are now nearly in 1992 and you've missed a whole decade! Get real!' He wasn't used to traffic on the streets either. It really was like looking out for a child.

Because at first things were difficult with Adrian emotionally, I felt I needed to speak to people who'd been in the same situation. I went to the library but there are no books to help you. I went to probation, to family support groups and various organizations. But I think there is a lot of prejudice against people who choose to be with a criminal partner. I know there are what I'd call 'prison groupies'—people who get their kicks out of going visiting prisons. I felt very few of these organizations were geared up to lifers' wives whose husbands have been released. There aren't that many of us around, and those of us who are about are usually 'hiding'. I'm not ashamed of Adrian but we do very much want to be anonymous, and I'm very keen for him to have a normal life. The neighbours here don't know about his background. It's a small community and Adrian's come too far to have to put up with hassle now.

•   •   •

Adrian has changed and I'd like to think we are equals. Even now, ten years later, we really enjoy each other's company. We're quite happy to be in our home, or pottering round the garden. Talking is still very important for us. When Adrian gets in from work in the evening we always spend the first half hour sitting down with a cup of coffee, talking about the day. He's as interested in my day as I am in his. He has given me as much as I've given him. As soon as I met him I was completely bowled over by him. His crime just happened to be how we met. I'm very much into fate and karma and this was obviously meant to be. When I was doing my counselling course we were all asked to tell our favourite fairy tale. Mine was always *Little Red Riding Hood* and afterwards when the tutor analysed our stories he said, 'That's your favourite because you like dangerous relationships.' He knew nothing about my marriage until I spoke to him privately after the session. Where did that come from? Perhaps there is something in me that needs to be with the Big Bad Wolf!

ENDNOTE

[1] See p. 191.

Philomena and Rob Donovan

When I interviewed Philomena in November 2000, she showed me a framed photograph of herself, her three children and her partner Rob together at what looked like a family picnic in a park. But in fact the picture was taken in the grounds of HM Prison Grendon.[1] Philomena's story is an extraordinary one of nearly 30 years of loyalty. Philomena, 45, is a housekeeper, responsible for looking after the homes of working families. She was brought up in London in a strict working-class Irish Catholic family—her father worked on the London Underground and her mother was a cleaner. Philomena was educated at a convent grammar school.

She first met Robert Donovan in the 1970s when she was 17 and he was 16 and just out of borstal. Philomena fell in love with him at first sight, but before they had even gone out together Rob was arrested for the murder near Charing Cross of pop star Tommy Steele's manager in a robbery that went wrong. Philomena visited him constantly in Aylesbury Young Offenders' Institution during the six months he was on remand, and she attended his Old Bailey trial every day. Rob was found guilty of murder and jailed for an indeterminate period at Her Majesty's Pleasure. Under great pressure from her family and the prison authorities Philomena was forced to give him up. She worked in childcare, including several years as nanny to Christine Keeler's son.

She married, divorced, had other relationships and three children. But she never forgot Rob, and finally wrote to him again just as he was completing his 13th and final year in jail. On his release they had a brief relationship but parted because of his involvement with other women. Then seven years ago Rob contacted Philomena again. He was back in jail, and had become a heroin addict in prison. The relationship started up again, the couple got engaged and eventually Philomena took Rob's name. They remain together but Rob is still in jail, because once he had served his sentence for the robbery, his life licence[2] came into force, and this has to be reviewed every two years. Twice he has been refused parole. Philomena still lives as his wife and continues to help him fight his addiction. She writes and speaks about her experiences to help outsiders understand the pressures on prisoners' families.

Philomena is a slim woman with short, fair hair and blue eyes and a very soft voice. Her appearance seems deliberately understated—the day we met she was wearing a cream sweatshirt and matching leggings—and her manner is quiet and thoughtful. We met in her comfortable sitting room, with its large sofas and vast array of ornaments. Philomena has lived in this maisonette for the last 16 years and has brought up her three children here.

The estate is rather run-down, with burnt-out car wrecks here and there, but Philomena's home is immaculate and her children, aged eleven, 14 and 16, are all doing well at school. You feel that beneath Philomena's mild manner lies a very strong character indeed.

* * *

I knew instantly I saw Rob that he was the person for me. I was 17 and we lived in Battersea. Rob's parents lived on a council estate on one side of the road and we lived on the other, though I didn't know him or his family. I'd left school at 15 and worked for a couple of years as a telephone operator, then I left home and worked as a nanny.

Though I'd moved away from Battersea, my friends were all still back at home. One particular evening I'd been home for a couple of days and was out with one of my girlfriends. We left a pub and we saw three boys walking in front of us. My friend said, 'I know this family—there's three brothers and a sister'. We caught up with them and that's when I first saw Rob. He was very attractive with jet black hair. He was slim and quite short—about the same height as me—and he was a year younger than me. He was the youngest of the three brothers. I didn't know it at the time but he was not very long out of borstal. He'd been in trouble all his life—in and out of court for robberies from when he was young.

We went back to the boys' house and I got the impression that it was very much open house and that his mum made everyone welcome. She would put up people who came over from Ireland and had nowhere to stay.

Rob wasn't going out with girls seriously then but there were always a lot of girls around him. When I told my friend I liked him she said, 'He's a bit of a Casanova, he's always in trouble. Why not one of the older brothers?' I was quiet and shy with very long, dark hair and I didn't have a steady boyfriend.

What I didn't know was that just very shortly before I met Rob something had happened. There'd been an incident. I told my parents that I'd met this Donovan family, and within a couple of days my mum suddenly said, 'I don't want you to go near them or have anything to do with them.' For the first time in my life I started rebelling a bit and I asked her why, but she wouldn't say.

The community we lived in was so close that everyone knew everyone—and my dad and Rob's dad drank in the same pub. A few days later my mum came into my room and put one of the national newspapers on the end of my bed. In it was a photofit picture that was definitely Rob, and the headline said he was wanted for murder. I can still remember that moment. I sat down and I was totally... totally... I was just shaking. I went straight round to my friend and she said she knew what had happened. She told me, 'They were on Hungerford Bridge. It was an intent to rob that went wrong and the police are looking for them.' So the night I met Rob it must have virtually just happened.

Apparently Rob was with his older brother and another male friend. The robbery had gone wrong, and a man in his late thirties had got knifed—it was a stabbing to the throat. The victim staggered to the bus stop and he stayed alive another 24 hours in the hospital. He turned out to be the manager of the pop singer Tommy Steele, and the papers were full of it —they called it The Charing Cross Murder. A down-and-out gave a description of boys running off the bridge and he caught the description of Rob better than the others.

My friend said that as soon as it was in the papers, Rob and his brother were staying housebound. But the other lad that was with them was out one night with his girlfriend and he phoned the police and said he could tell them who did the murder on Hungerford Bridge. Then the police raided Rob's house and he and his brother were remanded in jail.

•   •   •

Rob did about six months on remand in Aylesbury Young Offenders and I visited him all the time. I used to say to friends close to me, 'I will end up with him—I know I will.' And they would laugh and say, 'It's just infatuation'. But it wasn't like that at all—it wasn't about being with a notorious criminal—because there was no prison or anything like that involved when I first met him.

Then in the December his case came up at the Old Bailey. I went every day to the trial, and it was like I was in another world. I'd keep saying to myself, This didn't happen, it's not real! Rob's mum and his aunt attended as well and I remember going out at lunchtime and going across the road to get something to eat, and I just felt physically sick. I kept thinking, This can't be him! This can't be real. Yes, he did do it, but it was like it was another person, somebody completely different. There had been no violence in his other offences. They were just small robberies. But this time Rob was the one with the knife and he pleaded Guilty. He was sentenced just after Christmas and because of his age he got sent to prison at Her Majesty's Pleasure. His brother got five years.

He stayed in Aylesbury and I went on seeing him. I remember first going to visit just after he was sentenced. In those days, when you began a life sentence they'd drug you up. One day I asked what was wrong and they said he was taking Largactil.[3] He was on that drug for a while. He would sit opposite me and I'd think, This is awful, I'm coming to see him and he's not really together at all. Things seemed really, really bad. I remember going to visit Rob one day and in those days you got called in by the prisoner's surname, 'Visitors for Donovan'. This time I knew where I had to go and I started off down the main corridor. But then one of the officers said to me, 'No, it's not for the visit at the moment.'

He took me into a room where three quite official-looking people were sitting, and there were two officers at the door. I was told to sit down. One of the officials was a probation officer, one was a governor. I was only 18, and I didn't understand much about prisons. The probation officer said to me, 'Don't look so worried—this is just a friendly chat. But we're concerned about your relationship with Robert Donovan. It seems to be getting too serious and we don't think it's a good idea for you to carry on your relationship with him.' At the time everything seemed hazy and I couldn't quite understand what they were saying.

I was getting so much pressure from my parents that I hadn't been home for two or three weeks. I was still staying at Rob's mum's, though my own family only lived down the road. One night I'd gone out for a drink and my friend said, 'Your dad's outside the pub—he wants you.'

I met my dad and he said, 'We're going to Ireland for a couple of weeks' holiday and I want you to come with us—I'm buying the ticket and everything. I think you should get away.'

I went home that night and my mum was hardly speaking to me. She said, 'This isn't my idea, it's your father's. I don't want you anywhere near me. I want nothing to do with you.' I thought, How can I be with my mum for two weeks?

But I ended up going to Ireland with them. I was totally devastated while I was over there. I kept thinking about Rob, thinking what I was going to do. My dad said, 'Come back home to live. Make a fresh start, do things you've always wanted to do.' When I think back, this just didn't help, on top of everything and all the pressure I was under at the time.

I just couldn't see the end of a life sentence. I couldn't really see beyond the next week, let alone years and years. So I wrote Rob a 'Dear John' letter. I didn't know till way down the line, years later, that Rob was absolutely devastated to get that letter from me. It really cut him up to pieces. I did go on seeing his mum though she was really hurt. But my parents were pleased and I felt that a lot of pressure was lifted from me. I got a flat in Essex and started work looking after children in a crèche in a battered wives' refuge.

•   •   •

About a year later I was home on a visit to my parents. My younger brother was living at home and he said, 'A letter came here for you'—and he went upstairs to get it. I could see from the envelope that it was from HMP Coldingley in Surrey and I threw it away unopened. I went back to Essex but I kept thinking and thinking about the letter. I thought, Rob's somewhere close, he's in Surrey somewhere.

I got no more letters, and I was visualising to myself that there would be somebody else with him, somebody else writing to him, and if I got in touch I'd end up stepping in the way. So I didn't get in touch.

I was 27 by this time and I had no inclination whatsoever to get involved with anybody else. I didn't ever live with any boyfriend. I didn't want to be attached to anybody, I didn't want a man in my life. I really did hold strong feelings for Rob, and I had this feeling that it wasn't ended between us. But I did feel I wanted children. I was with a man a very, very short time when I fell pregnant with my daughter and then later we had a son. But Rob had never left my mind. I always wondered where he was, what prison he was in, what he was doing. My children's father loved me and he wanted to make a relationship out of it. He knew about Rob and he always used to say, 'I don't understand you. You're living in the past holding on to this'.

It was about that time, when my son was a few months old, that I moved to the maisonette I'm still in now. I had a friend who used to come round with her children. By this time I was wondering whether I needed counselling about Rob, but she said, 'Why don't you just write to him and find out what's happened to him?'

I was no longer in touch with Rob's family, but I knew from a friend that he was last in Wormwood Scrubs. So I phoned the prison, and finally someone came on the line and said that if I was looking for a Robert Donovan then I was through to the right place. He was in the Wormwood Scrubs hostel. I hadn't got a clue what that meant, but I wrote to Rob. It was a very short letter. I just told him where I was living, I said he'd been playing on my mind, I wondered what had happened to him, and could I come and see him.

About two days later I was pottering around in the kitchen with my little girl. She was standing on a chair playing with water in a bowl in the sink and the baby was outside on the balcony in his pram—it was really hot weather. The doorbell rang and I lifted her down off the chair and ran downstairs to open the door. On the doorstep was this tall black chap, and there was a car parked right in front of the door. He said, 'Philomena?' And as he said my name, Rob moved out in front of him!

I was absolutely dumbfounded! I was sitting waiting for a prison letter to come, and the very last thing I expected was to see Rob! The prison hostel system allows prisoners at the end of their sentence to go out to work every day, and Rob had got a job in a car showroom. The day he got my letter, a chap at work said he knew where my address was, and at lunchtime he drove Rob round to see me.

I can remember it like it was yesterday. I was sitting on the sofa feeling really sick and faint and the black guy offered to make me a cup of tea. He said, 'Are you okay? I can see that it's a shock'. I said, 'Yes, I'm in shock. You can't believe what a shock this is'.

It was 12 years since I'd last seen Rob. He was 19 then and he was 31 now. I was totally devastated but Rob was smiling. I was trying to find out quickly what he'd been doing but I was also lost for words.

He told me he lived in the prison hostel but he came out at weekends. He'd already seen my daughter running about but then the baby started crying and I went out on the balcony. Rob said, 'Whose baby is that?' and I said, 'He's mine'. Rob asked me if I was with somebody and I said, 'No, I'm not'—though the baby was only a few months old. I asked him if he was married and he laughed and said he wasn't. After his visit I rang my friend and asked her to come round. When she got here I said, 'You better sit down, I've got something to tell you!' She said, 'Oh, you've had a letter. Thank goodness, now you'll stop going on and on about him! Are you going to go and visit him?' And I said, 'I don't need to—he's been here!'

After that Rob used to come over here at weekends to stay, then he'd go back to the hostel during the week. Piece by piece I learned what had been happening. A girl had visited him near the end of his sentence, but he said he had no intention of settling down, and getting married was the last thing he was thinking about. In fact Rob was catching up on the years he had lost. Though he was in his early thirties when he came out, it was like he was a 16-year-old, running round everywhere. I thought I was holding together really well about it, but then somehow this girl he'd been seeing got hold of my phone number and started making phone calls in the middle of the night telling me not to see him.

One night I woke up in terrible pain and I thought I had appendicitis. An ambulance got me to the hospital and the doctor examined me and said, 'You're miscarrying.' I said, 'That must be a mistake—I'm not pregnant!' But I was 16 weeks pregnant with Rob's twins, and I lost them. I was absolutely devastated, and I couldn't even tell my family.

I went on seeing Rob though I knew he'd been seeing a lot of girls, including the one who phoned me late at night. Then one day he came over and he said, 'I've got something to tell you'—and he told me that girl was pregnant. I was really upset, really devastated, and I told my friend that I wasn't going to see him any more. It was breaking my heart and I was cut up, really badly cut up, but when Rob came over I told him it was ended.

I watched him get on a bus and I just stood there and I thought, So that's it, is it? Is that what I had to find out after all these years? Is that what it was all about?

The very next month I met someone else and I married him. We got married in church, my family liked my husband and they were very pleased, and we had a baby—my second daughter. But I still thought about Rob. I used to have these visions that he was settled he'd probably got married.

•   •   •

After a few years I decided to apply for a divorce. One day I said to my closest friend, 'Rob's in my mind all the time. I'm never going to be able to make a relationship with anybody else. I know that now.' She said, 'I don't think there's any point you looking for him. You made your decision, and if I were in your shoes, I'd feel that any move should come from him.'

Not long after that I came down one morning to get my post and there was a prison letter on the mat. Instantly I knew the handwriting was Rob's and I thought, No, I can't believe this. It's like a nightmare!

I opened the letter. It was very short and it said, 'Phil, I'm in Belmarsh prison in London. I've been in prison over a year for armed robbery.' He said he'd got a six-year sentence, but after that he'd have to carry on because his life sentence recall[4] would kick in. That means they continue with the life sentence and you have to go before a Discretionary Lifer Panel every couple of years till they think you're ready for release. He went on to say he'd got three children from two different women but he hadn't seen them or his children for a long time. He ended, 'You don't know how long it's taken me to write this letter.'

Rob sat down to write that letter on a Good Friday, and on that day I'd gone shopping with my parents. My mum went off with the children and I sat on a bench with my dad. My dad said to me, 'You're not really with us, are you?' I said, 'No, not really.' And my dad said, 'I know where your mind is. Phil, you've got to do something about this. Put him out of your mind. He's taken over your whole life so far—do you understand that?'

What was so odd was that the day I was having that conversation, Rob was sitting down writing to me. I read his letter over and over again. Then I wrote back. I said, 'I'm still here', and I made arrangements for him to phone me at my friend's house. He phoned and said he was moving to a prison in Kent, and he asked me if I would come and see him.

My friend said she'd drive me there so I put her name on the visiting order. When we drove up to the prison I was really, really nervous. Outside I said to my friend, 'I don't know what's going to happen, but I just feel like my whole life has changed.' She said, 'I know what's going to happen. This isn't going to be a one-off visit'.

We went in and waited for him to come out, and I thought, 'I wonder what he looks like? Will I recognise him?' He came out and he was exactly the same. He hadn't changed one bit. He walked over and he was all bubbly. He kept chatting and I didn't get a word in. It was a really strange feeling, like no time had passed between us. At the end of the visit he said, 'Are you going to come and see me again?' and I said I would.

Then I started going regularly. After I'd been visiting for about four weeks, he was wondering if I'd be in his life in six months' time. I said I would be. I said, 'I am sure, I'm certain.' Then he told me that after that first visit he had walked back to his cell and he knew what he wanted.

I gave it a lot of thought and I said to myself, 'I don't want to be anywhere else. There's no point in me trying to make a life, or going out and looking for somebody else, because he's the one that I want.'

I went on visiting Rob and at first my children didn't know about him. That was pulling me apart because I'd always had an honest and open relationship with my eldest daughter—she was ten by now—so I found it really difficult.

•   •   •

After I'd been seeing Rob again for about a year, I said, 'I don't know what to do. I don't want to walk away again, but I don't think you and I want the same things.' He said, 'Look Phil, I want to marry you, but I don't want to get married in prison. I've spent half my life in prison. I want to do something for *me* out there.'

Some people think that men have a better chance of parole if they're married with a stable home waiting for them outside. But Rob said, 'I'll never do that, because I'm not having everybody think that I'm only marrying you because you're my way out.' I feel quite proud of him because he wants to show that he's done it on his own, not through marrying someone half-way through his sentence. We'd both seen people get married in prison and I felt very sorry for a lot of the women because they didn't even know exactly what the man had done. Then there are some women who are only 'married' while they're in the visits room. On the outside they've got their own life, then they transform themselves again the following week. This is quite a widespread thing, I've found. I'd say that 70 per cent of women treat this thing in prison as a drama. They think it's great to go and visit somebody in prison, regardless of what they've done.

At first I think Rob and I were both really frightened of saying how we felt. I had never in all my life told anybody that I loved them, never. I'd never said those words. But then one day Rob asked me to get engaged and I said yes.

•　　•　　•

One thing I have with Rob is honesty. About 18 months after I'd been seeing him again, he asked for a private visit. I already knew something was wrong and he told me he'd got introduced to heroin in prison. It was horrendous going down that road with him. He had a period of two years in Grendon (see endnote 1), a therapeutic prison. He said, 'I'll be okay in a new environment, I'll give up drugs.' And he did leave heroin alone. But at Grendon he was caught smoking cannabis and he got sent back to the same prison he'd left in Kent. He said, 'They can't send me back there because I'm not strong enough—I'm not able to fight the drugs.'

Because I didn't understand at the time, I was always blaming him. I used to say, 'If you want to do something you can do it. You can pull yourself out of this'. But then I began to get more understanding of what drugs are like in prison, and I started trying to do things to help Rob. I got him a new solicitor, and I got involved with his probation officer. I knew that in the end he'd got to get off drugs by himself—I couldn't come off the drugs for him. But I do think that prisons ought to have some sessions where the family is brought in. I used to badger the people on the drug treatment unit—for instance if I was worried about him because he hadn't phoned and I thought he was back on the drugs.

Back in Kent Rob was accepted on the rehab unit but he made a muck of it and got thrown off. Then he got himself put down the block for about ten weeks and the prison put us on glass visits.

I wrote to the area manager and I caused a real storm. I was absolutely hated by all the staff. The lifer governor spoke to me on the phone and said, 'You've caused a big stink here'. The staff treated me very badly, making me wait and so on, and I was treated very coldly. They did really stupid things, like visiting orders not being sent out to me. I was quite polite at first. But as time went on I began to wonder how they could get away with things like that.

•　　•　　•

About a year ago, six years after Rob and I got together again, his mum died. I'd got very close to her since I began visiting him again. She was housebound and I'd go and see her every week and tell her how he was. She was just so pleased I was back in his life.

For my wedding ring I'm going to have the eternity ring that Rob's dad had bought for his mum. I wore it round my neck at the funeral, then when I went to see Rob shortly afterwards I expected to take it off the chain and give it to him. But then he put it on my finger, and that meant a lot to me. I'd like a small wedding in a church, if that's something Rob would like. I don't really think we've got to prove anything—I have taken Rob's surname and in every way we live as if we were married.

●　　　●　　　●

Rob's mother died in the August, and the following January he got on to the drug free unit. The prison had promised him that if he got through six months on the unit they would move him to another prison that did a special drug rehab course. By the July he had completed the six months successfully, but they didn't send him on. Instead they kept stringing him along. I kept making phone calls to the Home Office. I said, 'You can't leave him on the normal wing in that prison where there are so many drugs! He'll soon be back where he started'. But they told me he'd have to wait as there was a waiting list for the unit in the other prison.

In the August I went to visit Rob as usual and I could tell immediately that he was back on the drugs. People on drugs lose concentration with you, their personality changes. I had the children with me, and when they had all gone up to the refreshments counter I said to him, 'You're using drugs again, aren't you?' and he said, 'Yes I am. But I can beat it if I can get out of here.'

I was devastated, and after that I got very paranoid. I've always supported him financially and I used to send him money weekly. But now I told him, 'I'm doing nothing till you move. You're not getting anything out of me.' I kept ringing the prison he was in and the one he was supposed to be going to. Then at last one day the lifer clerk at the Kent prison rang me here at home and told me the move had finally happened.

Rob is now in his third week at his new prison, and he's going to need a lot of reassurance to go on to the next course.

●　　　●　　　●

My parents are still not at all happy about my relationship with Rob, but my children are fine. My elder daughter was about ten when she found out. She knew of Rob, she knew I had phone calls from him and I'd say he was working away. I used to keep saying to him, 'I've got to find a way to tell her. I don't keep anything from her.' On her very first visit with me to the prison she was holding on tight to her seat and Rob asked her if she was all right. She said,

'Could I be sitting near a murderer?' Rob said it cut him up inside to hear that. When she went up to get some sweets at the counter, Rob said, 'Let it be me that tells her. I'll tell her when you bring her again.' But by the middle of that week she kept asking me, 'What's he done? What's he done?' So I had to tell her myself instead of waiting for Rob to do it. I found it so difficult. I thought, I'm telling my own daughter that I'm involved with someone that's murdered. I remember her looking at me and she said, 'I asked you if I could be sitting next to a murderer.'

Many times I've thought, I really love Rob but how can I get over this fact to my children? But they saw a big difference in the way I was, and they could see I was totally committed to him. They saw the difference in me and they wanted me happy. I take them to see Rob at weekends and in the holidays. My youngest daughter hit it off with him straight away. The oldest girl isn't particularly fond of visiting, particularly when Rob was in Grendon (see endnote 1), because there are so many sex offenders there. She used to say, 'I can't bear it, Mum, I can't bear thinking I'm sitting at a table next to somebody who's looking at me and gloating.'

•   •   •

Rob is quite protective of me. He doesn't like to think I'd go out with a group of women to a pub or anything like that—so I don't do things to put our relationship in jeopardy. When you realise how strongly you feel about somebody, loads of other things go by the wayside. I don't really have a social life as such, unless it's somebody's birthday or a gathering of some sort. I find it difficult because we can't go to things together as a couple, and I don't like being questioned. I've had to break away from a lot of people who were good friends. I've isolated myself, which I feel I've had to do because of what I call the small-mindedness of people.

I think people can feel threatened. I had a friend I'd known about ten years and after a year of seeing Rob again I plucked up the courage to tell her. I sat down one evening and told her the whole story. She was very nice to my face and I thought, Oh, that was easy! Why did I worry about it so much? Then after a week she phoned me and said, 'I've decided we'll cut ties with each other. We'll have nothing to do with each other any more.'

•   •   •

About four years ago I began writing. On the coach to visit Rob I used to meet a lot of women going to visit their men too, and I decided to write an article for a group called Prisoners Wives that I belonged to. The article was called *Women who Wait* and it went into the newsletter. After that I got asked to write for other prison journals as well and I enjoyed it.

Then I was asked to do a talk in a lifers' prison. I was speaking to lifers newly into their sentences, about the families outside. I just stood up and talked. I was nervous at first but soon they made me feel quite comfortable and they were giving me feedback and talking about their own families outside.

Then a woman in America asked me to write something for a newsletter that goes round all the Death Row jails over there. The response that I got from Death Row inmates was unbelievable. Now I've written for the *Howard League Journal* and the *Prison Service Journal* about life the other side of the wall.

•　　•　　•

It's now seven years since Rob and I got back together, and nearly six years since I took his name and started to live as his wife. He's had two lifer discretionary panel hearings, and each time he's had a two-year knockback.

I'm not one of these women who thinks that when the gate opens, that's when all the problems end, and everything is going to be hunky-dory. I know there's no rosy life about it. I know it'll be very difficult for Rob to get a job. He's not trained for anything, he's not done any courses in prison. And when you've done that length of time in prison, you're in a totally different frame of mind.

I've prayed when Rob was doing drugs because I needed some sort of guidance. My religion is important to me and I still go to Mass. The convent school I went to was very, very strict, run by an order called the Poor Clares. They had quite an influence on me, and I've found they still do today. They have to dig a piece of their own grave every day.

Someone asked me the other day why I had put all these years on hold. Was it to do with first love, or maybe he was the only person I had ever loved?

Yes—Rob is the only man I have ever loved, and what's more, I never wanted it any other way.

Postscript: Just before this book went to press, Philomena contacted me to say that in May 2001 Rob had had another parole 'knockback'. He now has to wait until May 2003 before applying again. 'To say the least this has been an awful year and the loneliness doesn't get any easier for me,' she said. But the estate where Philomena lives, so run down at the time of my interview, has now had a facelift, with new homes where a tower block once stood, and Philomena is looking forward to the birth of her first grandchild.

ENDNOTES

[1]　See p. 39 and endnote 2 p. 61. Also see index for further mentions.
[2]　See p. 184.
[3]　Brand name for Chlorpromazine, an anti-psychotic drug used in the treatment of schizophrenia and mania. Sometimes produces serious side effects including movement disorders, slow reactions and blurred vision.
[4]　All life sentence prisoners remain on licence for the rest of their lives following their release, and are subject to recall to prison during that time.

Kay and Jeff

Kay used to run a guest house in a picturesque spa town. Now she is a writer and a campaigner in miscarriage of justice cases. In 1999 she fell in love with a Jeff, a lifer who has spent 19 years in prison for killing a two-year-old child. Kay is still married to her second husband but it is a marriage in name only. She has two adult children and a daughter of six.

Kay's 46 years have been a roller-coaster of a life. Raised in a poor Catholic family, she married at 16 as an escape. Her first child, a son, is now 22 and has been diagnosed as mentally disordered. Her adopted mixed-race daughter is now 20 with a baby of her own. After 20 years the marriage ended in divorce.

At 39 Kay married for the second time, and the couple now live in a neat house in a pleasant residential area on the outskirts of a Midlands town. On the wall of their spacious sitting room is a portrait photograph of Kay, her second husband and their daughter, now 6, when she was a baby. In the photo Kay looks plump, pink and beaming with maternal pride, while her husband appears to be the picture of solid, bespectacled fatherhood. But Kay says her second husband, like her first, is an alcoholic and he has recently become violent towards her. She says she hopes soon to get divorced for the second time.

Kay's face now looks drawn and often anxious. Wearing a pink top and grey trousers she chain-smoked throughout the interview as we sat in her kitchen. But throughout her many traumas she has never lost her sense of humour and her eyes sparkle as she recounts anecdotes about her life. She is a published writer and showed me a very well-written story that was included in a collection of Yorkshire writing.

Seeking an interest outside her loveless second marriage, Kay became involved in a high profile miscarriage of justice campaign and through the prison connections that resulted she began writing to Jeff, 41, who has so far served 19 years in prison for killing a two-year-old child when he was 23. He has always maintained that the crime occurred because his drink was spiked with LSD by his mates in the pub, and Kay believes him. Now she visits him weekly and they correspond and speak on the telephone daily. While I was interviewing Kay, Jeff rang and Kay handed me the phone. He sounded rather taken aback and nervous, but said in his pronounced Midlands accent that Kay was brilliant and was supporting him over a recent issue of prison discipline. This had led to the couple being shut into separate kiosks in the prison visiting room, only able to communicate through a glass partition.

●　　　●　　　●

When I was a child in Nottinghamshire, if anyone in our community did time in prison the adults would always tell the children that they'd gone on holiday. Now when anybody asks me where Jeff is, I say he's a long way from here—and that's why I chose the name *Zanzibar* for a lyric I wrote for one of the songs Jeff has composed. This is how it begins:

Black velvet dreams in Zanzibar
When you touched my world
You made me a star
Our fire of love
Broke free tonight
In a cold desert dream
There's no wrong and no right

I started writing poetry seriously when I was eleven. There was so much going on in my mind that I needed to express it. I went to a Catholic school and we were coached to be good little Catholic people. At this age I suppose I'd started to question the Catholic faith. One of my first poems began:

Bless me, Father, please do tell
Why I have to go through hell

I was always magnetized towards girls who had stopped caring about what anybody thought of them. But then when we were given essay assignments I'd actually come out top, and the embarrassing thing was that the teachers read my essays aloud. My rebellious mates couldn't understand that they'd got a friend who was winning brownie points from the teachers, and I became isolated—I was in no man's land.

There was a boy at school who kept smiling at me and I asked him where he lived. He said River House, and I asked my father where that was, and he said, 'That's a bad boys' home!' I asked this boy why he was in this institution and he said, 'For breaking and entering'. I didn't know what that meant so I went back and asked my father and he told me it was burglary. That made that boy even more attractive. I remember thinking, Wow! He's gorgeous good-looking and he's a rebel too!

I was good at art as well as poetry and when the careers officer came round I said I wanted to go to art college. But he said, 'Oh no, you can't do that! You're a secondary school girl. We've got either shop or factory work.' So I left school at 15 and went to work in a small Clark's shoe shop and I hated it.

•   •   •

At that point I met my first husband. I was still only 15 and he was 20. I met him in a pub and I thought he was very clever because he could speak fluent French. He was working at a steel works in Sheffield but he'd been to grammar school. At 16 I married him and I changed geography. I thought this was the passport out of the home I wanted to break away from.

By 1987 I'd had my son, adopted a daughter and we were running a guest house. I started going to evening classes in creative writing, and I began writing short stories about my time at school, the big Irish Catholic families, and how poverty played a part. I used to make the stories up during the day. When I wasn't cooking rashers and sausages and taking phone bookings I used to go into my own little world of writing.

At the class they asked me how long I'd been writing, and I used to get such joy from hearing them laugh when I told them my stories. Three pieces were published in a book brought out by the local university, and two more stories by a northern arts group, and I got an award of £25. My mother and I went on the train to the award ceremony. We were up there with all these celebrities, people we'd seen on TV, like Colin Welland.

I wanted to further my writing and go to an English O-level class as well as the creative writing class. But my husband said, 'Oh, you'll be out two evenings now, will you?' It really was like *Educating Rita*. The kids were about 12 and 14 and I was running the guest house, but my husband decided I wasn't giving it my full commitment and started saying awful things like, 'I'm going to quit my job'—and I knew that if he quit, we wouldn't have had the bread and butter money coming in.

But by then I was becoming very much my own person. I'd known my husband since I was 15, when I didn't know what potential I might have, then I was married for the next 20 years. So I ran away and got a bed-sit in the city, and in the end we got divorced.

•   •   •

At this point I started getting involved with radical politics—I'd always had a sense of the victim not having a voice in this country. When I first met my second husband, I suppose the attraction was that his professional job was connected with social injustice and I thought he was somebody I could talk to.

Then I got pregnant. I was 39 and it was a shock. I married him because of the baby and because I had to have a roof over my head. Circumstantially it may have looked fine, but emotionally it was all wrong. I have to say there have been no good times in our marriage, and I've only stayed with him for two reasons: bricks and mortar, and our daughter, who is now six.

Recently my husband has become physically abusive. But even before that he said to me one day, 'Look, I haven't got any time for you. You're going to have to find another interest'.

•   •   •

That's how I got involved in prison issues. I had written some letters to an Irish newspaper, and a group campaigning for Republican prisoners in this country picked up on my address and sent me a list of prisoners, asking if I would consider sending them a Christmas card. I corresponded with one of them for two years until he was eventually transferred to Ireland.

Then in the *Socialist Worker* I read about a prisoner who had been in prison about seven years but who said he was innocent and was fighting his conviction. Again, readers were asked to send cards and letters of support. I did, and I found myself part of a high-profile campaign. In 1999 that man's appeal was successful and he was released.

In October that year I had a letter from another prisoner asking if I had time to write to someone called Jeff, whom he described as 'a decent guy who knows about music and about life the same as you do, and like you he likes intelligent conversation.'

There was a lot on my mind at the time and I wanted to be in a more positive frame of mind before writing to a prisoner. Then I had this strange dream. I was in a dark room with a very soft floor. There was writing on the wall and beautiful music coming from somewhere. I was kneeling down in front of a man who was just in black silhouette. It progressed on to a lovemaking scene.

About a week later I wrote to Jeff and I sent him a tape I'd made with some of my favourite bits of music. He wrote back saying he had been convicted at 23 and had been in the prison system for 19 years. He added, 'Unlike most of the people you may have met in the appeals system I am guilty'. When I read the letter I thought, This is a man in pain. But I also thought, Oh, I don't know how I feel about this. I'd mainly been dealing with miscarriages of justice and I didn't quite know how to cope with someone who admitted he was guilty.

With that first letter he sent a tape of his own music. He plays the best blues guitar I know, and his music has impressed a lot of my professional friends. But when I played that tape for the first time I just went cold inside, and the hair stood up on the back of my neck—because it was the music in my dream!

•   •   •

Jeff and I went on corresponding but he would never tell me what he had done to get such a long sentence. He wrote, 'I'll tell you when I see you, because it's so awful'. He said that originally he'd got 14 years but then the Home Secretary of the time added six more years, making 20 years. For the 19 years he'd been inside, he hardly had any visits apart from family members, but even they had distanced themselves over the years. In 1993 his father, who used to be his mainstay, had died. Jeff told me he was a Category A prisoner and I wouldn't be able just to come and see him. He wrote, 'You have to be vetted by the police. I'll send you the forms if you want to come and see me.' So I went through that vetting process. I filled out all the forms, attached photographs to them and sent it all back to the prison.

While I was waiting to visit Jeff we used to write long letters to each other. The minimum length would be two sides of A4, though some letters would be five or six pages long. We discussed doing a musical concert in the prison to raise money for a children's charity. He had done this before with a group of other inmate musicians and they raised £800.

In my letters I would pour out all my domestic blues, the weird and bizarre things that my husband did. I would sit up in bed and write to Jeff, though I couldn't keep any of his letters in case my husband found them. Jeff would write to me at my elder daughter's address and I would collect the letters from there.

I haven't slept with my husband for years. We live separate lives, and I think maybe it was the starvation of love, and of normality, that I was missing. For a long time my first marriage was no good, and now I was in another marriage that was no good either.

And then Jeff started writing that he loved me and he was going to marry me one day! I was writing, 'No, you're not!' This went on for about three months, and there were still delays in the vetting process so I couldn't go and visit Jeff. And I still didn't know what he was in prison for. He wouldn't tell me and now I can understand why—he was frightened of losing me. The CID vetting officer didn't tell me either. I've had police checks before to visit other prisoners, and only once have the police asked me if I knew what the man I was visiting was in for. That man turned out to be serving 30 years for terrorist offences.

•　　　•　　　•

The reason Jeff didn't want to tell me was because he'd been jailed for the death of a child. In his letters he always stopped short of telling me. He wrote, 'I was in a car. Please tell me you know what happened next.' In the end he told me over the phone one night. I can't explain how awful it was. He kept saying, 'Tell me you know, tell me you know!' I was sitting on the stairs holding the phone and I said, 'If you want to tell me, tell me'.

So he said, 'I'll tell you what happened. I went out drinking with my mates one night and a man spiked my drink with LSD and I didn't know anything about it. I'd arranged to meet my best friend back at his house afterwards, and I kept going to the house and knocking on the door. I did it three times, and on the third time I must have woken up this little child and she came to the door. She was about two years old, she was my best friend's child. I didn't know what to do. Should I leave her alone and close the door, or should I take her in the car to find her dad?'

He told me he took the child and put her in the back seat of the car and drove off. Then he had a crazy hallucination. He said, 'The steering wheel was melting, the sides of the car were caving in on me. I didn't know what was happening and I slammed on the brakes. The child flew from the back seat to the front seat.'

That's when he stopped short and he said, 'Do you want to know how she died?' I said yes. Then he said, 'Asphyxiation'—and he just started to cry. I started to cry as well and I said, 'Jeff, I can't deal with this at all.' He said, 'If you don't want me to phone you any more I won't. I won't phone unless I get a letter from you saying that I can phone you again.'

I put the phone down, I was gutted. In my letters and the message tapes I'd sent in to him I had said, 'The worst of all crimes to me is child murder'—because at that point I'd got no idea what he had done. Now I thought, I've got attached to this person, he plays beautiful music, he's rational, he's a normal guy. Yet 19 years ago this thing happened. I left it that Jeff and I were not going to speak to each other again or communicate in any way.

But when I got up the next morning I felt that part of my life had died. Even though I'd never met Jeff, I'd really got to 'gell' with him and he with me. It was a feel-good factor that had now gone.

Then I thought, 'Come on, you're a strong woman! Put your coat on and go to town!' But when I'd only got 50 yards into the town the tears were streaming down my face. I kept looking in shop windows and all I could see was me crying. I went into Boots and forgot what I was in there to buy. I remember saying, 'I've got to go home, I can't cope with this!' I was distraught, I was breaking apart, breaking apart.

At about half-past-five that night the phone rang and the strong woman, the rational thinker in me, came back and I said, 'I thought I told you you weren't to phone any more!' He said, 'I just wanted to hear your voice.' And I started to cry, and he started to cry as well, just like he did the night before, when he was telling me about the little girl. He said, 'The only time the pain subsides, just a little bit, is when I'm raising money for children through my music.'

Jeff told me he'd panicked at first after what happened. He didn't know what to do and he ran off. But then he eventually went to the police and gave himself up. One of his friends came to visit him in prison to tell him how they had spiked his drink. He told his solicitor, who said he was going to plead diminished responsibility but he never did, nor did he explain about the circumstances.

At the time of the incident Jeff was a car mechanic who had been happily married for three years and wanted a family. He had never committed a crime and he had never done drugs, though he liked a drink. At the pre-trial hearing he pleaded guilty so of course he never got a jury trial as there was no point.

The police said the motive was rape—that Jeff wanted to take the child and rape her, then when he realised what he'd done he thought he'd better murder her. But there was no forensic evidence to establish rape. The police told him he'd raped the child in the same way they told him he'd strangled her. All the statements were written by the police and Jeff, being vulnerable and gullible, signed them. To this day he will not put his signature on anything, not even on the bottom of his letters to me.

For 19 years he has said, 'This was not me, it was LSD. I'm a regular guy'. But the prison psychologists have always responded, 'You can't blame a substance for your behaviour.' So for those 19 years he has had reports written about him by prison staff who want him to admit he's a cold-blooded child-killer. He said to me recently, 'I'll never ever admit that I strangled that child. I'd rather die in prison'. I said to him, 'Asphyxia doesn't necessarily mean strangulation. With a small child suffering a bad head injury, all sorts of damage could have been done.'

He couldn't expect his wife to wait all those years for him and he wanted her to have her freedom. In my opinion, by letting her go he displayed how much he loved her.

● ● ●

After Jeff told me about the offence I kept in touch but our letters changed, because now I had my own grief joining his grief. At first I found that paralysing, but then I told him how I felt. I hadn't really told him before. He was wanting me to tell him that I loved him the same way he loved me.

What I did love about his letters was his truthfulness, his honesty. He gave me his mother's phone number and he said, 'You can phone her at any time and check out that everything I've said to you is true.' I did ring his mum and she corroborated everything he said. I've since met his sister and she told me his whole trial was a farce.

He's in the prison VPU[1] but he's said to me time and time again that he is not a sex offender, and he's sent me all the documentation to prove it. I've also asked him why he's still a Category A prisoner after all these years, and he says he's never been given a concrete reason.

● ● ●

Finally I got cleared to go and visit Jeff. He'd sent me a photograph showing a slim, gorgeous-looking bloke and I went into the visits room looking for a bloke like that. I heard a Midlands accent and a voice said, 'Here's Kay'. I looked round and what I saw was this rather large man. He said that since the photo was taken three years earlier he'd piled on the weight, because he didn't want to live any more. He'd gone into a sort of Mars Bar frame of mind and just eaten and eaten. He went red when he saw me staring at him and he said, 'Are you disappointed now?' I said, 'Well, your mother told me you'd been eating a lot of curries!' Then he hugged me and picked me up and he was lovely.

On that first visit we talked about anything and everything. My kids, his life, him being alone for 19 years and never having anyone. And his music. He'd learned to play on a guitar he found lying smashed on the prison floor. It only had two strings and he methodically mended it. He plays music of a high professional standard but he's got no ego whatsoever. He always puts himself down, he's always self-criticizing. He says to me, 'Before you came along I didn't want to live any more.'

Yet I've had more emotional support from Jeff than I've had from any other man—ever. Like when my younger daughter had whooping cough for about six weeks earlier this year, he would ring me every day, sometimes three or four times, to make sure that we were okay. Now he still phones me daily and he's so reliable I can set my watch by his phone calls.

I talked to my elder daughter about Jeff and she's been vetted so she can come with me and see Jeff, and recently she did meet him. Like me she knows that the effects of drugs can make people do the most awful things. She's had her phone number approved so that if I'm not in, Jeff can phone her instead. He encourages her to be positive and to continue her studies.

Jeff suffers in prison because he's tried to make good. He's done all the courses on offer, though no amount of courses will make what happened 19 years ago go away. Condoning offences is something neither of us will do and Jeff has never even suggested that I should condone what he did. At no time has he sought to justify the death of a child. He has relived that terrible, terrible set of events every day of his life and he can never put it right. He can only suffer for the rest of his life. It's an awful continuing pain that he has to live with. He has gone to the point where he's wanted to take his own life because he can't live with himself.

I understand that the offence is not one that society is going to look on favourably, but I believe that there has to be a mechanism whereby Jeff can establish that the person who committed that offence was not the person he was before or the person he's been since.

●　　●　　●

As well as speaking to Jeff on the phone every day, I visit him once a week, when I can—he's got visiting orders that go back to the last century—literally!

One day I was with Jeff on a normal morning visit and he passed me a piece of paper on which he'd written the phone number of a music shop. He had some musical amplifying equipment which had got broken, and he'd arranged with the prison authorities to hand it out to me so I could take it away and get a replacement for it from this shop. The shop was one that was approved by the prison, and Jeff asked me to ring the music shop so I could tell him how much this would all cost. He said, 'Princess'—that's what he calls me, his princess—'Princess, go and ring the music shop and then when you come back on this afternoon's visit you can tell me what the cost would be.'

But when I left the visits room at the end of that morning visit, the officers took me into a room, confiscated the piece of paper and gave me a pat-down body search. They said Jeff had been shown on the security camera handing me a piece of paper. Me being the open and honest person that I am, with nothing to hide, I was shown quite openly waving the piece of paper in the air. Jeff said an officer had given him permission to give it to me.

This incident resulted in us being placed on closed visits for three months. A closed visit is like in those American jail films that show the inmate and the visitor with a glass partition between them. In this country we don't even have a telephone to let you hear what the prisoner is saying. We have a perforated metal grille, and you have to put your ear up close to it. I have a hearing impairment so it was very difficult for me, and I had to perch on the ledge in front of the glass, till an officer came rushing in and told me to sit on my chair. I found the whole thing very degrading, particularly as I was locked into this stifling room as well and I wasn't allowed to go and buy a drink for myself and Jeff like all the other visitors—the officers had to come and take an order from me. I felt criminalised by the whole process. The only way we survived was by finding some humour in the situation.

If ever there was a test to a partnership, we've had it all. But we've survived and become stronger. The weapon of isolation, putting us on closed visits, saw me continuing and increasing my trips to see Jeff, and we never abandoned each other. If the prison authorities did all this to try and undermine a positive relationship, it didn't work. In fact the reverse happened. Finally we threatened legal action about being kept on closed visits, and in August 2000 we were put back on open visits. Since we've been together I've encouraged Jeff to be more forceful about taking up the challenges he faces. For instance, last Saturday I had a heated debate with one of the governors about the way he is being mistreated. I was accused of being 'anti-prison'. I stood my ground and told the governor that his officers were immune to accountability. Apparently the lads on Jeff's wing cheered, but the governor told Jeff he thought I was ruthless.

I take that as a compliment, but I don't know whether what I'm doing is the right thing or not, because Jeff's the one in prison who'll have to face any repercussions. It's okay for me, sitting at home and telling him to challenge this and fight that. At the end of the day he's inside and there's hostility that he can't leave behind.

•   •   •

It's about a year since that Jeff and I have been part of each other's lives. His parole is due, but I know the score and I know we have a long way to go before we find ourselves pulling a Christmas cracker together and sunning ourselves in our own back garden. He's still Cat A and he'll have to work his way through Cats B, C and D. It's like starting a marathon, and you have to have staying power to finish it.

What Jeff did all those years ago he calls his one night of madness. He has never been violent before or since, though he has been provoked many times. He has risen above it when most of us would have lost our cool and I'm proud of him for doing so.

Postscript: In Autumn 2001 Kay rang to let me know that Jeff had won the Brian Eno Merit Award in the annual Koestler Awards for prison arts. She said, 'The feedback to all Jeff's music has been brilliant'.

ENDNOTE

¹ Vulnerable Prisoners Unit. See *Glossary*.

Tracey and Rob Walker

Tracey, 31, met Rob, 34, when he was a serving prisoner nearing the end of his sentence. She was married and had given up her job in the accounts department of a London company to look after her two young daughters. Rob had been sent from the local prison to work in Tracey's neighbour's garden as part of his community service.

Tracey is a very attractive woman with remarkably striking, bright blue eyes and shoulder-length, wavy dark hair. When we met she was bare-footed and casually dressed in short-sleeved black tee shirt and loose trousers, discreet gold chain and earrings—and she wore a beautiful aquamarine engagement ring. She has two daughters aged three and four and a half, and had recently moved into a pleasant council property in a town to the north of London. The sitting room has long cream leather sofas and a large digital TV and music centre. Most of the furniture and equipment was bought by Tracey's fiancé Rob out of his wages, because he is allowed to leave the prison and work full-time every weekday, returning to his cell each evening. On the wall is one of the many certificates that Rob has gained in jail, and on top of the TV is a large framed photograph of him receiving another certificate from the prison education officer. A set of small pictures taken in a passport photo booth show Tracey, Rob and Tracey's two children, looking like a very happy family. The room opens through patio doors on to a small garden full of children's toys.

Tracey, the second of three children, is the daughter of a successful self-made businessman. She had a comfortable middle-class upbringing in the south-east of England. She attended the local grammar school and then worked in the accounts departments of a number of London firms. She met her husband when she was 15, and married him at 20. Her husband, family and friends were horrified when at the age of 29 she took their two children and left what appeared to be an ideal marriage—seemingly for the love of a serving prisoner with previous convictions.

During my interview with Tracey the phone rang three or four times. Each time it was Rob, asking how she was. They only spoke for a minute or so, but Tracey would run from the phone, eyes sparkling and face flushed like a young girl.

•　　•　　•

By February 1997 I was beginning to feel extremely unhappy in my marriage. I'd been married for six years, and I'd been feeling quite disenchanted for about a year—but I kept hoping things would improve. But however hard I tried, I didn't feel the way I should about my husband.

He used to put me down all the time. He made me doubt myself so much that I couldn't drive. I passed my driving test first time when I was 17 but he made me so nervous I was terrified to get behind the wheel of a car. It's only recently that I've started driving again—since I met Rob in fact.

I'd always planned to give up work when I had children. But this meant I never had any money of my own. I had to ask my husband before I went and bought anything—he'd give me enough money each week to cover the playgroup fees and the milk bill.

He never saw the girls during the week and he never spent any time with them at the weekend either. By the time our second daughter was born I'd completely fallen out of love with my husband. I wanted to leave but with no means of support I didn't have the first clue how I was going to manage that. Also I knew how upset our families would be if we split up.

On my birthday I woke up in the morning and I thought, I'm 29. Am I still going to be in the same position at 49? That's when I made the decision that I was going to stop trying to please everyone else and I was going to try and work out how I could leave my marriage.

I had a very close friend called Mary whom I'd met at work. She lived in London and though we rarely met, we used to spend hours talking on the phone. So now I confided in her and told her I was unhappy in my marriage But she had her own problems so she didn't have the time to really listen to mine. That made me feel very alone and even more nervous about taking the step of ending my marriage.

●　　　●　　　●

That May my elderly neighbour had asked for a new gardener to be sent from the local prison. For years she'd had men working there who were let out from the prison doing community work. I didn't understand that they'd have lifers there who were at the end of their sentences. When I'd talked to my neighbour she always told me what the men had done, but mostly it was drugs offences. She only told me the last one was in for murder just before he left, the first time I realised these prisoners could have committed more serious crimes.

My neighbour just didn't like this latest man. He was a very strange character and she wasn't very comfortable with him. It so happened that Rob had volunteered for community work at about the same time as my neighbour asked the prison to replace this other guy. So they sent him along to have a look.

When I saw Rob from my window I thought he was gorgeous. I was just going out to fetch my elder daughter from playgroup and as I walked up the road past my neighbour's garden I looked at him and said hello. And what I felt was unlike anything I'd ever felt before. It was an overwhelming feeling that I should be with this man. It felt like I was supposed to be with him. I knew I should be living my life with him and in a strange way I knew I was going to have a relationship with him. The feelings were so intense—and what reinforced those feelings was the look on Rob's face as he looked at me. It was like everything I was feeling was exactly what he was feeling. I walked up the road dying to turn round and look back at him, but I didn't. Rob told me afterwards that if I had looked back I would've seen him standing on the pavement watching me.

I told my friend Mary about Rob and how gorgeous he was. But as soon as I told her that he was a prisoner she automatically said, 'He's in prison. Forget it!'

●   ●   ●

The first week Rob was working next door my daughters started talking to him over the fence. One thing that struck me immediately was how good he was with them, unlike their father. You could see he just had a way with children. They'd ask him what he was doing and he'd always explain. He'd never ignore them and he'd make them laugh so much. It was so lovely to see.

One day that first week we were all out in the garden and Rob was talking to the girls as usual and he told me that they were about the same age as his own daughters, who were aged five, three and two. So I went over to the fence and we started to talk about his girls. He told me he missed them but even more so because he was getting divorced from his wife and she no longer brought them on visits. It seemed such a shame because you could tell he must have been a wonderful father. We started to talk every day he was there and I remember feeling very at ease with him. I found myself getting excited on the days I knew he was going to come to work. We were always talking and laughing and I'd mess about with the girls in the garden with water guns and their toys—and life didn't seem so bad.

One of the days that Rob hadn't been at work next door I found I really missed him and I was looking forward to the following day when I knew he'd be working again. That evening my husband came home and promptly burst into tears because he couldn't cope with some pressure he had at work. I couldn't comfort him with words or in a physical way and it really brought it home to me that I couldn't stay in this marriage any longer.

The following day Rob came to work and he noticed that I wasn't so cheerful as I normally was. After a while he asked me whether there was something wrong because I looked really sad. Because Rob had told me that he was going through a divorce I thought he would understand, so I poured my heart out to him and told him how unhappy I was. Rob was brilliant. He was sympathetic and supportive and he reinforced my thoughts, telling me that I had to think about myself and stop trying to please everybody else.

We started to talk more about ourselves and we both started to make it more obvious that we liked each other. It was clear that we were becoming closer and neither of us wanted to lose touch.

I asked Rob about his offence and he told me without any hesitation what had happened. He'd agreed to take some money to Spain for some acquaintances and in return he was going to get a holiday and a car—things he couldn't have afforded at that time by conventional methods. He knew he was breaking the law by taking the money but at no time did he think that drugs were involved. Whilst he was on holiday the drugs were put in the car. He pleaded not guilty at his trial because to his mind he hadn't set out to bring drugs back, so he didn't consider himself to be guilty of the crime. Now though, he's looked back at the events and realises that those amounts of money don't change hands like that for no reason, and that people don't get nice cars and holidays just for taking money abroad. So he's now come to accept that he did play a part in the drugs crime, albeit unknowingly. He got six years and when I met him he'd done two of them.

I also asked him if he'd been in prison before, which again he answered without hesitating. Looking back he was surprisingly honest. He'd been convicted of false declaration and forgery and he did about twenty months. He told me about his family background too and how he was adopted at ten days old. His adoptive parents weren't involved in crime at all, but Rob started getting into trouble at about 18.

We were getting to know each other very well at this stage and it felt to me as if all my initial thoughts and feelings had been right. I was falling in love with him and I knew for sure I wanted him to be part of my life. It was strange that he'd come into my life at that time, but looking back it was the right time. I suppose that's why everybody thinks I've walked away from a happy marriage to be with someone else—because it happened at the same time. But it wasn't like that. I'd already decided to end my marriage.

Near the end of June we'd discussed the fact that he wouldn't be working in the garden forever and I gave him my phone number so that he would be able to contact me if necessary. He gave me the prison's phone number, address and his prison number so that I'd be able to get in touch with him. He also told me that I'd be able to visit him at the prison, but at that point I put the idea out of my head thinking 'Me? Go into a prison? I don't think so!'

•   •   •

I was dreading the two weeks' holiday that my husband was about to take at the beginning of July and I started to think seriously about going to visit Rob at the prison. When my husband's holiday started he seemed to be watching my every movement. The first morning I suggested to him that he should take our elder daughter to playgroup and I waited for Rob to arrive. I felt guilty and sneaky but I missed Rob so much and I knew that I would have to try not to speak to him quite so much for the next two weeks. I really wanted to have a few minutes with him alone.

We were standing talking over the fence but we were both as close to the fence as we could possibly get, and as we were talking, Rob slowly leant forward and kissed me gently on the lips. And then he kissed me a second time in the same way. I hadn't been expecting it but it didn't shock me either. They were such beautiful kisses. He told me afterwards that he didn't know whether he was going to get a slap, or what was going to happen. He was taking a big risk because there was always the chance that I could've reacted badly, phoned the prison and complained. But he said he just had to take that chance. He wanted a relationship to start and he wasn't prepared to let it go without trying. He'd felt the same as me from the start, he'd felt that I was 'the one' and he didn't want the opportunity to pass and then spend the rest of his life wondering, What if? As I've got to know Rob I've discovered that it's very much in his nature to act on impulse. He does things here and now.

That night my husband got very angry and he said to me, 'The girls are not to talk to Rob or play with him any more! That's it!' then he went off upstairs. After a while he came down again and went out of the front door. He'd left a note saying he just didn't understand what was happening and he had to get away for a while.

A couple of hours later he came back and he was about to leave again but I stopped him. I said, 'We've got to talk about this now you've brought it up.' And that's when I told him our marriage was over. He broke down and cried. That week was very difficult, being in the house with my husband.

The next Monday Rob brought me some visiting orders and gave them to me over the fence and I arranged to visit him at the prison that Thursday.

●　　　●　　　●

I was so nervous about going to the prison—I'd only just started driving again after 12 years. That Thursday I told my husband, 'I need some time. It's no good me just wandering round the village. I'm going out shopping in the car.' So I got in the car and set off to drive to the prison. Luckily, from our house you could get there down a very quiet lane with not much traffic and I thought I could manage to do the drive.

When I arrived I parked the car and wandered round trying to find out how to get into the prison. I was a bit late and all the other visitors had already gone in. Eventually I saw a building outside the prison and heard voices and I asked the men there what to do. One of the officers walked along with me and explained that I had to go through a door and hand in the visiting order Rob had given me.

Then I saw Rob standing on the other side of a fence watching the main gate waiting for me to arrive. It was a really hot sunny day and he'd got dressed up for me. He had a nice pair of jeans on and a smart shirt and he looked absolutely gorgeous. I was half an hour late but he'd stood there waiting for me all that time. As soon as I saw him I was so glad I'd come and my nerves completely disappeared. I walked into the visits hut and Rob was waiting at the door for me. We threw our arms around each other and kissed properly.

It was then that I noticed that one of the prison officers was a man that I recognized from the playgroup. His child and mine were both there. So he obviously knew that I was married with children and he seemed to be looking at me in a funny way.

Rob and I got a drink and went and sat on a bench outside on the grassy area and I noticed that this man walked past us a couple of times as if he was watching. In fact all the other prisoners seemed to be watching us as well. It was almost like they were wondering about Rob, 'What's he doing with a visit? Where's she from?' We spent the whole time kissing and talking. I'd really only planned to stay for about half an hour because I thought it might look strange to my husband that I was away that long. But once I was there I just couldn't leave and the time went so quickly.

Leaving was hard. As I was walking towards the main gate I turned to look back at Rob and he was standing by the fence again watching me. I started to get a bit upset because that was the first time I'd seen him in the prison environment. I'd known from the minute I set eyes on him that he was in prison, but it was at that moment—seeing him standing behind that big high fence knowing that I was leaving and he couldn't—that I really started to think about what being in prison meant. He was locked in there. He *had* to stay. I started to think about how his loss of freedom must feel.

I was so sad because of all of these thoughts and because I'd had to leave him. But I was so happy too because I'd seen him and we'd had such a wonderful couple of hours together where our feelings could finally flow.

When I got back my husband asked where I'd been and I said I'd been to the local town and had a look round the shops. He didn't question it.

•   •   •

Rob and I talked each day on the phone and I arranged to go and see him again on the Sunday. The following week I had two more lovely visits and it wasn't getting any easier to leave.

On the following Saturday I was talking to Rob on the phone in the evening when my husband listened in. Rob was saying he couldn't wait to get out of prison to see his children again, and my husband must have misunderstood and thought he meant our girls, not Rob's own.

When the phone call finished I went downstairs and that's when my husband started to become violent. He didn't touch me—it was the threat of it. I was sitting on the sofa and he came over and he had his face an inch from mine and he was shouting at me. He had his fist raised and I thought he was going to hit me.

That night I could hardly sleep because I was worried that my husband would take the girls and leave. The following morning he went out and came back at lunchtime and then I went out in the afternoon to visit Rob.

The next week I kept phoning the council and eventually someone found me a place in a refuge not too far away. That evening I started getting some papers together and phoned my sister to arrange for her to come round the next day. She helped me put some clothes in a couple of bags and took me to the station with the children where I met the woman from the refuge. I had no money and I was in a complete state. I had no idea what to expect. I'd been living my nice, comfortable, easy life and I was stepping into the unknown.

•   •   •

The refuge house was filthy and I kept breaking down in tears. I spoke to Rob and told him I was okay because I didn't want him to worry. The other children in the house were between nine and 12 years old and they were showing my little girls how to stand on top of the banisters, and then my younger daughter cut her thumb on a razor. I panicked completely.

I didn't know what to do and eventually I phoned my dad who lived about a 20-minute drive away and asked him to come and get me. It was at this point that I told my parents about Rob and where he was. They took it quite badly— they weren't comfortable with it at all and they're still not. My dad especially is very anti-drugs. He's said to me that he doesn't want anything to do with people involved in drugs in any way. He said about Rob, 'Look, if you're going to continue with this I don't want to meet this man till he's out. As long as he comes out and proves himself and he can look after you, then maybe things will be all right.'

My mother was upset that my marriage had ended. She got on very well with my husband—and then to find that I was starting a relationship with a prisoner! Her attitude was, 'What's happened to Tracey? She's taken leave of her senses!' It was almost as if she thought Rob had forced me to leave a happy marriage.

I finally got to speak to Rob and he was so supportive and understanding. By the Wednesday I'd started to calm down but I was back to not knowing what to do—I couldn't stay with my parents indefinitely. Then one night my husband came round with my brother-in-law and they stayed shouting at me for an hour—I felt so intimidated. I discovered that my sister was passing information to my husband about where I was and what I was doing. Since then I haven't had any contact with my sister at all, though we were quite close.

Rob had suggested I try the council in the area north of London where he was from, and eventually I was offered a place at a refuge in that area. The next morning my dad gave me a bit of money and my mum paid for a taxi to get me to Euston. She was worried about me travelling on trains and tubes with two young girls, a pushchair and bags.

Through all of this I was speaking to Rob several times during the day and he gave me the strength to carry it through. He was so loving and so supportive. I couldn't have managed without him. But then throughout the entire journey I felt so calm.

I got to the refuge and it was lovely. I could not have wished for a nicer place. I felt so relaxed and totally at ease. This time I told Rob I was okay and I meant it. He had nothing to worry about. I was fine and I knew I was going to cope.

•   •   •

However, by the following week things were a little less settled. Rob rang to tell me the prison had started an investigation into claims made by my husband who had phoned the prison making allegations that Rob and I had been having an affair. As soon as the prison found out, Rob was taken off the gardening job. Then a big investigation started. Some prison officers were sent to interview my husband and neighbours to try and establish what had happened, and both Rob and I had to write statements. My elderly neighbour told the prison that

Rob hadn't done much work towards the end because we were talking so much over the fence.

My husband kept phoning the prison telling them they weren't doing their job properly. And he kept threatening me, telling me he was going to ring social services and tell them I was an unfit mother. That terrified me in case they believed him. I'd chosen to set up my life with a criminal and I thought it would look bad and they might want to take the children away.

Then Rob rang to tell me he was being shipped back to a Cat B prison. The prison had decided to send him back there to try to stop any adverse publicity by the media, because my husband had threatened to give the whole story to the newspapers. They told Rob that he'd breached the conditions of his licence.

The following day I went with Rob's dad to see him and I'll never forget the look of despair on his face. It was devastating. I felt so guilty and I told him so. I said I thought I was causing him too much trouble and that if he wanted to end it I'd understand. He told me that nothing was further from his mind. He loved me and he knew I was worth it. He said he'd do anything to be with me. While we were there one of the senior officers came over to speak to us. He said he was sorry this was happening to Rob and the prison didn't really want Rob to go as he'd been a good inmate.

As we were saying goodbye I was trying so hard not to cry, but Rob was so upset as well and we couldn't let go of each other.

•   •   •

Rob was taken to his new prison a couple of days later. I was still worried about him, because we'd talked about what it was like in prison, so if I didn't hear from him at the time when he usually called me I'd be terrified that something had happened to him. I went to a solicitor and applied for a divorce. My husband wanted to contest it at first but in the end he just went for custody of the children.

I couldn't even contemplate not seeing Rob for a fortnight. So I got on a train with the girls at six in the morning, travelled on the tube to Victoria, got an eight o'clock train from there to Sittingbourne, changed there to get to Sheerness and got a taxi across to the prison because the bus didn't leave till eleven-thirty. The girls were tired and bored and playing up and it was complete hell. But I visited every Thursday and every Sunday, getting the train when I couldn't get a lift. I'd have done anything to get to Rob because I missed him so much.

Rob used all his money on phone cards—he rang me every chance he got. He was so worried about me as he could do even less for me now he was in a bang-up jail.[1] But I was fine. The refuge was lovely. They'd helped me sort out my benefits so I had money coming in to feed the girls. We had a roof over our heads and beds to sleep in, in a clean, warm, comfortable house in a nice area. I'd been very lucky and I'd toughened up a bit.

Rob and I used to talk about so many things on those visits. We've found there are so many ways in which we are similar—even silly little habits that we've both had for years. Rob told me more about his past—things he really didn't have to tell me, but he has always been very honest with me. He's never lied to me and he's told me things that could potentially have made me think about ending our relationship. He didn't know how I was going to react but he wanted everything out in the open, so that I knew everything and I was fully aware of all the facts, rather than me finding things out at a later stage.

But I can honestly say that nothing he told me made the slightest difference. I was more certain about my feelings for him than I'd been about anything before in my life.

•   •   •

Rob finally got his D Cat, which was a huge relief, and now we felt a bit more able to make plans for the future. Rob asked me what I'd say if he did ask me to marry him, and I told him I'd say yes. He asked if I wanted to wait and just get married when we were both divorced, or did I want to get engaged. So I told him I'd like to get engaged. We looked at rings and chose the ones we'd pick for each other—and they turned out to be the ones we'd have picked ourselves.

The council offered me a temporary place in a hostel. I was a bit nervous about what it would be like because Rob had told me about hostels he'd stayed in. But it would mean that he had somewhere he could come on his town visits. When I saw the place I couldn't believe my good fortune! It was a three-bedroomed flat in a newly-built block. It was furnished and clean and it was lovely! I felt so lucky and it was like we were being shown again that we were meant to be together. Everything was going to work out for us. Rob came out that weekend on his town visit and with my parents he helped me move the last of my things out of the refuge. That day we exchanged rings and got engaged.

•   •   •

Meanwhile my custody battle for the children was still going on. The next time I had to go to court, Rob got compassionate leave so that he could be there with me, because we were going to find out who would get custody of the children. Oh, it was horrible! I just wasn't sure how the courts would look at it. When I was in the refuge I spoke to the solicitor and she told me the welfare officers would do all they could to get the children back into the matrimonial home, the home that they knew. And that devastated me. I'd been there for them since their birth, I'd been their full-time carer, I'd never done anything ever to damage my children—I hadn't abused them, I hadn't neglected them. But then I thought because Rob's was a drugs crime the court would say, 'Drugs! That's not a good model for children!' and might take them away.

But the welfare officer recommended I got custody and my husband didn't contest it after all. In fact I don't think he ever wanted to take the girls away from me. It was just that he didn't want Rob to take his place. It was a gamble I took, I suppose—a big gamble.

Personally I think that it worked out for the best. I couldn't live without my children and now my husband actually spends time with them, which he never did before. So it's actually strengthened his relationship with his daughters. If anything, it's shown him how to be more of a father.

• • •

Last Christmas Rob was allowed out for the day and for Boxing Day. My parents decided to invite me and Rob to their place for Christmas dinner. It was okay but my aunt and uncle were there and my parents hadn't told them Rob was a prisoner. They haven't told anybody that, though people know I'm divorced. For a Christmas present my dad helped me get a car, and Rob got me driving. He was brilliant—he just made me believe in myself.

My parents have come to a certain acceptance of the situation, but more because they love me and they don't want to lose me, rather than looking at how much happier I am now. I don't feel they've really taken the time to get to know Rob. They've held on to all their preconceived ideas about what he's like and why he's with me and I don't think they've given him a chance. All the time they're looking at what he's getting out of the relationship, not the support he's given me. They think he'll leave me and won't love the children. My mum very much hopes that when Rob comes out that'll be the end of us and we won't be able to live together—it doesn't matter what I say. My sister has cut all ties because my brother-in-law has decided they feel sorry for my husband. They don't want their children associating with Rob. The only thing I've had to give up through meeting Rob is my family. Even though I'm still in contact with my parents, I don't feel there's the same closeness as there used to be.

My friend Mary seemed as if she was supporting me and I wanted her and Rob to meet. We met up in London for a meal but it went wrong right from the start. She was annoyed that I'd had my tongue pierced like Rob's, and she said to me, 'You're don't seem to be the person you were'. Rob said he wasn't having her talking to me like that and she went storming out of the restaurant saying, 'I've always been there to support Tracey, and I'll still be there when this finishes!' I just couldn't believe how she treated him and I haven't spoken to her since. It seems so strange from someone I was so close to.

The council has now rehoused me in a lovely little house with a garden for the girls and we couldn't be happier. People round here know where Rob is but they don't seem to be fazed by it as they were in the village where I used to live.

• • •

Throughout all the hard times and setbacks neither of us has ever thought of ending our relationship. We've both always been so sure about our feelings for each other. We've gone from strength to strength—and we couldn't be closer or stronger than we are today. We've both had hard times to deal with but throughout them all we've been there for each other and we've got through everything together.

Thinking about it now, it really does feel as though we were brought together for a reason. Rob could have been sent somewhere else other than the garden next door. He hates gardening so he could have turned it down. If I'd left my husband already I wouldn't have been there to meet him. There are so many 'what ifs?' But I'm sure we were meant to meet and be together. I don't think things would have turned out so well if it wasn't right.

The girls have always been close to Rob. I explained that one day we'd get married and he would be their step-dad. They know he's not their real dad but they're very proud of him and love telling people about him. They know he's in prison. When they first met him they used to ask him where he lived and he'd say, 'In a big house with a yard'. I never wanted to take the girls to a prison and my family thought I shouldn't but in the end I had to take them with me. I used to tell them it was just a place where Daddy had to live for a little while, but then they met other children and heard them say it was a prison.

●　　　●　　　●

Knowing Rob has changed my views. I always used to think you should go to the worst possible prison so you don't want to go back there. But until you know a prisoner personally you have no idea how they are treated.

My divorce is through and I'd marry Rob immediately if he got his. I wouldn't mind if we married in a registry office, as long as it's a quiet little ceremony. We would like children together and I hope we see more of Rob's own daughters. Rob now comes home to me and the girls every weekend but until he comes out for good my life can't get going again. I still write letters to him, though not every day as I used to when I first came to the refuge—now he gets a letter a week and I write a bit of it every day. We have just heard that Rob's been granted parole and he'll be out in August 2000. We're both ecstatic that we'll finally be together after all this time.

I feel I've changed in myself. I've become much more independent. I have a very close relationship with a man I adore and who adores me. We can discuss anything and everything and we're both working towards the same goals. Rob's made me believe in myself—he tells me he knows I can do things, rather than putting me down like my husband did. I've found a new confidence and happiness and I finally feel like I've started to live my life.

Postscript: Tracey contacted me just before Christmas 2000: 'Rob did get his parole —he was released in August and moved into our home. Things are going really well—so well in fact that I'm expecting our baby in June.' In September 2001 she rang to tell me that their son was born on 5 June. Rob has a good job as assistant site manager on a house building site, and the couple married in August 2001, a year after his release.

ENDNOTE

---

[1] A prison with more secure closed conditions than the Category C establishment he was in before, which allowed him out to work.

Moira and Alan

Moira, 40, is a qualified saddler living in the home counties. She also has an HGV licence and currently drives a refuse disposal lorry for the local council. She is divorced with a 14-year-old son. She and her partner, Alan, 38, have been together five years. Moira does not want their real names disclosed because Alan is a convicted sex offender serving a six-year sentence.

Moira is a very tall woman with a pleasant manner when she smiles. However, much of the time during the interview her voice sounded rather dispirited, except when she grew angry talking about her ex-husband and about social services. Then she became the opposite, very feisty. She was casually dressed in sweatshirt and mauve leggings with jodhpur-style pads inside the knees: her hobby is riding and she has her own horse. It was early December 1999 when I interviewed Moira, and the living room of the maisonette she shares with her teenage son Shaun was already decorated with a Christmas tree and other trimmings. Shaun was with us most of the time: although we discussed some difficult issues Moira said there were no secrets between them.

Both Moira's parents were driving instructors. As a child she was very keen on horses and after school she studied saddlery at a specialist college and later ran her own saddlery business. Her first marriage ended after nine years when she divorced her husband for mental cruelty.

She met Alan in October 1994 when he was working as a milkman in her street. They formed a firm friendship but he was soon to tell her that he had served a number of prison sentences for indecent exposure and was currently on bail yet again, charged with another offence. Their relationship has grown deeper during the six years since they met, though they have spent a total of only eight months together 'on the outside' and he has served two further prison sentences for similar crimes. Moira believes Alan is innocent of the crime for which he is currently in prison, but nevertheless she will face a serious dilemma when he is released. Her son will still be a minor and he and Alan will not be allowed to live under the same roof.

•   •   •

I met Alan because I forgot to sign a cheque! I left out an unsigned cheque to pay the milk bill and he called in to let me know. Actually I'd seen him before on his rounds because at that stage I was working nights. Shaun was about nine then, and because I was a single parent I'd drop him off to sleep at my mum's each evening before going to work. Then at about 2 a.m. when I had a half-hour's break I'd come home and let my dogs out for a run. Alan was doing his early round and he thought it was odd to see someone's door open. So he called in about the cheque, and after that, if I was home I'd offer him a cup of coffee and we'd have a chat.

I don't know really what we talked about. We do have quite a lot in common, but as far as I was concerned at the time it was just a bit of fun—just a friendship.

We talked about anything and everything. Within two or three days of knowing him he'd told me about the trouble he was in. He was honest and open and up-front about things, and I think in a way that was one of the things that did attract me to him—his honesty.

I remember the evening he told me about his record of sex offending. I met him when I went to get some money out of the cash machine in our local high street—I was about to go to work actually—and as I got back in the car, he said, 'Can I get in the car? There's something I've got to tell you'. I said, 'Can't it wait till we get home? I've got to get to work'. And he said, 'No, I've had to pluck up courage to say this and I've got to tell you now.'

He said he'd been in trouble—he had been in trouble several times—and he told me the trouble he was in at the time. And then a couple of days later, he took me down to the solicitors' and got them to open his file and said, 'There you are'. He told them that he wanted me to have access to any files I wanted to read. His convictions were for exposing himself to women. He was a flasher.

•   •   •

I could have refused to read the files, but as I said, more than anything it was Alan's honesty that I respected. And I thought about it and I said to myself, It's taken a lot of courage for him to come out with this. The honesty was more important to me than anything really because it was something that I value in a relationship, and it was something I certainly never had with my ex-husband.

My husband used to have me followed, he used to check up on absolutely everything. He laid traps all round the house. To see if I'd used the phone he'd leave little tiny pieces of paper—tiny, tiny, tiny little threads of paper—that he'd put under the telephone receiver, so that if I took the receiver off I'd disturb them and he'd know that the phone had been used. He'd lie to me about what money we'd got in the bank, and he'd lie to me about where the money'd been spent.

The reason I got out of that relationship was because I found myself sitting at the bottom of the stairs one day and thinking to myself, Please God, let the next person that calls be a policeman, saying that he's been killed on the motorway.

But with Alan there was never any deviousness. Of course I'm like everybody else, and obviously the first thing that sprung to my mind when I heard the words 'sex offence' was, Oh my God, I don't want to know! But then I went to the solicitors and actually saw the charge sheet and the offences written down in black and white, what Alan was actually supposed to have done, exposing himself to women. And when I walked out of that office I found myself laughing at him.

He asked me what I was laughing at and I said, 'I can't believe that no woman has ever clumped you one. My immediate reaction would not be to run off to the police station—it would be to turn round and give you such a belt!'.

And he said, 'No, no, nobody ever hit me'. I said, 'Well, if you'd exposed yourself to me you'd have been wearing your balls for earrings! I'd have done something to you you'd never forget!'

I know some of his victims were under-age, and I can understand how they would be frightened and they would react the way they did. But a lot of them weren't that young. And I just couldn't believe that nobody had ever given him a decent put-down or given him a slap round the face. But nobody ever had.

So I sat down and I said to him, 'What you've done—yes, okay, they're crimes, but they're ridiculous nonsense!'

He said, 'Oh, but I've really frightened people, and I really regret that now'. And I said, 'Well, that's as maybe, but to me you're just a complete and utter pillock!'

●   ●   ●

I met Alan at the end of October 1994 and at the beginning of December he was sent to prison for four years. I think his longest sentence before that had been 18 months. During those few months we spent together we talked a lot about what he'd done. Now that I've known him for some considerable time I can see reasons for what he did. I can't see justification because I can never see justification for things like that—but I can see reasons.

Alan's only two years younger than me, but I'm a lot more mature and he's had to do an awful lot of growing up. In many ways he was very much still a child when we met, and this is where I think a lot of his problems stem from. His behaviour is adolescent behaviour, but of course it's totally unacceptable adolescent behaviour from a man in his thirties. He is very inexperienced in all types of life and he's very, very young emotionally. As I understand it his father was exceedingly violent and Alan says that when he was about five, he saw him raping his mother. Alan went to live with his grandparents when he was very young, then the grandparents died and Alan came back to the family home. And something must have happened then because he was put into care when he was about eleven, and that's when he committed his first offence.

Now of course his name is on the sex offenders' register. It doesn't matter how serious the offence—it can be flashing like Alan did, right the way through to rapists and murderers—all sex offenders are now put on the list.

I know that experts say that offences like Alan's can lead to something worse, even rape or murder, but in his case I don't think this will ever happen. I believe him when he says he didn't commit this latest offence he's been done for. This was a very unfortunate thing. He had no alibi, but there was no evidence against him either, so he was convicted purely on verbal evidence, which I think is dreadful. He had a long record and this time they just threw the book at him and gave him six years. The previous one he got four years for—that's the offence he was jailed for soon after I met him. He came out on 22 July 1997 having done two years and eight months. He finished off his sentence at HMP Albany on the Isle of Wight.

When Alan got sent to prison I never had any doubt that I would support him. But I must say, visiting someone in prison for the first time was a very different experience—totally different to anything I'd ever been involved with before. That first visit I ever made, back in 1994, was to HMP Winchester. Alan had been convicted and they'd put him there because it's our local prison. They do that until they disperse them round to other prisons. And funnily enough, on my first visit I met a lady barrister who was there visiting her boyfriend.

She was sitting there, wearing very nice clothes, and I was sitting there looking smart too, though not in the sort of clothes she could afford. We both seemed to be giving out the message to each other: 'Neither of us belong here, do we?' And it was very nice to talk to her. Alan was sent from Winchester to Maidstone, then to Wandsworth, and then he went to Albany. He was there for the sex offender treatment programme.

When he was released in July 1997 I had to drive Alan to a special centre not far from here—sex offenders have to continue with the treatment programme out in the community. They really broke people down on that programme at Albany, but what happened at this centre I found very dangerous. Part of the sex offender programme is to make men feel like the lowest of the low—which I think is stupid because someone like Alan has terrible self-esteem to start with. The blokes used to come out of that centre feeling very angry and very bitter, very alone. And I used to think, How stupid can you be? You send these blokes out, who already have very low self-esteem anyway, and then you kick them into the gutter and then you wonder why, on the way home, they grab some poor girl and throw her into an alleyway. I used to wait for Alan outside in the car and I would see these blokes come out at the end and of course you know they're all sex offenders. Some of them are rapists, some of them are murderers. I'd see the anger and the bitterness in their faces, and I thought it was just so dangerous.

I know they've got to face up to what they've done and learn to deal with it. But surely at the end of the session they could be sent out on a good note. Maybe someone could say, 'You haven't offended this week, that's really good, it's a positive note, you've done something really good. Keep working on that till next week and we'll see how we do!' If only they could send them out at least feeling something's been achieved. But they sent these guys out with a weight on their shoulders. They'd tell them, 'You're a horrible pervert. Nobody's ever going to want to look at you, you're evil'. I suppose there must have been 15 or 16 men at the session—and the centre was right in the middle of a housing estate. I'd see them walk out and I'd think, Oh my God, you're just sending out time bombs!

Alan used to get in the car very angry, *very* angry. But he was lucky because there was somebody waiting for him when he came out. He could talk his anger out with me. But as for the others, I don't know how far they had to go home, I don't know how they got home. But nobody seemed to take that point seriously.

Despite these weekly sessions, those six months between July 1997 and the end of January 1998 we had some good times together and we had some good laughs. Everything was absolutely fine until Alan was arrested again. Before that he didn't have a court case hanging over him or anything. It was a complete shock when he was arrested on 31 January 1998.

• • •

By this time we had a normal boyfriend/girlfriend relationship—though obviously he couldn't live here because Shaun was living with me—he was about 12 then. But Alan could come and stay here when Shaun was at his father's—he used to go and see his father once a fortnight for the weekend. I must admit that when Alan's been about, the times we have been able to stay together here, my life has been very much easier. He would do the housework, the dinner was on the table and everything neat and tidy. There was never any hassle or worry about it.

Alan's a totally different person when he's outside prison. He's not worried about silly little things. But when people go into prison, everything becomes magnified and the tiniest little difficulty suddenly becomes an insurmountable problem that everybody must get involved with because it seems so important. Prisoners' self esteem goes down and down and down—and then people wonder why they fly off the handle and end up committing more crimes. But those weekends when Alan would come here I could imagine what a normal relationship with him would be like. It was very nice, very easy-going.

Unfortunately social services got involved because of Shaun and they contacted my ex-husband and told him about Alan. Then they insisted on Shaun going to live with his dad. It was supposed to be permanent but it only lasted seven weeks. I knew it wouldn't work because of his father's attitude. But those seven weeks put a rift between Shaun and his father. His dad hasn't sent him a birthday card or a Christmas card for the last two years.

Then after Alan was arrested and sent to prison again, social services told me they weren't interested in Shaun any more, now that Alan was back in prison. I was very annoyed. I told them, 'You've destroyed the relationship between my son and his father. You've walked into a family situation, you've set your time bomb, you've watched it explode and now you're just going to walk off!'

They've taken Shaun's name off the 'At Risk' register now because of Alan being back inside. But then Alan got pulled to one side by one of the governors in the prison to say that he wasn't allowed to speak to Shaun on the telephone. He said, 'If we find out you've spoken to Shaun on the phone we'll stop your phone calls'.

It has never occurred to me that Alan could be any risk to Shaun, because what he did was expose himself to females. I told Shaun all about it because he wanted to know. Obviously when Alan disappeared to prison he asked questions. We don't have any secrets from Shaun.

• • •

My mum found out about my relationship with Alan and she was totally against it. She knew because an ex-boyfriend of mine had sent her the newspaper reports of Alan's case. A couple of friends have said, 'You must be bloody mad!' but I just said, 'It's my madness'.

At the moment, the situation is that Alan's got at least another two years to serve in prison, and I don't know what will happen to our relationship in that time. He's still going on about getting married. In fact he wrote to me today and said, 'I want to know where this relationship's going. Am I going to live with you when I come out?'

Social services are saying Alan can't live with us till Shaun is 18. He won't be quite 16 when Alan is released. So I've said to Alan, 'It depends on so many factors. Where am I going to be in two years' time? What am I going to be doing? What's Shaun going to be doing? We don't know.'

•   •   •

Alan has changed an awful lot since we met and he finds it much easier to cope with things now. The experts say it's his very low self-esteem that is the trigger for his offences, and I don't think his self-esteem would ever again drop as low as it used to be. Intellectually he's very bright, and he's now got qualifications. He's passed all sorts of computer exams, and now he's doing book-keeping. I suggested him doing accountancy because then he can open his own business when he's released. He does worry about that too: he said, 'What if I get a female client? She might just call round the house.' I said that all he'd have to do to do is make sure an appointment is made for her when I'm at home, then I can be his chaperone. I don't think he fears he might do something—I think he fears being accused of something.

I know Alan says he can't understand why I stay with him because of all this hassle. I met Alan probably at the right time for Alan more than me. I certainly wasn't looking to get into another relationship.

I do think prisoners can become dependent on people outside—to stop them reoffending, as in Alan's case. He's said that many times. But I said to him, 'No, Alan, that's not the reason. *You're* the one who's got to stop. It's not fair to put it on to me.' I do something I call 'putting the mirror up'. I make Alan look at himself and look at what *he's* got to do about things—not what I or anyone else has got to do. I've told Alan, 'I'll help you, I'll help you to the ends of the earth. But if I find you do commit another offence it won't be the police you'll have to worry about—it'll be me!'

•   •   •

Alan was the one prisoner partner who insisted on my visiting him in prison, where he was held in the Vulnerable Prisoners Unit. A round-faced, quite jolly-looking man with a toothbrush moustache, he looks about ten years older than his age. He was wearing a tee shirt with the word 'WIN' across the front.

I used to be a milkman delivering milk, and Moira was delivered to me really! I called on her when she left me an unsigned cheque and after that she would always wave to me as I did my rounds on my milk float. One day I stopped and said, 'You seem to keep following me around—do you fancy me or something?' She said, 'Yes, I do actually!' and from there it really took off.

I'm on the sex offenders' list because I exposed myself in a public place to complete strangers, including children. But I don't believe I'm any threat at all to Moira's son Shaun. When I first met Moira he was only about nine or ten and I was left in charge of him and I took him out for the day. We went to the market and bought food for tea and we came home and cooked it so Moira could put her feet up next to the open fire. She said nobody had ever done anything like that for her before.

When I'm released, which should be in two years' time, social services don't want me to go and live with Moira because Shaun will still only be 16. But I feel I'm much more at risk of reoffending if I'm put in a bedsit on my own But living with Moira I'm sure there'll be no risk at all.

I've been through the Sex Offenders' Treatment Programme and they went back over my past life and it came up how I saw my father rape my mother when I was five. The other guys in the VPU are okay and we don't see much of the main prison, but when we do we're always expecting to be attacked. Most of the officers in the VPU are okay too, but the ones running the programme do put you down and make you feel you're the lowest of the low.

But I believe people like myself can change. I think Moira has changed my life. Meeting her was the highest point in my life. She's a very respectable woman who has never been in any trouble at all, not like me —I've been in trouble since I was 13 and I was sent to a detention centre for stealing. I do wonder sometimes if she has other relationships, but she says she doesn't.

I do get very agitated if I can't speak to Moira, for instance if she's on the phone when I ring. She doesn't seem to realise that I have to queue up for ages to get to the only phone on the wing, and if she's engaged when I reach the front of the queue I have to go to the back again.

We write long letters to each other as well as phoning. Mine are now down to six pages though they used to be even longer. I find it therapeutic to write down my feelings throughout the day.

I do ask Moira why she bothers with me, with all the hassle it causes her and Shaun. But she just says she loves me—and that's all there is to it.

George Delf and Sara Thornton

George is a journalist and writer. In August 1990 he read a letter printed in the *Independent* newspaper. It came from Sara Thornton, a prisoner in HMP Durham. She had been convicted a few months earlier of the murder of her abusive alcoholic husband, and jailed for life. He wrote to her and his letter was the start of a short but intense relationship.

George is 66, 21 years older than Sara, 45. He lives in Durham in a 250-room castle of Norman origins, rebuilt in the 1820s by a wealthy coal magnate and now converted into apartments—though only about 15 people live there. George, the longest resident, says he feels like 'the ghost of the castle'—and he could certainly be described as a genuine English eccentric. With his floppy grey hair and debonair manner he has a donnish image, but in fact he took the decision in the late 1970s not to take on any work that earned him enough to pay tax. He says he did not want his taxes to make any contribution to nuclear weapons, which he has opposed since his student days.

The son of an army officer, George was brought up in India and first came to England at the age of 12, with the result, he says, that England 'has always been a slightly foreign country.' At his public school, Sedbergh, he was a contemporary of Lord Bingham, former Master of the Rolls and Lord Chief Justice. After Cambridge George got a job on a boat belonging to the Duke of Newcastle and sailed with his French girlfriend through the canals and rivers of France to Marseilles, then hitch-hiked to Kenya where he worked as a journalist on a paper called *The Colonial Times*. When he was still in his twenties he wrote an acclaimed biography of Jomo Kenyatta. Other books include *Asians in East Africa* and *Humanizing Hell: The Law versus Nuclear Weapons*. He went on to work in North America and Europe.

George was divorced in the 1970s and has two adult sons. Before he began corresponding with Sara he had had no contact with prisons at all. Yet soon after they began writing he took on the campaign for Sara's freedom.

At her retrial in 1996 (following her second appeal) she was convicted of manslaughter and finally freed. In that year, she and George collaborated on a collection of their letters[1] which was serialised in *The Independent*, the newspaper through whose letter columns Sara and George first met. The book is a moving account of the extraordinary intellectual and physical intensity of their short relationship. They still remain friends.

•   •   •

When I read Sara's letter to the *Independent*, two things struck me straight away. One, it was exceptionally well-written, which made an impression immediately. And second was the fact that there seemed to be an obvious injustice there. The letter spelled out a number of things that had not worked when Sara had appealed to them—like the Church, social services and the police—while this violence was going on in her home.

Sara was in Durham prison, not far from where I was living, so I wrote and asked her if she wanted to meet and discuss it, and that's how it all began.

That was the first time I'd ever had any connection with a prison or a prisoner, but I'm interested in the idea of justice. I'm interested in the way the law works and doesn't work, and I'd become a specialist—self-taught—in international law and had a book published about it.

That September I went to visit Sara in Durham prison's H wing[2] The whole thing was quite a shock to me, going through eight or nine locked doors to get to someone you're seeing. It was the whole violence and intimidation, the wretched impression of a big prison like that. And then to end up in this rather cosy little visitors' room with coffee easily available! There were two women prison officers in the corner chatting, and they obviously weren't interested in what we were saying—and that in itself interested me.

On the first meeting we just shook hands—there was nothing more than that. I didn't know what to expect. I just asked Sara a lot of questions about what was behind her letter to the newspaper, and what it all meant. Then we just chatted generally. It was all very easy.

After that when I visited her it was often just us and occasionally one or two other people, but that visits room was never crowded and it was always rather easy-going. It was really a little point of sanity in the middle of that completely insane place.

It's pretty obvious from the book of our letters we published that there was a very quick rapport between us. I don't think anything happened gradually—it all happened within a month, with one visit a week. We couldn't talk on the phone at all—it wasn't allowed at that point, though later there was a very small amount of that. The rapport between us was very quick, because Sara was incredibly articulate. I thought she had a very dynamic face—a small woman with curly hair. Soon we were writing to each other three or four times a week and I was seeing her once a week.

•   •   •

Sara said in one letter that she was certain we were each other's destiny, that we'd get married, and in a kind of way I shared that certainty. But it was odd because of the fact that she was in prison and we couldn't do anything—so talking about things outside the prison was, in a way, fantasy. But the hopes and the feelings were there.

The governor gave me this special status—it was marvellous! Sara didn't have a solicitor at that point and there was no legal aid, so I went in as her unofficial sort of legal adviser. The social visits were on alternate weeks, but every other week I went in on legal visits as well—that's how I was able to visit weekly. For the legal visits we had to go to the legal advice room where we sat across a table. We were supposed not to touch each other and she of course made all sorts of jokes about it, which was quite funny. There was a lot of humour mixed up in our relationship because Sara's got a pretty waspish sense of humour. Her mind was sharp, working ten times quicker than anybody else's in the prison and always ahead of the game. I think the prison was very pleased to get rid of her in the end. People in the Establishment generally were quite intrigued by this woman who was quite obviously educated and articulate and middle-class and just like them in a sense.

In one of her letters Sara said that for other women prisoners and even for the staff, our relationship was like a fairy tale. We did have wonderful dreams about being in the castle where I live, with a log fire, playing Sibelius—even going to Finland together. All human beings have peak experiences, some more than others, and this was a peak experience for me in the sense that it was highly unusual, it was running against the system, it was unlike anything I'd ever done before.

As Sara said in one of her letters to me, the women in H wing and the prison officers were fascinated by what was happening. One of the prisoners, an IRA woman, actually made desktop published wedding invitations for us! But the other half of the fascination, for both prisoners and officers, was: 'This won't work, it can't work, it mustn't work. Because if it works it means *my* life is meaningless'. So their first reaction was very positive and sound, and the second reaction was very negative and destructive.

I did think marriage was possible—we were trying to get her out, the first appeal was coming up, she could have got out. But I also knew that we didn't know what each other was like outside a prison environment.

I was certainly completely intrigued by Sara. I admired her courage. She is very brave, and she's very intelligent and very articulate. I think what's really unique about the book of our letters is that I've never come across a woman in prison for a murder conviction able to write in the way Sara did about what was happening to her on different levels. You've got the mixture of challenging the system, the humour, the wit, and the love element. I've always had a long-standing interest in psychology. It just interests me. And obviously Sara was a fascinating sort of person. I was completely intrigued by her background, her relationship with her parents.

•　　　•　　　•

Quite early on Sara was predicting the end of the relationship. I had talked about the need for 'debriefing and decompression' for several weeks if Sara got out. She wrote and said life wouldn't be a bed of roses, and she said, 'If you're going to end it, give me a lot of hints'. That was partly because it's just human to do that, but also partly because she was so used to being knocked down by life. But I hung on in there for a long time. It's a characteristic I have and both my sons have it too. Once we've got our teeth into something we're very intense and we're very concentrated—for better, for worse. That's what I felt with Sara. I respond much better to that sort of challenge. I need that spur.

The whole thing was a pretty mind-blowing experience for me. It was taking me into a new territory completely in terms of being in a women's prison, in being involved emotionally with a woman prisoner who was a convicted murderer. I think in terms of my own psychology I'd been interested in violence for some time. I'd been curious about domestic violence. I think anyone's got to be, because we're all capable of violence and I think it's something we're never that far from, even if we think we are. I'd had no personal experience: I'd never been violent, I'd never suffered it and I didn't know at first hand anyone who'd been through that mill.

But I grew up in the Second World War and my father was in the army and I did National Service. So I've been intrigued by violence and still am—because in my opinion the whole culture we live in is still traumatically affected by the First World War. The role of men is, to some extent, crippled by that experience, down the generations—not just people who fought—in the sense that men became cut off from women to a dangerous extent in their experience.

Sara can be aggressive and she can be very quick, very volatile. But I've never had the feeling with her that she would suddenly flare up and attack me. I think she is absolutely committed to non-violence, probably more than 90 per cent of the population.

I don't think I ever over-idealised Sara—in the sense that I knew what she'd done and it was quite appalling. Killing anyone for any reason is appalling, and I put that in the context of me growing up in a society that's rationalized killing people by the million and has covered it over with a lot of smarmy monuments and history and rubbish, and is still doing so. So in a sense I saw Sara and anyone like that as being the scapegoats of a culture that's adept at hiding its own guilt and imposing guilt on the weakest people in society.

So I suppose in that context, Sara to me was someone who was in the middle of the whirlpool. We were both in a way odd people out within the wider circle, though for different reasons. So my hope was that we would be able to be together, cooperatively, inside that total problem, however we each defined it. And I think that could have happened. She'd got the intelligence and the energy and a lot of insight.

•　　　•　　　•

We came from very similar backgrounds in a sense. Like Sara I spent my early childhood abroad and England has always been a slightly foreign country to me. I was brought up in India and she was brought up in Fiji. Like her I was sent to boarding school in England—I was at Sedbergh, a boarding school in Yorkshire, where I helped organise a mutiny on a big field day for the cadet force. There was an end-of-term parade in the school yard and we managed to get somebody to undo the fire hydrants so the whole place was flooded. Tom Bingham, who became Master of the Rolls and Lord Chief Justice, was in the boarding house next door and I remember him leaning on the gatepost and he had a sardonic smile on his face, watching this mayhem going on.

At the time I met Sara my sons would have been in their mid-20s. They were intrigued by my relationship with Sara though it wasn't the first off-beat relationship I'd had since I was divorced back in the 1970s. They regard me as basically lunatic anyway, but we do have a very good equal sort of relationship where they're my best critics. They regarded my relationship with Sara as interesting and they paid a lot of attention to it and they read the book of our letters. Then when Sara was released they both met her in London.

I did write to Sara that I felt I needed a whole new world for her. I wrote, 'At first I tried to fit you into my world, but now I realise I need a whole new world for you.' Most of us have this feeling occasionally—that we need our habits broken, we need to be tested to destruction, to be forced to think of new things in a new way for new reasons. That's happened periodically in my life for different reasons and this was one such moment. I felt that there was something very healthy within the problem: for Sara and me it would actually force us into a new thing. But then unfortunately for various reasons it sort of took a step back and didn't happen quite in that way.

I've come to feel, based I suppose on my own experiences, that love as such is doomed without a strong creative element to it. I'm very much a fan of Keats, because I think that Keats understood how these things are absolutely entwined—beauty, truth and love. If you start disentangling them it falls apart.

Sara wrote to me that some men are only able to love what's unattainable. She was challenging me, and I wrote back, 'How come I've never loved another woman before like that?' It was a defensive comment, I suppose, as if to say, 'OK, if that's me, if that's my habit, where's the evidence?' There could have been something of that in my feeling for her, absolutely, but I wouldn't have admitted it at the time.

●   ●   ●

In the book of our letters there isn't much about the part I played in the campaign for Sara's release. That's because during the six months of our relationship, the campaign was only just getting under way. I was the one who initiated public interest in Sara and gave her the contacts, because I'd been a journalist and I could talk to the journalists who were forever phoning me. It was just unbelievable at the castle—the phone was ringing all day long.

I was trying to make the campaign more specific. I tried hard to get Sara to think about using justifiable killing—self-defence—as her defence, but she wouldn't have it. My argument was basically that a woman looking after a young child has a very specific defence role, and anyone attacking that woman is attacking the child through the woman. And therefore her defence is to do with the child as much as it is to do with herself. I thought you could build a really good defence on that. But by that time too much water had gone under the bridge and it was too late to reverse it. I think that was my gripe with Sara in the end: I trusted her with everything she told me about prison, but she wouldn't trust me with everything I told her about what was happening outside. I felt she didn't have any feel for the political reality outside prison and she was operating on an incredibly self-centred, limited sort of perspective. In a sense I felt that this was unfair, and I got a bit fed up with it.

I think you come back to the fact that Sara felt she deserved punishment. I felt she had a very good case for being released. But I suppose she would then have had to say to herself, 'Look, I was under extreme pressure from my husband. He was threatening me, and through me my child. What I did was totally justified. It was terrible, it was awful and I'll never do it again. But it was justified at that point.'

But Sara never quite crossed that line. All she could fall back on was this feeling she had that, 'I'm basically pretty wicked, nobody really loves me, I've done an awful thing and I've got to be punished.' Sara was like a lot of people who have an ability to shoot themselves in the foot: they succeed in one direction and immediately sabotage their success because at a certain basic level they just don't believe in themselves. So they are constantly undermining their success.

Sara's first appeal was turned down and then she went on hunger strike and that attracted a vast amount of publicity. She'd left Durham in March, she was in Holloway for the appeal, then during the hunger strike she was still in Holloway, then she was moved to Bullwood Hall in Essex, then later she went to Styal prison in Cheshire. It was getting more difficult for me to actually communicate with her because now I was so far away from the prison, so we didn't have the time and we didn't have the physical contact through meeting on visits. After that her campaign was really taken over by Justice for Women.[3]

•   •   •

The way things were going between Sara and me at this stage—well, we were beginning to lose contact a bit. After she went from Durham our relationship and everything else started to come apart at the seams. By then it had lasted six months. What we didn't realise at the time we first used to meet in Durham was the protective factor of the control there. Sara was very, very good at challenging absolutely everything and they hated her in the system. But she was all over the place emotionally and being held in like that, it was reassurance in a way, even though she might be resentful.

I didn't follow Sara when she moved prisons. I had a sense of my own balance in my own life and I wasn't going to risk that. To me that was the quickest way of destroying what I had with Sara. I don't think two people can love each other if they don't have any balance. It's like two people dancing — they can't dance on each other's feet—you need your own place. So that was very important to me. I had to keep some kind of coherence.

I was in a mad situation in a way—I mean I regard the whole prison system as mad. And everything that was going on was very complex and very difficult. We were confronting the law without being lawyers, and we were up against the whole system. Both Sara and I felt we could do things better than people who were supposed to do them better than us. But it needs a lot of concentration to maintain some sort of balanced approach to that, otherwise no-one will take you seriously.

After the hunger strike Sara was obviously weakened physically and she was disappointed. But the odd thing was the ambivalence within her, which used to exasperate me because I felt that half the time I was more focused on getting her out than she was on getting out—even though she wrote, 'I want out of here—I only feel alive when I read your letters'. That ambivalence was an element that became noticeably worse after the failed appeal and the hunger strike. I also think it was about losing touch. I did go down to Bullwood Hall, where the only other person I met was Kiranjit Aluwahlia.[4]

Mentally Sara and I couldn't keep up our relationship. I think we hadn't known quite how important that physical contact was, and once that was lost, we were kind of drifting in this very complicated theoretical abstract world, and it was just out of control. Our relationship became like a balloon that was floating around adrift. One thing I did was support Sara at each point along the way. I might criticize her or argue with her but I always supported her. She still keeps saying this, so I suppose it's true. I think what I did do for Sara was to give her the green light for loving herself, for thinking things are all right.

Sara Thornton, whom I have known for several years, suggested George as an interviewee. Here is a brief comment she made on their relationship:

I had loads of men writing to me when I was in prison, wanting to rescue me. One man wrote and said he had a big house with five bedrooms and he would look after me. Men want their masculinity affirmed. They are often men who have had powerful mothers and are looking for vulnerable women to rescue.

George wanted to come along like a knight in shining armour and rescue me. He liked that role. He said he would take me away to his castle, but that would have been going from one prison to another. As I became more powerful he couldn't handle it. He wanted to get me out on my first appeal for my sake—but I wanted to get out to do something for other women. I think a lot of men are frightened of powerful women because they want their ego boosted all the time. And women look to men for things like getting their beauty affirmed. We are in a battle of the sexes which we ourselves have created. Men and women both try to act in the way society has told us we should act. I was brought up to believe that men knew best and I did that in my trial. But at my second appeal I believed in myself and I took power. Women can take back their power.

But George did give me a lot. He was an important part of the jigsaw puzzle which helped me when I was released, because he said he believed in me.

ENDNOTES

[1] *Love on the Wing: Letters of hope from prison*, Penguin 1996.
[2] The top security wing holding, at that time, about 45 women, all lifers.
[3] A campaigning group that fights to help women involved in domestic violence, prostitution and unjust imprisonment. One of its best-known cases was that of Emma Humphreys: each year JFW awards an Emma Humphreys Prize for a woman or group dedicated to fighting women's injustice.
[4] Another survivor of domestic violence who was jailed for murder. Her case was taken up by JFW and her conviction quashed by the Court of Appeal in July 1992.

Martha and Billy McFetridge

Martha, a 43-year-old nurse, was brought up in her native Switzerland in a strict religious group called The Brethren. In 1986 she left nursing to become a missionary in that faith. On a mission to Dublin to work with street people she met and fell in love with Billy, now 50, a former Loyalist terrorist serving a long sentence in the notorious H blocks of Belfast's Maze prison, jailed on 58 counts under anti-terrorism laws. They married eleven years ago on his release and have a young son and daughter.

Martha is a very tall woman with large brown eyes, dark curly hair with a touch of grey, and a ready, open smile. She came to pick me up from the railway station in what she calls her 'old banger'—a red left-hand drive car. Her strongly accented voice at first sounds Irish, but then you realise it has other overtones—the result of being a Swiss national who learned English in Dublin.

Martha is the second of five children—three girls and two boys—whose upbringing was very strict. Their father, a businessman, was an elder of their church and Martha was not allowed to watch television, cut her hair or wear short skirts or trousers. When she decided to marry Billy her parents were even more concerned about his being divorced than about his former terrorist activities.

As well as family opposition, Martha and Billy have had other great difficulties to overcome. After their marriage they set up home in Northern Ireland where their first child, a son, was born. He is physically and mentally disabled, though he was six years old before he was diagnosed as atypically autistic. When the child was nine months old, Billy's life story about his rejection of terrorism was published in a local newspaper. This led to death threats and the family had to leave Ireland at just two hours' notice and take refuge in Switzerland where they lived for seven years. They have only recently returned to live in England with their son, now eight, and their daughter, four. Martha works as an agency nurse but continues to take Christian literature into prisons. Billy, a born-again Christian, speaks publicly about his life here and abroad, and hopes to go into full-time ministry.

Although Martha is a strong and positive woman she broke down in tears at several points during the interview when describing the hardships the family have had to face.

●   ●   ●

The first time I saw Billy I thought, This man's going to influence my life in a big way. I hadn't even spoken to him but I knew I could trust him. I think that was what really attracted me to Billy from the very beginning. For me it was never 'Billy the ex-prisoner': it was 'Billy the man'.

I was living in Dublin and occasionally I used to go with friends to the Elim church in Larne. That evening in February 1987 there was a group over from Northern Ireland and Billy, who was still a prisoner in the Maze at that stage, was giving his testimony. He'd been invited by a friend of mine called Liam, who is a singer. I still think it was a miracle that Billy got permission to cross the border. I only understood about half of what he was saying because his accent was very strong. He said he'd been involved with the paramilitaries for a long stretch but he would not glorify violence, because he knew what he did was wrong. He'd done a lot of bad things but while he was in prison he'd become a Christian and experienced forgiveness.

After the talk I had to find an excuse to speak to Billy. I had just finished reading my first English books and one of them was by a woman who had been a prisoner in Northern Ireland—so I introduced myself and asked him if he had met her. I said I was a missionary and we went on chatting for ages. Through Liam I got the address of the Maze and I started writing to him and we became penfriends.

Billy was released on 24th April, and in August he came to stay with Liam and his wife Marie. That week Billy and I met up twice and we got on well together. But by this time I knew Billy was a married man and I'd met his nine-year-old son. Billy was going through a divorce but it wasn't complete at that stage. His wife had left him for another man by whom she had had two sons. Though we were just penfriends and we weren't dating or anything, I realised I was developing feelings for Billy—me a missionary and him not even yet a divorced man! And him with a nine year old son! To me that was *terrible!* It was something I struggled very, very hard with. I thought to myself, What are you thinking about? Stop!

●　　●　　●

I'd had a very strict upbringing in a country village in Switzerland, in a family belonging to a religious group called The Brethren. My father was an elder in the church—he still is to this day, at the age of 75. They are born-again Christians but very strict, even legalistic I would say, on certain points like physical appearance. I was not allowed to wear trousers until I was about 20 and I had to wear my hair in a bun—I couldn't have it cut. At home nobody had television, and at family meals we would pray. I think they had the idea that to bring up children you have to break their will, so there was physical punishment too. Looking back, I was never a teenager, I never rebelled. But I don't think I felt resentful at the time. That was just the way it was done—you couldn't do anything about it. Things were never discussed in our family and I do remember always thinking, If I have a relationship and a family, I want to work things through—I don't care if we have arguments.

We were a very close family. We didn't have too many friends outside the home and we didn't go to other people's houses, but people did come to our house. My parents wanted me to take people home rather than me go to their places.

If friends came to my house there would be praying before and after meals. But the main difference was the way the women dressed. It was the Seventies and most girls wore short mini-skirts. I was never allowed—my skirts had to be mid-calf length. At school I was always sticking out—I was very unusual. The children of Brethren families did go to state schools, but there were none in my class. I wouldn't be allowed to go to school parties and I've never smoked or taken alcohol in my whole life. When I left school at the age of 16 and I was confirmed, I signed a pledge that I would never drink.

After I left school I spent six months in Dublin working as an *au pair* for a Swiss missionary from our church, and that's where I learned English. Then I trained as a nurse, specialising in midwifery, and by the age of 25 I was a hospital midwife in the next village to my parents'.

But during all those years of nursing and midwifery back in Switzerland I was wondering whether my life was just about working as a midwife—or was there more? I was thinking about missionary work for a long time. I was single, I had no relationship and I thought of India or Africa. But I couldn't quite take on the responsibility of being a nurse out in the jungle on my own. I was tossing and turning back and forward and I was praying very hard.

Then out of the blue the missionary couple in Dublin that I'd lived with all those years before contacted me and asked me if I would come over and work with them for a year or two. They worked in a suburb of Dublin called Tallaght—a huge housing estate with probably 100,000 people. It was a very, very needy area at that time. Things have improved now because the area has been given a lot of European money. But at that stage there was extremely high unemployment, small houses, a lot of drinking, a lot of violence, no future, no jobs and no hope.

So in 1986 at the age of 29 I went to Ireland. I was leaving a good, well-paid job. I had my own apartment with another girl, a nice car, a nice boss, a very structured life. I'd always said I could not leave Switzerland and everything I had unless I was 100 per cent sure I was doing the right thing. And from the start I was sure—or I would never have been able to cope.

When I first started I went through a huge crisis. It was the end of October and the Irish weather is lousy at that time of year. But I grew to love those people and I set up a fellowship which grew to about 50 adults and the same number of children. I was there three years, and that's the work I was doing at the time I was invited by my friends to the meeting where Billy was speaking.

•　　　•　　　•

Billy and I went on writing as friends for quite some time after that August when we'd met up at Liam's. And then I happened to mention in a letter that I was going to visit somebody in Northern Ireland. After his release Billy had gone to live with his mum and he invited me to come and visit.

And that's when I really started to question myself. 'What am I doing? Who am I supposed to be? What's happening here?' Billy was my first boyfriend—I fancied plenty of men before but there was never any feedback. So I didn't trust my feelings whatsoever.

Billy wasn't in fact the first prisoner I had encountered. In my early twenties I had corresponded with a prisoner through an organization in Germany. I don't even remember his name now. I wrote him a few letters but he must have been coming on pretty heavy because I stopped writing immediately—that turned me completely off. I also remember that when I was a child, my parents did have an ex-prisoner staying with us for a few weeks, because through their church they helped people with problems. Subconsciously I think this had a great influence on me.

I couldn't talk with the friends I lived with about my feelings for Billy. So I went to Liam's wife Marie and I said, 'If I'm going to Billy's house, what will his mother think? I'm not his girlfriend! What will people think? What will the church think?'

And Marie, being typically Irish, said, 'Just go and enjoy yourself! Take a few nice clothes and just be Martha—that's all you have to be! Just be yourself. He just looks on you as a friend.'

That really helped me and I just went and tried to relax and be myself. Billy's mother was a beautiful woman. I was just Martha from Switzerland who lived in Dublin and I don't think she asked another question. I met Billy's son Christopher again as well.

I went home to Switzerland for Christmas but I didn't mention Billy to my parents. My father is the kind of person who would have said Billy had to ask him for my hand in marriage! I did tell my eldest brother who is a minister in our church and I explained about Billy's background. I remember my brother saying to me, 'God never promised us a straightforward, easy life—not you, not me, not anyone.' He didn't encourage me—he said, 'Just be 100 per cent sure of what you're doing, and don't do anything stupid.'

When I got back to Dublin I felt the pressure more and more, and I knew that we would have to speak about what was happening. I would have been willing just to stay friends, but I had to know where we were. I hate unclear situations—that's something I can't cope with. I think it was really me challenging Billy about what would happen.

One day Billy and I went out for a walk, and—I can't remember how I said it, but I think I just asked him, 'Where are we? What's happening?' And there and then he said he wanted us to get engaged! That was too quick for me! I had to ask him to go a bit slower.

As it turned out we didn't get engaged until the next Christmas, because it was now that the problems started with the bible college Billy had started attending.

•   •   •

Billy had been brought up in a household where he was made to go to Sunday school and church—his mother sent him. But it didn't change anything. Before he was involved in terrorism, Billy was in the British army. Then a cousin of his father's was murdered by the IRA. Family links in Ireland are very, very close, and Billy had just left the army and was used to guns. So the paramilitaries approached him, knowing that he was full of anger.

He was arrested in September 1980 for being a Loyalist terrorist and held for over a year on remand in the Crumlin Road prison in Belfast. It was there that he knew that God had forgiven all his wrongdoings. He thought this was marvellous after all the things he had done—and he had done plenty that was wrong. I think he was very high up in the paramilitaries, much more than I'll ever know.

In court he was charged on 58 separate counts under the Prevention of Terrorism Act. One of the charges was a murder he did not commit, but he pleaded guilty to many other offences. The charges included: manslaughter, accomplice to murder, robbery, armed resistance to arrest, possession of deadly firearms, fire bombings, pipe bombings, and possession of seven hand guns, one sub-machine gun, one rifle, two zip guns and a quantity of ammunition. The total number of years to which he was sentenced added up to 152, but because he took part in a plea bargain and admitted manslaughter, he ended up only doing six. In 1981 he was transferred to the Maze H block where Bobby Sands, the Republican leader, starved himself to death. There was a lot of tension there because Loyalists and Republicans were held together.

In the Maze Billy met up with James McIlroy, Director of the Prison Fellowship Northern Ireland, a Christian ministry to prisoners. He also did a correspondence course through the London Bible College, then when he was released, he immediately enrolled at the Belfast Bible College.

• • •

Billy was the first ex-prisoner and the first ex-terrorist they had ever had at the college. I think they thought Billy had met me more or less overnight and wanted to get engaged. They challenged him and said he could either continue with me and leave the college—or he could forget about me and stay.

They sent a letter saying all this to the people I lived with in Dublin and these friends said they had to talk to me about Billy. I thought they must have something really terrible to tell me that he hadn't already told me himself. Then they told me about the Principal's letter.

I said to Billy, 'What are you going to do now?' and he said, 'Carry on going out with you!' I wasn't at all happy with that, because I believe in Biblical authorities, and we had big arguments about it. I said, 'What will the Principal say?' Billy just didn't see it was a problem.

But I have to have clear situations. So I wrote a long letter to the Principal, explaining the whole situation in detail. I said I wanted Billy to finish his studies at the college—I didn't want to take him away. I never got a letter back from the Principal and I held that against him for a long time.

Billy wanted to get married as soon as possible—but I didn't. We finally came to an agreement. I knew he wanted to go into full-time Christian work, and obviously he would be better equipped if he'd had training. So we decided he would do two years in the college instead of three, and we would not get engaged then—we would wait till Christmas.

I wrote and told my parents that I was planning to get engaged, and my father wrote back. They were not happy at all. I was 32 years old but they were still worried about me. The problem was the divorce, which to them was much more important than the fact that Billy had been a terrorist. I think they were also concerned about the past before he got married to his first wife—he was pretty promiscuous in his relationships. Also there was his prison past. Dad thought he would be institutionalised. Billy'd been in the army for almost six years, then in prison for another six. He had had no training—would he be able to support me and later on support a family? Would he be able to stick at a job? Dad just expressed his concern, and I think, looking back, there were a few things he saw pretty clearly in perspective. Of course all this hurt me, but I was 100 per cent convinced that God had brought Billy and me together.

•　　•　　•

About six months before we got married I had a huge crisis. I suddenly thought, Do I really want to get married and maybe have children? Or do I just want to stay single and have an independent good life? Because if so I'd rather stop it now. I was almost torn apart —it was *dreadful!*

I prayed for a week and after that I said, 'I want to get married.' I knew absolutely that I was not going for an easy life, because of the hurt Billy had had. I never knew what kind of person he'd been before all that happened to him. Would I be able to cope?

Billy always wanted to give me a church wedding, but my home church in Switzerland would never have married us because of Billy being divorced. And for the same reason they wouldn't marry us in Billy's church in Northern Ireland. But one of the tutors at the bible college had always said that if we were to get married he would marry us in church—so we agreed to get married in Northern Ireland.

After we got engaged Billy came over to Switzerland for Christmas. The visit was fine. My parents don't speak English very well and their main concern was, was he really a Christian? There is a German saying about marriage: 'Those that pray together stay together.'

I asked my dad if he would do it the Irish way and walk the bride into the church. And he did. The evening before the wedding he told me straight that he wasn't happy, but I thought, 'You can tell me what you want but I'm getting married tomorrow!'

Our wedding was lovely—it was beautiful. A friend made me my wedding dress. It was ivory with a peach-coloured belt and a small veil. I just had one bridesmaid and a flower girl. My next-door neighbour in Dublin was a singer and she sang *Ave Maria*, and my Swiss guests sang some songs in German. We were allowed to have the reception in Billy's own church hall, even though we couldn't get married in his church. The church ladies did the catering because we didn't have much money. We had about 50 guests including my parents and both my sisters came and one brother, Billy's sister and a whole bunch of my friends from Dublin.

Irish weddings are all speeches, but Swiss weddings are hilarious because they do little sketches. So we had a mixture of an Irish and Swiss wedding. Then we went to Switzerland on our honeymoon.

• • •

We started our married life in Larne, north of Belfast. To begin with Billy worked on a government scheme to give work to the unemployed and they sent him to the Prison Fellowship. He worked there for three years and though the money wasn't very good, at least it was a job. After the first year they offered him a permanent job on the staff, travelling round visiting prisoners and speaking in schools. For those three years we often had ex-prisoners living with us.

At first I was told I was not allowed to work because I didn't have a work permit, then I started work as a nursing auxiliary because I wasn't qualified to work as a midwife in the UK. I had to work in a hospital for three months unpaid before I could get registered. It was hard, but I loved the work.

Billy obviously introduced me to his friends. Some of them were from way back, but they all accepted that Billy had left that world they'd all been in, that it was finished. All his friends—and I really mean *all* his friends in Northern Ireland—have been in prison at some stage, all for political reasons.

When we'd been married two years our son Danny was born. I remember a lovely boat holiday we took in Northern Ireland when I was pregnant with him. When he was six months old, he was a beautiful boy, but people started asking me what was the matter with him. He was too quiet—he hardly moved at all. I can't understand now why I didn't realise that there was something wrong with him. But my mother-in-law always told me that as a baby, Billy had been very quiet too.

• • •

We'd been living in Larne about three years and Danny was nine months old when Billy's life story was published. It was called *Prisoner of Hope* and it was published in the local newspaper. But it turned out to be a thorn in some people's sides. One day we were out shopping and Billy met a man and spent some time talking to him. After that I asked Billy, 'Who was that man?' and Billy said, 'He's a former boss of mine. He asked me if he was mentioned in the story.' Billy told him no names were mentioned. He said, 'It's just me and my life, and if anybody was mentioned they were all under different names.'

But soon after that we were more or less told they didn't want us in Northern Ireland any more. A friend of ours told us, and we left with Danny within two hours—just like that—it was awful. We were both very, very low emotionally.

We went to Switzerland—I phoned my parents from France and said we were on the way. We didn't know how long we were going to stay—it was just,

'Please give us a bed.' In the end we stayed in Switzerland for seven years. We only came back to the UK last year—to England not to Northern Ireland.

In the beginning I thought Billy had overreacted. For a long time he'd wanted to get out of Northern Ireland and I thought he'd jumped at the chance because he felt so low. I held a grudge against him for many months. But now looking back, I do have to say he did the right thing. Since Billy came out of prison, so many of his friends have been killed, all of them ex-paramilitaries. So many have been murdered in the last ten years.

We stayed with my parents for the first three months and then we got an apartment. I worked as a nurse and Billy started to work in my dad's factory. Of course my parents wanted to know what had happened, and they did say, 'We told you so, we warned you.' I was very much hurt by that though I didn't say anything. I should have said to my father, 'You could tell me something else, you could encourage me.'

●　　●　　●

After we'd decided we'd stay in Switzerland we went to a doctor to see if Danny was healthy. He was about a year old by now and we could see that he was physically different from other babies his age. He didn't start to sit up till he was a year old and when he did his back was bent over. He showed no sign of standing. He couldn't crawl till he was about 18 months old. He was four years old before he started to walk.

Danny had all the tests under the sun but they didn't really find anything out. I am very much a nurse in my thinking, and I said to Billy, 'I want to know, I *have* to know what is wrong with him'. I was heavily pregnant with my daughter Natasha when Danny went into hospital for five days and had every possible check he could have. And after five days they knew as little as before. We only had this questionable diagnosis—that it could be a very severe metabolic disorder that actually gets worse.

While I was pregnant with Natasha I would never have any tests done, because I would never have agreed to have an abortion. But throughout the pregnancy I was anxious, and being a midwife I knew that all that comes out during labour. Danny's birth had been no problem, but this time I was so tense, as if I didn't want to let the baby go—I didn't want her to be born. I was in such pain—and nothing happened. But when she was born she was perfectly all right.

●　　●　　●

After Natasha was born, for the next two years Danny became really, really bad. From the quietest boy you could possibly imagine he became the loudest. You could not talk over his shouting and screaming the whole day long. Yet for a long time Billy said to me, 'There's nothing wrong with Danny'. He seemed to ignore it, he just wouldn't accept it. He just *loves* Danny.

When Danny was about six and a half we got the diagnosis of atypical autism—though autism is not really a diagnosis—it's a spectrum of symptoms. Now we're back in England he's in a very good school half an hour from home.

At first I thought having a disabled child was a punishment, maybe for doing something my parents didn't want me to do. But that was a long time ago and I do know that God doesn't punish. It's just that it was really, really hard, and I always wondered, Why? Why? I still get emotional about it.

Going back to our life in Switzerland: three months after I had Natasha I went back to work. I worked nights while Billy looked after the children. By now he was officially long-term unemployed, because people there don't speak English—so he had to learn the language. Unemployment is a curse in itself. It was terrible, *terrible*. Billy was so depressed. I've made big mistakes myself in the past, but I'm a doer and a goer and a very active person, and Billy's the opposite—he's very passive.

One of the reasons we came back to the UK after seven years was because Billy has always wanted to go into full-time Christian ministry. When we moved to England we agreed we'd do job sharing. I never used to accept a late shift because he would have to collect the kids from school, give them their tea and get them to bed—and I thought he couldn't do it. But then I said, 'How about me working from two in the afternoon till nine at night? ' He said he could manage that—and it actually works. I can't understand why I didn't do it before. I think Billy needed to be challenged more. I think it's the curse of being a nurse that you're used to carrying so much responsibility on your own. So I have had to learn to let go.

•   •   •

If Billy gets depressed, I want to talk to him about it there and then—at that moment. But I've had to learn with Billy that this is just not possible. I don't think he was like that before he went to prison. Every time he's come out of his depression he has talked. One thing I am finding it very hard to learn is not to push him to do anything he doesn't want to. He's very stubborn and if he doesn't want to do something, he won't.

One of the things he struggled with after all those years in prison was that it was very difficult for him to make decisions—and it still is. He still turns decisions back to me. He asks me what I think about everything, even the most simple things. Of course he made the decision to leave Ireland and go to Switzerland—that was a big one. But it's more the simple things, like what to wear when he goes anywhere. He'll ask me at least five times, 'Does that look okay? How do I look?'

We still go back to Belfast on holidays, though Billy has finished with living over there, absolutely. But a good part of our life still circles around prisons. Billy has been cleared to go into our local prison once a week and what he would really love to do is to become a community prison chaplain. At the moment I'm going through the process of security clearance to go into prisons as an agency nurse. I do have a feeling for prisons. I know there are crooks there who will never change, and we have to accept that. But I also know there are plenty who want to change—yet the reoffending rate is incredible. A lot of prisoners are like alcoholics: deep inside they are very, very vulnerable, almost too scared to face life. I believe God can forgive everybody, whatever crime they have committed.

●　　　●　　　●

We'll definitely tell Natasha about her dad's past when she's older. We'll say that everybody has done bad things and he was in prison—we don't have to go into detail.

I don't regard my husband as an ex-criminal. He is an ex-terrorist, and in my eyes he was a political prisoner. When I first met Billy I didn't know much about Irish politics—I had read very little, though since we have been together I've read more Northern Ireland history. But from the start I thought I understood why Billy had done the things he did. I know that he broke the law, and you could argue that anyone who breaks the law is a criminal. But he only did what he did for the terrorist cause. He would never have done anything criminal otherwise. So I feel he's not a criminal as a lot of others are. That's my opinion, though I know a lot of people might feel different.

He has recently been ordained as a pastor by an American church and now he is a minister travelling round this country and abroad, mainly sharing his life experiences in a lot of different churches, and he was filmed by Swiss television talking about forgiveness. He talks about the situation in Northern Ireland and about how there is a solution to it. He does still get angry—he was very angry a few years ago when the bomb went off in Omagh. It's his father's home town and that day he was so frustrated and really, really angry.

The other day my sister phoned me from Switzerland and she said, 'How are you? How are things?'

'We've had better times and we've had worse,' I said. 'Let's put it like that. It goes up and down, up and down. But I know it can only get better.'

Tracy and Tony

Tracy is 37 and has a post of considerable responsibility with a major building society, a job she has held for the past 12 years. She has been married for eleven years to Tony, who was convicted of murder when he was still in his teens and has served 17 years of a life sentence. The story of their relationship is a most unusual one. They fell in love when they were both 16 and at college. The relationship did not last and Tracy moved to London to work. A year later Tony was arrested for murder and at the age of 17 he was sent to prison for life. Tracy believed he was innocent, visited him when he was on remand and wrote to him for a while after he was convicted. She married another man but the couple divorced after six years and Tracy began visiting Tony regularly. They married in 1991, and their eight-year-old son was illicitly conceived when Tony was allowed a few hours' home leave. Tony is still in prison hoping to get his parole soon. The couple do not want their surname revealed.

Tracy has short, dark, curly hair and a slim figure and she smiles a lot. Her hobby is DIY and she has transformed the small terraced house in Greater Manchester that she shares with her eight-year-old son Aaron. His bedroom has a bunk bed unit with desk and computer suite underneath. All the carpentry was done by Tracy and she has painted the walls and ceiling with stunning murals on a seaside theme. The rest of the house is beautifully designed and decorated too. Tracy inherited her artistic skills from her father who retired after years of farming to become a painter. On the living room wall is a lovely watercolour which Tracy commissioned from him, showing a spot in the Pennines that she regularly passed on her way to visit Tony. There is also a framed pencil drawing of Tracy and Aaron, done by Tony. On the mantelpiece is a photograph of father and son on one of their few days out together. It shows a handsome athletic-looking mixed-race man and a small boy looking up at him with obvious love and admiration.

After the interview we went out for a meal in a nearby pub close to the picturesque Cheshire village where Tracy, an only child, was born and brought up on her parents' farm. Her mother has worked for 25 years at a local restaurant, and Tracy comes from a very close, stable family. The gently trickling river and the neat stone-built primary school which she attended were a delightful picture of rural tranquillity, a far cry from the forbidding walls of Strangeways Prison in Manchester where Tracy first visited Tony.

●   ●   ●

I was only 18 the first time I went to Strangeways, and oh, it was horrible! Tony was still on remand and there was this horrible, grotty side room where they made us sit for ages and ages waiting. There were three of us—me, Tony's mum and a friend of his. He was on closed visits behind a screen. There was mesh all round the screen and you could see where people had tried sticking cigarettes through. There was an officer with a dog behind Tony, and an officer with a dog behind us. Tony was just 17 years old and obviously very, very scared as if he didn't know what was going on. It was all horrible.

•   •   •

I was at college sitting on a radiator when I first saw Tony and I said, 'I'm going to marry him!' It was the first time I ever saw him, I was only 16 and my friend said, 'Don't be stupid!' But I said, 'I *am* going to!' He was nearly a year younger than me and I was in the second year, doing catering and hotel management. It was break time and we were all sat there watching the new first-years come in when I spotted him and I thought, That's it! That's the man! Perhaps it was because being mixed race he was unusual—his mum's white but his dad was from Sierra Leone.

So I decided I was going to get him! One day he walked up with his mates and I remember saying to him, 'Want something to eat?' and I went and made him a sandwich spread butty, which used to be one of our staple diets as students, and it went on from there. The college we were both at was a residential college in Buxton—I lived there during the week and went home to Cheshire at weekends. So Tony and I started going out together and soon we were inseparable.

He was doing business studies but he only stuck it out for a term and then he quit. I think he spent all his year's grant in the first term—he'd blown it and there was no way he could go back. It was probably a good job that he did leave, because I'd started missing my lessons to be with him and if he'd stayed I'd probably have failed everything. What I didn't know when I first met him was that at home he lived about four miles down the road from me, though we'd never met before. I lived right on the border, and I went to school in Cheshire. Tony lived on a council estate and went to school in Derbyshire. When he was at home he'd come round to our house quite a bit and my parents didn't like him. It wasn't to do with race, though Tony still thinks it was. But I think they found him arrogant and my mum wasn't very impressed that he lived on the council estate. I think they thought their daughter could do better.

I stayed on at college and gradually, because of the distance between us now that Tony lived back in Cheshire, we split up. When I finished college I moved down to London, just to get Tony out of my system. I got a job as an *au pair* for a wealthy family in North London.

•   •   •

About two months after I moved down south I remember being woken one morning at seven o'clock by my radio alarm clock as usual. On the news it said there had been a murder in my home area. My first reaction was to wonder whether I knew the victim. Then everybody started phoning me. I found out I didn't know the victim, but friends back at home told me that the police kept taking in all these people that we knew, and arresting some of them, and I remember people saying they'd arrested Tony. I remember thinking that was a bit daft, but he was only one of a lot of people it was happening to. Apparently there'd been a party on the Saturday night, someone had been beaten up and strangled and the victim's body was found the following Wednesday, and everyone at the party was being questioned by police.

The following weekend I went home to Cheshire and I saw Tony at the pub. I think we were giggling about Tony being taken in and questioned by the police and I let him walk me home. Bearing in mind that I lived in the middle of nowhere, if I'd had the slightest doubt about him I wouldn't have done that. I actually remember leaving the pub and making a joke about it, shouting out to my friends, 'See who I'm leaving with!' We were all laughing and joking. But as we walked along the High Street a police car followed us very slowly for about 200 yards. That was a Saturday night and Tony said, 'Right, I'll meet you at the pub tomorrow.'

He never turned up—but that wasn't unusual. He used to have a habit of saying 'I'll be there' and not being there after all. I went back to London on the Sunday night. Then the next day this lad I knew phoned me and he said, 'I want you to know before you hear it on the news that they've charged Tony with that murder.'

And I just laughed! It was probably a nervous reaction—but I just couldn't believe it. Tony'd been in the usual scrapes that all teenagers go through, but nothing like this, no violence, nothing like that at all. I remember phoning his mum and she was in a right state about it, so I arranged to go with her and visit him in Strangeways. I went three or four times while he was on remand. Then he went to trial and he was convicted. He was only just 17—his birthday's in March and the trial was in June—so he was given HMP. That meant he was to be detained at Her Majesty's Pleasure. The judge suggested ten years but later the Home Secretary upped it to twelve.

I remember writing him a letter. God, it was hard—I just didn't know what to write, it was so horrific. I can't remember what I wrote, I just remember thinking, What the hell can I say? What can you say to somebody in that situation? He was sent to Aylesbury Young Offenders' Institution as a Category A prisoner and he stayed in that category for about four or five years. I applied to visit him but they wouldn't let me—I still don't know why. So we just wrote to each other, but only every six months or so—Christmas cards, birthday cards and so on.

When Tony was first arrested he was seeing somebody else and she stuck it out for the 12 months that he was on remand, then she finished with him.

•　　　•　　　•

I'd had a number of jobs after that first *au pair* job. I worked as a waitress and at an estate agents, then in 1987 I got a good job working for a building society, the same one I still work for now—I transferred to the Manchester branch when

I moved back to this area. Soon after Tony was arrested I met my first husband when he was working behind the bar of a pub I used to go to with my friends. We got on really well to start with—maybe it was on the rebound from Tony. We started seeing each other and eventually moved in together, bought a flat and married about 18 months later. We were married in my home village—a small registry office wedding but it was a nice family day with about 40 guests.

About a year after we married, things started to go wrong. My husband started staying out all night and when he'd had a drink he'd become violent to me. Actually he was an alcoholic. He worked at an off-licence and at ten in the morning he'd start on the Special Brew. But we were together five or six years.

•   •   •

Near the end of the marriage I wrote to Tony and told him that if he wanted to see me I'd come and visit. Ever since his conviction he'd been a Category A prisoner and I wouldn't have been allowed to visit him, but by now he was a Category B prisoner in Wakefield prison, and a visiting order arrived from him right away. I phoned Tony's mother and told her I'd be going to see him one Sunday, and when I got back home I called round to see her but for some reason I couldn't get hold of her—she wasn't in. Looking back now, that was definitely Fate, because that meant I went to see Tony on my own.

On the visit I sat there being all chatty. Because Tony was now a Cat B prisoner it was no longer a closed visit but a normal visit. God, it seemed like the quickest visit ever! At the end of the time we stood up, gave each other a peck on the cheek, not a proper kiss, and then changed our minds and went for the real thing—and that was it!

I remember, going back on the train to my husband I wrote Tony this really massive, long letter. And at the same time he was writing exactly the same letter to me! I was writing, 'If you want me to come and visit again I will—it's up to you.' And he was writing, 'I'd like you to come and visit again but it's up to you—you don't have to'. I think it was about another month before I visited, and then after that it was once a fortnight, and then every week, as soon as the prison allowed it.

That first visit was probably one of the deciding factors in me splitting up from my husband, but at the time I probably didn't think of it as one. I just wanted to get out of the marriage. My husband found a couple of letters—one I'd half-written to Tony and one he'd written to me—and he wasn't at all happy about them.

Eventually I moved out and found myself back in a bedsit, paying the mortgage on a house I couldn't live in and leaving my husband to pay all the other bills. He never paid them so I ended up in mega, mega debt. In the end my parents had to lend me thousands of pounds to buy him out. I had to move back home with my family because it took months and months for me to sell my house in London in the recession. I was about 24 years old and it's never easy going to live back at home after you've been away and had your own place.

My parents knew I was visiting Tony and they were all right about it to start with. They'd never liked him very much but they knew him and they couldn't see him committing a murder like that. But as they saw my relationship with Tony getting more serious they said, 'He's in prison and it'll have changed him an awful lot. We'd rather you didn't get into this.'

But the thing that really scared my mother was when she realised that I was actually going to get a divorce. It panicked her because she knew what was coming. She said, 'You can't! You can't!'

•   •   •

I got my divorce papers through in April 1991 and Tony and I got married in the August. I don't think I ever actually told my parents about our wedding, though I knew they knew, because everyone else knew, and they must have heard us talking on the phone. I don't think they've ever even seen the wedding photos. I do remember my auntie talking to me and saying, 'Do you know what you're getting yourself into?'

We'd been planning the wedding inside Wakefield jail but then Tony was recategorised as Cat C and moved to Featherstone prison in Wolverhampton, which meant he could be allowed an outside wedding. He had been in prison nine years and our wedding day was his first day out. We got married in a little registry office in a gorgeous idyllic country village with a cricket field. It was a baking hot August day and I went down with a few friends of mine from work—one brought her husband and little girl. Everyone at work knows I'm married to a lifer—I'd rather tell people than have them find out and I've never had any problems, though you never know what people say behind your back. Another lady came who'd been a sort of mother to Tony. Tony's brother was there with his wife and son. Tony came with an officer, who was brilliant.

When Tony arrived with the officer, Jim, in a taxi he was wearing a suit I'd taken in to the prison earlier. It was a bit long so one of the staff had turned up the hems. Jim didn't make Tony wear handcuffs or anything. The wedding was at 11 o'clock and Tony had to be back by 1 p.m. After the ceremony Jim said, 'What are you all hanging round here for? Come on, let's go to the pub!' He took us to the pub and then he told his taxi to disappear for a while. My mate had put ribbons and everything all over her car, and Jim gave us her car keys and left us on our own for half an hour in the car to consummate our marriage! The car was parked out of the way round the back of the pub. We didn't know it was right opposite a police station—nobody told us that!

Jim went back to the prison with Tony in the car covered with ribbons and all the prisoners working outside in the grounds cheered them as they went past. In the afternoon I went back on my own to the prison in the dress I wore for the wedding—that's why I didn't choose a long dress. I was still covered in confetti. I went to stay at my friend's place for a few days, and then went home again. But one of the women who came to the wedding worked with my mum, and she told me that after the wedding my mum thanked her for going to support me.

After the marriage I think I was allowed to visit Tony three times a month and for about five years I never had a holiday from work because I had to take a day off in the week for a visit and that used up all my holidays.

● ● ●

The December after we married, Tony was allowed his first escorted home visit. I was still living with my parents so we ended up in Manchester wandering round the Arndale Centre which was packed because it was just before Christmas. The escorting officer walked about ten yards behind us, and he nearly killed himself laughing when a woman came up and asked Tony to do a survey about shopping! The officer was in plain clothes and it looked like a store detective was following us around. Then we went to my work place to introduce Tony to everyone.

By the next home leave I'd got my present house, so Tony was allowed to come here, and he came a good few times. He used to arrive between 10 and 11 a.m. and he'd stay till about 3 or 4 p.m. Sometimes he came with one officer, sometimes with two. They would come with Tony all the way from Wolverhampton to Manchester by taxi, about 80 miles, and leave the taxi waiting all day. I was told the officers got 150 quid extra pay for just coming here and finding a fridge full of beer and food to keep them happy. The first time the officer followed Tony about like a hawk. The officers were even supposed to stand outside the toilet when he went in, but they soon grew to trust him. Tony never did a runner and I don't believe anyone did. It got really lax—it was great but actually it was ridiculous.

I think it was on Tony's third or fourth home leave that our son happened. It was an accident but it was lucky, otherwise we'd probably never have had any children. Considering that we weren't meant to be left alone at all it was a bit embarrassing for the escorting officer. When I found out I was pregnant Tony had to break it to him and he said, 'Right, the story is I went to get the car and it happened then—a quickie!' The rumour's gone round the prisons though. When Tony was moved to Channings Wood prison in Devon somebody came up to him and said, 'You're the one who got your missus pregnant on a home visit!'

When I discovered I was pregnant, part of me was dead chuffed, but I was also absolutely panic-stricken. The girls at work made me do a pregnancy test at lunchtime so they knew before Tony did. That night he phoned as usual and I thought, I've got to tell him now, to give it time to sink in before I see him. So I told him and he said, 'You're joking! You're joking!' I think he went round saying, 'Guess what I did on my home leave'. Then I had a scan and I found it was a boy and we kept saying, 'It's a lad! It's a lad!'

Our son Aaron was born in June 1993. When I went into labour it was about half past eight at night and when I phoned the prison to tell Tony they said I couldn't speak to him because he was banged up for the night. They'd have to tell him in the morning. All night I was saying, 'They've got to tell him!' I found out later they had. When the baby was born the nurses wheeled the phone in to me and I spoke to Tony. Prisoners aren't allowed incoming calls unless it's something really important, but the officers dragged him into the wing office to speak to me.

It was nine days before I could show Tony his new son because a week after the birth he got shipped out to a prison in Doncaster, and at first they refused him home leave because his wife and baby were both well. If we'd been sick he'd have been allowed to come. Finally they agreed to give him a compassionate leave and he came here with a couple of officers, handcuffed to one of them. I was trying to give him the baby to hold but he couldn't because of the cuffs. Then after a few minutes the officers took off the cuffs and went off down the pub, leaving us together for the whole afternoon.

●　　●　　●

I'd told my mother about the baby as soon as I found out. It was awful—that's the only time we've ever stopped speaking. To my parents I think it was a case of, 'There's no way you're going to be able to cope. You'll be stuck there with a baby on your own. Tony won't be there to help. You won't be able to do your job, you won't be able to manage financially.' My dad was upset because my mum was so upset about it. They were on holiday when the baby was born.

But once Aaron arrived it only took about a week for them to come round and see him. It was very strained at first and it took a few months before I started going round to them. My parents have made a real effort for their grandson's sake, and now I'm there nearly every weekend. Our son is eight now and he loves the farm.

I've said to my parents, 'Right, do you want to come and visit Tony?' but it's always been, 'No, we can't go in a prison!' But when Tony started getting town visits I took him to their house. I was absolutely dreading it, but it was all right. My mum said later that they'd remembered this person who was really arrogant but now he was totally different. My dad more than anything is concerned about how prison will have affected Tony, being banged up for all those years. My dad and Tony are very, very similar. They both live for football. My dad still plays every Saturday and Tony does too, so I've got him lined up to play in my dad's team when he gets out! And both of them are into art. It's a shame they've had to meet in this way.

Having our son has made a big difference to us all. I'll never forget the day of Tony's first unescorted visit home. I collected him at 8 a.m. and brought him to our house. Due to cutbacks in the Prison Service it was the first time in four years that he had been here. We spent the day together then collected Aaron from school. He didn't know Tony was home, and the look on his face as he left school with his dad was just amazing.

I would love another child. Tony says, 'You've still got to give me my daughter!' But it depends when Tony is released, and I'm getting on a bit now. I think Tony missed too much of our son's early life—though he was lucky to miss getting up in the nights! Tony still doesn't believe me when I tell him that the first time Aaron ever walked was to his dad on a visit.

I was determined that Tony should see Aaron as much as possible. The furthest away I've ever had to travel for visits was the six-hour drive each way from Manchester to Devon for three months when Aaron was two. I only missed one weekend in all that time. I think I was mad! I used to get the baby up at 2 a.m., leave Manchester and drive to Devon for the Saturday morning visit. Then I'd go and stand by the fence and watch Tony play football for most of the afternoon. He'd often manage to get injured and then we'd be able to talk through the fence. Then I'd take Aaron back to a hotel for the night, have another visit on Sunday morning, then drive back to Manchester. I was working nine-to-five all week and doing that every weekend. It did make me ill doing that journey—I ended up really worn out. Most prisons Tony's been in have been about two hours' drive each way. I'm lucky I have a car—I feel so sorry for families who have to go on buses and trains.

I also feel very sorry for some women whose men seem very selfish. I can remember talking to one woman who used to take a load of kids to visit their dad. One day she showed me this list and on it were written the names of about 20 cassettes that this guy wanted his wife to go out and buy for him—these were proper shop tapes he wanted, not copies. And she was going to get them too, though the kids had holes in their shoes, holes in their clothes.

Now we've got the visits properly sussed. As soon as we walk into that visiting room Aaron is Tony's responsibility. If Aaron's naughty it's Tony who's got to tell him off. He has to take control on visits—otherwise when he comes home he'll suddenly turn into the dad who shouts at his son. Luckily Aaron's never had his dad at home—Tony's always been in prison so he's never known anything different. Aaron waltzes into the prison and doesn't get fazed by it at all. He treats it as his second home.

When I first visited Tony with Aaron, I used to tell Aaron that prison was 'Daddy's work' because it was easier, but I don't think that lasted long. Now we've explained it briefly, but not in detail. We told him that the policeman said Dad was in a fight and somebody got hurt, so that's why he's there. Aaron's immediate reaction was to say, 'I'm going to tell the misters now that you should be home!' We had to stop him heading off to tell the officers! His best friend at school knows, but I don't think many of the other kids do, and so far he's not had any problems.

Tony and I have written thousands of letters to each other—I've got a big box full of his letters. We write five letters a week—two sides of A4 at least every day—and the weekend letter is a big long one. Everybody says, 'What do you find to write about?' But if you write every day you can write trivia, whereas if you only write to somebody every six months you have to tell them something important. He also rings me every night as long as he can get to the phone.

•　　•　　•

When I got back with Tony all those years ago, I thought he'd only got about three years left in prison. When we married I thought he'd be out pretty soon, but that's eleven years ago now. He keeps getting knockbacks on his parole. He was first made a D category prisoner about three years ago but unfortunately the prison he was sent to was awful—a horrible, horrible place. The first time he met the lifer governor he sat Tony down and said to him, 'So you're the little shit who killed some fucker, are you?' There's racism too: Tony got injured playing football and had to have a knee operation. The prison probation officer told our own probation officer, 'You can't miss a nigger on crutches, can you?'

In another prison he got set up and heroin was found in his cell, though he's an absolute fitness fanatic and has never taken smack. He's also got too much to lose at this stage in his sentence to have drugs anywhere near him.

When he does come out he's got a job to go to with a big landscape gardening company run by a friend. And he's got me and Aaron to come home to. They say there are seven elements you need for successful rehabilitation. I can't remember what they are but Tony's got them all. He just needs the chance to put them into practice.

There are obviously going to be some problems when he finally does get out, but Tony is confident so his confidence will probably come through. Several times when he's been home we've gone to the estate when he was brought up, and he's insisted on wandering round on his own. Most people will come up and shake his hand.

•　　　•　　　•

If I was asked to give any advice to other people in the same situation as us, I would say, 'Just get on with it'. I also find it helps to be up-front with people. It stops all the gossip, and believe me, the people you least expect can turn out great.

These last few years I don't know how Tony's kept his head with all these setbacks. We hoped he'd at least be out by the Millennium. But when he wasn't, on New Year's Eve both of us went to bed at 5 p.m., waiting for it to be over. But I've never for a minute regretted my decision to marry Tony. I don't think our love for each other ever died, and when we met up with each other again we knew that. And once he's home it'll just be a case of putting it all behind us and making the most of the time we have together and with Aaron. I think we're so determined to make it work because everybody said it wouldn't.

Postscript: A few months after this interview Tracy left the building society where she had been working for 12 years and got a job at a solicitors' firm specialising in prison law. She is very happy there. She also works several evenings each week in the visitors' centre of a local prison. Tony had just applied for parole but he was told to re-apply in two years' time. By then he will have served 20 years in prison—double the trial judge's recommendation of ten years.

Anthony and Grace Hall

Anthony, 46, married Grace, 40, when she had spent 13 years in prison. The seventh of eight children, Grace became a prostitute at 15. She stabbed a man to death and at 21 was sentenced to life imprisonment for murder. She was released in March 2000 after 18 years, making her one of Britain's longest-serving women prisoners. Both Anthony and Grace are born-again Christians. In October 2000 a television film about their relationship was screened in the BBC *Everyman* series. Entitled 'Life after Murder', it focused on the theme of forgiveness and received much critical acclaim.

Anthony is a highly-skilled painter, decorator and carpenter, a pleasant, rather diffident man with a soft Lincolnshire accent. Like Grace he comes from a large family. He is the youngest of seven children and he had an unusual upbringing. His father was a high-ranking army officer who won the Military Cross for heroism in World War II. For many years the family lived a life of colonial privilege in Africa and China and at the age of seven Anthony was sent to a private boarding preparatory school in England. But when Major Hall was invalided out of the army and the family returned to England, everything changed. He became a lay preacher and as he moved from church to church his large family moved with him. There were 21 moves before Anthony was 15, with accommodation varying from an elegant Georgian house to a tiny caravan.

At 16 Anthony left home and was soon involved with local Hell's Angels biker groups. He grew a long beard, became a heavy drinker and drug-user and was constantly in fights with rival gangs. At 26 he married another alcoholic and they had two children but the marriage was tempestuous and they divorced. Anthony had worked sporadically and managed to buy a house which he used his carpentry and building skills to renovate. But over the years his drug and drink habits worsened and at the age of 34 ended up homeless, sleeping in his battered car. He drove to Maidstone and began attending a hand-out service for the homeless. Grace worked for the charity as part of her rehabilitation at a nearby open prison and that is how they met.

•   •   •

The first time I saw Grace it was like I couldn't take my eyes off her. She was handing the food out and I remember that I was staring at her all the time, just looking at her. She told me to stop staring at her—but I couldn't! Then the place shut, so I went back another day—it was open two or three times a week and you got a meal and chat. I was still on the streets taking drugs and booze every day.

I knew this bloke on the street, Michael his name was, and after a couple of weeks of me going there and staring at Grace he said to me, 'I'll fix you up with her—you can go for a walk together.' I said, 'Oh, I can't be bothered with that. I just don't want to know women.' I'd had enough of that, I just didn't want to know. But he was very persistent.

So eventually I went for a walk with Grace down by the river Medway, just feeding the ducks. I've always got on well with animals—that was another form of escape. If you get on well with animals you don't have to bother with people. At the centre they gave out big bags of bread and we took a bag and went to feed the ducks. I used to get the swans to feed out of my hand and I could touch them. Grace was amazed—they don't normally do that sort of thing. Because of that she sort of knew I was okay.

I knew right from day one that she was in prison and on a day release scheme, helping at the handout centre. It didn't bother me. I think fairly soon she told me why she was there, and that didn't bother me at all either. People make mistakes. On the streets I've come within an inch of killing somebody in a fight. It can just happen when you lose your temper. If she'd been a cold, compulsive serial killer—that's a bit heavy! But a one-off, in an argument where you end up killing somebody, I can quite understand that.

We went for a few more walks, and I found that I could talk to her—that was one of the greatest things with us. When I first met Grace I never used to speak to anybody else at all. And although Grace had conversations in the jail there wasn't anybody there that she could talk to easily. But we could talk about anything. And I think her being in jail and me being outside was like a release for her. The barrier of the jail actually helped too. It meant we could say things that we wouldn't maybe get into as deeply if we were both outside.

Basically that's because there was no threat there to either of us. Say you're in a relationship on the outside. Say the two of you meet in a nightclub or pub or wherever. The relationship quickly becomes intimate. Whereas with us there was a distance, so we could become intimate personally not physically—we could tell each other things about ourselves. There was never anything physical, nothing like that for a long time. We could talk about our problems, what we felt about things, our past, all those things, without the problem of actually having a relationship. We were building a friendship more than a relationship. In relationships, you bring all the garbage from your past, and all the defence mechanisms against things that have hurt you over the years. But we were just friends for about 18 months before we got married.

Then Grace began to be allowed out of prison for the day on Saturdays—she'd have about six hours out. So I'd pick her up in my old car—it was chucking oil but it was still just about going—and we'd go out somewhere for the day.

It was a good six months before our friendship got to the stage where it was becoming a relationship, and it was at least a year after we met before we decided that yes, we'd got a good thing going here. But we still didn't want to rush into things.

●   ●   ●

Grace had told me she was a Christian, she'd got born again. I'd always read in the Bible that God made a difference. One day me and Grace were sitting in the gardens in Maidstone and we were eating a kebab and some biscuits. The little birds wouldn't come down and eat the crumbs we were throwing. So Grace prayed and praised God and they all came down. And I knew that there was something in it—that there was the power of God to change circumstances, like He did in the Bible.

From that moment I knew that Grace's religion wasn't just a scam to get out of jail, and she wasn't talking a load of garbage like most people I've ever met. So I started going to church with her, every Sunday, and later that year I decided I'd give my life to Jesus too. I had nothing anyway, so what difference did it make? And from then on, that's what really changed me. I gave my life to Jesus on a Thursday night, and from that very day I haven't touched anything—drugs, booze, nothing. I've never had any cravings, nothing. That all stopped instantly.

When I first got born again, I was still living in my car. So I prayed to have somewhere to live. By the end of that week I had a really nice bedsit in the town and the people from the homeless centre paid the deposit for me.

After Grace and I had known each other about eight or nine months, Grace saw an article in a Christian magazine and it said, 'If you still feel the same in a year's time, then get married—or take it a step further'—something like that. So we decided, okay, we'll give it a year and see if we still feel the same.

We were good, good friends. It was great to see her on her days out, but it was also great for me to have my own time to get myself fixed. I was outside getting my life sorted out and Grace was getting her life sorted out in jail. I think we needed this time apart to get to know each other, to get to know how to have a relationship. Because we neither of us knew how to do that. We'd had relationships before of course, but we didn't know anything about how to actually run them.

Then Grace was allowed out to work in a women's refuge, and we started working together every day. I was mending things in the refuge and I was helping Grace out in the office and driving the van so I was seeing her every day. We got to know each other very, very well.

After that year we decided we'd get married. What would be the practicalities of it? Grace would say, 'I might have to stay in jail another four or five years!' And I'd say, 'Well, that's okay. We know that, we'll go on from there.' We weren't looking at it through rose-tinted glasses: the relationships we'd both had before had always peaked and then crashed, and that wasn't what we wanted. We wanted something that would last.

I prayed again and within eight weeks we had a council flat. It was a dump when we got it, but since then I've stripped it all out and done it all up. Grace was still at East Sutton Park, an open prison near Maidstone. But she had a couple of problems there with a few girls that she'd had flare-ups with, and she got shipped back to Cookham Wood, a more secure prison in Rochester where she'd been before. We'd planned to get married in December on my birthday, but then she got shipped back in September or October.

We'd wanted to get married when she had a day out from East Sutton Park. So in Cookham Wood she put an application in to get married, have the day out. But the prison authorities said, no way—she couldn't have it. They did say they might allow her to have two hours out one morning. But right up till the last minute we didn't know if they'd even allow that. The day was set for us to get married on Saturday 2 December, and it wasn't till the Friday they said, yes, okay, a couple of hours out. So that was quite hectic.

A friend of hers who'd been in jail with her has got a florist's shop up in Vauxhall, and her husband promised to bring the wedding flowers down to my flat the night before. But by the morning he still hadn't turned up! He finally arrived about an hour before I had to go to the wedding! But they were *fantastic* flowers—absolutely really, really beautiful. There were bouquets, buttonholes, the lot.

The wedding was great, really great! The registry office in Maidstone is in this fantastic room in a very historic building called the Bishop's Palace. There were 50 or 60 people there. I've never really had a lot of friends, never ever. There were lots of people that Grace knew, and some people from the streets that we both knew. All through the wedding Grace was on a chain called a closeting chain, about 15 to 20 feet long, with two prison officers in plain clothes. She was chained to one and the other one was a sort of supervisor.

We were very, very nervous, both of us, in front of all these people, and we clung to each other. Grace was wearing a white dress that we'd got from a second-hand shop on one of our walks in the town. One day she'd picked out this white dress. It was knee-length and she tried it on and she looked very nice in it. So she bought it for a couple of quid.

The chain was really long, and that was quite good because you could take all the photos and the officers would stand out of the way. They were behind Grace, a long way behind, and when we sat down to sign the register they were 15 or 20 feet to one side and she could hide the chain down her sleeve. But you can still see it on some of the photographs.

Upstairs in the registry office there was a café so we went up there—me and Grace and about half a dozen others and the two officers—and had chocolate cake and coffee. Then the officers had to take Grace back to the jail. The rest of us stayed upstairs for about half an hour and had a little reception. In the afternoon I went over to the prison and they let us have a special visit in one of the solicitors' rooms—the legal visits rooms. The kitchen girls in the prison had made us a nice decorated wedding cake.

●　　　●　　　●

It took nearly five more years after we got married for Grace to be released from prison. It did get harder for us because although we always knew it could be years before she got released, our emotions were now involved. The hardest times have been when Grace got knockbacks on her parole.

Grace served eight years more than her tariff recommended by the judge at her trial—18 years in all, which I think makes her one of the longest-serving women prisoners. They said she was badly-behaved, so they wouldn't release her. In prison you must feel you're going round in a tin can. Sometimes I was able to help her, but the trouble with parole knockbacks is that prisoners tend to withdraw into themselves, and the person on the outside has to break down those walls again, to get through.

•   •   •

It's now a couple of weeks since Grace was released and I'm sure that after 18 years in prison she is going to find problems, there's no doubt about it. But she knows that I'm always there. I can't solve all the problems but I can help her with them. I don't think there are going to be *vast* problems but I think one of her biggest difficulties is that there aren't going to be a lot of people around. In jail there's people around you all the time and now she's out she's only got me!

We knew that from the beginning she might miss her women friends. That's why I didn't hog the visits. In any case the jail wanted her to see a wider circle of friends. I think I'm a little bit possessive, but I think from what Grace and I have learned from past relationships, we know the bad side of being possessive. We've had to get past all the walls of damage that are in us.

We've both been damaged. She's been damaged by blokes, I've been damaged by women. Grace has been in relationships where blokes have been overpowering and beaten her up, and she sometimes thinks I'm like that. And I've been in relationships in which women have been possessive of me. My ex-wife used to get drunk and throw a fit. So I thought Grace could be like that. As you go along you put characteristics from people you knew before on to the new partner. But we've realised that that isn't the way we are. I think we've learned from that and we've grown up. We're wary of the pitfalls you can fall into, and maybe the trigger points that put you into them.

I don't argue any more. I used to fight because I was angry at the world, angry at everything. You come across a pattern of behaviour in yourself, but being with Jesus is about change. It's about deciding you're not in a right pattern of behaviour, and changing into a good pattern. I don't lose my temper any more, and instead of walking away I've learned to stand and talk about things. If we've got a problem we'll sit down and talk about it. Over the five or six years I've known Grace I've seen massive changes in her too. We've both decided that the way we were wasn't the right way to be, and that doing it God's way is the right way to do things. We're both going on the same path now.

Though we've never said it to each other, I think there's been times when we've both—not actually regretted getting into our relationship, but there have been times when we didn't want to go any further. Because it meant we'd have to open up more and more and more to the other person. But being a Christian and being a grown-up is about opening yourself up to the other person and having a deeper and deeper and deeper relationship. Grace likes to break down the barriers with people, take off the mask. Now I think we've reached a plateau, and the relationship will stay at that sort of plateau.

My relationship with Grace is fantastic! It's the first relationship I've ever really had—my first *real* relationship, the first relationship I've ever really wanted. This is forever, it's not going to be for just a few years. We said this before we got married. We said, 'This is a serious thing, there's no way out of this. If we're going to do it we'll do it for life.'

• • •

I told my family all about Grace. My children by my first wife are now aged 15 and 20, and for years before I met Grace I wouldn't even tell them where I lived. Then me and Grace talked about it and decided I should get in touch because my family would be worried about me. So I went to visit my dad—my mother died years ago—and I've talked to my son about Grace and now he comes down here on holidays. He's very accepting about it. When he first met Grace he said, 'Oh, she's not like I thought she'd be!'. People have this picture of a murderess, a lifer in prison, a crazy woman looking at you as though she wants to kill you, that sort of thing. But Grace is a fun-loving woman, and he's realised she's a normal person. We've been out for the day together and things like that. Grace has met my daughter and I've met Grace's family and we get on fine.

I think God brought me and Grace together. Grace prayed that she wanted somebody to hug and I turned up. For years in my mind I had built up a picture of my ideal woman. Well, really it was three pictures, and I believe those pictures definitely came from God. And Grace ended up a mix of all those three. I worked in Scotland for about seven years, so the first picture was of a Scottish woman, strong-willed, brave, bold, courageous like the women on the prairies who used to sit on the covered wagons—and of course Grace comes from Scotland! The second one was a gypsy. I went to see the film of *Far from the Madding Crowd* at school and there was a gypsy girl in that. Very happy, free, jolly. And my third fantasy was of an Arab concubine in a harem. She was very dark, alluring, attractive, warm—you could melt into her embrace. I had all those pictures in my head and it's weird that they stayed with me—some of them for 30 years. All those pictures culminate in Grace, and that's what confirmed to me that Grace was the right partner. I believe God said, 'This is the woman I want you to be with'. Grace believes the same about me. We've made our choice and we'll change, take our masks off, bring down the walls.

• • •

I interviewed Anthony again almost exactly one year after the first interview and six months after Grace's release. Anthony and Grace lived together for the first few months, but then Grace decided she needed some space and went to live in a hostel for released prisoners, and then moved to a flat on her own. The couple still saw each other regularly and went out together for meals and to the cinema—and they went for a weekend to

Paris. Anthony embarked on a counselling course which he felt might help him understand more about the problems of their relationship. He still hoped that Grace would one day live with him again:

I knew there would be problems when Grace got out, but I didn't know how it would actually work out in reality, in everyday living. People coming out of prison get 'gate happy'. They say, 'I'm out—*yeah!*' and I've known people who've gone absolutely berserk because of that. There was an element of that with Grace but it's fizzling out now. There was the element of euphoria in us moving in together, because we've wanted that for a long time. But Grace had been in prison 18 years, and no matter what anyone says, there is an element of institutionalisation in any long-termer who's released.

That shows itself in their rigidity—there's no give and take. The prison system treats you like a child, so you end up being a child and you lose the ability to see the other person's situation. In prison you've got to create your own little world and you don't let anyone into it because there are situations where you will get hurt—and Grace has been hurt in jail. She's mellowed a lot over the six years since I've known her, and she recognises the problem, but I don't think she knows how to get out of it. She's out of jail, but it'll take a few years to get the jail out of her.

For instance Grace wanted a TV set and though she knew I don't like television, she just went out and got a licence. There was no interaction and she didn't consider all the aspects of it. In jail you make up your mind to do something and then you take the consequences. Grace has been in jail but she's been in her own prison as well. She created that barrier for protection. And before I met Grace I was alone for ten years—so in a way I've been in a self-imposed prison too. We are two people with fixed views who have always done things our own way, which is why our relationship was very full of friction when we were living together.

I don't think it would have made any difference if we'd waited until Grace was released before we got married. I knew there would be problems but I didn't think Grace would leave. I thought we understood the problems enough to be able to work round them. But I don't think I realised how vulnerable Grace really is.

•   •   •

I still think splitting up is the wrong way to go, because the way I see it, how can you work on the problems in a relationship if you're not actually together? I don't see how we can work on the problems with her living in the hostel and me living here. We go out, for instance to the pictures, but that's just two hours out of any day. In a 24-hour-a-day relationship you've got a completely different set of problems. You have to say, 'Okay, I'll climb down a little bit', then hope the other person will climb down a bit too.

I do think we've grown in understanding of each other much more since Grace has been out. But being more open with each other has opened a can of worms. I had to make myself vulnerable to let Grace in, to show her that person behind the wall, the person who has been hurt. And she has to make herself vulnerable to let me in. So we have had lots of friction, and we've recoiled from it, instead of staying together and working at our relationship.

•   •   •

Of course there are lots of good things too. We can pick up the phone without Grace having to buy a prison phonecard. We can see each other whenever we want to. There's a freedom to the relationship, going out for a meal, going to the pictures, without that rush to go back to the jail like she did on her day releases.

But I think people coming out of jail, specially long-termers, need psychological help to get readjusted into society. There are a lot of jail courses to stop people reoffending but they don't do any courses for the development of the person. After a long jail sentence you need to be debriefed, but all Grace does is go to see her probation officer once a week. That's not really aftercare, it's not helping her interact with society—it's just to keep tabs on her so she doesn't reoffend.

If somebody gets involved with a prisoner, as I did with Grace, and if they are going to be committing themselves to a long-term relationship with the prisoner, then they should be involved in the rehabilitation programme. Grace's probation officer said to me in a roundabout way, 'You do know what you're letting yourself in for?' But he doesn't know Grace and most of the prison officers didn't know her at all either. They all thought she was a very hard tough woman, but she's not.

I have never felt in any danger from Grace, because I understand completely why she ended up killing that bloke. She has always been honest with me, right from the beginning. She is sometimes loud, but that's only defensive—a front she puts up. Inside she is like a vulnerable little child. All she's had is being battered at home and being lost in a big family, then she had the streets, prostitution, drugs, booze, then 18 years of jail. Now it's the start of her life, and she needs big help.

It's a very slow process getting over jail. You've got no past for a start. Grace has only got 18 years of jail she can talk about—nothing else—so she's totally limited in the 'now' situation, which is frustrating for her because she's intelligent. She had problems with men, which is understandable, given her background. But jail compounded those problems.

I do pray about all this, and I get the answer back that time is the main thing. Grace is learning more about society, more about people, more about herself, and so am I. I'm going to college now and doing a counselling course and I'm learning a vast amount.

But I have never ever regretted my relationship with Grace because we are great friends. We got together on the basis of being friends and helping each other out. I admit I'm disappointed that we're not living together, but there's no element of blame at all, because this is a growth situation, an opportunity for us to grow in friendship. We went into this to help each other, to walk together along the way, and that's what we will try to do. If there's a possibility that we can live together again, then great. But if not, we'll just be good friends.

•　　　•　　　•

By March 2001, a year after she was released, Grace had decided that she and Anthony should part. Here she gives her reasons, and describes the couple's problems after she finally left prison:

Coming out of jail was a real revelation for me in a lot of ways, although to be honest I knew I had seen changes in Anthony as soon as we got married. When we'd first met in 1995 he was the most laidback, easy-going, non-judgemental person I'd ever known. It seemed to me though, that as soon as the ring was on my finger, he thought he didn't have to bother pleasing me in that way any more, and showed himself to be the exact opposite.

I'd been sent back to a closed prison because of an altercation with another inmate, and at first I thought our problems started because Anthony was mad that I'd messed up us seeing each other every day, as we had done when I was in the open prison when I did community work and went to church events. I tried to talk to him about it but he said that wasn't what he thought—it was all in my imagination. In reality, we fought so much on visits that my personal officer tried to get us marriage guidance counselling, but the powers that be wouldn't facilitate it.

In all honesty, I just hoped Anthony would calm down and go back to how he'd been temperamentally. We went to marriage guidance counselling for a couple of months after my release, and all the time we were in there he agreed with the counsellor. But then when we left he moaned about how stupid the counsellor was. I felt defeated.

When I came out of jail I found that the power struggle that had begun in there was only getting worse. The balance had changed so dramatically and suddenly, and things that I'd been able to ignore weren't so easy to ignore any longer. Whereas in jail I'd been totally reliant on Anthony, I wasn't any more, and I felt I should be able to assert myself and be able to grow as I needed to. I had been growing in various ways all along, but perhaps it wasn't so obvious.

Anthony had always been so good about getting me clothes and other things that I needed. I'd tell him colours and give him pictures, and he'd generally get me what I wanted. Only occasionally I'd be disappointed when he got me things he'd like to see me in. Then when I came out, I took to wearing leggings and trousers more than skirts and dresses, and I don't think he really liked it. He didn't say anything overt—just comments here and there that annoyed me. But I couldn't really say anything about it without looking like I wanted a fight. I'm not all that good at keeping quiet and putting up with things. I never could do that, even with all my years in jail. I'd just end up frustrated and yelling. Anthony hates yelling, I hate being frustrated.

More and more after I was released I began to see that Anthony was a real people-pleaser. He'd lived by himself in the flat that I came out to, but together we decided to redecorate it more to suit me. At least, I thought we'd decided together. But then later in an argument I discovered he'd never liked how it was done.

That really hurt me, but by that time I was getting used to being hurt in my relationship with him. He said I could make changes because I had to make the flat my home too, but when I actually did, he'd moan about it. Then when we went to church he'd be pleasant to people to their faces, then really critical when we left. I'm a really upfront person and that drove me mad.

•　　•　　•

I had a lot of hopes and dreams when I left prison, as I'm sure Anthony had too, though I can't really speak for him as he never shared them with me. In fact since coming out I've said to him many times that during that time we lived parallel fantasies. We thought we had common goals, so we convinced ourselves we could talk and sort things out. But what really happened was that we talked around things and then went on our own sweet ways. When we started to live together more than the odd weekend, I found this out in a big way. Strangely, Anthony didn't seem to agree—we never seemed to agree on much from then on, unless I just went along with him. As long as I was agreeing with him we were okay, but if I had a different opinion we were fighting or sulking.

For example, before I went to jail I'd always lived in hotels and bedsits, and as an adult I'd never had to share intimate body odours with people. Then in jail for 18 years, you'd be walking down a corridor and you'd know when other prisoners had been to the loo and I hated it. So when I got home I put air freshener in the toilet and would always use it—but Anthony wouldn't do the same. I'd been badly sexually abused as a child, and I knew that was partly the reason for my dislike of body smells. But to Anthony I just needed to get over it or put up with it. He didn't care and he wasn't going to change.

Sometimes our past relationships seemed to be being lived out in our relationship with each other. I felt that he was often controlling with money as he'd never been when I was inside. I put it down to his ex-wife being a drunk who wasted his hard-earned money, and because of that he found it hard to trust me. I'd always had my own money in the past and now I felt out of control. I'd lived for years with crazy controlling guys and that, coupled with screws telling me what to do for years in jail, was enough for me to have my radar tuned in full to any hint of it in my relationship with Anthony. He disagreed. He thought the past was past and I was imagining things. There were too many things I thought affected us from the past, and too many he thought didn't.

I guess that living alone inside or outside prison, a person gets selfish, and I know that in the end I was as guilty of that as he was. But I think that if that had been our only problem—getting used to living with another person—we would have been able to overcome it. But Anthony's absolute denial of any need for change in himself was another thing. I'd spent years with counsellors and on social skills courses, learning how to relate in socially acceptable ways, and I tried to use all this to get on better with Anthony. But I ended up feeling this was just a one-way process.

●　　　●　　　●

I know I've left Anthony. I know I can cope if he's not around. I didn't realise it till recently, but I actually felt quite alone and lonely a lot of the time when he was at work and I was at home. I'd been so used to having others to talk to. I was used to the affirmations of the other women I'd lived with and suddenly I was alone, and finding affirmations few and far between. I never knew Anthony to tell me I'd done well.

But then, I shouldn't really need that, as I didn't marry him to make myself complete. I am whole because of my relationship with Jesus and I've never really been alone at all because I have Him. So there is one good thing that has come out of all this—the strengthening of my faith in God.

I've always wanted an equal—a partner, not a child and not a father—and I believed that as a Christian living Christian principles, that's what I'd get. But the Bible and its principles are just more of the things Anthony and I don't agree about any more. I pray a lot still, but mostly I pray for Anthony to be able to leave me and find the happiness he wants.

For the last six months I've lived alone—without feeling lonely—in a flat run by an ex-offenders' charity. The council have offered me a property which I'm just waiting to go and see. I prayed about it and I'm sure it will be the right place. I feel that I can finally be my own person, in my own place, in my own right, safe in the knowledge that Jesus is the only husband I'm ever going to need.

Aisha and Muhammad

Aisha is 48 and shortly before I met her she had married Muhammad, 31, a life-sentenced prisoner, in a prison Muslim wedding at which she was not present. It was conducted by the prison Imam who later telephoned her to let her know that the ceremony had taken place. Aisha became a Muslim nine years ago and her husband embraced that faith quite separately during a previous prison sentence. They first made contact when Aisha began corresponding with Muhammad through a penfriend scheme. For three years they corresponded as friends, but then Muhammad wrote to Aisha declaring his love for her and asking her to visit. As a strict Muslim who eschews all physical contact with men, she refused to visit as his girlfriend. When he proposed marriage she accepted, and the ceremony took place early in 2001. It was not until six weeks after the wedding that the couple finally met.

Aisha drove to my house in Kent from her London home. When she arrived in her car on a blazing July afternoon she was wearing a flower-patterned *hijab* covering her hair and forehead, a light blue, floor-length robe, and dark glasses for driving. Alone with me for the interview in my kitchen she was able to remove her scarf, as there were no males present.

The only daughter of hard-working parents, she rebelled against their discipline and had only recently re-established a good relationship with her mother. She has always been a high achiever, took a degree in sociology and psychology and held a number of high-powered administrative jobs.

Aisha had a long relationship with her childhood sweetheart whom she met when she was eleven and he was 14. They stayed together until she was 24, despite the fact that he was in trouble with the law from the start of the relationship and spent years in borstals and prisons.

Like Aisha's first boyfriend, her husband Muhammad was also in trouble with the law from his youth and has served previous sentences, though he does not come from a criminal family.

•   •   •

Muhammad and I met through a penfriend organization. We are both white British and we are both reverts[1] to the Muslim faith. I think he became Muslim about the same time as I did, which was nine years ago, long before we knew each other, and our faith is a very big bond between us.

I'm 48 and he is 31. Before we got involved in a relationship, we were just friends, and we never discussed ages. And then one day after we'd been writing for over two years, he wrote and said, 'I've been waiting two and a half years for you.' And I was shocked. I thought there was a big age difference between us—and this is when age became an issue for me. I was aware of how old he was, but he wasn't aware of my age, and I was really worried that it would make a difference to him. But he wrote back and said, 'Your age has no bearing on anything at all.'

•   •   •

Though Muhammad's background is very different from my own, we are as if we came from the same mould. We are very, very alike.

I come from south-west London and my parents worked for the council. There were two of us children—I have a brother five years younger than me. It was a stable family, in that my parents are still together though they argued constantly. I don't really remember much of my childhood relating to my mum and dad. I do remember my childhood with my grandparents, and it was excellent. They lived in south-west London too and I saw a lot of them. I didn't want for much. I'd say my family were lower middle class, but my dad's parents owned a huge house. My grandfather was a taxi driver who owned his own cab and bought two of his sons cabs as well.

But I did lack affection from my mum and I got on better with my dad. I was very rebellious and as a teenager I was always running away from home and going to places like the Isle of Wight Festival.

We moved to Surrey when I was eleven and I passed the 11 plus and went to an all-girls grammar school. After I left I did an art foundation course, then I went to Croydon College then on to Hull University where I did a degree in psychology and sociology. At the time I was quite a hippy with very long hair and long dresses.

•   •   •

I didn't find it easy to relate to people at school. People infringe on your space and they're so demanding. I love my own company and I hate crowds. They called me 'the gypsy' as a child. My grandparents owned eight caravans near Clacton and I spent most holidays there. As soon as I got there I was gone and they didn't see me all day. I used to go off for miles and play on my own, with my own fantasies.

At school I was physically bullied. The bullying had to do with my boyfriend that I met when I was eleven. He was 14 and I stayed with him until I was 24. All the girls fancied him and they didn't like the fact that he'd come and pick me up from school on his scooter. He came from the council estate and my mum and dad weren't at all keen on him. He was Anglo-Indian and my parents were quite racist, like most of their generation.

He was also a bit of a tearaway to say the least. He started getting into trouble at the age of 13 or 14 nicking pushbikes. Then it got more serious and he went to borstal at 15. Finally he got a seven-year prison sentence for conspiracy to armed robbery. I was never in any trouble myself but I never tried to stop him because I suppose at the time I thought it was a bit of a laugh. But it meant I spent a lot of my youth visiting borstals and prisons.

That last sentence he got, I was with him for two years of it, and then I found out he'd been writing to somebody else. At that stage I'd finished at university and I would have been prepared to wait for him if he hadn't written to that other girl. But instead I went and told him it was finished between us. His probation officer got me moved out of the area because he threatened to kill me—he was so obsessive. He'd always been like that. I was his, and that was that. I coped with that—it didn't worry me at all. I belonged to him, and that was fine. I've had several boyfriends in my life and men are very possessive of me. I think they want to control me—but I'm not somebody that you can control.

• • •

After I finished at university I went into the accounts department of a big company and I progressed and picked up a lot of skills, as an administrator as well. But I wasn't really happy in the job so I went back to my sociology roots and worked for social services for over two years. But I had a bad experience. I was a family social worker and I had a little girl in one of my caseloads. My recommendation was that she be moved from her home, but they chose to ignore it and in the end she died. I was heartbroken and I felt I couldn't do that job any more.

So I left that and went into credit control in a big public limited company. But I don't fit into the office environment world because I get on with my work, I don't chitchat and because of my faith I don't flirt around and make lewd jokes and things like that, and I don't interact with men at all. People at work found that very, very hard to cope with.

At the time I reverted to the Muslim faith, I was working for the Chinese government in an import/export shipping business. I did that job for four years, between the ages of 36 and 40. All the Chinese people I worked with were absolutely horrified that I became a Muslim! It wasn't anything to do with how my character changed or anything. It was the scarf, the hijab. One morning I just turned up in my normal clothes but wearing the hijab, and they were horrified. They just kept staring and they didn't know what to say. But as time progressed they started telling me that they didn't want me to be dressed this way because it didn't help business. So that's why I left that job.

• • •

I was 39 when I became a Muslim—nine years ago now. Neither of my parents practised religion but I've always been interested. I did go to church with my grandmother, who was Church of England, and I went to Sunday school as well, then I looked at the Jehovah's Witnesses. As a youngster and all through my growing-up years I was interested in religion. I am definitely a spiritual person.

But one religion I was never going to look at was the Muslim faith—Islam— because I believed in the media image that women were treated like second-rate citizens. A friend of mine who was West Indian had joined a group called the Nation of Islam, so he kept trying to get me interested in it. Then someone gave me a book called *Towards Understanding Islam,* by Sayyid Abul A'la Mawdudi[2] and I thought, Oh, I'll read it some time. And then one day I found it in my coat pocket when I was on a bus and I read it and I was interested. So I went to a local mosque and met some women there, because I wanted to see what their idea of Islam was all about.

I went in as me and I came out a Muslim! I had no intention of doing any such thing and when I came out I just stood there and thought, God, what have I done? You make a declaration which is called a *shahadah,* which is when you testify that there is only one God, and that Muhammad is His prophet. Once you take the *shahadah* that is it, you're a Muslim. You don't have to have instruction first. I think what convinced me was the women, but I can't even recall what they said. In our faith we believe that it wasn't my decision to become a Muslim— it was God's will for me.

When I came out of the mosque I felt a bit lost, so I enrolled in a college which taught Islamic subjects, and I spent five years doing that in the evenings after work.

What attracted me about the Muslim faith was equality. People who believe what is put in the media need to read the Qur'an which tells you that men and women are equal, though one has a degree over the other, and that degree is to provide and protect. That's what it tells you quite clearly. It all makes logical sense and I'm a logical person. When you read the Qur'an and start thinking about it, maybe there are some things that as a Westerner you find hard to accept. For example women are supposed to be in after the early evening prayer which is at sunset, and obviously that is much earlier in the winter. You might think that's a bit harsh, but then you realise the reason behind it is for your own protection, and you look at society today and you understand that it makes sense.

If you're doing a nine-to-five job you can't do that, but you are given leeway—there's nothing hard and fast. Everything is made easy for you—it's man who complicates things. In my situation, my husband's in prison, so I have to go out to work. It's not me or my husband that's forcing that situation—it's what's happened to us. So I have to do what I have to do to survive. But if Muhammad was at home, I wouldn't go to work—he would go to work and I would stay at home—and very contented I would be too.

•   •   •

About five years after I became Muslim, Muhammad and I started writing through a penpal organization. His letters always made me laugh—always. There was never anything out of order, nothing at all sexual, but I'd read his letters and I'd smile and start chuckling. I'd get on the bus and I'd be laughing all the way—he used to have me in hysterics. One day his letter had me laughing so much that everyone on the bus looked at me because the tears were just rolling down my face!

So gradually we built up a relationship. Muhammad had been in trouble with the law from an early age—just small things, though he doesn't come from a criminal family. He had been in prison on this sentence nearly four years before I made contact with him. I didn't even know what he was in prison for, or how long he'd got. I never asked him, because I felt that if he wanted to tell me, that was his business.

But after he made it clear that we were becoming more than friends, then I told him that there were three reasons which would mean that I wouldn't be prepared to take our relationship further. I said I had my own boundaries, and I wasn't prepared to overstep those. He asked me what they were. I said, 'If you're a sex offender, if you're a paedophile, or if you left Islam'.

Then he asked if he could phone me, and I gave him my number and got it cleared. The first time he phoned me it felt really strange talking to him. He sounded so young, so soft—I had a big smile on my face. I had never seen a picture of him and I still didn't know the offence he was convicted of. But I knew that he was a Category A prisoner, so I knew that whatever it was, it was something serious.

So I wrote and said to him, 'Look, I really do need to know about your offence. I've never asked you this before, but I do need to know.' But he still wouldn't tell me. He kept saying, 'When you come up and see me I'll tell you face to face.' And I said, 'No, no, no—I need to know.' I was very smitten by him—that was the word I used to a friend.

That's why I said to him, 'I really need to know'. He said, 'I don't want to tell you on the phone. You'll have to wait till you come up and see me.' And then he said, 'You're going to have to be cleared by the police anyway.' So I wrote to him and I said, 'I'm sorry—you're not doing this to me. I'm not having the police coming round here and telling me what offence the man that I'm involved with has committed. I don't want them to see the shock in my face. I need to be able to tell them that I already know. I don't want to be put in that vulnerable situation and for them to have that power over me. If you can't safeguard me from that as a Muslim, then I'm not going to do it.'

And then he told me what he was in for and I said, 'Okay. Fine' and he was shocked. He said, 'Are you all right with that?' and I said, 'Yes, it doesn't come into the categories that I've mentioned'. And then he told me his sentence, and I just couldn't believe it. Because it's a long, long time—life times two.

I believe you're responsible for yourself and if you don't protect yourself, then you've got nobody to cry to. The prison authorities can't tell you about the offence—they're not allowed to because of confidentiality. I don't believe they should be allowed to either, because confidentiality is an issue that you can't divide. You either operate under the confidentiality rules or you don't. You can't have special circumstances, and if a woman chooses to marry someone and she is not aware of the situation, then more fool her. If Muhammad had said to me, 'I'm not going to tell you,' then I would have thought, If he's not going to tell me this, which is a big issue, then what else will he hold back from me? And what sort of relationship is that? It's not an open, trusting relationship. So I wouldn't have gone further.

My husband asked me on the phone to marry him. He wanted to ask me face to face, but I refused because I knew what my feelings were and I knew that if we were face to face we'd have to hold hands and kiss each other and I wasn't prepared to do it, not unless we were man and wife. That's part of the Muslim religion. There is no such thing as boyfriend/girlfriend relationships. I knew that if we met I'd do something that was wrong, so I wasn't prepared to do it. That's why I told him, 'I am not going to visit you except as your wife. Unless you ask me, I'm not coming to visit you.'

So on the phone he said, 'Will you marry me?' and then the pips went! I shouted, 'YES!' and the phone just clicked and I thought, Did he hear me or not? So I wrote a card saying, 'The answer to your question is, Yes'.

I spoke to the Imam, who is the Muslim priest, and he asked me if I was aware of the situation and I said, 'I'm fully aware.' He asked me if I was aware of the sentence so I said, 'Yes, I am—fully aware.' So he said, 'Okay, that's fine. Have you got a *wali*?' (a guardian). I did—he was a male friend of mine.

I spoke to my *wali* and he wrote to the Imam saying he was my *wali* and that he was authorising the marriage. I had accepted my husband's proposal—and that was it. So he was sent the paper and he received it, and once it was in writing, nothing else had to be done. There was a ceremony at the prison but I didn't have to be there, because it had been written. In Islam all law contracts have to be authorised in writing, everything should be in writing. If I lent someone 50p I should write it down and I should sign it.

We got married at the beginning of the year [2001] before I visited Muhammad. This visit took place about four weeks after he proposed. Muhammad was present at the prison marriage ceremony and he had to witness it before other Muslim prisoners and the Imam. I don't know what they did because I wasn't there. I didn't even know I was married.

The Imam phoned me and told me, 'Congratulations—you're married!' I was shocked because I was doing housework at the time. I was so excited I was ringing everybody up, then my husband phoned and he told me we'd got married at three minutes past four and I said, 'I can't believe it!'

Since I got married I've had my name changed by deed poll. I went to a solicitor and my name now is Aisha, wife of Muhammad.

•   •   •

It was another six weeks before I visited my husband. I was already married to him but I was terrified—absolutely terrified in case he didn't like me, what I looked like. Of course, our age difference was still at the back of my mind. I thought, Well, okay, I can accept what you're saying, that age isn't a problem, but you haven't seen my face yet—you don't know what I look like. I suppose it was my own ego, because I was concerned about what he might think once he saw me.

I didn't know what he looked like at all, to the point that when I spoke to him on the phone I had to ask him what colour he was—I really didn't know. I have a feeling I asked him that before I married him, not after, but it didn't make any difference anyway because I fell in love with the person, not what he looked like.

Then I got cleared to visit Muhammad and I went along to the prison. On that first visit I wore my hijab and a long dress. I went into the visits room and they told me the table number. I was looking for it and I was concentrating so much on finding it, that though Muhammad was standing there calling me, I just ignored him! I looked at him and walked past him. He kept calling me and all of a sudden it just clicked that it was him and I went and sat down. He sat opposite me and he couldn't even look at me. I was sitting opposite him and he was talking to me but looking over his shoulder to the side. He picked up my hand and looked at my wedding ring and said, 'That's nice', but then he dropped my hand really quickly because he felt awkward and I did too.

I suppose after about three quarters of an hour, he started to actually look at me and talk to me—I can't recall what we were talking about. And eventually he came and sat next to me and he held my hand, and that was it—I was with my husband.

I visited Muhammad three days in a row that first time. The second day I visited we were like an old married couple, then the last day of the three it was very emotional. It was awful, absolutely awful, because he should have been coming home with me.

I just walked out of there and when I left I had a big, big smile on my face for him, and it wasn't until I got outside and actually got on the train that I just broke down. I was heartbroken and I was sobbing my heart out. But all the time I was with him I thought, I'm not going to show any emotions whatsoever, because if I do, he might react and I don't want to put him in the situation where he's going to be showing himself to other people.

When I got home I sent him a tape straight away, though it took weeks and weeks for him to get it. The tape was of me speaking—he's allowed to have tapes. I wrote to him as well and sent him some money. Muhammad tells me I shouldn't keep spending my money on him. He's very concerned about my wellbeing. If he asks for things he'll ask me to go into charity shops and get them. He doesn't want designer clothes. He said, 'I don't want to wear some guy's name on myself!'

•   •   •

When the prison officers search me coming in to the prison, I absolutely refuse to take off my scarf in front of male officers and that is my right. They're okay with me now they know I know my rights. They take me into another room and I take my scarf off.

I think it's unproductive when partners of prisoners challenge the system by confronting the prison officers. I could make a lot of trouble, but at the end of the day they've got my husband and I'm not going to put him in a vulnerable position because of what they can do. As a prisoner's wife, my attitude to the guards is: You have my husband. You classify him as a criminal, not me. I have done nothing wrong. You do not treat me like I am a criminal, because in this country you are innocent until proven guilty. I just treat the guards as human beings. As a Muslim, part of our character is to be polite and respectful at all times. So I'm polite, I'm respectful, I say hello, goodbye, I do not converse with them any more than I have to. I do enough to ensure that I get to see my husband on my visit.

My faith gives me patience and tranquillity. I think that is why this religion found me. As Muslims we do believe that on the day that you are born, the angels blow your breath into you and everything in your life is predestined. It is written—the time you are born, the time you die, and what happens between. My husband actually believes—he said to me—'We are the same unit, but we were divided by time.' We talk sometimes and I say, 'Really I don't need to phone you any more, because you answer before I even ask you the questions.' I've written to him and asked him a particular question and the next day I've got a letter which has obviously crossed with my letter, and he's answered the question before I've even asked him. That happens a lot to us— an awful lot. In the Qur'an it tells you: 'We made a mate for each of you.'

•　　　•　　　•

My mother and father are fine about my relationship with Muhammad. My mother knew before I even told her. I think that now she is quite intuitive where I'm concerned, because my relationship with her only really started properly when I was 40. Now I talk to my mum every day. The majority of my friends were okay about my relationship with Muhammad. Just one in particular, who'd been my friend for a very long time, gave me a lot of grief about it. When I married I was working, but I never told anybody at work. It's not their business. I only tell people that need to know, because I don't share my personal business with people.

I don't feel isolated by my marriage because I like my own company, and also Muhammad and I talk three or four times a week and we write constantly. Silly things do upset me though. Last Tuesday I cooked a chicken, though I don't often cook because I'm on my own and I can't be bothered. I took it out of the oven and I got quite tearful because I was thinking, He should be here to eat this chicken with me. Little things like that. There are two things that I would like—and Muhammad is fully aware of this because we've discussed it. The two things that I would want to do when he's released is that he leads the prayer that we say together, and also to cook for him as well. That's what I want to do.

What sacrifices have I had to make for this relationship? Well, celibacy is a sacrifice—a very big sacrifice. And I miss him not being with me. It's things like if something goes through my mind, I can't ring him up and ask him. So it's always waiting. I might write it down for later, or I talk on a tape.

We are both very, very similar. He probably is stronger, because I'm a woman and I have my emotional self to deal with. Really I think we are equals—intellectually, emotionally and definitely morally.

Sometimes we both sit there in the visits room and we don't say anything, we just chill. We buy loads of sweets and chill out. We talk about what books we've read and we don't run out of things to talk about. But every now and then we'll stop and just sort of sit back, just like Sunday afternoons. What would be nice, what I'd really like, is to just spend a Sunday afternoon with him and read a book, with him being there, in our front room. We would be totally at ease with that sort of thing. That's how it would be if we were together.

One thing I did, I sent him photographs of my flat, which is *our* home now, so he could piece them all together. The flat is in our joint names now. I bought it and now I've put it in both our names. So now Muhammad has a home, and if I die it's all left to him.

Of course the truth, the crux of it all, will be when my husband comes out and we live together. But we've written for these three years as friends —and there's the big difference. I fell in love with the person—the character. The relationship grew, so much so that I, the Westerner, who had been raised in this country, was able to marry somebody who hadn't even seen me, because it was the person that I fell in love with. It didn't make any difference what he looked like.

When he gets out he says he doesn't care if he's a roadsweeper as long as he's able to maintain me, and that's all that matters, and that we can live our lives Islamically.

I have grown Islamically through my relationship with Muhammad. My knowledge is even wider now because we go through books together and reference things and he's really made my faith a lot stronger. Muhammad has helped me to try and analyse what I want out of life. I am more at peace with myself now.

ENDNOTES

[1] Aisha explained that Muslims prefer the word 'revert' to 'convert' as they regard themselves as reverting to the one true faith.

[2] Published by The Islamic Foundation 1980/1400AH (after Hijra).

Maureen and Dave Chapman

I interviewed Maureen in mid-December 2000. She worked as the manager of a hospital for mentally disordered people, but by the time we met she was gravely ill with cancer. She was however very keen to talk to me about her relationship with her husband Dave, 48, whom she married in 1995 while he was still in prison. She had visited him regularly for eight-and-a-half of the ten years he served of his 16-year sentence for armed robbery.

Dave was released in time for the Millennium celebrations but their time together was brief: Maureen died on 20 January 2001 at the age of 49, just over a month after this moving interview took place. Her funeral was attended by 250 people and included a tribute from Terry Waite, who had befriended Dave in prison and visited Maureen during her final illness. Maureen was buried in her wedding dress and Dave wore his wedding suit to the service.

Maureen was a true East Ender, the daughter of a London docker. She had always lived in a very close community a short distance from the Millennium Dome. I met her in her neat house in a quiet street—though the flats nearby are home to heroin users. The front room downstairs, where she had slept since her latest operation, was cosy and eclectically decorated. In the corner was a Christmas tree, beautifully trimmed and surrounded with presents for her three children and six grandchildren.

Maureen was 49 but because she was so slim she looked younger, though her face was etched with pain. She looked very different from the fresh-faced woman in her wedding photograph having suffered a great deal of trauma in her life because of her own illness—she was diagnosed with cancer ten years ago—and the deaths of close relatives. First married at 18, she gave birth at 19 to a child suffering from spina bifida. He survived only a few hours and she spent months in a psychiatric hospital, her first marriage ending in divorce. Her second husband died of a drug overdose leaving her four months pregnant with her daughter; her next partner, the father of her two sons, was murdered when he was summoned by a local woman to help her sort out a drunken brawl. Maureen's final partner (before Dave) was abusive to her and her children. When she finally managed to break away from him she vowed not to enter another relationship. Instead she concentrated on her job and helped care for two of her grandchildren, both born withdrawing from heroin.

Maureen first met Dave, a friend of her brother, when she was just 12 years old. Dave was in trouble with the law from an early age. During the period when she was living alone, she heard that Dave was back in prison yet again, this time serving a 16-year sentence.

She wrote him a friendly letter and gradually began visiting him regularly and when Maureen was diagnosed with breast cancer in 1995 the couple decided to marry. The wedding took place in HMP Gartree that year. Dave was released four years later.

•　　•　　•

The day Dave came out after doing ten years in jail, he came and met me up Piccadilly Circus, under Eros. It was December 9th last year [1999] and he had a Father Christmas hat on. Two days before that he'd rung me up and said, 'I'll be home in two days!' and I said, 'Well—I'm going out!' I think I was in shock. He said, 'What do you mean you're going out?' and I said, 'I'm going out with people from work!' I'd never been out with them before. I was managing a hostel for mentally ill people and my health was getting worse. I'd had a breast cancer operation but the cancer had come back by then.

When I first went to visit Dave in prison he still had eight-and-a-half years to serve for robbing a post office. He was given 16 years but in the end he did ten. At the time I went on the visit I'd been living on my own for a couple of years. I was 40 and I'd left a very abusive relationship after eight years. I made up my mind I was going to stay on my own for five years and not get involved with any men. I went and got a job in care work with the mentally ill and I just worked and worked to try and get it all out of my system.

•　　•　　•

I was about 12 when I first knew Dave. We lived in the same road and he was always the one who was in trouble. My own brother was always in trouble too and that's how I knew Dave and what he used to do. I think it began when he was about ten years old and he stole something worth about two shillings. After that he was put away every time—approved school, borstal—the lot. Never probation, never, 'Let's give this boy a chance.' Then it went to jewellery robberies, then post offices. It was escalating all the time, each time he'd come out of prison. He was never out of prison for more than about three weeks before he'd done something else—he was actually 25 years in and out of jail.

When I was a teenager I did fancy Dave, but I was too shy to do anything about it. I never said anything to him and he never knew, though I kept in touch with the family. He didn't come from a criminal family—it was just him. His dad worked really hard, night work and things like that, trying to get money together for the family.

My family were hard-working too, and it was only my brother who got in trouble with the law. My dad was a docker and my mum was in care work with handicapped adults. I was the middle of three children and we've always lived in the East End. The only time I moved away was for four months, to Hythe in Kent. I was so depressed there that the doctor said, 'Get on a coach and go home to London. It's where you belong.' I'll never forget coming back into London on the coach. The depression lifted and I felt better—I was home.

I was never a rebellious teenager because my mum and dad were quite strict. I was terrified of doing anything like drugs because I thought my mum would know straight away. My dad was Catholic and I went to a Catholic school. He was Irish and he would quite happily have seen me become a nun. I did love going to church, and between the ages of about seven and eleven I used to come out of school and go in the church down the road for a little while before I came home. When I was in church it put me in touch with another world.

•   •   •

I got married when I was 18, in 1970. I was so shy I didn't have any friends of my own, and I suppose because of my brother, most of the people I knew had been in trouble and the man I married was another like that. And after the age of 18 my life took a bit of a twist.

My husband Tony was two years older than me and when I was 19 we had a little boy. He was born with spina bifida and he died a couple of hours after the birth. About two weeks after I had the baby I landed up in a mental hospital because I couldn't cope, and I spent four months there. I felt I'd let everyone down. I blamed Tony because he should have been there for me—but he was in prison for petty crimes. So the first bit of rebelliousness in my life was to go and get a divorce. Everyone said, 'You can't do that!' and I said, 'Can't I? Watch me!' And I went off and got my divorce.

While I was in the hospital I met a young man who was doing a two-year detox to get off drugs. We got together and when we both left the hospital he came and lived with me in my flat. By this time I was 20 and I was really in love with him and I fell for another baby.

But when I was about four months pregnant this man died. He took a lot of drugs and it killed him. We never knew whether or not it was suicide.

I had my daughter in the September, and again there was nobody there to help me. Then I met a man called Larry who I'd known since he was a kid. He was a few years older than me and he was very, very good with my daughter. But though I didn't know it when I met him, Larry was a heroin addict. In 1972 the drugs got the better of him and he packed up work. In 1974 we had another child, a little boy. And in 1975 we had a second son.

Then in 1979 Larry was murdered. A woman asked him to drive her home to Streatham because her kids had rung up saying there was trouble at a party in their block of flats. There was an Irish group drinking there and when Larry went up they dragged him into the flat and stabbed him. I was 27 and I was left with kids aged three, four and six. That's when I couldn't cope with the kids at all. I went on the booze for 18 months but we managed to stay together, though social services tried to put the kids in care.

Then I met another man. He'd come round to say he'd heard that my husband had died and he was sorry. And I landed up marrying him—he was my second husband. But he was very abusive, very bad to the children. I stayed with him for eight years out of fear. I was terrified of him—absolutely terrified. I don't know where I got the strength to break away. One evening when I was still married we bumped into Dave in a pub. He was married at the time too.

I was about 38 when I left this abusive husband and that's when I made up my mind to stay on my own for five years at least, and I got my job in care work.

Then one day I bumped into Dave's brother and he said he was in prison again. He said, 'Dave's just got 16 years'. I said, 'Oh crikey! What's he done now?' He told me it was something to do with a post office and I said, 'Well, tell him to drop me a line—I'm on my own now'. His brother said, 'I'll give you the address.' So I wrote to Dave and that's how it all started.

●　　●　　●

I wrote that first letter in the June and I said, 'Sorry to hear you're away again. What have you done this time?' Rightly or wrongly we treated it as a bit of a joke.

Then at the end of December I went to visit him in Whitemoor prison with his mother—he'd done about 18 months of that sentence by then. I'd been in prisons before, visiting my brother, so it was exactly as I'd expected it to be. I'd seen Dave only a couple of years before in that pub and he hadn't changed much. At first I used to go down on visits with Dave's mum, who was pretty old and frail by then, and I used to help her get there.

There was still nothing between me and Dave, and I kept my distance. It was just a peck on the cheek when I got there. That first visit Dave said, 'Will you come again and will you come on your own?' and I said, 'Oh, I don't think your mum's going to like that!' She used to cosset her boys a lot. When we went on visits we talked mainly about the family.

It was probably as much as a year before I managed to get to see him on my own. His mum was hanging on for dear life so I didn't tell her I was going! When I went on my first visit on my own it was more to talk about me, and that's when it got more personal.

We went on writing to each other, and I fell in love with the man who wrote me letters. One day I was visiting him on my own and the funniest thing he said was, 'Do you think you'll be around when I get out?' And I said, 'I don't know—how long have you got left?' and he said, 'Oh, I'll be out in 18 months.' In those days you'd get a long sentence but you'd get lots of parole. They changed it all in the early days of his sentence, and eight-and-a-half years later I was still visiting. Parkhurst was the best time for us because it was nice and easy, though most prisons treated visitors terribly.

Dave actually served ten years of his 16-year sentence. I never had any doubts that I would wait for him till he came out, but while he was still in prison we talked a bit about his crimes and I said that if he came out and committed any more crimes, I wouldn't wait another ten years.

●　　●　　●

When Dave was in Parkhurst I was diagnosed with breast cancer. I was frightened I was going to die and he was going to be stuck in there, so I started going to visit him weekly. He was very supportive and when I went into hospital he used to phone me there every day. I was convinced I was going to die, so we asked if we could get married in case things got worse, then he'd be able to see me in hospital.

I'd been determined to stay on my own, but for some reason I needed to know that somebody cared for me. And the easiest way was to communicate with somebody in prison, so I wouldn't have all the bad bits that can go with a relationship.

There were no real frictions between Dave and my family. My dad liked Dave and he was quite close to him and whenever he came to London he used to come and see my dad. But my children were in their twenties by then and they were a bit worried, because they'd seen the abusive side of other relationships. They said, 'Mum, you don't know what he's like'. I said, 'It's okay, I won't put up with any shit any more. I've been on my own too long.'

From Dave's letters he appeared to be kind. He was different from my last one—he didn't appear to me to be openly violent. So I thought about it and I thought, okay, we'll give it a try. I'd been divorced twice before and I thought, Well, if it doesn't work I'll just get a divorce. I had no big illusions. I didn't have rose-coloured glasses on. The only thing I was interested in was that Dave was good to women. And I'd seen Dave's antecedents—his previous convictions etc. He sent me those very early on—he volunteered them without me asking. They told me about the years where I didn't see him and I had a gap. They told me where he'd been and what he was doing.

Dave got moved from Parkhurst to Gartree near Leicester and we got married there the following September. The prison did say to us, 'Don't think he's going to get parole any easier because you're married'. But it was a lovely wedding. Somebody had got the money together to put me in a hotel the night before, and when I arrived there was a bottle of champagne. Some of the prison officers there were very good and we were able to choose the ones we wanted at the wedding.

The ceremony was in the Governor's office and I wore a white dress and a hat and I managed to get a bouquet. The wedding was on a Monday, as all prison weddings used to be,[1] and I took Dave a suit in on the Sunday. Then I came back to London that night and we had a reception in the pub down the road from my house. At first I didn't tell anyone at work about getting married.

After we were married, the prison allowed Dave a few compassionate leaves home. In the end they gave him 18 months' parole so he could come out to me, because things were getting worse for me by then. I had had a lumpectomy but then the breast cancer had come back.

On Dave's home leaves we did things together, like going on a boat trip round the Dome. It was just as well we did because that first Christmas Dave came out was all a bit of a daze. Everything was too much for me as well as for Dave. It was like a big whirlwind—all too fast.

●　　　●　　　●

There were a lot of problems for us the first seven months Dave was home. It's like prisoners have been living in a world where what they say goes. They get respect, but it's respect of a different kind. And then suddenly here was Dave with a woman who was very independent, a woman who could cope perfectly well on her own. He thought he was coming out to someone who was dying and he actually came out to someone who was going to fight for her life. He didn't even like me answering him back.

Even though my kids are all grown up and I'd got none of them living with me when Dave came out of prison, they still visited. But just the small amount they did visit, Dave couldn't handle it. Even though men in prison know you've got kids—and in my case I've got six grandchildren as well—they feel a bit jealous of them. Dave wanted me to himself.

I feel that in those first seven months we went through every stage you would have gone through if you'd met someone, courted them, got engaged to them. The arguments, the shouting at each other, the walking out on each other—no different from any other courtship, except we crammed it all into seven months. I think I'd had enough by then. I could have walked away, easy. But then we sat down and we said, 'Come on, where are we going from here?' So we gave it another try and it's worked.

• • •

I think the biggest thing was Dave managing to get a job, painting and decorating. He never really worked before—he was just into crime. I think the temptation to go back into crime has been there a little bit, when I've been ill and he's said, 'Oh, you know we could have had private medicine and everything would have happened quicker.' But we had a chat about it and I've said, 'No, you still get the same surgeon on the NHS.' And he told me that the times he was tempted, he thought, What would happen to Maureen if I got nicked? He would let me down, and he knows he's going to get life if he goes inside again. If he committed another crime I would have to walk away, whether I was ill or not, because I couldn't go through all that again. The only problem I have is when he gets a little bit mouthy when he goes past the police or anybody in uniform, even traffic wardens. He'll say, 'Why don't you go and get a proper job?' and I normally wince and say to him, 'Do you have to do that?' I think in the early days when he came out I used to challenge him a lot, and that was where a lot of our conflict came from.

I really have had a rotten life, and if I can get through it and keep on the straight and narrow and come out of it, then people shouldn't think they can come and tell me their sad stories, and I don't want people round me who are committing crimes.

But now Dave's as good as gold—I can't fault him, I really can't. He does all the shopping and he cooks all the meals. There have been odd times during those first seven months when I thought, God, what have I done? But then Dave would always come in just at the right point and put it all right.

On 18 January 2001 Dave called me to tell me Maureen had only a few more days to live. He spoke movingly of his gratitude for the interview transcript, which meant he now had a record of her life during their years apart. Had Maureen not spoken to me, he said, that period would have been a blank to him. He was also grateful to have Maureen's acknowledgement of their difficulties on his release, their success in overcoming them, and the testimony of her love for him. She died two days after his phone call.

Dave felt he would like to talk about their relationship and gave the following interview in March 2001. A stocky man with cropped greying hair, rimless glasses and a weatherbeaten face, he was in the middle of redecorating the front room where I had interviewed Maureen.

•   •   •

I can't bring myself to paint over Maureen's animal wallpaper. When I first saw it I said, 'You don't want to put that stuff up!' To me it was kids' wallpaper, but she loved it.

When I first saw her in her brother Terry's house she was a pretty little girl of 12, and she always stayed in my mind from when I was a kid. If she'd been brought up anywhere else she would have gone to college, been one of those educated women—all that was in her. But she had all these drug addicts and thieves and scumbags around her. She'd had terrible, horrible men and I used to say to her, 'The relationships you've had before are ruining you and me'. That was the hardest thing we had to get through.

I can understand women who write to men in prison because it's safer for them—they're not whacking them, they're safe. To some extent I think it was like that with Maureen. I think at first I just thought of her as a friend. Obviously the prisoner's the one who's in more need, but she could talk to me about things like plays and museums and things that she couldn't talk about with people round here. And I do remember Maureen saying to me, 'You've done as much for me as I've done for you.'

I'd sworn I'd never get married again, but there was nothing else I could do to help Maureen, because she had the cancer by then. So I ran round the prison ducking and diving and I managed to get together about £1,000 to pay for everything—the rings and the car. My friend's son had a pub across the road and he arranged a little buffet and a gorgeous motor to bring the bride to the wedding. I gave the kitchen blokes in the prison a tenner to make me a big cake, a proper one. Maureen looked lovely in her wedding dress—she was buried in it and at the funeral I wore my wedding suit.

•   •   •

The prison only told me on a Tuesday that they were letting me out on the Thursday. I phoned Maureen and said, 'Listen, they're letting me out Thursday!' and she didn't say, 'Great!' Instead she said, 'That's weird!'

I said I'd meet her at home and she said, 'Oh no, I've got the firm's do Friday, I'll have to meet you up Piccadilly.' I accepted that but really inside I was gutted—I'd been away all that time and I thought, She thinks more of them than me.

It was horrendous, that first meeting. I went up the 'Dilly and there was hundreds of people there. It was Christmas Eve and there was a bloke selling Father Christmas hats and I got one and stuck it on to look inconspicuous. Then I saw Maureen across the road. My main concern was getting across the road to her and not getting run over. We went in a pub and there was all these people singing and dancing. I just wanted to run off but I fought to control myself. I had a drink and it went straight to my head.

•   •   •

The first six or seven months I was out were really hopeless. I'd done nearly ten years inside and everything had changed. I couldn't get used to the bright colours—everything in prison is grey or dark blue. Then there were all those children and dogs—you don't see them in prison. Then the traffic—everything had changed, the one way system, the traffic wardens were terrible and I couldn't help saying, 'Get a proper job!' as I walked past, and Maureen used to have a pop at me about that. It took me ages to get back to driving a car.

Then I was jealous because Maureen was sharing herself with her kids and grandkids and I kept saying, 'I married you, not them. Let's just be me and you.' Maureen was like Mother Teresa round here. Everyone borrowed a couple of quid from her, or if people had problems she'd go round with a bag of clothes. For the first six months I was home people never stopped knocking on the door and the garden was full of kids.

It was a constant slog when I came home because I'd come back expecting someone who needed me. I expected to be useful but she made me like a bit of a eunuch. I think I had a little bit of the knight in shining armour about me, but Maureen was a fighter, right up to the end.

At first I didn't want to work. I expected things to come to me, and it took me three or four months to realise that if you want anything you have to get it for yourself. I thought I was owed stuff, but Maureen made me realise that you get nothing for nothing. Then I got work painting and decorating with a friend of mine and things got easier. Maureen wouldn't give up her job and I ended up working six days a week from seven in the morning till seven at night. And I think that's what she wanted. She wanted to get me into that routine. And by doing that she actually saved me. For the first time in 25 years I knew how to work properly and she made me value money. I started to quite enjoy it. I found I got a buzz from jobs where I was in charge and people were asking me what to do.

But then I was tempted to go back to crime to pay for Maureen to have private medical treatment. I went and asked at a private hospital and it cost £400 a day and it would have cost about ten grand for her to have the operation she needed. I was tempted and I was offered a couple of good things. I discussed it with Maureen and I said, 'I could get a lump of money at the weekend, you could have the operation and then we could book into somewhere nice or go on a cruise.' The thing that stopped me was the thought of getting nicked again. If anything had happened and I wasn't there to help her I would never forgive myself. But one of the hardest things that first six months was getting people to realise that I wasn't the same Dave, that we'd got nothing in common any more. For ages they'd say, 'Come on, got a vanload of videos. Pick it up, drive it round here and you'll get two grand for half an hour's work.' Most of my friends round here were thieves and I don't have anything to do with them now, and so I haven't got any mates.

It took me a long time to realise I was a parasite, living off other members of society. I used to say to myself, 'The insurance'll pay'. If you've shot a bloke in the leg you think, He'll be all right, he'll get compensation.

But thanks to Maureen my values have changed and I don't think I'll ever go back to crime now. If it hadn't been for Maureen and Terry Waite being my guarantors on parole I'd still be in prison now. The prison told me I was a dangerous man who was never going to get parole.

She made me enjoy things like getting on a bike and riding round the village, or if me and her just walked down the village holding hands or had a day in the park, spent about a tenner all day and had a great time. In all the neighbours' eyes it was a waste of time her marrying me, because they were sure I was going to go off. So it was great them seeing us holding hands and walking down the road—because I'd proved them all wrong.

When Maureen was so ill at the end, it was like the wheel coming full circle. When she was in hospital she used to give me a list of things to get, just like I did to her when I was in prison, and she used to say, 'Now it's you coming to visit me!' It was quite funny and we had a few laughs about it. It was a complete reversal.

Towards the end the doctors wanted to give her more chemotherapy but we'd discussed that and I knew she didn't want any more. The doctors put a terrible big metal cast on her and for three days I tried to get the hospital to take it off so I could take her home. In the end I went out and bought a big pair of cutters and me and two friends cut the thing off. The nurses couldn't believe it—they were threatening me with this and that but we discharged her and got her home. She died peacefully about a week later.

So I did end up doing a lot for Maureen. That's what I wanted to do—if only she'd let me do that from the beginning. But honest to God, Maureen had a profound effect on me. She has made me want to be a better person.

ENDNOTE

[1] According to the Prison Service Press Office there is nothing in any prison rule that says weddings have to be on a Monday, but often this is the day when there are no social visits, only legal visits, so governors may have chosen Mondays for convenience. It seems that nowadays a prison wedding can be arranged on any day of the week. See p. 46 and p. 172.

Bibliography

Anderson, Digby, *Losing Friends*, The Social Affairs Unit, 2001

Aungles, A, *The Prison and the Home*, Sydney, Australia: Institute of Criminology, 1994

bandele, a, *The Prisoner's Wife: A Memoir*, USA: Washington Square Press, 1999

Broadhead, J, 'Prison as a Dating Agency', *New Law Journal*, November 1999

Brown, Kelli, *No-one's Ever Asked Me*, Federation of Prisoners' Families Support Groups, London, 2001

Collins, Hugh, *Autobiography of a Murderer*, Pan Books, 1997; *No Smoke*, Canongate Crime, 2001

Delf, G and Thornton, S, *Love on the Wing: Letters of Hope from Prison*, Penguin, 1996

Devlin, A, *Invisible Women: What's Wrong with Women's Prisons?*, Waterside Press, 1998, reprinted 2002

Devlin, A, *Going Straight; After Crime and Punishment*, Waterside Press, 1999, reprinted 2002

Dibb, Liz, *Supporting Prisoners' Children in School*, Federation of Prisoners' Families Support Groups, London, 2001

Gray, J, *Men are from Mars, Women are from Venus*, Harper-Collins, 1992

Isenberg, S, *Women Who Love Men Who Kill*, Simon and Schuster, 1991; 'What Makes Women Fall in Love with these Monsters?', *Express*, 8 May 2001

Kennedy, H, *Eve Was Framed*, Vintage Books, 1993

Kray, K, *Hard Bastards*, John Blake Publishing, 2000

Lamb, J, *Feelings*, Avon Books, 1996

Mawdudi, S A A, *Towards Understanding Islam*, The Islamic Foundation, 1980/1400AH

McCrystal, C, 'Glad to be Kray', *Independent on Sunday*, 1 April 2001

Montagu, Fiamma, (Director), 'Life after Murder,' BBC Television, October 2000

Norwood, R, *Women Who Love too Much*, Random House, 1986

Prasad, Ashok, (Director) 'Dear Peter: Letters to the Yorkshire Ripper', BBC Television, 9 May 2001

Smartt, U, *Grendon Tales: Stories from a Therapeutic Community*, Waterside Press, 2001

Smith, J, 'Letters to the Ripper', *Guardian*, 3 May 2001

Van Mechelen, R, *Killers, The Backlash!*, USA: New Chivalry Press, 1991

Willcox, J and Piper, M, 'Barred Wives' (Australian TV documentary) 1993

Willcox-Bailey, J, *Dream Lovers: Women Who Marry Men Behind Bars*, Australia: Wakefield Press 1999

Ancillary Information

The following additional information is available free of charge at www.watersidepress.co.uk:

Media reports on prison relationships (in summary)

Questionnaire sent in advance to interviewees for *Cell Mates/Soul Mates*

Facts and figures drawn from questionnaire responses (as described in narrative form in *Chapters 1* to *3* but containing further specific information)

Glossary

ABH Actual bodily harm

Block Prison segregation unit where prisoners who break the rules are kept apart, or those at risk from others, or withdrawing from drug misuse, are held for their own protection. Also known as **Seg.**

Categories A, B, C and D Prisoners are categorised according to their security risk as they move through the system, A being the highest, D the lowest category.

CCRC The Criminal Cases Review Commission which looks into alleged miscarriage of justice cases, usually those where an appeal has already failed in the Court of Appeal.

Cell spin Surprise search of a cell looking for drugs, weapons or other contraband.

Closed visit A visit supervised by prison officers when the prisoner is in a closed booth and is separated from the visitor by a glass or mesh screen. Also known as **Glass visit.**

Dear John letter A letter bringing bad news, usually the end of a relationship.

Depositions Copies or transcripts of evidence given by witnesses and victims. Prisoners may ask other prisoners/partners to read them to scotch rumours that they are guilty of sex offences.

Electronic tagging Prisoners felt to be suitable may be released early on condition they wear an electronically controlled anklet or bracelet which is monitored to ensure they obey a curfew confining them to their home ('home detention curfew'), usually at night.

E-list Escape list of prisoners thought to be a high risk of attempting to escape.

Enhanced regime Highest of the three regimes under which a prisoner can be held. The other two are Basic and Standard. Being an Enhanced prisoner affords more privileges such as extra visits and more spending money.

Flying Squad Top police detectives, usually meaning Scotland Yard but sometimes applied to Regional Crime Squads.

Gate happy Exuberant, excited, moody or anxious about forthcoming release.

Glass visit See **Closed visit** above.

Groupie, prison Someone (usually female) who is said to find it exciting to correspond with and/or visit prisoners.

Hijab Scarf worn by Muslim women

HMP At Her Majesty's pleasure. While life imprisonment is the mandatory sentence for murder committed by a person aged 21 or over, if the offender is aged ten to 17 the equivalent mandatory sentence is detention during Her Majesty's pleasure.

Home leave/home visit When prisoners are allowed out of prison for periods prior to final release, at first with prison officer(s) escorting them, later unaccompanied. Now renamed 'release on resettlement licence' (RLED).

Knockback A setback, e.g. if a prisoner loses an appeal, is refused parole or is told that the next parole review will not be heard for some time.

Legal visit Lawyers are allowed to visit clients in prison without using a visiting order (see **VO** below).

Life licence Licences are given to prisoners who have received mandatory or discretionary life sentences for murder. He or she may be released on a licence which remains in force for the rest of his or her life. At any time it may be revoked and the person concerned returned to prison.

Life times two A double life sentence, e.g. for two murders.

Natural lifer A prisoner who has been told that he or she will remain in prison for the rest of his or her natural life, i.e. will not be released.

Offending behaviour course Prison course run by officers, psychologists or outside agencies to make sure prisoners address the reasons for their crimes.

Piss test Word prisoners use for urine test for drug misuse.

Pre-release hostel The prison hostel system allows prisoners at the end of their sentence to go out to work every day while living in a prison hostel during the week. They may be allowed to stay with friends or relatives at the weekend.

Pat-down/rub down search Prisoners and/or their visitors are searched quickly by officers running their hands over their bodies outside their clothes to make sure they are not carrying contraband.

Seg/segregation unit See **block** above.

Shahadah Declaration made by Muslims that there is only one God and Muhammad is His prophet.

Shipped out (or back) Moved from one prison to another (or back), often without warning.

SOTP Sex Offender Treatment Programme. There is widespread Prison Service provision of programmes run by prison officers, psychologists and others for sex offenders.

Spent conviction A conviction is legally 'spent' when a fixed statutory period has expired from the date of the conviction. Thereafter, the conviction cannot normally be mentioned outside criminal proceedings (where it is also marked 'spent'). This does not apply to prison sentences over two-and-a-half years.

Tariff The minimum period a prisoner must serve. Once it has expired, a prisoner is released only when the Parole Board, after due consideration, is satisfied that there is no unacceptable risk to the public.

Twirly Word used by some prisoners for a 'do-gooder'.

Temporary release Now called release on temporary licence. There are three types of licence allowing a prisoner to be temporarily released from jail. Each has its own set of rules, but all depend on prisoners passing a risk assessment test.

VO/visiting order A pass note which prisoners are allowed to send out to friends and relatives allowing them to visit them in prison.

VPU (Vulnerable Prisoner Unit) The wing in a prison where prisoners are held if they may be in danger from other prisoners, e.g. because they are sex offenders, former police officers or have got into debt to other prisoners. They may also be people who are considered a danger to themselves through self-harm or attempted suicide.

Wali Guardian for a Muslim woman.

Index

Other works by Angela Devlin from the Waterside Press catalogue

Criminal Classes Offenders at School

A highly acclaimed first work - which identifies areas at the schooling stage which influence and predict future offending behaviour. 'If you are in any doubt about the links between poor education, crime and recidivism, read it': Marcel Berlins *The Guardian*.1996 Reprinted 1997, 2000. ISBN 1 872 870 30 9 £16.

Prison Patter A Dictionary of Prison Slang

Words culled from prisoners, prison officers and other people working inside prisons together with their explanations and background material. 'Useful for the custody suite' *Police Journal*. 'Will help lawyers to understand the "ins and outs" of prison slang': *The Independent*. 1996 ISBN 1 872 870 41 4. £13.50

Going Straight After Crime and Punishment
Angela Devlin and Bob Turney
Foreword Jack Straw, former Home Secretary

Based on first-hand accounts, *Going Straight* seeks to identify turning points and key influences in the lives of criminals (some well-known) who - often against all odds - turned their lives around. Includes contributions by **His Honour Sir Stephen Tumim** and film-maker **Roger Graef**. 'Truly inspirational': Martin Narey, Director General, HM Prison Service. 'An absorbing read of interest to all sentencers': *The Magistrate*. 'A super read': *The Independent*. 1998 Reprinted 2001 ISBN 1 872 870 66 X £18

Invisible Women What's Wrong With Women's Prisons?

First-rate reviews – Angela Devlin's classic account of women's prisons: 'A seminal work': Baroness Helena Kennedy QC, 'What an excellent book' *Justice of the Peace*. 1998. Second reprint 2002 ISBN 1 872 870 59 7 £18.

Anybody's Nightmare The Sheila Bowler Story
Angela and Tim Devlin

As dramatised on ITV, starring Patricia Routledge. One woman's fight to clear her name of murder –successfully, in the end, and after four years as a life sentence prisoner in HM Prisons Holloway and Bullwood Hall. ISBN 1 901470 04 0 £12.50

WATERSIDE PRESS • DOMUM ROAD • WINCHESTER • SO23 9NN
Tel/Fax 01962 855567 e-mail:orders@watersidepress.co.uk

Direct mail prices Please add £2.50 per book p&p (UK): to a maximum of £7.50

VISA • MASTERCARD • SWITCH Etc

Catalogue: **www.watersidepress.co.uk**